JOHNS HOPKINS UNIVERSITY STUDIES

IN

HISTORICAL AND POLITICAL SCIENCE

EXTRA VOLUMES   NEW SERIES, No. 16

NATIONAL COLLECTIVE BARGAINING IN THE POTTERY INDUSTRY

NATIONAL COLLECTIVE BARGAINING IN THE POTTERY INDUSTRY

BY

DAVID A. McCABE, Ph. D.

Professor of Economics
Princeton University

BALTIMORE: THE JOHNS HOPKINS PRESS
LONDON: HUMPHREY MILFORD
OXFORD UNIVERSITY PRESS

1932

COPYRIGHT 1932
BY
THE JOHNS HOPKINS PRESS

The Lord Baltimore Press
BALTIMORE, MD., U. S. A.

PREFACE

The study of which this monograph is the result goes back more or less continuously over fourteen years. In 1914 I made a study of national collective bargaining in the pottery industry for the United States Commission on Industrial Relations, under the direction of Professor George E. Barnett of Johns Hopkins University, who had charge of the field studies on joint agreements. The report which I then wrote was not published. The field work on which the present monograph is based was completed, so far as details are concerned, in the summer of 1928, and the manuscript was written as of that date. However, circumstances delayed its publication. I have added the more important developments which have occurred in the industry down through the renewal of the agreement in May, 1931, but the descriptive account is, in most particulars, of the situation as it stood in August, 1928.

My indebtedness to the many men in the industry who have given me information is beyond measure. They have been most generous of their time and most patient in bearing with my repeated inquiries. I cannot thank all of them here by name, but I wish to acknowledge especially my indebtedness to Mr. Charles Goodwin, Secretary of the United States Potters Association, to Mr. W. E. Wells, until 1928 Chairman of the Labor Committee of that Association, to Mr. J. J. Dale, for many years Secretary of the Sanitary Potters Association and the Trenton Potters Association, to Mr. John A. Campbell, who was the leading figure in the sanitary agreement system on the manufacturers' side,

v

to Mr. Frank Hutchins, First Vice-President of the National Brotherhood of Operative Potters until 1922, to his successor, Mr. George Cartlidge, to Mr. John T. Wood, Secretary for many years and later President of the Brotherhood, to Mr. John McGillivray, since 1922 Secretary of the Brotherhood, to President James M. Duffy of the Brotherhood, and to Mr. Thomas J. Duffy, ex-President of the Brotherhood. I wish also to acknowledge my very great indebtedness to the late Edward Menge, Secretary of the Brotherhood from 1903 to 1911 and its President from that date to his death in 1922, and to record here my admiration for him and my respect for his memory.

For whatever is worth while in this monograph the reader may thank Professor George E. Barnett, my former teacher, and the director of the original study from which this monograph grew. He has also been kind enough to read the present manuscript and has, needless to say, made many valuable suggestions. To my colleague, Professor A. M. McIsaac, I am also indebted for undertaking the uninspiring task of reading the manuscript and for many helpful suggestions.

For such interpretations and judgments as are not supported by documentary references or references to statements made to the writer by men in the industry, or at one time connected with the agreement system, I assume full responsibility and express the hope that it may not prove too burdensome.

D. A. McC.

June, 1931.

CONTENTS

INTRODUCTION

THE INDUSTRY AND OCCUPATIONS

This study does not cover labor relations in the entire pottery industry in the United States. It is concerned only with the two divisions of the industry in which national collective bargaining prevails, or once prevailed, and primarily with those workers within these divisions who are, or were, members of the National Brotherhood of Operative Potters, the only union of any importance in the pottery industry in the past thirty years. The two divisions are known as the " general ware " and " sanitary " divisions. The first covers chiefly the manufacture of tableware, both "semi-porcelain " and " china." The sanitary division covers the manufacture of semi-porcelain toilet fixtures, such as closets, tanks and lavatories. National collective bargaining collapsed in this division in 1922.

Within the general ware division the manufacture of " semi-porcelain " and that of " china " constitute in some respects separate sub-divisions. The labor operations are of the same general nature, the union employees in both are in the same national union, their employers are in the same employers' association, and both subdivisions are covered in the same general system of collective bargaining. On the other hand, it has been assumed—until very recently, at least—that china requires more careful workmanship than semi-porcelain and higher piece rates were fixed for working in china than for operations of the same name in semi-porcelain; the " conditions " and working rules have also differed to some extent.

1

The generally accepted distinction between china and semi-porcelain is that china is practically non-absorbent below the glaze. China is accordingly called " vitreous " and semi-porcelain " semi-vitreous." It was until very recently supposed that the difference was caused not only by firing the former at a higher temperature but by a difference in the proportions of the materials entering into the composition of the " body "—a term applied to the ware before the glaze is put on; a " china body " is made from approximately the same materials as a " semi-porcelain body " but the percentage of feldspar and flint is higher in the china body and the percentage of " ball clay " lower. In the last few years, however, the temperature at which the body is fired has come to be recognized as the more important factor in producing the difference between vitreous and semi-vitreous ware, if not the real determinant. At least one manufacturer has recently offered as " china " a product of which the body has been declared to be technically a " semi-porcelain body " but which has been made vitreous by firing at a higher temperature than has ordinarily been applied to semi-porcelain.

Nearly all of the china manufactured in the United States and practically all made in plants operating under the national system of collective bargaining is intended for use in hotels, restaurants, dining cars, etc., and it is on that account often called " hotel china." It it heavier than ordinary semi-porcelain. " Hotel china " does not compete with American semi-porcelain ware for household use, to any considerable extent. The production of semi-porcelain general ware greatly exceeds that of china, although the proportion of the latter has increased greatly since the first national wage agreement in the industry (1900). Quantitatively semi-porcelain is still over three-fourths of the total, although the proportion in terms of the value of the product is more favorable to china.

The semi-porcelain sub-division of the industry is highly localized. The chief center is the " East Liverpool district," which includes East Liverpool, Ohio, and Newell and Chester, West Virginia, two towns just across the Ohio River from East Liverpool. At least half of the semi-porcelain production is concentrated in this district. The next largest center is Sebring, Ohio. Trenton, New Jersey, once the leading center of the industry, has declined absolutely as well as relatively, and now (1928) possesses only three small semi-porcelain potteries in actual operation, producing not more than five per cent of the ware.

The china plants are more scattered. For the most part they are not found in the same localities as the semi-porcelain tableware potteries. There is no china plant in the East Liverpool district, nor is the State of Ohio, which accounts for over three-fourths of the semi-porcelain production, an important china producer. Syracuse, New York, leads as to localities and with Buffalo gives New York first place among the States. Trenton, the original leader in china, as in semi-porcelain, has now only one large plant in operation, but it also possesses a small plant which makes a very high grade of china for household use.

The manufacture of semi-porcelain sanitary ware developed later than that of semi-porcelain general ware. At the time of the breakdown of national collective bargaining (in 1922), the sanitary division was less than half as large, whether measured in value of product or the number of employees, as the general ware division. In the production of sanitary ware Trenton was again the earliest center, but in this division Trenton was still preëminent in 1922, with over half the production, although the industry was developing rapidly in other towns widely scattered. A few of these were towns which also possessed one or two general ware potteries. Thus well over half of the production of sanitary ware was carried on in localities in which the general ware industry was also represented. The converse was far from true, however. The greater part of the general ware production was, and is, carried on in centers in which there are no sanitary potteries. There is no sanitary pottery in either the East Liverpool district or Sebring.

The operations and separate occupations in the general ware industry are numerous. About forty per cent of the operatives are rated as skilled workers. Over a third of the employees are females and not more than ten per cent of these are in the skilled class. Among the skilled workers craft demarcation prevails to a high degree and a considerable percentage of the semi-skilled are employed as helpers by journeymen.

It is customary in the industry to group the operations and the operatives into several distinct " departments." The first is concerned with the preparation of the clay before it goes to the workers who form it into ware, and with the " slip " used in the " casting " process of ware-forming. Machinery is used to a much higher degree in the " clay and slip " department than in any other. The workers in this department are now unorganized, although a considerable minority of them are rated as skilled men.

The next department in order is the " clay shop," the ware-forming department. It is the largest department in the pottery in point of numbers, including approximately a fourth of the operatives. The proportion of the total number of skilled workers found in this department is even higher; it is nearer a third than a fourth. It is in this department that craft demarcation is most striking. It is here, too, that the employment of helpers by journeymen is most prevalent; indeed the helpers employed by journeymen in this department exceed the journeymen in number.

The most important clay-shop branch in point of numbers are the " jiggermen." The jigger consists of a power-driven horizontally revolving " head," in which the mould containing the clay is fixed, and a pull-down equipped with a shaping tool which is applied to the clay in the revolving mould. Although the jigger may be classed as a machine the jiggerman is regarded as a skilled potter rather than as a machine-operator. He has to apply the shaping tool separately to each piece of ware and he must know how to treat his clay under various conditions.

The jiggerman usually employs three helpers —a " batter-out," a " mould-runner " and a " finisher." The batter-out cuts off a lump of clay of the necessary size from the supply of clay on the bench and puts it on the mould, ready for the jiggerman. If the piece is " flat ware," such as a plate or saucer, he has to " bat out " the clay before putting it on the mould, hence the name. If he is employed to fill moulds for cups he is usually called a " cup baller." The mould-runner carries the moulds from the jiggerman's bench to a stove-room, where the ware is dried in the mould; he also removes the dried ware from the moulds and carries the empty moulds back to the jiggerman's bench. The work of the mould-runner requires less skill, of course, than that of the batter-out. In some plants the mould-runner has been superseded by " improved " stove-rooms equipped with sliding or revolving shelves or chain conveyors on which the jiggerman can place the moulds directly. A mechanical " spreader," operated by the jiggerman himself, has also been introduced, but not widely, to eliminate the need of a batter-out. The finisher works over the ware after it has been through the stove-room, in order to give it a smooth surface and a smooth edge; it is chiefly flat ware which is finished in this way. The finishers are almost exclusively women.

Cups and some other classes of ware of similar type are " turned " after they have been through the stove-room. This operation is the work of a distinct skilled craft, the " turners." The turner uses a tool on the ware while it is revolved on a lathe. The turners ordinarily employ helpers known as " spongers "; frequently two turners employ the same sponger jointly. " Handling "—the putting of handles on cups, etc.—is also the work of a separate skilled craft, the " handlers." The handler ordinarily does not make the handles himself, but employs a " handlemaker " to do this work. The handler confines himself to putting the handle on and sponging the joint to smooth it out.

The " dishmakers' " branch is one in which the craft distinction is based on the kind of ware made. In the industry the term " dish " is confined to the large oval or oblong pieces used for vegetables, etc.; it is not applied generally to all tableware. Under the older method the dishmaker shapes the dish against a revolving mould with his hand and a hand-tool. Dishmakers using this method are now called " bench dishmakers." What is essentially a jigger was later introduced for making oval dishes, and was called for a time a " dishmaking machine." Men operating a " dish jigger " are now called " dish jiggermen " but they are still classed as " dishmakers." The dishmaker frequently employs a helper.

The method of fashioning the ware by " pressing " the clay in a mould has given way almost entirely to

jiggering or to casting. There are only a few " pressers " left. Another almost extinct branch is that of
" sticking-up." The " sticker-up " handled and finished
large ware, usually " after the big jigger." Sticking-up
has been almost eliminated by the reduction in the
quantity of this type of ware made and by the introduction of casting on much of that which remained.

All of the above branches are engaged in fashioning
plastic clay or on ware in the green state. The " casters " make ware by pouring slip—which is clay in solution—into moulds and pouring out the slip remaining
after the clay has been deposited on the inside of the
mould through absorption of water. When the ware is
sufficiently dry, it is removed from the mould and finished by the caster. If the cast ware is to have handles
the handles are usually " cast on." The casters do not
employ helpers. Casting was not widely introduced
until after the inauguration of national collective bargaining but the casters are now the second largest
branch in the clay shop.

As to relative numbers, the jiggering branch constitutes nearly half of the skilled workers in the clay
shop. The casters are about half as numerous as the
jiggermen. The turners, handlers and dishmakers rank
almost together, but the dishmakers have been falling
somewhat behind in recent years. When it is remembered that the jiggermen's helpers are more than twice
as numerous as the jiggermen, it will be seen that the
jigger dominates the clay shop.

After the ware leaves the clay shop it goes to the
" green room " where it remains until it is ready to be
fired the first time. The first firing is called the
" bisque " firing. After that firing the ware is dipped in
glaze and then fired again; the second firing is called
the " glost " firing. The firing is done in two distinct

2

sets of kilns, called respectively " bisque " and " glost."
Thus there are two sets of operations in the " kiln
department," with the operations of the " dipping "
department coming in between.

The outstanding group of workers in the kiln department are the " kilnmen." They place the ware in large
" saggers " made of coarser clay than the ware itself,
but also fired, and then place the saggers in the kilns.
They are essentially " kilnplacers " and are sometimes
called that. Kilnplacing is skilled work. The kilnmen
work in crews of several men each, under a " bench
boss " who is also a member of the crew. There are
usually separate crews for the bisque and the glost
kilns. It takes many more men to place the same
amount of ware in glost than in bisque, as the ware
requires more careful treatment in placing it in the
saggers after the glaze has been put on. The kilnmen's
branch is the largest single branch in the industry.

The firing of the kilns is looked after by a separate
group of " kiln firemen." There are usually two kiln
firemen in each plant. They are rated as skilled workers. After the ware is fired, the kilns are " drawn " by
" kilndrawers," who remove the saggers from the kiln,
transfer the ware from the saggers to baskets, and
carry it to the bisque warehouse, or to the glost warehouse after the glost firing. The work of the kilndrawers is heavy, but it is not rated as skilled. The
number of kilndrawers is nearly two-thirds of that of
kilnmen.

The old style kilns, known as " upright " or " bee-
hive " kilns, are now being rapidly displaced in the
larger plants by " tunnel kilns." The ware is placed in
saggers as before, but instead of the saggers being
placed in tiers inside the kiln by the kilnmen, they are
placed on trucks which are moved slowly through the

kiln by automatic control. To be operated economically the tunnel kilns must be kept in operation continuously. They are therefore sometimes called "continuous kilns," in contrast with the old-style kilns which are now also called "periodic" or "intermittent" kilns because several days must be allowed between firings for cooling, drawing and placing. The chief difference, from the labor standpoint, between the two types is that where tunnel kilns are used the carrying of saggers into (and out of) the kiln and placing them in tiers or "bungs" in the kiln is eliminated.

There is a large group of women employees who work on the ware after each firing, in either the bisque warehouse or the glost warehouse. They are divided into several distinct classes according to the operations which they perform but the group as a whole is known as the "warehousewomen." Their work requires little skill on the whole.

The "dipper" stands at a tub filled with liquid glaze and dips the bisque ware into the glaze. It is his job to see that each piece takes on sufficient glaze and that the glaze is properly distributed. Some kinds of ware have to be dipped singly. Dipping china takes more time and care than dipping semi-porcelain. The quality of the dippers' workmanship has a very important bearing on the quality of the finished ware. In a small plant there may be only one dipper; in a large plant there are several. In number the craft ranks with such clay-shop branches as the handlers and turners. The "dippers' helpers" sponge the ware after it has been dipped, to remove excess glaze. They are not employed by the dippers, but by the firm. Nearly all of them are women and they are usually included in the "warehousewomen" group.

Not all of the ware is decorated in the potteries, but in recent years most of it has been. The decorating department covers a large number of employees, the relative number varying with the proportion of the ware decorated and the amount and kind of the decoration. Generally, however, the decorating department ranks next to the clay-shop department in point of numbers.

Nearly all of the " design " decorations are now put on by the decalcomania process. The older printing process is nearly extinct in semi-porcelain but there is a considerable amount of printing in china. The " printers " are a skilled craft. The women employed in decalcomania work, known under the group name of " decalcomania girls " make up the majority of the employees of the decorating department. They are not classed as skilled workers. The chief group of skilled workers engaged in putting the decoration on the ware are the " liners " or—if the line is gold—" gilders." Generally the number of liners and gilders will not run much over half the number of decalcomania girls. The majority of them are women, although in the East Liverpool district the males are still in the majority.

The decoration is ordinarily put on the ware in the glost state and ware decorated at this stage has to undergo a third firing, in a " decorating kiln." The crew consists of a " decorating kiln fireman," who is in charge, and " decorating kiln-placers and -drawers "; all are called " decorating kilnmen." It is not one of the larger branches. In recent years tunnel kilns have been introduced in a few plants for firing the decorated ware. It is generally conceded that not as much skill is required, of some members of the crew at least, on the tunnel kilns.

Two branches which handle the ware but do not participate in the manufacturing process are the " warehousemen " and the " packers." The warehousemen's branch is the more numerous of the two, ranking next to the jiggermen among the skilled branches. Not all of the operatives called " warehousemen " are doing skilled work, but the selection of the ware for the filling of orders—the warehousemen are employed in the glost warehouse—is responsible work. The packers, rated as a skilled branch, are less than half as numerous as the warehousemen.

Two other skilled branches, which do not work on the ware itself, are the " saggermakers " and the " mouldmakers." The " saggermakers " are one of the less numerous branches. In a small plant there may be only one saggermaker. In many cases the saggermaker employs a helper. Most saggers are made by hand but in some plants a saggermaking machine is used; the saggermaker in charge of the machine is classed as a skilled saggermaker but the helpers on the machine, who are paid by the firm, are not. The mouldmaking branch is also one of the smaller branches. The moulds are made of plaster-of-Paris. There is a distinction within the branch between the work of the " blockers and casers " and that of the ordinary mouldmakers, the former being regarded as more highly skilled; the majority of the mouldmakers cannot do blocking and casing.

In addition to the workers included in the above classes there is a considerable number of employees engaged in various tasks, most of which require little or no skill. Some of these workers have distinctive names but many others are known simply as " laborers " or " odd men." In the aggregate this residuum accounts for at least ten per cent of the employees. They do not, however, figure in this study.

The most important difference between the sanitary division and the general ware division, from the stand-point of labor operations and the classes of workers employed was, during the period of national collective bargaining in the sanitary division, the much smaller proportion of unskilled or semi-skilled workers in the latter. There were almost no female operatives in this division. The difference was due mainly to the large size of the pieces and the absence of any decorating process. There was no group of employees comparable to the warehousewomen or the decalcomania girls or the liners. Nor was there any large group of helpers comparable to those employed by the journeymen in the general ware clay shop.

Another important difference in the clay shop was the almost exclusive use of the pressing process. Casting did not attain any considerable importance in union shops until the last few years of the agreement system and even at the end the casters were in a relatively small minority in the union shops. There was no other clay-shop branch of any importance in the sanitary division. The pressers not only dominated the clay shop but they made up over half the skilled workers in the division. Next in numerical importance among the skilled (and unionized) branches came the kilnmen, both bisque and glost. The dippers, packers, saggermakers and mouldmakers—all relatively small branches numerically—completed the roll of the organized branches.

PART I
THE ORGANIZATIONS

CHAPTER I

THE UNITED STATES POTTERS ASSOCIATION

The manufacturers in the general ware division of the pottery industry are represented in the national system of collective bargaining by the United States Potters Association. This Association was organized in 1875, thirty years before it made its first real national agreement with the union. During its earliest years it was primarily a trade association, not an employers' association. Indeed, it disclaimed any purpose of fixing the rates of wages to be paid by its members. There were occasional reports on and discussions of wages in its meetings, but no combined action on wages was taken through the medium of the Association itself until 1894.

EARLY HISTORY

The initiative in the formation of the United States Potters Association came from Trenton. On December 18, 1874, a call was sent out for a convention of the manufacturing potters of the United States with a view to the formation of a permanent association of earthenware manufacturers.[1] The circular met with an encouraging response and at the resultant meeting, held in January, 1875, a permanent organization was ef-

---

[1] The circular is reproduced in *Proceedings, U. S. P. A.*, 1875. The initials " U. S. P. A." will be used in the footnote references wherever this is necessary to distinguish the *Proceedings of the United States Potters Association* from those of the National Brotherhood of Operative Potters. For the latter the initials " N. B. of O. P." will be used where necessary.

fected. The " general objects " of the Association were
stated in its first constitution to be

to procure, regularly, the statistics of the trade, both at home and
abroad; to provide for the mutual interchange of information and
experience, both scientific and practical; to collect and distribute
all information relating to the various branches of our art, and to
take such means as will diffuse theoretical and practical information
to our trade in all its branches.[2]

In the forefront of the Association's concern at the time
of its formation, as today, was " the important subject of tariff, Custom House entries, or any other undue
and unfair competition in our home market."

There is no doubt that some of those who responded
to the call for the formation of an organization of
manufacturing potters cherished a hope that the new
body would lend its support to the stabilization of selling prices. But the Association did not assume for
itself the function of price regulation. The question was
raised in the first meeting, only to provoke a decision in
the negative. The conclusion was that " combinations
on either selling prices or working prices would weaken
the Association." [3] For one year, 1878-1879, it did
attempt to maintain a " standard price list " for the
convenience of the trade and to fix the discounts which
might be given from it in quoting actual selling prices,[4]
but the next year the Association officially withdrew
from regulation of selling prices and that function was
delegated to a representative committee of manufacturers.[5] Whatever attempts were made thereafter to
fix the discounts that should be given from the " stand-

---

[2] *Constitution*, Article I—printed in *Proceedings*, 1875.

[3] *Proceedings*, 1875, p. 10.

[4] " No local society, association or firm [was to] be permitted to
publish any lower rate of selling prices or increase of discounts."
Proceedings, December, 1878, pp. 8, 21, 22.

[5] *Ibid.*, 1879, pp. 22, 25, 26; 1885, pp. 8, 9.

ard list" were made through other organizations.[6] They appear to have been regarded as not highly successful and were given up many years ago.[7]

The exclusion of the regulation of the wages of labor from the objects of the Association did not prevent the creation of an "Aid Committee on Labor," to which was assigned the duty of giving information on labor matters when called upon for this service by any of the members of the Association, or the frequent discussion in the earlier meetings of what was a proper wages policy. Indeed, for a few years there was an attempt to use the Association meetings as a medium for securing the observance of a uniform wage list. In 1877 the manufacturers of Trenton had forced through a general reduction in wages, in spite of a strike, and had set up a new " working price list." Although the Association did not officially adopt this list, the " importance and necessity of adhering to the new rate of wages proposed by the Trenton Manufacturing Potters Association " was urged upon the members.[8] The next year the Trenton 1877 list was recognized as " the standard of prices paid for potters' labor throughout the country " and a committee was appointed to undertake a revision of it.[9] Apparently the proposed revision was not carried out, at least not through the Association.

There is no further suggestion of concerted action on a wage list in the reports of the Association meetings until 1894. From time to time the declaration was made

---

[6] *Ibid.*, 1890, pp. 6, 12; 1897, pp. 11, 15; December, 1900, pp. 19, 23-25; 1904, p. 38; 1907, pp. 15, 50.

[7] Statement of Secretary Goodwin to the writer; also *Proceedings*, 1919, p. 28. The practice of publishing the standard price list in the *Proceedings* was discontinued after 1921.

[8] *Ibid.*, 1877, pp. 10-11.

[9] *Ibid.*, December, 1878, pp. 6, 10, 20.

that the Association as such regarded the regulation of wages as outside its province.[10] Such general observations as appear from 1885 to 1894 were to the effect that the general level of wages was no more than adequate and should not be reduced unless a tariff reduction should make it necessary. It was obviously the policy of the Association to enlist the support of the workers for the existing tariff rates.[11]

In the meeting of January, 1894, concerted action to enforce a wage reduction was the primary business.[12] A recommendation for a general wage reduction was accepted through a roll call vote of the firms represented. There was then adopted a form of agreement to be signed by each member, which included an obligation to place in the hands of a treasurer the sum of $50.00 for each general ware kiln. Separate treasurers were named for the East and the West and a committee was appointed in each section to take charge. The reports of the Association indicate that no extraordinary expenditures were made through its own treasury for the conduct of the six-months strike which followed.

The next meeting of the Association at which labor matters were in the foreground was one called in 1897 to consider a proposed agreement with the organized workers. A labor committee of seven members, three

[10] *Ibid.*, 1885, pp. 8, 12; 1888, p. 5. Ex-District Master Workman O'Neill, testifying before the United States Industrial Commission in 1901, ascribed the failure of the operative potters organized within the Knights of Labor to reach a uniform scale in the industry largely to the fact that the United States Potters Association would not "take up the wage question at all," and to "cut-throat" competition among the manufacturers. *Report of Industrial Commission* [Washington: Government Printing Office, 1901], XIV, 655. The abbreviation "*U. S. Ind. Comm.*" will be used hereafter in citing this report.

[11] *Proceedings*, 1886, p. 13; 1887, p. 15; 1888, pp. 5, 19; 1893, p. 8.

[12] *Ibid.*, 1894, p. 7.

of whom were from Trenton, was appointed, with authority to deal with the operatives' representatives " on all questions that may arise relative to the adjustment of wages." [13] Thus the Association had advanced from collective action on wages to collective negotiation with the organized workers. No agreement was made by the Association itself with a labor organization at this time, but this outcome was due to the inability of the eastern and western unions to agree on a wage list to be presented to the manufacturers, not to a refusal by the Association to enter into a wage agreement.

In 1900 the Association again entered the field of collective bargaining. The eastern organized workers had meantime joined the National Brotherhood of Operative Potters, the union with which the Association has dealt continuously since 1905, and this simplified the task of making an agreement of national scope. However, some of the eastern members of the Brotherhood refused to accept the wage scale agreed upon. The Association then took the ground that this cancelled the agreement so far as it was concerned and it withdrew from the field of national collective bargaining. It took a hand again in 1903 in order to bring about arbitration when a strike was threatened in the West. Finally, in 1905, after the terms of the western agreement had been extended to the East, it again carried on the negotiations and concluded an agreement with the Brotherhood in its own name.

SECTIONAL EMPLOYERS' ASSOCIATIONS

Prior to 1905 most of the members of the United States Potters Association were also members of sectional organizations which acted for them in labor mat-

[13] *Ibid.*, 1897, pp. 7, 10, 11, 12, 14.

ters. The Trenton manufacturers were much more active in this respect than the western employers down to 1897. Reference has already been made to an association of Trenton manufacturers which as early as 1877 forced through a reduction in wages and set up a new wage scale. The Trenton manufacturers also came to collective bargaining before the manufacturers of the West, where the workers were relatively unorganized before the 1894 strike. As early as 1885 there was an agreement between the Trenton Potters Association and the Knights of Labor, making effective a new—and reduced—scale of wages. When the negotiations conducted by the United States Potters Association with the operatives failed to result in a national agreement in 1897, and again in 1900, the Trenton Potters Association reappeared as the representative of the Trenton manufacturers in dealing with the organized workers in Trenton and acted in that capacity until 1905. Thereafter it played little part in labor relations. It was not exclusively a general ware organization; some of its most important members were sanitary manufacturers, and for these members the Sanitary Potters Association [14] performed the same functions in labor matters as the United States Potters Association did for the members in the general ware division. The primary interests of the Trenton Potters Association after 1905 were with such matters as transportation rates and facilities and proposed state legislation.

The western manufacturers first negotiated collectively with the Brotherhood in 1897, after the breakdown of the attempt to make an agreement of national scope. At that time they apparently had no formal association for dealing with labor. The agreement with the

[14] See below, ch. xiv.

Brotherhood to restore the 1893 level of wages in the West was made by a " committee of western manufacturers." But in 1901, after the United States Potters Association had declined to deal with the Brotherhood again, the " Western Manufacturing Potters Association " came forward with an offer to treat with the Brotherhood on behalf of those western members of the United States Potters Association in whose potteries the agreement of 1900 was in force. It was this Association which dealt with the Brotherhood from 1900 to 1905. After 1905 it disappeared from the labor scene.[15]

THE INTER-ASSOCIATION COMPACT OF 1903

Meanwhile the United States Potters Association had sponsored a defensive alliance between the three associations actively dealing with the organized operatives—the Western Manufacturing Potters Association, the Trenton Potters Association, and the Sanitary Potters Association. The Brotherhood had threatened to call a strike of sanitary pressers in 1902. Now, in 1903, there was danger of a strike against the western general ware manufacturers; the agreement between the Brotherhood and the western association was to expire June 30 and the negotiations for a renewal of the agreement had revealed little prospect of agreement. In June, 1903, the three associations pledged

[15] The *Eleventh Special Report of the Commissioner of Labor,* " Regulation and Restriction of Output " (Washington: Government Printing Office, 1904) gives the erroneous impression that the United States Potters Association had been confined to the " East, or Trenton field," and had dealt with the eastern operatives, in contrast to the Western Manufacturing Potters Association which had dealt with the western operatives, and that " these facts " had " tended to keep the workmen of the two fields apart." (p. 666.)

themselves to united action under the leadership of the United Potters Association, in case of a strike against the members of any one of them.

The 1903 treaty required each association to attempt to settle its labor difficulties peaceably with " a committee representing the workmen." If it should fail to secure a settlement after " an earnest attempt," it must, " without resorting to lockout or submitting " to a strike, lay the matter before a joint committee representing all three associations. If the joint committee should in turn fail to secure an amicable adjustment of the difficulty, the entire matter was to be referred to the combined membership of the three associations. No action resulting in a strike or lockout was to be taken except upon vote of a two-thirds majority of the aggregate membership. If, after such a vote, the action taken should result in a strike or lockout in any of the plants of any of the three associations, all three associations were to close their potteries until the matter was adjusted. The United States Potters Association was to have general supervision of the carrying out of this compact.[16]

The inter-association agreement was invoked by the western association in September, 1903, when the Brotherhood, after the failure of protracted negotiations, threatened to call a strike against it. The president of the United States Potters Association intervened, and following a conference of representatives of the three associations,[17] the manufacturers made an offer of arbi-

---

[16] MS. *Memorandum of Agreement between the Western Manufacturing Potters Association, the Trenton Manufacturing Potters Association, and the Sanitary Potters Association,* June 11, 1903.

[17] MS. *Minutes of Special Joint Meeting of Committees from the Western Manufacturing Potters Association, the Trenton Potters Association, and the Sanitary Potters Association,* September 17, 1903.

tration, which was accepted by the Brotherhood.[18] This seems to have been the only important result of the compact of 1903. By 1905 the reason for it had disappeared in general ware, and the sanitary division had set up its own national system of collective bargaining.

THE UNITED STATES POTTERS ASSOCIATION SINCE 1905

Membership.—In 1905 the United States Potters Association had 51 members in general ware, with 432 kilns. There were then 35 potteries, with 226 kilns, outside the Association.[19] It was the policy of the Association to bring within its membership all general ware manufacturers, at least all who were willing to comply with the terms of the agreement with the Brotherhood.[20] This consummation has never been achieved. But for the past dozen years there have been few general ware plants outside the Association. The non-member plants are new or small, with two exceptions. Both these firms left the Association because they were involved in disputes with the Brotherhood and both plants are non-union.

Full participation in the labor agreement has not been made a condition of continuing membership in the Association in every case. The largest china manufacturing firm in the Association, the Onondaga Pottery Company, located in Syracuse, New York, does not recognize, and has never recognized the Brotherhood. This firm had been in the Association for years when the joint agreement of 1905 was made. In the following year the Brotherhood attempted to organize the shop

[18] *Proceedings, U. S. P. A.,* 1903, p. 20; *Proceedings, N. B. of O. P.,* 1904, pp. 9-10.
[19] *Proceedings,* 1905, pp. 73-75.
[20] *Ibid.,* 1908, p. 23; 1911, p. 19.

3

but the head of the firm, who was in that year President of the United States Potters Association, made it clear that he did not wish his employees to join the union, and the attempt was not successful.[21] Nor has the union been able to secure the allegiance of any considerable number of the employees of the company at any time since then. On the other hand, four firms, two in china and two in semi-porcelain, have resigned from the Association in the last dozen years upon refusal to abide by the terms of the labor agreement and the Association has not attempted to get them back.

The absolute membership has declined recently on account of the depressed condition of the industry. In 1928 the Association had 54 active members with 690 kilns in general ware.[22] Ten of these firms were engaged in the manufacture of china ware. Approximately one-sixth of the kiln capacity covered by the Association was in the china ware subdivision of the industry. By December, 1930, the number of kilns had been reduced to 624 and the number of members to 38; one of the members had, as a result of a consolidation, succeeded eight formerly independent members.[23]

Internal Organization.—The constitution of the Association and its methods of functioning have changed but little since 1905. The officers of the Association are elected at the annual meeting.[24] This is ordinarily held in December. Each firm has one vote in the annual

[21] *Report of President,* 1907, pp. 8-9. This abbreviation will be used for the annual *Report of the President and First Vice-President of the National Brotherhood of Operative Potters.*

[22] *Proceedings,* 1927, pp. 11-12, 32. The number of kilns is still given in terms of periodic kilns, the old unit; tunnel kilns are counted in each case as a number of periodic kilns of equivalent capacity.

[23] *Ibid.,* 1929, pp. 13-14, 36; 1930, pp. 10-11.

[24] The Constitution and By-Laws are published in the annual *Proceedings.*

meeting, regardless of its kiln capacity. It is the practice to elect a new president each year. The office of secretary-treasurer is a salaried office. The present incumbent, Mr. Charles F. Goodwin, has served continuously since 1914.

The committees of the Association are also elected at the annual meeting. The two most important committees are the executive committee and the labor committee. Other committees are concerned with transportation rates and facilities, manufacturers' costs, art and design, research, machinery, and types of kilns and fuels. There are also three smaller committees which have to do with the labor agreement. These committees meet with similar committees from the Brotherhood as joint " standing " committees for the adjustment of disputes arising under the agreement. Their function is to deal with disputes within the terms of the existing agreement, not to negotiate new terms. The latter function belongs to the labor committee, which acts as the policy forming committee of the Association in labor matters. It has been the practice of the Association to preserve continuity of membership on the several committees, as far as possible. The most striking example of unbroken service is that of Mr. W. E. Wells on the labor committee. He served as chairman of that committee from its establishment as a regular committee of the Association, in 1906, until December, 1928.[25]

Finances.—The financing of the activities of the Association is cared for by annual dues and occasional assessments. The annual dues are $80.00 for all active members.[26] The executive committee is authorized to levy assessments when necessary. These are made on

[25] *Ibid.,* 1905, p. 13; 1906, pp. 5, 17; 1928, pp. 8, 20, 69.
[26] *Ibid.,* 1924, p. 89; 1927, p. 78.

a kiln basis, at a flat rate per kiln. Two Trenton sanitary firms are members of the Association, having retained membership through many years. They are not subject to assessment on their sanitary kilns. The total receipts of the Association for the year ending December 1, 1927, were $31,587.48. Its balance was $2,435.11. It will be readily seen that the Association is not a financially powerful employers' association. It has no strike fund or defense fund of any kind. Nor has it levied assessments for the conduct of a strike since the beginning of the agreement system. In 1922, when the potteries of the members were closed for ten weeks by a strike, the receipts and expenditures of the Association were approximately the same as those for the years immediately preceding and following the year in which the strike occurred.[27]

[27] The receipts and expenditures are given in the annual *Proceedings*.

CHAPTER II

THE BROTHERHOOD—HISTORY

The National Brotherhood of Operative Potters dates from 1890. It had its origin in a secession movement from the Knights of Labor. Until 1897 it was confined to the West and until 1899 practically to the general ware division of the industry.

Such organizations as had appeared among the operative potters before the advent of the Knights of Labor in the industry were of a limited and apparently ephemeral character.[1] The first organization among the pottery workers in Trenton was formed in 1868, through the efforts of John D. McCormick.[2] If this union maintained a continuous existence,[3] it made little impression upon the operatives as a whole. When the Trenton manufacturers proposed a reduction in wages in 1874, " there was no organization in existence " among the operatives.[4] The workers did resist the reduction of 1877 for four months before they were compelled to submit, but if they had an organization of a general character at that time it did not long survive the struggle.[5] McCormick said in 1890 that " he had

---

[1] *Eleventh Special Report of the Commissioner of Labor*, p. 665.

[2] *Official Souvenir of the Convention of the Potters National Union*, 1893. McCormick was a member of the Executive Council of the Potters National Union at the time of the publication of the *Souvenir*.

[3] One of the witnesses before the United States Industrial Commission (in 1901), a Trenton jiggerman, stated: " Our first organization was created in this city in 1869, and has continued ever since." *U. S. Ind. Comm.*, XIV, 644.

[4] *Official Souvenir*, 1893.

[5] *U. S. Ind. Comm.*, XIV, 655.

fought with the potters in the old trades unions long
before the Knights came, and they could never accomplish any permanent good. Branch jealousies and race
prejudices would spring up and prevent united action." [6]

ORGANIZATION WITHIN THE KNIGHTS OF LABOR

The widespread organization of the potters by the
Knights of Labor did not come until 1882. The East
Liverpool operatives preceded those of Trenton in the
formation of local trade assemblies but the Trenton
organizations were soon more numerous and proved
more lasting. The first local assembly in Trenton made
up exclusively of potters (L. A. 2185) was not organized until late in 1882. It was made up of general ware
pressers.[7] It was soon followed by one of kilnmen
(L. A. 2474).[8] Between the 1884 and 1885 general conventions of the Knights of Labor, local assemblies of
printers and transferers (L. A. 3549), sanitary pressers (L. A. 3561), jiggermen and dishmakers (L. A.
3573), and turners, throwers, and handlers (L. A. 3594)
were organized. These six local assemblies in Trenton
had on July 1, 1885, an aggregate membership of
approximately 950.[9]

In the West, East Liverpool boasted two local assemblies early in 1882. The larger of these (L. A. 1853) had
557 members.[10] But in June, 1882, the Order was
plunged into a fight in East Liverpool which resulted

[6] *Proceedings, D. A. 160*, p. 26. This abbreviation will be used
for the *Proceedings of the Operative Potters' National Trade District
Assembly 160, Knights of Labor.*

[7] *Official Souvenir*, 1893; also *Proceedings, Knights of Labor*, 1883,
p. 550. This abbreviation is used for the *Record of the Proceedings
of the Sessions of the General Assembly of the Knights of Labor.*

[8] *Proceedings, Knights of Labor*, 1883, p. 552. It is not clear whether
this local included dippers and saggermakers at that time.

[9] *Ibid.*, 1885, p. 204; *Official Souvenir*, 1893.

[10] *Proceedings, Knights of Labor*, 1882, p. 378.

disastrously for it. The manufacturers gave notice to their employees that each one must, if he wished to retain his employment, sign a statement that he did not belong to the Knights of Labor and would not join any labor organization. This precipitated a struggle which lasted for nine months. The locked-out men were dependent for financial support on District Assembly, No. 3, of the Knights of Labor, a geographical district centering in Pittsburgh. Owing to a strike in the iron and steel mills the District Assembly was unable to furnish adequate assistance. The General Assembly of the Knights of Labor was appealed to but the response was not satisfactory to the East Liverpool potters. The employers won a complete victory.[11] The failure of the union to win its fight on the vital issue of " the right to organize," combined with the belief on the part of the potters that they had not been properly supported by the Kights of Labor, led to the speedy decline of the Order in East Liverpool.[12]

In July, 1886, the potters' local assemblies of the Knights of Labor, hitherto under the jurisdiction of their respective geographical districts, were gathered into a district assembly of their own, known as District Assembly, Number 160.[13] Its full title was " The Operative Potters National Union, National Trades District Assembly, Number 160, Knights of Labor." [14] It was a national trade union in form, subordinate to the Knights of Labor. Although it was for several years an important factor in the industry in Trenton

---

[11] *Ibid.*, 1882, pp. 305, 326-327; 1883, pp. 453, 455, 469; *Proceedings, D. A. 160*, 1890, pp. 29-30.

[12] *Proceedings, Knights of Labor*, 1883, p. 530; 1884, p. 823.

[13] *Ibid.*, 1886, pp. 19, 328.

[14] *Constitution and By-Laws*, 1887.

and established a considerable measure of local collective bargaining, it never became in reality a national union of pottery operatives, as it failed to secure the adherence of the majority of the workers outside of Trenton.

By 1890 a large proportion of the western members had concluded that a national organization could not be effected within the Knights of Labor. Accordingly they proposed that the Potters National Union should withdraw from that Order and launch out as an independent national union. When the convention met in September, 1890, the most important matter which it had to consider was a resolution from the Toronto, Ohio, assembly calling for just such action. The reasons for the proposed step, as given in an appeal accompanying the Toronto resolution and reiterated in the debate in the convention, may be briefly summarized. There were too many assessments on the members and too little forthcoming from the Knights of Labor in payments to the members when called out on strike. The potters owed such organization as they had to their own hard work and not to the Knights of Labor. The success of the English potters and of the Flint Glass Workers in America showed that much more could be done through an independent organization. It had been clearly proved that the employers would concede nothing to the operatives as members of the Knights of Labor. The western operatives would never join the organization in large numbers as long as it was connected with the Order; indeed, the threat was made that all the western assemblies would withdraw from the Potters National Union if that organization did not leave the Knights of Labor.

The resolution for withdrawal was finally defeated through the adoption of a motion to postpone the question until the next annual meeting. The vote was 19 to 13. An appeal made by a member of the executive board of the General Assembly of the Knights of Labor to stand by the Order had considerable influence in securing this result. Much was said also of an energetic campaign that was to be made to organize the West.[15] Nearly all of the western local asemblies then withdrew from the Knights of Labor,[16] and although the response to the project for an independent national union was not at all encouraging the sponsors of the movement did launch a new organization, to be known as the National Brotherhood of Operative Potters, in December, 1890.

The eastern organization continued its existence until 1897. However, its connection with the Knights of Labor had become shadowy by 1892 and in 1893 it ceased altogether.[17] Several of the Trenton local assemblies were then reorganized as " local unions " of the Potters National Union.[18] The kilnmen, dippers and saggermakers of Trenton did not join the Potters Na-

[15] *Proceedings, D. A. 160,* 1890, pp. 23-35, 38, 42, 50, 60; Thomas J. Duffy, *History of the National Brotherhood of Operative Potters from 1890 to 1901* (Pittsburgh: Commoner and Glass Worker, 1901), pp. 3-4. This work will be cited hereafter as " Duffy." T. J. Duffy was in 1901 National Secretary of the Brotherhood.

[16] *Proceedings of the Executive Board, D. A. 160,* December, 1890; *Proceedings, D. A. 160,* 1892.

[17] The convention of January, 1892, selected a delegate to the General Assembly of the Knights of Labor but neither District Assembly No. 160 nor any of its Trenton local assemblies was represented at the 1892 convention of the Knights of Labor. *Proceedings, Knights of Labor,* 1892, p. 30. Nor does the name of District Assembly No. 160 appear in the 1893 *Proceedings of the Knights of Labor.* The title page of the *Souvenir* of the 1893 convention of the Potters National Union contains no mention of the Knights of Labor. See also *Eleventh Special Report of the Commissioner of Labor,* p. 665.

[18] MS. *Minutes, Trenton Jiggermen, Local Union No. 4.*

tional Union but maintained an independent organization until they went into the Brotherhood in 1897. There were some sanitary pressers in the National Union in 1893 but a short time later they, too, formed an independent organization.

EARLY HISTORY OF THE BROTHERHOOD (1890-1899)

For the first three years of its existence the Brotherhood made small impression on the potters of the West. So dark was its outlook at the end of that period that some of the local unions requested a meeting of the executive board for the purpose of formally disbanding the organization and a meeting was actually held to consider this proposal. President Hughes and a few others vigorously opposed dissolution. It was rumored that the employers were about to reduce wages on account of the proposed reduction in the tariff on earthenware and President Hughes was able to persuade the members of the board to continue the Brotherhood, weak as it was, in order that the operatives might have some sort of organization around which to rally in case the manufacturers attempted to enforce a wage reduction.[19]

The posting of notices by the manufacturers in January, 1894, announcing a reduced wage scale, and the almost universal determination of the operatives to resist the proposed reduction, created the first situation favorable to the organization of the western operatives which the Brotherhood had encountered. The officers of the Brotherhood now seized the opportunity of proving the usefulness of their union by organizing resistance to the reduction in the various potteries and by leading in the conduct of the strike as a whole.[20]

[19] Duffy, pp. 5-16.
[20] *Proceedings, N. B. of O. P.,* 1894, pp. 6-7; Duffy, pp. 17-19.

Starting out with a very small, apparently moribund, union with an empty treasury they carried on the strike for six months without a serious break in the ranks of the operatives and surrendered then only because the acceptance of the reduction by the eastern operatives seemed to make further resistance hopeless.[21] At the conclusion of the strike, in July, 1894, close to half, if not a majority, of the skilled operatives of the West were nominally members of the Brotherhood.[22]

Nevertheless, the Brotherhood had to suffer a loss of membership for over two years before the tide turned again in its favor. In July, 1896, it had but 457 paying members.[23] It was the series of negotiations with the western manufacturers in 1897, resulting in an agreement that the wage level of 1893 be restored, which established the Brotherhood firmly in the industry in the West.[24] In these negotiations the Brotherhood was recognized by the western manufacturers. This, and the successful outcome of the negotiations, convinced many of the western operatives that the Brotherhood could again be very helpful to them and they joined in large numbers.

Another important outcome of the 1897 wage restoration and the negotiations involved in it was the adherence of the Trenton operatives to the Brotherhood. The leaders of the Brotherhood had hoped from the beginning that the eastern operatives might even-

[21] Proceedings, N. B. of O. P., 1894, pp. 8, 19, 22; 1895, p. 4; Duffy, pp. 19-20; U. S. Ind. Comm., XIV, 627.

[22] Proceedings, 1894, pp. 6-7; 17-18; 1895, p. 4; Duffy, p. 18.

[23] Proceedings, 1896. The pages of the 1896 Proceedings are not numbered.

[24] President Duffy said in his 1908 Report (p. 3) that prior to this series of conferences the organization appeared to be " doomed to failure and extinction. . . . . The real perceptible progress of our organization dates from this conference."

tually be brought together with the western in one national organization, but down to the 1894 strike the Brotherhood was so weak even in the West that there was no chance of its attracting the eastern operatives away from the Potters National Union. The fight waged against the wage reduction of 1894 by both the eastern and the western operatives brought the unions of the two sections closer together for a time; but the acceptance of the reduction by the eastern operatives, without regard to the wishes of the West and without consultation with the representatives of the Brotherhood, upset the accord.[25] Early in 1897 the Brotherhood officers again approached the eastern operatives with a request to consider the question of consolidation, or at least to agree upon a plan of common action to secure the restoration of the wage cut of 1894 and the establishment of a uniform wage list. This produced many gestures toward immediate combined action on a wage advance and a uniform scale, and even toward later consolidation.[26] However, the two organizations failed to agree on a wage list to be presented to the manufacturers, the eastern representatives fearing that they stood to lose by accepting a common base, and each group made its own terms with its respective employers.[27]

Then, rather unexpectedly, the eastern operatives decided to join the Brotherhood. Their adherence was the result of aid given them by the Brotherhood officers in a dispute with their employers over the new scale. The Trenton manufacturers contended that their rates should be based on the new western prices which, they

[25] *Proceedings, N. B. of O. P.,* 1894, pp. 8, 19, 22; MS. *Minutes, Trenton Jiggermen, Local Union No. 4; Proceedings, N. B. of O. P.,* 1895, pp. 4, 8.
[26] *Ibid.,* 1897. The pages of the 1897 *Proceedings* are not numbered.
[27] *Ibid.,* 1898, pp. 3-5; Duffy, p. 27.

insisted, were lower than those asked by the eastern operatives. During the controversy the Trenton union of kilnmen, dippers and saggermakers, then an independent union, asked the Brotherhood to send someone to Trenton who could give it reliable information as to the prices, conditions and customs in the West. The Brotherhood sent two of its national officers. These visits led to the affiliation of the general ware local unions of Trenton with the Brotherhood.[28] When the Brotherhood met for its 1898 convention it was the only organization of general ware potters of any consequence in the industry. Its reported membership was double what it had been the year before.[29]

The Brotherhood was greatly helped to this position by the attitude of the western manufacturers toward it. The great gain in membership in the West and the adherence of the eastern operatives were largely the result of the recognition of the Brotherhood by the western manufacturers and the granting of the restoration of the 1893 prices through agreement with it. Had the manufacturers ignored the Brotherhood and restored the wages of 1893 on their own initiative without negotiation with the Brotherhood it is difficult to see how it could have gained much in prestige or membership at that time. Or had the manufacturers refused to increase wages and stubbornly resisted the attempt of the Brotherhood to force the restoration, the success of the union would have been at least doubtful. The Brotherhood had in July, 1897, but 502 members and total cash resources of but $5,600.[30]

In December, 1899, the Brotherhood finally established itself as the only important union in the pottery industry by absorbing the remnants of the Sanitary

[28] *Proceedings*, N. B. of O. P., 1898, pp. 5-7; Duffy, pp. 28-29.
[29] *Proceedings,* 1898, p. 16; 1899, p. 10; Duffy, p. 31.
[30] *Proceedings,* 1897.

Pressers National Union. This union had been launched in May, 1895, through the initiative of the sanitary pressers of Trenton, and it had gathered to itself a number of sanitary ware pressers in the West who were at that time members of the Brotherhood.[31] President Hughes of the Brotherhood had opposed the movement to form a separate national union of sanitary pressers. He expressed the opinion that all workers in white ware should be in the same organization, and cited the experience of other unions in support of his thesis.[32] Apparently the western sanitary pressers who were in the Brotherhood also favored having a single national union of pottery operatives, but when the eastern sanitary pressers would not accept that view, they left the Brotherhood to join their craft brothers.[33]

Fortunately for the Brotherhood the attempt of the sanitary pressers to establish a national craft union apart from the other skilled workers in the industry met with failure. After an auspicious start it found the financial problem too much for it and its membership began to decline. By 1899 the " national union " had been reduced practically to a Trenton local union. On December 7th, the remaining members voted unanimously to " amalgamate with the National Brotherhood of Operative Potters." [34] This action was followed by the enrollment of many sanitary pressers in the Brotherhood in other localities and of workers in the other sanitary branches as well.[35]

[31] *Ibid.*, 1895, p. 5; 1896. It was preceded in Trenton by another organization of sanitary workers. MS. *Minutes, Sanitary Pressers National Union.*

[32] *Proceedings, N. B. of O. P.*, 1895, pp. 5-6.

[33] *Ibid.*, 1895, p. 26; 1896; Duffy, p. 23.

[34] MS. *Minutes, Sanitary Pressers National Union; Report of President, N. B. of O. P.*, 1906, p. 14.

[35] *Proceedings*, 1900, p. 8; Duffy, pp. 33-34.

THE ESTABLISHMENT OF NATIONAL WAGE SCALES
(1900-1905)

In May, 1900, the Brotherhood reached the goal toward which it had long been working, an agreement with the United States Potters Association on a national wage scale for the general ware division. Disappointed in 1897, unable to make any headway in 1898, it had set out determinedly in 1899 to establish a uniform wage scale in general ware " with or without the cooperation of the manufacturers." After months of preliminary negotiations an agreement was reached without even a threat of strike. As the result of this achievement and the accession of the sanitary workers, the membership of the Brotherhood was increased by " some 1,500 " between July, 1899, and July, 1900, an increase of over 100 per cent.[36]

The attitude of the general ware manufacturers toward the Brotherhood and toward its proposal for a uniform list had again enabled it to attain an important objective—and so greatly strengthen itself with the operatives—which it is very doubtful that it could have secured by force. In the summer of 1899, when the Brotherhood decided to push the uniform list proposal, its membership in good standing did not exceed 1,300,[37] and it had but $15,700 in its defense fund.[38]

But in the moment of its apparent triumph the Brotherhood received a severe setback. There was much dissatisfaction in the East with the new uniform wage scale and two of the Trenton local unions,

[36] *Proceedings,* 1900, p. 7.

[37] This is the figure reported to the American Federation of Labor. *Report of Proceedings of the 19th Annual Convention of the American Federation of Labor,* held at Detroit, Michigan, December 11th to 20th, inclusive, 1800, p. iv.

[38] *Proceedings, N. B. of O. P.,* 1899, pp. 40-41; 1900, p. 36.

the jiggermen and dishmakers' union, and the kilnmen's union, refused to accept it. The jiggermen and
dishmakers' union even withdrew from the Brotherhood and attempted to reorganize a general union of
eastern general ware operatives under the auspices of
the Knights of Labor. The secessionists succeeded in
detaching a number of kilnmen, turners, and handlers.
The Brotherhood local of turners and handlers dissolved and the membership of the kilnmen's local was
reduced by more than one-half. The Brotherhood also
lost heavily in those groups which had looked for
advantages from the adoption of the uniform scale; the
local unions of the pressers and packers in Trenton
turned in their charters.[39]

The persistence of the Brotherhood in the policy of
securing a national uniform list even at the cost of
accepting " an average of prices East and West " had
thus nearly wrecked the organization in the East. The
kilnmen and the jiggermen and dishmakers of Trenton
had been too long organized and had too recently joined
the Brotherhood to allow the latter to sacrifice them to
the principle of uniformity in prices. A uniform list
was desirable but it should have been obtained, they
held, by bringing western prices up to eastern.[40] For

[39] *Ibid.*, p. 9; 1901, pp. 6, 7; *U. S. Ind. Comm.*, XIV, 636, 639,
640-641, 644-645.

[40] Witnesses representing the jiggermen and dishmakers' organization of Trenton before the United States Industrial Commission in
1901 expressed resentment at the national union's attempt to reduce
their wages. (XIV, 641, 645.) It is interesting to note that John A.
O'Neill, who, as District Master Workman of D. A. 160, had opposed
the withdrawal of the western operatives from the Knights of Labor
in 1890, told the Industrial Commission in 1901 that if he were to
return " to the bench," he would consider it his duty to join the
Brotherhood. " I would join the Brotherhood if I went to the bench,
even if I were all by myself." XIV, 653.

the next few years the policy of the Brotherhood toward the eastern operatives was to leave the matter of a national uniform wage scale in abeyance and attempt to reorganize the trade in the East.[41]

The reversal suffered in the East did not prevent progress by the Brotherhood in the West. The agreement rejected in the East went into operation in the West on May 1, 1900. The Brotherhood was thereby recognized by all the western manufacturers who had been parties to the agreement—and this included nearly all of the western general ware manufacturers—as the representative of the workers in the branches covered by the agreement. A system of settling new prices and adjusting other points of difference was also established which made this constantly manifest. Between July, 1900, and July, 1901, the total membership was increased by over 500 in spite of the defection of the eastern operatives.[42]

Up to this time the Brotherhood had been practically an organization of and for skilled operatives alone. This was not so much the result of conscious exclusion of the unskilled as of inability to interest them in the organization. In the 1901 convention, following the recommendation of the president, a program was adopted for the organization of the less skilled workers in the industry. President Hughes urged this step largely for the protection of the skilled workmen. The batters-out and the finishers, for example, groups which he urged specifically that the Brotherhood should organize, could be expected to learn in time to do the work of journeymen jiggermen and stickers-up, respectively. The warehousewomen, whom he urged that the Broth-

[41] *Proceedings,* 1902, pp. 15, 79, 80, 82.
[42] *Ibid.,* 1901, p. 9.

4

erhood should attempt also to include in its organization, were already organized as an independent local of
the American Federation of Labor and had demon-
strated their ability to tie up the potteries by striking.[43]

For a time the attempt to include the less skilled
workers, particularly the female workers, appeared to
meet with considerable success. In all, five local unions
made up primarily of female operatives were organized in the year 1901-1902. The membership jumped
nearly two thousand from 1901 to 1902, the greater
part of the increase coming from the inclusion of the
women operatives. However, by 1904 the Brotherhood
had lost most of these female recruits.[44]

In the year 1902-1903 the Brotherhood made important gains in the sanitary division. The sanitary pressers secured a uniform list by agreement with the
employers in June, 1902. The next year an agreement
was made with the manufacturers establishing uniform
scales for the other organized sanitary branches and
a joint standing committee for the adjustment of
disputes. The system of national collective bargaining
then set up lasted until 1922.

In the general ware division in the East, also, the
tide turned in 1902. The local unions of pressers, turners and handlers, and packers were reorganized and a
separate local union of saggermakers was established.[45]
The kilnmen's local received back those who had
deserted in 1900 and regained its old membership.
Even the jiggermen and dishmakers came back into
the fold, but only with the promise that no attempt
would be made to force the " uniform list " upon them

[43] *Ibid.*, pp. 6, 71-72.

[44] *Ibid.*, 1902, pp. 6-7; 1904, pp. 12-13.

[45] These local unions of packers and saggermakers in Trenton
included both general ware and sanitary workers.

if they were still opposed to it after the 1903 convention. With the reorganization of the general ware operatives and the increased membership in the sanitary shops the Brotherhood's eastern membership increased by a thousand in this year.[46]

The next milestone in the progress of the Brotherhood was the extension of the western uniform list to the East in the teeth of the opposition of the Trenton jiggermen. Thomas J. Duffy, who had been National Secretary since 1899, was elected president in the 1903 convention upon the retirement of President Hughes. President Duffy regarded the bringing of the East under the " uniform list " as the most important task before the Brotherhood. He made it the keystone of his policy and directed the energies of the Brotherhood toward its realization until it was acomplished.

In the 1903 general ware negotiations in the West, the Brotherhood concentrated on increases for the jiggermen and kilnmen in order to make the " uniform list " more acceptable to the members in these two branches in Trenton. No gain was made on this front, although the Brotherhood stood out to the point of breaking off negotiations and threatening a strike; it was forced to submit these demands to arbitration and lost the decision in both branches. Nevertheless, President Duffy and First Vice-President Hutchins succeeded, in May, 1904, in getting the Trenton kilnmen to declare for the western list. Their hands were further strengthened by the action of the 1904 convention, which empowered them to proceed with the enforcement of the list in Trenton " for the benefit of those branches that are willing to accept it." [47]

---

[46] *Proceedings*, 1903, pp. 8, 10-11, 16-18.
[47] *Ibid.*, 1904, pp. 19-20, 60-61, 106.

In September, 1904, a conference was finally secured with the Trenton manufacturers.[48] The latter then declared their position to be what it was in 1900— willingness to accept the list if the Brotherhood could give them satisfactory guarantees that the list would be accepted in its entirety by all branches. They were not willing to grant the list to the branches which would gain by it and continue to pay the higher eastern prices to the jiggermen. Nor were they willing to court a strike of the jiggermen. Until the jiggermen voted to accept the list the manufacturers would not, they stated, agree to adopt it.

The Brotherhood officers did not deny that the jiggermen did not want the list. Their position was that the Brotherhood was prepared to force the jiggermen to accept it so that the other branches which did want it might have it. If the manufacturers would agree to accept it the Brotherhood would see to it that the jiggermen would work under it. If the manufacturers would not agree to put in the list, the officers would have to let the branches which wanted it strike for it. The manufacturers were finally brought to an agreement to take the list, with the understanding that the Brotherhood officers would assume the responsibility of compelling the jiggermen to work under the agreement made for them by the Brotherhood.

The jiggermen did not submit without putting the Brotherhood to the test. The local union notified the manufacturers that " eighty per cent of the jiggermen of Trenton refuse to accept the uniform list." The next day, at a conference between the manufacturers and

---

[48] This account of the September-November negotiations in the East is based on the verbatim reports of the conferences between the Brotherhood and the manufacturers. See also *Report of President,* 1905, pp. 3-6, 19-20.

the Brotherhood officers, the manufacturers agreed that they would put in the list if the Brotherhood would keep the jiggermen at work or furnish men to replace those who quit. President Duffy assured the manufacturers that if any considerable number of jiggermen refused to work the Brotherhood would furnish men to take their places. The jiggermen quit work in several potteries, but the national officers got the jiggermen together in a meeting and after a long and stormy session persuaded them to work under the list. Within the next few months the uniform list was extended to the other union shops in the East. The logical consequence was a national joint agreement with the United States Potters Association in 1905. The national joint agreement system in the general ware division was then established essentially on the basis which it has since retained.

DEVELOPMENT UNDER THE TWO NATIONAL AGREEMENTS (1905-1922)

From 1905 to 1922 the two national agreements were the outstanding factors in the life of the Brotherhood. These were years of peace and development. Except for a suspension for ten days in the general ware division in 1917 there was no general cessation of work in either division during these seventeen years.

Throughout this period the Brotherhood maintained a strong position in the semi-porcelain part of the general ware division. At no time from 1905 to 1922 were there more than a few semi-porcelain plants making ware of the kind covered by the uniform scale which were not working under that scale and dealing with the Brotherhood. In 1922 there was no large semi-porcelain plant in the country operating " non-union." Not all of the union shops held membership in the

United States Potters Association but the few which
were outside observed the terms of the " wage scale and
agreements " between the Brotherhood and the Association, except those relating to the adjustment of local
disputes.

In china ware the union did not fare so well. The
largest china plant in the country, the Onondaga at
Syracuse, remained beyond the pale throughout. It did
not refuse to employ union members but it refused to
recognize the Brotherhood. The union at no time declared war on it; union members were not expressly
forbidden to work there. The other china shop in Syracuse, the Iroquois, went non-union in 1917. Early in
that year the firm became involved in a dispute with
the Brotherhood over the discharge of three men. The
Brotherhood officers requested that the case be sent to
the joint discharge committee, in accordance with the
agreement with the United States Potters Association.
The firm refused and resigned from the Association.
A strike was called but the firm weathered it.[49]

In the sanitary division the union maintained close
control of the plants making ware by the pressing
process. A shop in New Castle, Pennsylvania, went
non-union in 1905, refusing to comply with the terms
of the agreement and withdrawing from the manufacturers' association. It was then the only sanitary shop
in the country which did not recognize the union and
operate under its wage scale. This shop later gave up
the attempt to press ware and went over to casting.[50]
In 1910 the union attempted to organize a non-union
shop which had been opened in Lambertville, New Jersey. As a result, its members were locked out. How-

[49] *Ibid.*, 1917, pp. 13-14.
[50] *Ibid.*, 1906, pp. 15-16; 1907, p. 7; 1908, p. 15; 1909, p. 13.

ever, in November, 1912, the firm came to terms with the Brotherhood and the shop was unionized.[51] There was no further non-union competition in pressing semi-porcelain sanitary ware until 1922, when a firm in Tiffin, Ohio, which had operated a union shop for years, went non-union a few months before the sanitary strike. However, non-union competition had been growing through the use of the casting process as a substitute for pressing and by 1922 it had become a serious factor. Indeed it was the decisive factor. The refusal of the sanitary membership to meet it was the fundamental cause of the 1922 strike.[52]

The growth in membership from 1905 to 1921 was steady. In the earlier year the membership was approximately 5,600. In 1921, the peak year, it was 9,360; this was 122 more than the figure for 1922. Approximately 2,400 of the members were employed in the sanitary division.[53] The figure for the total membership includes two groups not employed under a national agreement system—138 " grogware " or " heavy porcelain " workers, and 43 members of a Canadian local who had been technically " on strike " for several years.[54]

Most of the increase in numbers from 1905 to 1922 came in the general ware division. It reflects not only the growth of the industry but an increased degree of organization among the employees in the union shops.

[51] *Ibid.*, 1911, pp. 6, 18-20; 1912, pp. 15-16; 1913, pp. 11-12.

[52] See below, ch. xiv.

[53] Estimate made by President Wood. Exact figures are unavailable as several of the local unions included members employed in the general ware division and members employed in the sanitary division.

[54] For the membership of the local unions the writer is indebted to the Secretary of the Brotherhood.

The Brotherhood improved its position in this period in several of the branches which were unorganized or but slightly organized—in the trade centers, at least—in 1905, although one branch included in the list of organized branches in East Liverpool in 1905, the kilndrawers, was lost. There were temporary losses, too, in one or another of the organized branches, due to dissatisfaction with some action of the Brotherhood. There were also marked fluctuations in the female branches. Yet the net result of these changes and fluctuations was to leave the Brotherhood representing more branches in its dealings with the employers in 1922 than in 1905 and with a very high percentage of organization in nearly all of these.

One of the most important extensions of activity during this period was the establishment of beneficiary features, other than strike benefits.[55] It began in 1910 with the inauguration of a death benefit.[56] The plan eventually adopted was in its essentials urged upon the Brotherhood by Vice-President Hutchins in his 1907 report. He was convinced of the necessity of offering some form of benefit, in addition to the strike benefit, as an inducement to members to keep in good standing. The practice of signing a wage agreement for a specified period had freed the members from anxiety over wages and this caused some to lose interest in the organization. The practical elimination of strikes also

[55] The system of strike benefits is described below, pp. 67-69.

[56] The original constitution of 1890 had called for the payment of death benefits, for which the necessary funds were to be raised by assessments upon the local unions, but this provision was never operative. *Constitution*, 1890, Article XXVIII. District Assembly 160 had had a death benefit. It was abolished, however, in the 1892 convention. *Proceedings, D. A. 160*, 1890, pp. 11, 40-41; January, 1892, p. 2.

made the members reluctant to pay assessments for a fund from which strike benefits alone could be paid.[57] The death benefit plan makes the amount of the benefit vary with the length of time the member has been in good standing and the funds are derived from the interest on the invested defense fund, without any additional tax on the members.[58] It was followed in 1913 by provision for sanatorium treatment for members suffering from tuberculosis, without charge to the members so treated, a provision which was later extended to members suffering from asthma.

From 1921 to 1923 the Brotherhood also paid unemployment benefits. An assessment of one-half of one per cent upon wages was levied for this purpose. The workings of the plan caused widespread dissatisfaction among the members. Unfortunately for the experiment, before it had been tried for a sufficiently long period to test the possibilities of overcoming the difficulties which had appeared, the 1922 strikes intervened to divert the energies of the organization and impose a severe strain on the financial resources of the membership and the 1923 convention abolished the unemployment benefit.[59]

[57] *Report of President,* 1907, p. 18.

[58] *Ibid.,* 1910, pp. 11-12; *Rules and Regulations,* 1910, Secs. 81-91; *Constitution,* 1925, Secs. 124-140.

[59] An appendix which I wrote in 1928, describing the unemployment benefit plan and its history, was used in the preparation of the account of the Brotherhood's unemployment fund in *Unemployment Benefits in the United States,* by Bryce M. Stewart (New York: Industrial Relations Counselors, 1930), and it is therefore omitted from this book. D. A. McC.

THE 1922 STRIKES AND THE LOSS OF THE SANITARY AGREEMENT

The autumn of 1922 brought a decided break in the progress of the Brotherhood. National collective bargaining in the sanitary ware division was ended by a disastrous strike. In the same autumn there was a strike of ten weeks in the general ware division, but in this division the old system of dealing was resumed upon the conclusion of the strike.

The Brotherhood has lost over 2,000 of the 2,400 members it had in the sanitary division in 1922.[60] The sanitary strike also contributed to a temporary loss of membership in the general ware division. The conjunction of the strikes in the two divisions in the autumn of 1922 had depleted the defense fund and in January, 1923, the executive board called for an assessment of 5 per cent on wages, to make possible the payment of benefits to the sanitary strikers. This caused considerable irritation among the general ware members. Their own strike of ten weeks had ended only a few weeks before. They had received an increase in wages of but four and one-fifth per cent, after having accepted a reduction of seventeen per cent in the previous year, whereas the sanitary members were striking against a reduction from the " peak " wages of 1920. Although the 1923 convention withdrew the assessment the Brotherhood membership in East Liverpool on March 31, 1924, was 536 below the figure for the corresponding date in 1922. However, in the first two months of 1925 an intensive membership campaign in the East

---

[60] The *Report of the Executive Board* for 1928 refers (p. 12) to " the practically complete disorganization of the sanitary branch of the trade." In July, 1930, Vice-President Cartlidge resigned " because of the seeming hopelessness of reorganizing the sanitary industry." *Proceedings*, 1930, p. 17.

Liverpool district brought back 353 members and secured 164 new members as well. The East Liverpool membership on March 31, 1925 was but 32 less than the 1922 figure.[61]

Since 1925 the depressed condition of the business has caused a further decline in the general ware membership. By 1930 the total membership had fallen to 6,060, a loss of 3,178 since 1922. As a result of the disorganization of the sanitary division and the continued decline of the general ware industry in the East, the Brotherhood has become once again little more than a general ware organization and one confined almost entirely to the West.[62]

The union has suffered little loss of control of shops in general ware since 1922. It has lost only one semi-porcelain plant which was organized before the strike. In 1923 a large plant at Mt. Clemens, Michigan, went non-union.[63] A small plant at Paden City, West Virginia, which was unionized in January, 1924, broke away from the union in September, 1925.[64] These are the only two semi-porcelain potteries now listed as "unfair" (in 1928).[65]

[61] The aggregate membership is given for East Liverpool and for Trenton in the *Reports of the Executive Board* for the years 1924-1928.

[62] The Trenton local unions had but 603 members (of whom 49 were in the grogware local union) on March 31, 1928, as against 1,892 in 1922. There are now three local unions of grogware workers in the organization, with an aggregate membership of 195. The Canadian sanitary local union finally acknowledged the uselessness of further struggle for life in October, 1925. *Report of Executive Board*, 1926, p. 7.

[63] See below, pp. 261-262.

[64] *Report of Executive Board*, 1924, p. 6; 1926, pp. 10-15; *Proceedings, U. S. P. A.*, 1924, p. 23; 1925, p. 32. The local lapsed in October, 1926. *Report of Executive Board*, 1927, p. 7.

[65] A member may not work in a shop which has been declared "unfair" without written permission from a national officer. *Pro-*

In china ware the Onondaga and Iroquois plants in Syracuse have remained non-union. A small china shop in Trenton, the Lenox, which had come under the agreement system a short time before the 1922 strike, also went non-union in 1922 as the result of the strike.[66] In September, 1924, the union officially called off the strike against this plant and has since allowed its members to work there.[67] It does not, however, operate under an agreement with the union. Moreover, the second largest china plant in the country, the Shenango, at New Castle, Pa., broke with the union in October, 1928.[68] It had been threatening for some time to break away,[69] and at the close of the 1928 conference gave formal notice that it reserved the right to withdraw from the agreement at any time.

---

ceedings, 1920, p. 73; Constitution, Sec. 241. The references are to the 1925 edition of the Constitution unless some earlier edition is specified.

[66] Report of Executive Board, 1923, pp. 53-57; Proceedings, U. S. P. A., April, 1923, p. 15.

[67] Report of Executive Board, 1925, p. 37.

[68] Ibid., 1929, pp. 38-40, 53-57; 1930, pp. 92-94, 97-98; Proceedings. U. S. P. A., 1928, pp. 23-25, 33.

[69] Report of Executive Board, 1928, p. 20.

CHAPTER III

THE BROTHERHOOD—STRUCTURE, FINANCES AND
MEMBERSHIP POLICIES

STRUCTURE

There are certain features of the internal organization of the Brotherhood which have an important bearing upon the workings of the system of joint dealing. The local unions, the convention, the conference committee, and the national officers all have some part in the agreement-making process or in the execution of the terms. What are the respective powers of these bodies and of the national officers and where does the decision rest as to the policy to be followed with the employers? How far have the different occupational branches within each division, more especially within the general ware division, been recognized in those features of the internal organization of the Brotherhood which affect the making and administration of the agreement?

The Local Unions.—In dividing its members into local unions the Brotherhood has adopted the plant basis in towns in which there is only one pottery, but in East Liverpool and Trenton " branch "—or craft—organization predominates. Indeed, in Trenton craft organization has prevailed to a considerable extent over the distinction between general ware and sanitary. In that city there were unions among the kilnmen, dippers, and saggermakers which included those working in sanitary potteries and those working in general ware potteries, before the eastern operatives joined the

Brotherhood. The clay-shop branches, on the other hand, were organized apart from each other, as between general ware and sanitary, because, apparently, of the preference of the sanitary pressers for separate organization, a segregation which was accepted by the Brotherhood when it instituted local unions in Trenton. Within the general ware division, there are a few local unions which include both workers in china and workers in semi-porcelain, but most are china or semi-porcelain locals exclusively; Trenton is the chief exception.

In East Liverpool the branch basis has been followed since 1894. When the Brotherhood had its first real opportunity to organize the East Liverpool operatives in that year, it was found easier to get the operatives to join craft local unions than to organize them into local unions on a plant basis. At that time as many as eleven separate local unions were organized on the branch basis.[1] The branch has been the normal unit of organization in the East Liverpool district ever since. There are now twelve separate local unions in East Liverpool. In 1926 there were fourteen, but in that year the three local unions of warehousemen, decorating kilnmen and decorators were consolidated. In Trenton the recent trend is toward consolidation, owing to the falling off in numbers. In 1925 the three Trenton clay-shop locals (general ware) were consolidated into one.[2] The mouldmakers have also given up their independent local union and merged with this clay-shop local. There are still, however, five branch local unions in Trenton— the kilnmen, the dippers, the saggermakers, the packers, and the decorators. In Sebring there are three locals, the members being grouped by departments.

[1] *Proceedings*, 1894, p. 7.
[2] *Report of Executive Board*, 1926, p. 7.

Outside East Liverpool, Trenton and Sebring, the " mixed " local union, including all branches in its membership, prevails.

The Brotherhood officers early found the branch basis of organization for local unions unsatisfactory. In 1895, after a year's experience with it in East Liverpool, President Hughes recommended that it be given up in favor of the plant as the basis of local grouping. He failed to convince the convention, which left the matter to the discretion of each locality.[3] President T. J. Duffy, in his first year as president, renewed the attack on the branch local system. Again the proposal to change to organization by potteries was decisively defeated after a whole day had been taken up in debating it.[4]

The preference of the two presidents for the local union with the pottery instead of the branch as its basis of jurisdiction, often called the " shop local," was for the most part due to a conviction that it would result in more effective pressure upon those individuals who were inclined to be indifferent or too disgruntled to adhere to the organization. Where the branch local system prevailed, the men in a given branch in a particular pottery, if few in number, could be in bad standing or even remain out of the organization altogether without the operatives in the other branches in the same pottery knowing much about the situation or being appreciably concerned over it.[5] Moreover, organization by branches seemed to discourage membership on the part of those in branches not well enough organized in the trade centers to have branch locals. Another point

[3] *Proceedings*, 1895, pp. 8, 30; 1896, 1897.
[4] *Ibid.*, 1904, pp. 13-15, 108.
[5] *Ibid.*, 1895, p. 8; 1904, pp. 14-15; *Report of President*, 1908, pp. 9-10.

emphasized by the presidents was that the branch local plan left the members in the several branches unacquainted with the problems, difficulties, and needs of the other branches. It tended to encourage each branch to work for its own interests without sufficient regard for the welfare of the other branches or the policy of the national union. There had been manifestations of branch particularism, too, in matters affecting the agreement system, such as demands for an automatic referendum by each branch on the particular terms of proposed agreements, and for branch decision on grievances and on the question of striking. There were also instances of branch disregard of the constitution, in the holding of unauthorized branch " delegate meetings," and even rebellions by branch locals against the decisions of the national body.[6]

The members in the trade centers, especially in the branches longest organized, prefer the branch system primarily because they are convinced that it affords greater protection of their interests. It is the only way, they believe, in which they can keep abreast of the developments in the various potteries affecting their respective branches, such as changes in facilities or other conditions, and the prices fixed on new articles. These things are of great importance to piece workers. With branch local unions, too, they can maintain more direct branch control over the action of the shop committee, the union negotiating body which takes up all questions with the employer in the first instance. In East Liverpool and Trenton each of the larger branch locals has its own shop committee in each plant, appointed by the local. In the smaller plants there are

[6] *Proceedings,* 1900, pp. 9, 10; 1903, pp. 6-8, 83; 1906, pp. 34, 36-37, 44-45; *Report of President,* 1906, pp. 14-15.

only a few men employed in the less numerous branches and for these there is no standing shop committee of the particular branch, but the practice has been to have a committee from the local act with the members of the branch employed in the shop when a grievance has to be taken up. Proposals to change to a single shop committee for each department, or one shop committee for each plant, to be made up of a member from each branch, have repeatedly been rejected.[7]

Furthermore, the existence of a branch local in a trade center insures the branch of representation in the convention. Obviously a delegate from a branch local can give greater attention to the interests of his own branch. In fact the delegates from the mixed locals are inclined to look to the delegates from the branch locals to take the lead in matters particularly affecting their respective branches which come before the convention.

The Convention.—The convention is the union agency for the consideration of the proposals to be presented to the manufacturers. It is also the normal agency for legislation and changes in the union constitution. Although provision is made in the constitution for direct legislation through the initiative of local unions and a referendum vote of the membership, and although the executive board may also, on its own initiative, submit proposals for changes in the law to referendum vote, these methods of enactment have been infrequently used, comparatively.

The Brotherhood continued to hold annual conventions until 1930, although since 1921 there had been no national wage conference to prepare for in the odd-numbered years. Down to 1921 the sanitary and the

---

[7] *Proceedings,* 1917, p. 75; 1921, p. 50; 1925, p. 21.

5

general ware conferences had been held biennially and in different years; since 1922 there has been only the biennial general ware conference. The value of the exchange of opinions and information which the convention makes possible was held sufficient to warrant the continuance of conventions in the " off years " in spite of the expense both to the locals and the national body. But in 1930 the economy argument prevailed and it was decided to hold no convention in 1931.[8]

The National Officers.—The officers of the Brotherhood have played, and still play, an important part in the workings of the agreement system. The influence of the officers has at times counted heavily in the negotiations for the agreement, although it has not by any means been always determining. In the carrying out of the agreement, however, their policy has been all important. It is not too much to say that the continuation of the agreement in the general ware division has been due primarily to the attitude of the Brotherhood officers. And the downfall of the system in the sanitary division came as a direct consequence of the rejection of the policies advocated by them.

There are three salaried national officers who devote all of their time to the affairs of the Brotherhood—the president, first vice-president, and the secretary-treasurer.[9] These and six other vice-presidents make up the executive board. The board is practically " the Brotherhood " between conventions. After the change to direct election of officers in 1912, the president and

---

[8] *Ibid.*, 1925, p. 20; 1926, pp. 19, 20; *Potters Herald*, July 8, 1926; *Proceedings*, 1928, p. 30; 1930, p. 10.

[9] The 1928 convention added another salaried position, that of organizer, to be appointed by the executive board. However, the organizer is not a member of the executive board. *Proceedings*, 1928, p. 17; *Potters Herald*, July 6, August 30, 1928.

the first vice-president tended more and more to seek the support of the executive board before taking actions that in earlier years they would have taken on their own responsibility. In this they followed the tendency toward more "democratic" government which was responsible for the change to direct election of officers. Moreover, certain powers that were earlier in the hands of the president were later specifically given to the executive board. The change in title in 1918 from the "Report of the President and First Vice-President" to the annual convention to the "Report of the Executive Board" to that body was significant of this transfer of authority and responsibility.

The sectionalism which appeared in the history of unionism in the pottery industry left a deeper furrow in the assignment of offices in the Brotherhood than did the division between general ware and sanitary. The constitution requires that the offices of the president and secretary shall be located in East Liverpool and the office of the first vice-president in Trenton. Four of the vice-presidents—the second, fifth, sixth and seventh—must reside west of the Allegheny Mountains and the other two in the East.[10] The geographical limitations do not extend to the locals which may place candidates in nomination nor to the voting for national officers. Any local union may place any member of any local

[10] Three places on the board had been assigned to the East in 1912 but the recent loss of membership in the East was followed by proposals to transfer one or more of the eastern vice-presidencies to the West. After proposals of this character had been defeated in earlier years (*Proceedings,* 1925, p. 22; 1928, p. 21) the 1929 convention reduced the eastern vice-presidencies to two, in addition to the first vice-presidency, transferring the fifth vice-presidency to the West. *Proceedings,* 1929, p. 22. In 1928 the convention voted to reduce the size (and expense) of the eastern headquarters. *Proceedings,* 1928, pp. 18, 30-31; *Potters Herald,* July 6, 1928.

union in nomination for any national office to which he
is eligible; and all members in good standing are eligible to vote for all national officers.[11] Proposals for the
assignment of places on the executive board by branches
have been persistent, but unsuccessful.[12]

There is no explicit constitutional allotment of the
national offices between the general ware and sanitary
divisions. When the present geographical distribution
of offices between East and West was made, in 1912,
the sanitary industry was located mostly in the east
and the general ware industry mostly in the West; the
western vice-presidencies were therefore naturally
filled by general ware men and the eastern vice-presidencies for the most part by sanitary men. The constitution made the first vice-president the chief administrative officer of the sanitary division but it did not
require, nor has it since, that he should be chosen from
the sanitary division. Neither has it specified that the
president or the secretary should be a general ware
worker, although both have always been chosen from
that division. Specific assignment of national offices to
divisions of the industry, it was feared, would encourage centrifugal tendencies.

Down to 1911 the officers of the Brotherhood were
chosen by the annual convention. In that year, following several earlier attempts to secure direct election,[13]
the constitution was amended to provide for election by
the membership from candidates nominated at the convention.[14] The next year the change was made to direct
nomination in January, followed by a primary elec-

[11] *Constitution*, Secs. 35, 48.
[12] *Proceedings*, 1912, p. 21; 1917, p. 88; 1920, pp. 26, 49, 73; 1923,
p. 26; 1928, p. 15.
[13] *Ibid.*, 1906, pp. 35, 36; 1907, pp. 17-18, 38-39; 1910, pp. 22-23.
[14] *Ibid.*, 1911, pp. 63-64, 90-92, 94; *Report of President*, 1912, p. 8.

tion in March. The two highest candidates for each office at this election were to be voted on in a final election in May. This system of nomination and election is still followed.[15] Prior to 1923 the officers were elected annually. The convention of 1922 changed the term to two years, in order to reduce the expense and the drain on the time of the national officers which the election procedure involves.[16] In case a vacancy occurs between elections, a temporary appointment, to hold until the next regular election, is made by the executive board.[17]

From 1905 to 1922 the Brotherhood was favored by noteworthy continuity in the offices of president and first vice-president. Thomas J. Duffy, who was advanced from the secretaryship to the presidency in 1903, in succession to Albert S. Hughes, who retired after continuous service through eleven trying years, served without a break until 1911, when he resigned to accept an appointment as a member of the Board of Awards created under the newly enacted Ohio Workmen's Compensation Act. The building up of the national agreement system in the general ware division on a firm foundation was largely due to the leadership he exercised over the Brotherhood membership and the confidence which he inspired in the leading manufacturers in the industry.

Mr. Edward Menge, who had succeeded Mr. Duffy as secretary in 1903, was appointed by the executive board for the remainder of his unexpired term as president. Mr. Frank Hutchins, the first vice-president, who would normally have assumed the presidency, declined the office. Mr. Menge was elected president in 1912

[15] *Proceedings,* 1912, pp. 51-52, 56-57; *Constitution,* Secs. 35, 43-51.
[16] *Proceedings,* 1922, p. 79; *Potters Herald,* July 20, 1922; *Constitution,* Sec. 54.
[17] *Ibid.,* Sec. 53.

and reëlected every year until his death, in 1922. In November, 1920, he tendered his resignation on account of illness but instead he was voted a leave of absence until his health should be restored.[18] He returned to active duty for a few months in 1921 and was in charge of the union side in the 1921 general ware conference. He was forced to retire from active duty shortly thereafter and died in April, 1922. His death was a great loss to the Brotherhood. He was mourned by operatives and employers alike.[19]

Mr. Frank Hutchins served as first vice-president from 1900 until 1922. In that year he declined to stand again for reëlection, on the ground that his health would not permit him to retain the responsibilities of the office. The practical resignation of Mr. Hutchins, coming so soon after Mr. Menge's death, was another severe blow to the Brotherhood. With Mr. Duffy and Mr. Menge he had helped to build up the organization and the system of agreements. The success of the agreement system in the sanitary division was largely due to his efforts and his leadership.[20] However, signs were not wanting in the autumn of 1921 that the sanitary membership was no longer willing to follow his counsels. Mr. Hutchins was appointed "Adviser" to the Brotherhood by vote of the 1922 convention and again by the 1923 convention. But after the latter convention the office was abolished by a meagre referendum vote and Mr. Hutchins refused to allow a new vote to be taken.[21]

[18] *Potters Herald,* December 30, 1920.
[19] *Proceedings, U. S. P. A.,* 1921, p. 23; April, 1923, p. 68.
[20] *Ibid.,* December, 1923, p. 24.
[21] *Potters Herald,* October 11, November 1, November 8, 1923; January 10, 1924. A resolution of appreciation of his services, proposed by the executive board, was adopted by the 1924 convention. *Proceedings,* 1924, pp. 63-64.

Since 1922 the Brotherhood has had two presidents. Mr. Menge was succeeded by Mr. John T. Wood, who had followed Mr. Menge as secretary-treasurer, an office which he held until he became president. He had also acted in Mr. Menge's stead, at the request of the executive board, during Mr. Menge's incapacity. He held the presidency continuously until 1927, when he was defeated for reëlection. This was the first time since the presidency was made a salaried office in 1892 that an incumbent of the presidency had been defeated. Mr. Wood retired with the good will of the Brotherhood members and the manufacturers.[22] In April, 1928, he was appointed Postmaster at East Liverpool.

Mr. Wood's successor is Mr. James M. Duffy, a younger brother of ex-President Thomas J. Duffy. Unlike his brother and Mr. Menge and Mr. Wood, he did not come to the office through the secretaryship. In fact he had held no national office before his election. He also shattered another precedent in that he is the first worker in china ware to hold the presidency of the Brotherhood. He was reëlected in 1929 and in 1931, in the latter year without opposition.

The first vice-presidency was held continuously from 1922 to 1930 by Mr. George Cartlidge, who was elected upon Mr. Hutchins' retirement. Mr. Cartlidge had served as fifth vice-president from 1917 to 1922.[23]

Mr. John McGillivray, the secretary-treasurer of the Brotherhood, who succeeded Mr. John Wood in that office, has also served continuously since 1922. Before

[22] *Proceedings, U. S. P. A.,* 1927, pp. 22, 37; *Proceedings, N. B. of O. P.,* 1927, p. 17.

[23] Mr. Cartlidge tendered his resignation in July, to take effect October 4, 1930. *Proceedings,* 1930, p. 17. He was succeeded by Mr. Joseph Smith, who had been a member of the executive board some years before.

that he had held the office of seventh vice-president for one year.[24]

FINANCES

The financial policies and resources of the Brotherhood have an obvious bearing on the extent of its membership and upon its bargaining strength. The amount of the fee which it charges for admission and the dues and assessments which it levies on its members are in substance a part of its membership policy. The financial resources which it has accumulated, or which it can mobilize, may be assumed to affect its bargaining position. On the other hand, the diversion of a considerable part of the resources gained through assessments primarily for strike funds to other purposes was a significant reaction to the many years of peaceful settlement.

The expenses which the national body has to meet fall into several fairly well-defined categories. First there are the costs of the ordinary administrative and legislative machinery such as the salaries of the national officers and the costs of the annual convention. Closely akin is the net cost of publishing " The Potters Herald " and distributing it gratuitously among the members—" net " because the total cost is met to some

[24] Of the other members of the executive board, Mr. Thomas M. Woods, of Sebring, has served as sixth vice-president continuously since 1908. He is the only member of the present board whose service on the board goes back to the days when the officers were elected by the convention. Mr. George Chadwick has held the second vice-presidency without interruption since 1916. Mr. Louis Driber, of Trenton, also began service as a vice-president in 1916. Except for an interval of two years (1926 and 1927) he has served as third vice-president since that date. Mr. Frank Hull, who resigned the seventh vice-presidency in 1928 to accept the position of organizer, had held the former office for six years.

extent by receipts from advertising, job printing, etc. These expenditures are defrayed from what is known as the " general fund." The cost of operating the specific machinery of the agreement system—conferences, standing committees, special committees, etc.—has always been met from the " defense fund," a fund which was inaugurated in 1894 to provide for the payment of strike benefits. Strike expenditures also are, of course, paid from this source. Finally, there are the payments for death benefits and the tuberculosis and asthma treatment. These, too, have been drawn from the defense fund indirectly; the so-called " insurance fund " from which these benefits are paid has been derived from the interest on the defense fund investments and, for a time, from a share of the defense fund assessment.[25]

Ordinary Revenues and the General Fund.—The normal sources of revenue for the general fund have always been the per capita tax and the national union's share of the initiation fee. In the earlier years these did not yield enough to meet even the modest expenditures of that period. The per capita tax was but ten cents a month; the national body received but fifty cents as its share of the initiation fee; and the membership was small. It was not until 1899 that the general fund showed an appreciable balance on the right side.[26]

The 1899 convention increased the per capita tax to fifteen cents. This, with the enlargement of the mem-

[25] Down to April 30, 1928, the Brotherhood had paid 1,417 death claims, aggregating $253,568.30. The largest amount paid in any one year was $25,040.00 (in 1924-1925). For 1927-1928 the amount was $16,170; in addition, $5,166.52 was paid for members suffering from tuberculosis or asthma. *Report of Executive Board*, 1928, pp. 3, 7.

[26] *Proceedings*, 1894, pp. 9, 10, 12-14; 1895, pp. 7, 20, 34-35; 1896; 1897; 1898, pp. 41, 42; 1899, pp. 9, 35-36, 40-41, 44.

bership, enabled the general fund for many years thereafter to meet its expenditures comfortably. In 1906 the
per capita tax was reduced to ten cents for females.[27]
It remained at fifteen cents for males and ten cents for
females until 1918. Increases in 1918 and 1919 brought
it up to twenty-five cents for males and twenty cents
for females, where it has remained.[28] The per capita
tax is collected for the national body by the local union,
in addition to its own dues for local purposes, and
forwarded quarterly to the national office.

The initiation fee was fixed at $3.00 in 1901. This
applied only to male entrants; for females it was but
half of that. Fifty cents of each initiation fee was to
go to the national union.[29] The locals have not been
allowed to increase the initiation fee. These figures
have remained the same since 1901, except that since
1912 females receiving the same wage rates as males
have had to pay the full initiation fee.[30]

The general fund has also derived some revenue from
the reinstatement fee. In 1902 the reinstatement fee
was fixed at $5.00. For females it was one-third less.[31]
In 1912 the rule was adopted for reinstatement, as well
as for initiation, that females receiving the same rate
of wages as males should pay the full fee.[32] These distinctions still hold, as does the provision, adopted in

[27] *Ibid.*, 1906, pp. 19-20.

[28] *Report of Executive Board*, 1918, p. 35; *Proceedings*, 1918, p. 79;
1919, p. 51.

[29] *Ibid.*, 1901, p. 65; *Rules and Regulations*, 1902, Local Rules
and Regulations, Article II, Secs. 5 and 6.

[30] *Proceedings*, 1912, pp. 37, 46-47; *Constitution*, 1914, Sec. 153;
1925, Sec. 167.

[31] *Proceedings*, 1902, p. 107; *Rules and Regulations*, 1902, Local
Rules and Regulations, Article XI, Sec. 6.

[32] *Proceedings*, 1912, pp. 37, 46-47; *Constitution*, 1914, Sec. 154.

1902, that one-third of the reinstatement fee shall go to the national union.[33]

The amount of the reinstatement fee has had a chequered history. It has been dictated by conflicting considerations and each has been at different times controlling. The reinstatement charge is obviously intended to serve as a deterrent to falling into bad standing. On the other hand, once a member has been suspended, it becomes a barrier to readmission. At certain periods the fee has been raised in order that it might more effectively act as a discouragement to individual lapses, only to be lowered again, in campaigns for increased organization, to make it easier for those who had been dropped to return to the fold.

The latest departure from the traditional $5.00 level came in 1923, after a large number of members had incurred suspension rather than pay the five per cent assessment. It was obviously incongruous that a man who had dropped out to escape the assessment, and so avoided paying an amount several times the $5.00 fee, should be allowed to get back into good standing for a mere $5.00. On the initiative of several locals a rule was put through by referendum that a suspended member seeking reinstatement should be required to pay all arrears of dues and assessments standing against him at the time of suspension, as well as the $5.00 fee. The next year there was the usual reaction. Even after modification by the 1924 convention [34] the reinstatement charges were thought to handicap too heavily the efforts to win back the ex-members and in November the executive board submitted to referendum a pro-

---

[33] *Ibid.*, Sec. 168.

[34] *Report of Executive Board*, 1924, pp. 21-22; *Proceedings*, 1924, pp. 46, 48.

posal to return to the old fee of $5.00, without any
extras, for a period of sixty days—from January 1 to
March 1, 1925. This was adopted by a substantial
majority.[35] The results of the remission were encouraging and the 1925 convention voted to return to the
flat charge of $5.00 for a period of one year, a precedent
which was followed by every subsequent convention
through 1929.[36]

From 1921 to 1925, the general fund was also allotted
forty per cent of the interest received on the defense
fund investments, this being diverted from the insurance fund in order to avoid an increase in the per capita
tax.[37] After the subsidy was withdrawn in 1925 in
favor of the insurance fund, the receipts of the general
fund were no longer equal to the expenditures. As
there was a strong sentiment against increasing the per
capita tax, the convention again sought relief for the
general fund from the defense fund, and again at the
expense of the insurance fund. The latter fund had
been receiving since 1925 a subsidy of twenty per cent
of the defense fund assessments—in addition to the
interest on the defense fund investments. That twenty
per cent was now diverted, in 1928, to the general fund,
for a period of one year.[38]

---

[35] *Report of Executive Board,* 1925, p. 32.

[36] *Proceedings,* 1925, pp. 26, 30; 1926, p. 32; 1927, pp. 9, 10, 14;
1928, p. 24; 1929, p. 15; *Report of Executive Board,* 1926, p. 17;
1927, pp. 30-31. In a revision of the constitution in 1930 the fee was
made ten dollars (five for those employed in the semi-skilled
branches) " plus all dues and assessments owed at the time of
suspension." *Proceedings,* 1930, pp. 51, 52.

[37] *Ibid.,* 1921, pp. 22, 45-46; *Potters Herald,* July 14, 1921.

[38] *Proceedings,* 1928, pp. 40, 54. *Report of Executive Board,* 1928,
pp. 2-3; 1930, pp. 4, 5. The expenditures from the general fund in
1927-1928, inclusive of expenditures for the *Potters Herald* in excess
of the revenues from the *Herald,* were approximately $26,000, or

Strike Benefits and the Defense Fund.—As failure
to furnish adequate financial support to members on
strike was one of the most damaging complaints made
by the western operatives against the Knights of Labor,
the founders of the Brotherhood naturally gave the
provision of strike funds a prominent place in their
plans for the new organization. They laid it down in
the constitution that benefits should be paid to all members engaged in duly authorized strikes and adopted
an assessment of one per cent on earnings for a " resistance fund " to insure the means.[39] But this program
proved altogether too ambitious for an organization
struggling to obtain and hold members and the assessment law was repealed in 1892.[40] The 1894 strike was
financed in East Liverpool, so far as it was financed in
an organized way, not by the Brotherhood itself, but
by a relief committee, which solicited subscriptions and
held entertainments and picnics to raise funds.[41] The
1894 convention, impressed by the urgent need and
hopeful that the operatives would be similarly impressed, re-established the one per cent assessment, for
a " defense fund." [42] This fund lived and in time grew
to very respectable proportions. As early as 1895 strike
benefits were paid from it.[43]

The amount of the strike benefit was not fixed in the
constitution until 1904 and then it was put at the comparatively low figure of $5.00 a week, where it remained

---

about $3.75 per member. For additional expenditures from the
defense fund for the administration of the agreement system,
see below, pp. 69-70.

[39] *Constitution,* 1890, Articles VII and VIII, Article IX, Sec. 1.

[40] Duffy, p. 11.

[41] *Ibid.,* pp. 18-19.

[42] *Proceedings,* 1894, p. 19; *Rules and Regulations,* 1895, Article
XVII.

[43] *Proceedings,* 1896.

for ten years.[44] In 1914 it was raised to $7.50 a week, for " sectional or local " strikes, and in 1917 to $10.00; for a " general strike " it remained at $5.00.[45] After the general strike of 1917 the benefit for a general strike was increased to $10.00. The payment for a local strike was raised to $12.50 at that time but in 1923, when the defense fund was in a precarious condition, it was reduced to $10.00 per week.[46] Under the present rule a member is allowed to earn $15.00 outside without reducing his eligibility for the benefit, but members working in regular positions are ineligible. A member who refuses to accept a position in a " fair " shop is also ineligible.[47]

Strike benefits are not paid unless the strike is of more than one week's duration, but if the strike lasts two weeks or more, the benefits are paid from the beginning. This rule dates from 1904.[48] Down to 1926 there was no limit to the time for which strike benefits should be paid. In some cases, notably that of the Canadian strike, they were continued long after all chance of winning the strike had passed. In the case of the sanitary strike, benefits were paid for more than two years. In 1926 a limit of twelve weeks was adopted.[49]

For many years the Brotherhood paid out relatively little in strike benefits. In the ten year period, 1900-1910, the expenditure for this purpose was only $24,000,

[44] *Ibid.*, 1904, p. 113; *Rules and Regulations*, 1904, Article IX, Sec. 6.

[45] *Proceedings*, 1914, pp. 20, 21; *Constitution*, 1914, Sec. 91; *Proceedings*, 1917, pp. 78-79.

[46] *Ibid.*, 1918, p. 41; 1923, p. 45; *Constitution*, Sec. 123.

[47] *Proceedings*, 1918, p. 41; *Constitution*, Secs. 103, 105.

[48] *Proceedings*, 1904, p. 113; *Rules and Regulations*, 1904, Article IX, Sec. 7; *Constitution*, 1925, Sec. 101.

[49] *Report of Executive Board*, 1926, p. 12; *Proceedings*, 1926, p. 24.

of which all but $655 was incurred prior to 1906. The first heavy strike benefit expenditure was incurred for the Canadian strike, or lockout, which began in 1913. That strike cost the Brotherhood $122,747.49, as contrasted with $33,297.01 for the general ware strike of 1917.[50] The strikes of 1922 took a heavy toll in benefits. The general ware strike cost $538,458.62.[51] The sanitary strike cost even more—$594,402.41.[52] These two strikes thus took over $1,100,000 of the $1,376,672.44 expended for strike purposes from 1895 to 1926.[53] Only $540.00 was paid out in the next two years.

Down to 1922, the expenditures from the defense fund for other than strike purposes were almost as great as the amount paid out in strike benefits. If the interest on the defense fund investments, which was diverted to the insurance fund after 1910, be added, the amount paid out for non-strike purposes was more than double that paid out on account of strikes.

The practice of paying the expenses of committees which dealt with the manufacturers from the defense fund was begun in 1897. The convention decided that the work of the negotiating committees was intended to secure gains by peaceful agreement which otherwise would have to be fought for, and to secure them much more cheaply.[54] The precedent was followed with the " uniform wage " committee of 1900 and the practice was later extended to all joint committees.[55] In 1926-

[50] *Report of Executive Board,* 1924, p. 6; 1919, p. 5.
[51] *Ibid.,* 1923, p. 5; 1924, p. 6.
[52] *Ibid.,* 1925, p. 5.
[53] *Ibid.,* 1926, p. 6.
[54] *Proceedings,* 1897.
[55] *Ibid.,* 1899, p. 48. In 1902 the word " defense " was substituted for the word " strike " in the definition of the purposes of the fund in the constitution. *Rules and Regulations,* 1902, Article XVII. In

1927, a conference year, the expenditures from the defense fund for the standing committees, conference, etc., amounted to approximately $6,000 or less than one dollar per member.

The receipts from the defense fund assessment were meagre in the first few years. But with the increase in membership after 1897, and the paucity of strikes, the fund grew rapidly. By 1910, the year in which the death benefit was established, the annual receipts had grown to $46,431.47 and the balance stood at $322,-163.58.[56] Within a few years the increase in the yield from the assessments overcame the reduction in receipts occasioned by the transfer of the interest on the invested funds to the insurance fund. With the increases in wages from 1916 to 1920 the receipts from the one per cent assessment mounted still more rapidly. For the year ending April 30, 1921, the receipts were $119,444.37, the highest figure attained under the one per cent assessment. The balance in the fund stood at its peak—$706,451.20.[57] In the following year it was reduced by approximately $39,000. The receipts were approximately $19,000 less than in the previous year; there were two wage reductions in general ware, in August and November, 1921, and 1921 was also a bad year for employment. But the real cause of the reduc-

recent years even the expenses of trips undertaken to bring the unorganized workers into the union have been charged to the defense fund.

[56] *Financial Reports of the National Officers,* for year ending May 31, 1910, pp. 83, 86.

[57] Since 1919 a financial summary has been published in the *Report of the Executive Board.* The figures given here for the balance in the defense fund are $10,000 below those published in the *Reports of the Executive Board.* The latter still include in the defense fund balance the sum of $10,000 " loaned " to the *Potters Herald* in 1914, which has not been repaid.

tion in the balance was the transfer of approximately $90,000 to the unemployment fund to meet the excess of benefits paid over the amount received from the one-half of one per cent levied for that purpose.

The 1922 strikes rapidly depleted the defense fund. Even the assessment of five per cent—inclusive of the one-half of one per cent unemployment tax—imposed in January, 1923, was not enough to pay $10 a week to the sanitary strikers, who were almost one-third as numerous as the members paying the assessment. The hard-pressed executive board determined to draw on one of the other funds to aid the defense fund. The insurance fund was the only one with a large surplus. On February 1, 1923, the board transferred the debt of the unemployment fund to the insurance fund and transferred an equal amount, $66,736.52, from the insurance fund to the defense fund.[58]

When the 1923 convention met it was apparent that the majority of the members were unwilling to go on paying an extra assessment either for the sanitary strikers or for unemployment benefits. The convention not only cut down the assessment for the defense fund but changed its form from a percentage assessment on earnings to flat rates. The unemployment benefit and the unemployment assessment were also abolished. The chief cause of the change to the flat rate form of assessment was the belief that there were " wholesale eva-

[58] From April, 1921, when the payment of unemployment benefits was begun, until the end of the next fiscal year, April 30, 1922, the expenditures for benefits amounted to $151,960.00 and the receipts from the unemployment assessment to but $53,065.30, leaving an adverse balance of $98,894.70 which was met by a transference of funds from the defense fund. However, by the spring of 1922 the receipts had begun to run ahead of the expenditures and by February 1, 1923, the indebtedness of the unemployment fund had been reduced to $66,736.52.

6

sions " of the percentage assessments.[59] This was no
new charge. It had been widely believed for years that
the percentage assessment was not paid in full by all.
Many members did not want their exact earnings
known. Some, too, objected to a percentage assessment
on earnings when strike benefits and death benefits
were paid at flat rates, irrespective of earnings.

The new rates were fixed at forty cents a week for
those classed as " skilled " and twenty cents for the
" semi-skilled " and " unskilled." [60] It was recognized
that these rates would yield less than the one per cent
assessment on earnings would yield if all were employed
steadily and all paid the percentage assessment in full,
but taking these two conditions as improbable, it was
expected that the new rates would yield as much as
the one per cent assessment would yield in practice
and cause much less dissatisfaction.

On April 1, 1924, the assessment rates were raised
to 50 cents and 25 cents, respectively. This action
was taken by referendum vote, on the initiative of
several local unions, in order to build up the defense
fund and to hasten the rehabilitation of the insurance
fund.[61] The receipts of the defense fund for 1924-
1925—$132,078.09—exceeded by some $13,000 the
receipts under the one per cent assessment in the peak
year of 1920-1921, a year in which the membership was
larger and the wage rates higher than in 1924-1925.
In 1926, the convention reduced the assessment to the
original rates of 40 and 20 cents a week. It was believed
that the situation which had caused the increase had
been met; the insurance fund showed a favorable bal-

[59] *Potters Herald*, July 12, July 19, 1923.

[60] *Proceedings*, 1923, pp. 27, 28, 32, 45, 52.

[61] *Ibid.*, p. 59; *Potters Herald*, March 6, 1924; *Proceedings*, 1924,
pp. 13, 46; *Report of Executive Board*, 1924, p. 21.

ance of nearly $5,000 on the year's operations and had a surplus of approximately $50,000. Moreover, employment had not been good during the year and it was thought undesirable to continue to assess at the higher rates members who were working only two or three days a week.[62] The lowered rates are still in force. The receipts from assessments have fallen off, of course, with the large amount of unemployment. For 1927-1928 they were but $86,652.78.

Meanwhile, the expenditures from the defense fund had continued at a heavy rate through 1923 and 1924. Payments on account of the sanitary strike were not ended until February 4, 1925; since May 1, 1923, approximately $230,000 had been paid to sanitary strikers. With this drain ended, the defense fund was able, from its receipts, to pay off the debt of $45,338.99 to the insurance fund which it had inherited from the unemployment fund on the demise of the latter fund on August 1, 1923, and to bring its balance up to $73,956.22 by April 30, 1925.[63]

In 1925, the defense fund was again obliged to come to the assistance of the insurance fund. That fund had practically lost its source of revenue when the defense fund investments had melted away in the 1922 strikes. The 1925 convention voted to turn over to it twenty per cent of the assessment receipts of the defense fund " until such time as the interest from the defense fund will adequately meet the obligation of the death insur-

---

[62] *Proceedings,* 1926, p. 32; *Potters Herald,* July 15, 1926.

[63] The 1923 convention had voted that the indebtedness of the unemployment fund to the insurance fund should be reassumed by the defense fund when its condition would allow it. The receipts of the unemployment fund from February 1, 1923, to August 1, 1923, had exceeded the expenditures by $21,397.55, reducing the debt of $66,736.52 (on February 1, 1923) to $45, 338.99.

ance fund." [64] In spite of this diversion of one-fifth of its receipts and of the reduction in the yield of the assessment because of the reduction in employment, the defense fund had been raised by 1928 (April 30) to $264,031.93.[65]

The total financial resources of the Brotherhood on April 30, 1928, were given as $463,919.20. This includes an estimated value of $100,000.00 for the headquarters building, printing plant, fixtures, supplies, etc. The remaining $363,919.20 is made up of $264,031.93 in the defense fund,[66] $80,940.62 in the insurance fund and $18,946.65 in the general fund.[67]

MEMBERSHIP POLICIES

The Unorganized Workers.—The Brotherhood has always been predominantly an organization of the male workers in the skilled branches of the industry. This was true in even greater measure of the sanitary division than of general ware. In the former division the members came almost exclusively from the skilled

[64] *Proceedings,* 1925, p. 13. This arrangement has been continued—except for the year August 1, 1928 to July 31, 1929, for which year the twenty per cent was switched to the general fund. *Proceedings,* 1926, p. 27; *Report of Executive Board,* 1927, p. 31; *Proceedings,* 1927, p. 14; 1928, pp. 40, 54; *Report of Executive Board,* 1930, pp. 4, 5.

[65] Approximately $50,000 was used for the enlargement of the headquarters building at East Liverpool.

[66] *Financial Reports of the National Officers,* 1928, p. 100. In its statement of "Resources" the Brotherhood does not count the $10,000.000 "loan" to the *Potters Herald* which it includes in the defense fund in its other statements.

[67] The balances reported as of April 30, 1930, were (*Report of Executive Board,* 1930, pp. 4-5):

Defense Fund	$269,528.43
Insurance Fund	76,354.16
General Fund	28,342.57

branches and in that division all the workers in the skilled branches were males. In East Liverpool, where the local unions are organized on the branch basis, only two of the twelve local unions, in 1928, represented branches not classed as " skilled." [68] These are the finishers' and warehousewomen's locals; both are women's locals. At least five-sixths of the female membership in East Liverpool was in branches outside the category of skilled as contrasted with the male membership which was almost entirely recruited from the skilled branches. The proportion of female membership in the Brotherhood as a whole, although it has increased since 1922, due to an absolute decline in male membership, was but 25 per cent in 1930.

Not all of the male branches which can be classed as skilled are organized, in the trade centers at least. The male groups " unorganized " in this sense include two skilled branches once organized in East Liverpool—the clay- and slip-makers and the kiln firemen. Neither is large numerically. The great majority of the unorganized males are, of course, outside the skilled branches. The kilndrawers, who rank high among the male branches in point of numbers, were once organized in the West, but have been practically unorganized for the past ten years. The large group of " boys " or young men employed as helpers by the journeymen in several of the clay-shop branches have never been organized. They are not rated as apprentices, although the apprentices were ordinarily drawn from them in the days when it was customary to put on apprentices. The unorganized males who have never been organized

[68] It is the Brotherhood itself that classifies these branches as not " skilled." Since 1923 the Brotherhood has differentiated between the " skilled " branches and the others in the size of the assessment levied for the defense fund. *Constitution*, Sec. 85.

also include the men and boys employed directly by the firm for relatively unskilled work, such as laborers and " odd men," and some " helpers " employed directly by the firm as, for example, the helpers in machine saggermaking. In the aggregate, the males outside the organized branches will reach at least two-thirds the number of those employed in the organized branches.[69]

Among the female operatives there is at present no large group totally unorganized in East Liverpool, but only two branches—the finishers and the liners—are well organized. The finishers are employed by the jiggermen but since 1903 they have had a national wage scale, agreed upon by themselves and their jiggermen-employers, and approved by the Brotherhood.[70] The liners have been organized along with the male liners in Trenton since 1913 and in East Liverpool since 1920. In both these localities the women liners are in a minority. In the other pottery towns, where the women liners are in a majority, they are not well organized. The two largest groups of female workers, the warehouse-women and the decalcomania workers, are but partially organized.

The warehousewomen are covered by the union scale to a large extent but their earnings are much lower than those of the finishers, or the decalcomania girls. Although the Brotherhood has found it difficult to keep

----

[69] The statements in this chapter as to the degree of organization in 1928 are based on estimates made for the writer by Brotherhood officers and by Secretary Goodwin of the numbers employed in the several branches in the union general ware potteries. They are borne out by the figures given for the number of employees in the various occupational groups in *Bulletin No. 412 of the United States Bureau of Labor Statistics:* " Wages, Hours, and Productivity in the Pottery Industry," 1925. (Washington: Government Printing Office, 1926.)

[70] *Proceedings,* 1904, p. 18.

the warehousewomen organized, this group twice had an independent union in East Liverpool. In 1899 their organization was affiliated directly with the American Federation of Labor. In the autumn of that year they were strong enough to carry on a strike which crippled the operation of the potteries.[71] In its campaign in 1901-1902 for extension of organization to the female operatives, the Brotherhood attempted to bring the warehousewomen within its ranks and a local union was established for them in East Liverpool. However, they left the Brotherhood the next year, apparently because they were dissatisfied with the results of the 1903 wage conference; they then remained unorganized for several years.[72] In 1910 they again went on strike in East Liverpool and secured an advance in wages. The manufacturers found them very difficult to deal with, as they " were unorganized, recognized no authority (and) had no responsible head." [73] In March, 1913, they once more went on strike in East Liverpool and their demands were referred to arbitration. The award gave them substantial wage increases.[74] The Brotherhood officers then succeeded in bringing them into the Brotherhood again. Their local union in East Liverpool had a membership of 500 in 1914 and covered three-fourths of the ware-room women in the district. However, the membership had fallen to 205 by 1928.

The decalcomania girls have been partially organized in the West at times [75] but less than half of them are now in the Brotherhood. In Trenton they were organ-

---

[71] *Ibid.*, 1901, p. 6; *U. S. Ind. Comm.*, XVII, 459.

[72] *Proceedings*, 1903, p. 9; 1904, p. 13; 1907, p. 51.

[73] *Proceedings, U. S. P. A.*, 1910, p. 28.

[74] *Ibid.*, 1913, pp. 31-32.

[75] *Proceedings, N. B. of O. P.*, 1902, p. 7; 1904, p. 12; *Report of President*, 1913, p. 5; 1915, p. 8; 1916, p. 17; *Report of Executive Board*, 1928, pp. 13-15; 1929, pp. 6, 58-59; 1930, p. 6.

ized in 1913, along with the liners, and have since maintained a good percentage of organization, considering the difficulties they have had to face.[76] There is no uniform scale for decalcomania work and the difficulties in the way of securing one are very great.

In summary, it would be safe to say that in the general ware division, at least one-half of the operatives in the union potteries are outside the organization. Of the male workers, it is doubtful if 60 per cent are in the Brotherhood and of the females the percentage is much lower.

The Policy Toward the Unorganized Branches.—It is obvious that the failure of the Brotherhood to include within its membership such a large proportion of the operatives in the union potteries is not due to a policy of deliberate exclusion. The constitution provides,[77] and has for years, that " all persons, male and female, who are connected with any of the branches of the trade represented in the National Brotherhood of Operative Potters and not under the age of sixteen years, may become members of the order, provided such persons are of sober and industrious habits." The word " branch " as used here means division of the industry, such as the general ware and the sanitary ware divisions. Not only has the Brotherhood taken no positive stand against the admission of workers in any of the unorganized branches, but conventions have repeatedly voted in favor of attempting to induce them to come in.[78] It is clear, too, that the initiation fees, per capita

[76] See below, pp. 84-85, 207.

[77] Sec. 164.

[78] The following resolution, adopted in 1915, is typical: " That this convention go on record as reaffirming its former attitude toward industrial unionism " and " that the locals of the N. B. of O. P. do all in their power to induce all employees in the potteries to join the N. B. of O. P." *Proceedings,* 1915, pp. 45, 72; also 1920, p. 64.

tax, and defense fund assessments, so far from being set prohibitively against the semi-skilled and unskilled, have been differentiated in their favor.

Although the policy of the Brotherhood has been that of the open door for all classes of operatives, it has not been in fact one of continuous campaigning to bring all branches within the organization. Drives for membership take money and energy, and for considerable periods the national officers believed that their limited supply of each should be devoted to the branches which had shown capacity for organization and had stood loyally by the Brotherhood through good times and bad.

Three male branches now unorganized in East Liverpool at one time had local unions in that district. All three of these became dissatisfied with the policies of the national union and attempted to secure their demands from the employers by independent action, but all three eventually became disorganized. The clay- and slip-makers went out in 1913, after their wage demands had been rejected by the convention.[79] They had been organized twice previously and had twice allowed their local union to lapse.[80] The kiln firemen gave up their charter in 1915, because their wage demands, like all others, were withdrawn as the result of a referendum vote; their local union had never been strong.[81] The kilndrawers were well organized in East Liverpool for many years. What broke the hold of the Brotherhood on this branch was an unauthorized strike in 1916. The Brotherhood punished the offenders by wholesale suspensions and the majority of the kilndrawers did not seek readmission.[82] It was not until

[79] *Proceedings, U. S. P. A.,* 1913, pp. 33-34.
[80] Duffy, pp. 18, 22; *Proceedings,* 1898, p. 10; 1904, pp. 12, 13; *Report of President,* 1908, p. 9.
[81] *Ibid.,* 1912, p. 7; 1916, p. 17.
[82] See below, pp. 350, 363.

May, 1923, however, that the East Liverpool local union of kilndrawers gave up its charter.[83]

The experience of the Brotherhood from 1901 to 1904 in attempting to organize the semi-skilled and unskilled operatives in the West has also been noted. The attempt met with partial success but was soon followed by the almost wholesale withdrawal of these workers because of dissatisfaction at the failure of the Brotherhood to secure the wages and working conditions for them which they had expected. This experience made a deep impression upon the officers.[84] For many years they made no further attempt to organize the mass of women workers. Nor did they attempt to organize the odd men, laborers, or other non-skilled males employed directly by the firm. The Brotherhood had little to offer them except its beneficiary features. It could not very well enforce a uniform scale for them in face of the differences in local wage rates for unskilled labor and local differences in what these workers are called upon to do. Many of the workers in this class are of the " floating labor " type.

As for the boys and young men employed as helpers by journeymen clay workers, although some of them do belong to the union in the outside towns and although conventions have adopted resolutions calling upon the journeymen to give preference in employment to those who belong,[85] the national officers have not, down to 1928, vigorously attempted to bring them into the organization in the trade centers. It is obvious that the officers cannot do much to organize them unless and until the journeymen who employ them are eager to

[83] *Report of Executive Board*, 1924, p. 7.
[84] *Proceedings*, 1904, p. 13.
[85] *Ibid.*, 1912, p. 22; 1916, p. 44.

have them in the Brotherhood. Apparently the journeymen have not been strongly in favor of organizing
them. They believe that the helpers are well paid now,
compared with what the journeymen earn. If the helpers were in the Brotherhood there would probably be
a movement to establish a wage scale for them, as for
the finishers, and that would present difficulties of its
own. Moreover, the journeymen have not always been
able to control their helpers in East Liverpool to the
entire satisfaction of themselves (the journeymen) or
the manufacturers and there has been fear that if they
were within the Brotherhood they might put the
national organization in an embarrassing position at
times with the manufacturers.

The Brotherhood never attempted to extend its
organization within the union potteries in the East as
far as in the West. Neither the kilndrawers, organized
for years in the West, nor the warehousemen, still
organized in the West, have ever been organized in the
East. The same is true of the warehousewomen. In
the East these groups have more closely approached the
category of " floating " labor than in East Liverpool
and Sebring, which are practically single-industry
towns. Vice-President Hutchins was always reluctant
to attempt to organize any group of workers which
could not be covered in the wage scale and of which the
personnel was so shifting as to make the task of controlling them a difficult one,[86]—whether in general-
ware or in sanitary.[87]

---

[86] Statement of Vice-President Hutchins to the writer; also *Report
of the President*, 1906, p. 26.

[87] *Report of Executive Board*, 1927, p. 44; also *Report of the
United States Commission on Industrial Relations*, 64th Cong., 1st
Sess., S. Doc. No. 415 (Washington: Government Printing Office,
1916), III, 2995-2996. This document will be referred to hereafter
under the abbreviation *Comm. on Ind. Rels.*

Thus the attitude of the Brotherhood officers toward the unorganized branches has usually been merely receptive. There was a renewed attempt to organize the female operatives in the West in the period from 1913 to 1915 but the results were not encouraging, except in the case of the warehousewomen in the East Liverpool district and they already had an independent organization. Then in the war years and the years immediately following, the Brotherhood was fully occupied with questions of wage adjustments for the organized branches. In the 1923 convention a resolution calling for a renewed attempt to organize the unorganized branches was defeated. The argument that finally prevailed, though but narrowly, was that the Brotherhood was not then in a position to do anything for these workers.[88] In 1927 and 1928 the officers again undertook an aggressive organizing campaign in some of these branches, particularly in the decalcomania branch, in spite of the fact that many of the older members were skeptical.[89] However, the earlier experiences seem to have been repeated; the " decal girls " left the Brotherhood in large numbers in the following two years.[90]

The Problem of Members in Non-Scale Branches.— The prospect or lack of prospect of securing a uniform wage scale for a particular branch in case it were organized has been an important factor in the success or failure of the Brotherhood in its organizing attempts. It has also had a great influence, at times a decisive influence, upon the attitude taken by the national officers towards urgings from within the Brotherhood that a vigorous campaign be launched for the organization of this or that branch. In a union in which so much of

[88] *Proceedings,* 1923, p. 50; *Potters Herald,* July 19, 1923.
[89] *Report of Executive Board,* 1928, p. 15.
[90] *Ibid.,* 1929, pp. 58-59; 1930, p. 6.

the activity of the organization is concerned with wage agreements, members not covered by those agreements obviously fall outside the union's normal method of functioning for its constituents. The national officers have been able to secure advances in wage rates or betterment in conditions for non-scale workers here and there who were clearly below the average for the shops in the section, but this has been accomplished, when it has been accomplished, by persuasion. Coercion is not practicable under the agreement.

Protection of non-scale workers against wage reductions or adverse changes in conditions presents an even more serious problem to a union working under a no-strike agreement. President T. J. Duffy declared as early as 1907:

> If we can not see our way clear to demand a wage scale for these branches, then we should decide whether or not we shall support these members, to the point of a strike, in maintaining whatever rate of wages they are getting, whether it be above the average price paid for such work, or not. To allow such members to pay their money into the organization and then give them no protection in return for it, does not seem altogether right.[91]

But the suggestion that the Brotherhood might support members of non-scale branches to the point of a strike to protect them against wage reductions, presents the very serious difficulty that the branches covered by the wage scale—and its corollary, the no-strike agreement—might become involved. This could not well be avoided if the Brotherhood went to the limit in support of them. The union constitution empowers the executive board to order the members in all branches to cease work if " any one part of a pottery shall be engaged in a legalized strike." [92] This clause is not

[91] *Report of President*, 1907, p. 10.
[92] Sec. 90.

mandatory but it creates a presumption as to what constitutes full support. And this, the manufacturers have always contended, would be a violation of the agreement.

Moreover, there was no joint machinery, until very recently, for the adjustment of disputes in the non-scale branches over wages or changes in conditions. It was the understanding that such matters should be settled on the basis of the prices and conditions which had prevailed in the particular shop. But if the firm and the workers failed to agree on terms, and if the national officers could not effect a settlement with the firm, there was no joint committee to which the dispute could be taken, as there has been from the beginning for the scale branches. The standing committees which act for the scale branches had no authority to render a binding decision for a non-scale branch. At least the Association would not concede that they had. It was not until 1926 that an additional " unofficial standing committee " was established for a non-scale branch—the decorating branch—and this was for the East Liverpool district alone. And it was not until 1930 that a similar committee was set up in Sebring.[93] Thus, so long as the manufacturers would not agree that a joint committee should protect the workers in non-scale branches against *ex parte* changes and so long as they insisted that any action on the part of other Brotherhood members which stopped the flow of ware would be a violation of the agreement, the Brotherhood was in an awkward position.

It is in the decorating department that the problem is most serious. The decalcomania workers in Trenton have experienced in recent years an unusual amount of

[93] See below, pp. 205-206.

trouble, largely because of the attempt of some employers to secure " western prices," which, they contended, were lower than their own.

The decal workers are very much discouraged because of the fact that they are kept in a turmoil attempting to meet the manufacturers' arguments and maintain their average earnings. In Local 91 this condition has caused a constant drain on the treasury taking care of the committees handling these disputes caused by the lack of uniformity in prices paid to decal workers.[94]

And the members in other branches have repeatedly been involved, or threatened with being involved, in the disputes of the decalcomania workers.[95]

Down to 1927 the issue as to how far the Brotherhood could go in protecting prices in a non-scale branch was not presented squarely. But in December, 1927, in a case involving lining prices in a china ware shop in New Castle, Pennsylvania, the officers of the Association denied the right of the Brotherhood to prevent the firm from reducing such prices, on the ground that these prices were not covered in the scale. In this case the Brotherhood went so far as to authorize a strike in the other branches.[96] There were also other serious disputes in the West over attempted reduction of decorating prices.[97] The " unofficial decorating standing committees " at East Liverpool and Sebring may protect existing decalcomania prices from reduction in those centers and take care of disputes on new work. But the decorators in china ware and all the decorators in semi-porcelain outside of East Liverpool and Sebring are still without any protection under the agreement.

[94] Vice-President Cartlidge, in *Report of Executive Board*, 1928, p. 46.

[95] *Ibid.*, 1927, p. 44.

[96] See below, pp. 358-359.

[97] *Report of Executive Board*, 1928, pp. 23, 24; *Proceedings*, 1928, p. 23.

PART II
THE GENERAL WARE AGREEMENT

CHAPTER IV

HISTORY OF RELATIONS

Prior to 1897 collective bargaining and joint agreements were the exception rather than the rule in the general ware industry. The Trenton manufacturers had dealt with the organized operatives for a dozen years or more, but in the West the opposition of most of the employers to the new Brotherhood, as it had been to the Knights of Labor, was "active and seemed impregnable."[1] When sectional bargaining appeared in the West in 1897, it was not as a development from a generally established system of shop bargaining. The employers were brought as a group to see the advantages of collective action for the section, and even for the country as a whole, before the majority of the manufacturers in the West had exhibited any willingness to treat individually with the operatives' organization.

COLLECTIVE BARGAINING, 1897-1900

The negotiations of 1897 began more or less informally in January. The occasion and the stimulus came from the common interest of the manufacturers and the Brotherhood in securing a restoration of the 1890 tariff duties on pottery. A committee from the Brotherhood had gone to Washington to plead before the Ways and Means Committee of the House of Representatives

---

[1] *Proceedings, N. B. of O. P.,* 1907, p. 4; *Report of President,* 1906, pp. 11-12.

for higher duties.[2] There it met a group of western manufacturers who had come on the same errand. The union committee took advantage of this opportunity to urge upon the manufacturers the fairness of restoring the pre-1894 wages if the old tariff rates were restored and also the advisability of making the "working prices" uniform in all the potteries.

The manufacturers in Washington gave the union committee encouraging answers on both points. They were obviously interested in the possibility of a joint agreement which would stabilize both wages and selling prices. They told the Brotherhood representatives that they would try to persuade their association to raise selling prices as soon as the new tariff bill was passed and restore the 1893 wages, if the Brotherhood on its part would extend its organization among the operatives and compel all manufacturers to observe the new selling prices. This plan looked good to President Hughes who commended it to the 1897 convention.[3]

The Brotherhood convention decided against the proposed agreement; the delegates objected to the manufacturers throwing upon the operatives the responsibility for maintaining selling prices. They voted to demand the unconditional restoration of "the wages paid prior to the passage of the Wilson bill," " in thirty days after the tariff bill now pending goes into effect." But they added that " if the manufacturers pledge themselves to pay the 12½ per cent in thirty days, that we, the operatives, will pledge ourselves to go to work immediately to establish a uniform wage list, and also help the manufacturers to maintain a uniform selling

[2] *Tariff Hearings before The Committee on Ways and Means,* 54th Cong. 1st Sess., H. Doc. No. 338 (Washington: Government Printing Office, 1897), I, 201-202.

[3] *Proceedings,* 1897; Duffy, pp. 26-27.

price to the full extent of our ability." [4] And a committee which had been appointed by the convention to meet with a committee of East Liverpool manufacturers had agreed that

if they would advise the employees of their different shops to join the National Brotherhood of Operative Potters so as to give us full control of said shops, we in return would do all we could to help the manufacturers to maintain a uniform selling price for their products, even to the calling out of the men of such manufacturers as tried to undersell; they in return agreeing to pay a proportionate share of such expense.[5]

The decision of the United States Potters Association to go ahead with the negotiations brought matters to the point of national collective bargaining for the first time. It had not been easy. Many of the manufacturers had been opposed to dealing as an association with the Brotherhood. The action of the 1897 meeting was due to the efforts of a small number of men in the Association who were willing to enter into a plan of regulating labor terms through organization on both sides and who were convinced that the Brotherhood was a responsible organization.[6] The manufacturers were undoubtedly influenced to some extent by respect for the fighting qualities shown by the western operatives in 1894, when they had resisted a reduction for months with very little prior organization and no money.[7]

The reluctance of the representatives of the eastern operatives to make a uniform list based on averaging eastern and western prices prevented the attainment of a national agreement at that time and the Brotherhood committee made a separate settlement with the western

[4] *Proceedings, N. B. of O. P.*, 1897; *Proceedings, U. S. P. A.*, 1897, p. 8.
[5] *Proceedings, N. B. of O. P.*, 1897.
[6] Statement of Mr. W. E. Wells to the writer.
[7] Statement of ex-President T. J. Duffy to the writer.

manufacturers.[8] In 1899, with the eastern operatives within the fold, the Brotherhood renewed its demand for a uniform wage scale. A committee was appointed to draw up a " uniform list " and the convention voted that the list be put in force thirty days after its completion whether the manufacturers coöperated in its formulation or not.[9] The manufacturers, when approached, declared that they could not take the time then to work over a list jointly with the union committee. The latter, anticipating that the Brotherhood would not be in a position to enforce its own list if the manufacturers refused to accept it after it had been presented, decided to wait until it could get the manufacturers to coöperate in drawing up the list from the beginning. It was not until the following year that the union committee and the executive committee of the Association met to attack the problem jointly.[10] The two committees worked on the problem for several weeks and finally concluded an agreement. " There was manifest a desire to be fair on the part of the representatives of the operatives and manufacturers alike, and both sides were willing to concede to the other, where necessary in order to secure adjustment." [11] The " Uniform Wage Scale " was to go into effect on May 1, 1900; [12] it was to cover 80 per cent of the general ware potteries of the country.[13]

[8] *Proceedings, N. B. of O. P.*, 1898, pp. 3-6.

[9] *Ibid.*, 1899, pp. 19, 41-43, 47.

[10] *Proceedings, N. B. of O. P.*, 1900, pp. 7, 8-9; *Proceedings, U. S. P. A.*, 1900, p. 30.

[11] *Ibid.*, p. 38.

[12] *Ibid.*, pp. 30, 35, 37 *et seq.*; *Proceedings, N. B. of O. P.*, 1900, pp. 7, 8.

[13] *Duffy*, p. 36.

SECTIONAL COLLECTIVE BARGAINING IN THE WEST
(1901-1905)

The failure of the Brotherhood to hold its eastern members in line under the uniform scale agreement of 1900 threw collective bargaining back to a sectional basis. The United States Potters Association immediately took the position that the action of the eastern operatives had nullified the agreement signed by the two committees.[14] Nor would the Association negotiate with the Brotherhood for a new agreement. To this suggestion, made immediately after the union convention of July, 1900, the manufacturers replied that their association could not deal further with an organization which could not hold its members to the agreements which its representatives made for them.[15]

The western manufacturers, however, were as a matter of fact observing the terms of the " uniform scale agreement " entered into at Pittsburgh. Under the name of " The Western Manufacturing Potters Association," they were dealing with the Brotherhood in the settlement of disputes arising in the West in the application of the " Pittsburgh Agreement." In February, 1901, when the Brotherhood again asked for a conference with the United States Potters Association, it was referred by the President of that association to the Western Manufacturing Potters Association as the body with which it should deal.[16] That association, for its part, not only accepted the rôle assigned it but used the assumption that the western manufacturers had recently entered into an agreement with the Brotherhood as a reason for not holding a conference at that

[14] *Proceedings, U. S. P. A.,* December, 1900, p. 15.
[15] *Ibid.,* pp. 14, 22-23; 1901, pp. 44-56; *Proceedings, N. B. of O. P.,* 1901, pp. 6-7.
[16] *Proceedings, U. S. P. A.,* 1901, pp. 46-48.

time to consider terms of a new one. The Brotherhood officers conceded in fact both of the manufacturers' contentions. They did allow the terms of the 1900 agreement to stand for a year, and they did deal with the western association, as the representative of the manufacturers in whose plants the 1900 agreement was in effect, on the terms of a new one.[17]

The agreement made in 1901 was not reached easily. It was only through the action of Thomas J. Duffy, then secretary of the Brotherhood, that an agreement was made at all. The conference had reached a deadlock, and the manufacturers had left the room after a final refusal to accept the terms insisted on by the Brotherhood committee. Secretary Duffy called them back and asked them to await the result of a further caucus which he had persuaded his colleagues to hold. He then urged his committee to make further concessions in order to secure an agreement.[18] The outcome was that the Brotherhood secured substantial gains at this conference, in spite of the fact that it was not in a position to compel the eastern manufacturers to concede the same things.[19] But more than that, the making of a western agreement in 1901 saved the agreement system. If it had lapsed then it is unlikely that it would have been reëstablished in the West for sometime, if at all. And if it had not been well established in the West in these critical years, it is extremely unlikely that it would have been extended to national proportions as early as 1905.

The 1901 agreement was made specifically for a term of one year. It was renewed in 1902 for another year without any important change.

[17] *Ibid.,* pp. 49-56; *Proceedings, N. B. of O. P.,* 1901, p. 8.
[18] Statement of Mr. W. E. Wells to the writer.
[19] *Proceedings, N. B. of O. P.,* 1901, p. 8.

In 1903 the agreement was not made until after a resort to arbitration. The concessions which the manufacturers were willing to make were so small in proportion to the union demands that the union conference committee did not believe that it should accept them as the basis of an agreement. The manufacturers refused to concede anything further " no matter what the consequences might be." The Brotherhood officers took a strike vote to see if the members were willing to back their demands to the point of a strike. Although more than three-fourths of those voting—the majority then required for approval of a strike—supported this course, only about one-third of the membership voted; moreover, business conditions were poor. The officers therefore " decided to play for a delay in hopes that the conditions of trade would improve." Fortunately for the Brotherhood the manufacturers made a counter proposal for an equalization of the list. The union agreed to this, with a reservation that the revised list should be submitted to a vote of the local unions before adoption. Meanwhile the terms of the old agreement, which expired July first, were continued.

The revision process did not result in a list satisfactory to the membership and it was rejected by the local unions. The union negotiators were now in a position in which they had to repeat the strike threat or back down. They took the bolder course and notified the manufacturers that they would have to order a strike.[20] The employers' inter-association agreement then came to the assistance of the union. The Western Manufacturing Potters Association, acting in accordance with that agreement, asked the union representatives to meet with a larger committee under the leadership of the

[20] *Ibid.*, 1904, p. 9.

United States Potters Association.[21] The union, nothing loath to treat again with the United States Potters
Association, readily agreed to this, but, to maintain its
bold stand, insisted that the meeting take place within
ten days. The committees met September seventeenth.
In this conference the union concentrated on two propositions, one for the kilnmen and one for the jiggermen,
which they hoped would help them, if obtained, to win
the eastern kilnmen and jiggermen to acceptance of
the uniform list. The manufacturers refused to grant
either of these and another deadlock ensued. The manufacturers then came to the rescue once more with a
proposal to submit these two questions to arbitration.
This proposal the union accepted. President Duffy
explained:

> In agreeing to arbitrate, we had an opportunity to establish the
> justice of our cause before an impartial tribunal; and in case the
> decision of the committee should be against us we realized that we
> could accept the defeat and at the same time preserve the strength
> and prestige of our organization, which meant a great deal.[22]

The decision of the arbitration committee went against
the Brotherhood on both points.

Before the decision was handed down the manufacturers had asked that the agreement be made for two
years. The officers of the Brotherhood submitted this
to a trade vote, which was favorable, and, at the request
of the parties, the arbitration board made its award
binding for a period of two years. Making the agreement for a two-year period was also favorable to the
Brotherhood. President Duffy said in 1904: "This, in
my opinion, was one of the best moves the organization
ever made, and if it was not for this agreement I think

[21] *Proceedings, U. S. P. A.*, 1903, p. 20.
[22] *Proceedings*, 1904, p. 10.

that we would have had a hard time this year to retain present prices and conditions." [23] It is well to remember that this proposal came from the manufacturer's association originally.

THE NATIONAL AGREEMENT THROUGH 1915

The 1903 agreement was the last made with the western association. In 1904 the uniform list was applied to the East and in 1905 the Brotherhood again carried on its negotiations with, and made its agreement with, the United States Potters Association. There was no reluctance on the part of the Association now to deal with the Brotherhood.[24] The Association asked only that the union conferees be " vested with plenary power to act in the premises "; this was granted by the convention.[25]

From that time until 1917 the agreement was renewed biennially without an adjournment of the conference or a strike vote because of a deadlock. In 1913 the manufacturers requested that the existing agreement, which expired October first, be extended until November first, in order to allow the conference to be postponed until the pending tariff bill had been acted upon by Congress.[26] The union officers, doubting their

[23] *Ibid.*, p. 11.
[24] *Proceedings, U. S. P. A.*, 1904, p. 14; 1905, p. 13.
[25] *Proceedings, N. B. of O. P.*, 1905, pp. 9, 30.
[26] A committee from the Brotherhood appeared before the Ways and Means Committee, in January, 1913, in opposition to reduction of the tariff duties on pottery and was active in trying to enlist support among Congressmen for their cause. *Report of President, 1913*, pp. 8-10; *Tariff Schedules Hearings before the Committee on Ways and Means, House of Representatives*, 62d Cong., 3d. Sess., H. Doc. No. 1447 (Washington: Government Printing Office, 1913), I, 631-636, 680-682.

power to grant this, submitted the question to a referendum vote. The result was a majority against extension, though the majority was but a slight one. The officers ruled that a vote against extension was a vote to cease work October first, and therefore a strike vote, and as the adverse majority was less than the three-fourths then required by union law for a strike, the extension was held to be carried. The conference committee sustained this interpretation by a vote of 22 to 2. The postponed conference was held in mid-October and resulted in an agreement for another two years.[27]

THE " VOLUNTARY " INCREASES OF 1916-1917

The unsettled labor conditions produced by the World War put the agreement made in September, 1915, for a period of two years, under a severe strain. The restlessness of the men in the face of an abnormal demand for labor and high wages in munitions plants and iron and steel mills and the rising cost of living made it difficult for the Brotherhood officers to keep the members from using pressure in violation of the agreement to get higher wages and for the manufacturers to hold their workmen. Twice in 1916, and again in May, 1917, the manufacturers attempted to meet the situation by granting " voluntary " increases in wages.

The negotiations for the first voluntary advance grew out of a request from the jiggermen for relief because of the increased difficulty of holding their helpers. The jiggermen and the warehousewomen were the only branches given increases in this first voluntary advance, effective in August, 1916. In September a general increase was granted. The advance was in the form of

[27] *Report of President*, 1914, pp. 2-3; *Proceedings, U. S. P. A.*, 1913, pp. 32-33.

a percentage upon the existing rates—in some branches 10 per cent, in others 5 per cent. These percentages upon " base rates " came later to be called the " plussages." In May, 1917, the manufacturers granted a second general voluntary increase; the plussages were advanced 5 points—those of 10 to 15 and those of 5 to 10.

THE 1917 STRIKE

In September, 1917, the regular biennial conference resulted in a deadlock. The amount of the general increase was the stumbling block. After six days of disagreement the conference adjourned to allow the manufacturers to prepare a counter-proposition. This carried some increases in the plussages for all departments. It also included a plan for dividing the rates for jiggering into specified rates for the jiggerman himself and each of his helpers. The union conferees expressed themselves as satisfied with the manufacturers' proposal for the jiggermen, both as to the level of the new rates and the plan of division, and suggested that a joint committee be appointed to work out the application of the plan in further detail. But on the increases to be given to the other branches, they did not accept the manufacturers' proposal. They presented a counter-proposition of their own which involved plussages ten points higher, in general, than those the manufacturers offered. The manufacturers refused the plussages asked for by the union. The conference committee in turn refused to assume the responsibility for accepting the plussages offered by the manufacturers. The union then submitted the manufacturers' counter-proposal to a referendum vote. The returns showed 2,791 against to 565 in favor. The size of the vote cast against the manufacturers' proposal was attributed to the opposition of the jiggermen.[28]

The executive board held a meeting with the labor committee immediately after the result of the vote was known. The manufacturers said that they could not make another proposition until after a meeting of the Association on October fourth. The union officers, therefore, had no new proposal before them which they could submit to referendum, nor any assurance that one would be made. The agreement had expired October first. The officers would not order their members to remain at work pending the possible receipt of a new proposal from the manufacturers and the outcome of a new referendum on it if one were received; they feared that the operatives would not remain at work under the circumstances, even if ordered to. The board therefore reluctantly issued the order for all members of the Brotherhood in semi-porcelain potteries to cease work on October eleventh.

Fortunately it happened that in this particular year it had been arranged that the executive board and a committee of manufacturers of china should hold a separate conference for china after the conclusion of the regular general ware conference.[29] This meeting was fixed for October fifth. The Association met on October fourth and formulated a new proposal for semi-porcelain, as well as china. Their revised propositions, the manufacturers said, were "less scientific than the original, but probably more in line with the views of your membership." They insisted that their previous offer was "eminently fair in principle as well

---

[28] *Ibid.*, 1917, p. 20; *Proceedings, N. B. of O. P.*, 1918, p. 26.

[29] The Brotherhood and the manufacturers of china ware had been engaged for some time in negotiations for uniform lists for china.

as in the amount of the advance proposed " but they were unwilling to submit to a strike " in the attempt to compel your people to accept, against their will, a plan that was designed for their benefit."[30] The new proposal eliminated the change earlier proposed in the system of paying for jiggering work. The percentage increases were, on the whole, substantially higher than those offered in September.

The new proposal could not be voted upon until October sixteenth. The manufacturers asked that the plants be kept in operation until it had been acted upon. The union officers did not believe that they had authority to rescind the strike order and the strike went into effect, as originally ordered, on October eleventh. The board members feared that if the strike order were revoked many of the members would quit work anyway. On the other hand, they believed that the fact of being actually on strike when the vote was taken would have a sobering effect upon many of the members and operate in favor of the adoption of the manufacturers' proposal.

The vote was 2,258 against accepting the manufacturers' proposal and 1,373 in favor. The executive board decided that the proposal had been accepted, because the vote against it was less than the two-thirds majority then required for a strike. After another conference with the labor committee, the board ordered its members back to work on October twenty-second. At this conference the manufacturers, in order to make the terms more acceptable to the jiggermen, had made further concessions to them in the form of relief from some " dead work." The decision of the executive board aroused great opposition in East Liverpool. An insurgent organization was hastily formed, which attempted to keep all the workers on strike until they got a 25

[30] *Report of Executive Board,* 1918, p. 13.

per cent increase. The officers finally suppressed the rebellion and work was resumed in all plants on the twenty-sixth.[31] At the next convention the law was amended so as to specify that a majority of the votes cast should be necessary to end a strike.[32]

FURTHER INCREASES, 1918-1920

The 1917 agreement was signed for two years, subject to reopening on ninety days' notice, not to be given earlier than July 1, 1918. The continued increase in the cost of living made it obvious that the Brotherhood would ask in July for a reopening. The labor committee met in June to decide whether to offer an increase voluntarily or await the action of the Brotherhood convention which was to meet early in July. The decision was to postpone action until after the convention and " in case that convention did not formulate extreme and unusual demands " to offer an increase to the Brotherhood officials and carry the matter through with them instead of holding a regular conference with an elected conference committee of the Brotherhood.[33]

The convention contented itself with instructing the executive board to ask for a general increase in wages. Only if a " satisfactory " increase could not be obtained in this way was notice to be filed for reopening the 1917 agreement. The executive board disposed of the matter itself with the labor committee. It proposed to the manufacturers that they offer to it the general wage increase that they were prepared to give, assuring them that if it were such that the board could accept it as

[31] *Ibid.*, pp. 2-17; *Proceedings, U. S. P. A.*, 1917, pp. 19-33; *Potters Herald*, October 25, 1917.
[32] *Proceedings*, 1918, pp. 22, 23-24.
[33] *Proceedings, U. S. P. A.*, 1919, p. 24.

"satisfactory," no request for a reopening of the agreement would be made. The manufacturers responded with a proposal which was accepted by the executive board, with slight modification. "From such little information as could be obtained as to the expectations of the Brotherhood officials, we are inclined to think," said Mr. Wells later, that " the offer was rather more liberal than they anticipated." [34] In a supplementary agreement made on September tenth, further increases were given the jiggermen and dishmakers. The percentage increases thus granted in 1918 were but slightly lower than those given in most branches in the 1917 agreement; in a few branches they were higher.

When the regular biennial conference convened in September, 1919, the union was again seeking a substantial increase in wages. The manufacturers now took the ground that the time had passed for wage increases. Finally, however, they offered a modal increase of 5 per cent, plus a substantial list of increases in base prices, " as the price of peace." They wished to avoid a referendum vote on the renewal of the agreement. It was accepted with a proviso that the agreement could be reopened after three months if the cost of living continued to advance. The warehousewomen were dissatisfied with the agreement, so far as it applied to them, and went out on an outlaw strike in the East Liverpool district. After they had returned to work their scale was revised upward.[35]

In January the Brotherhood called for a reopening of the agreement and obtained further increases.[36] It

[34] *Ibid.*, p. 25; *Proceedings, N. B. of O. P.,* 1918, p. 26; *Report of Executive Board,* 1919, pp. 11-14.

[35] *Proceedings, U. S. P. A.,* January, 1920, pp. 31-34; *Report of Executive Board,* 1920, pp. 11-12.

[36] *Proceedings, U. S. P. A.,* January, 1920, pp. 58-59; December, 1920, p. 42; *Report of Executive Board,* 1920, pp. 12-15.

8

was agreed that these rates should stand for six months, at least; unless there should be a " pronounced or radical change in labor conditions," they were to stand until October 1, 1921. Nevertheless, the convention instructed the officers, in July, to ask for a further increase of 25 per cent.[37] The manufacturers at first refused to reopen the agreement. They finally receded from this position, however, and at a conference with the board offered an increase of approximately 5 per cent in most branches and more in others. The executive board did not believe that it could assume the responsibility for accepting this offer as an answer to the demands of the convention and submitted the proposed terms to a referendum. The vote was favorable to acceptance, 1438 to 1258.[38] This was the last increase in the " war " series.

THE 1921 REDUCTION AND THE 1922 STRIKE

In May, 1921, the employers, for the first time in the history of joint dealings, asked for a reopening of the agreement for a reduction in wages, under the " change in conditions " clause. They requested that the new wage scale go into effect not later than July first. They also proposed the adoption of " a list of proposals looking toward an improvement in quality, and reduction of the extravagant waste now so generally prevailing." The Brotherhood officers answered that they could not appoint a general conference committee to meet with the manufacturers before the union convention, scheduled for the first week in July, but the executive board itself would meet the labor committee on June sixth.

---

[37] *Proceedings, N. B. of O. P.*, 1920, pp. 25, 45-46.
[38] *Report of Executive Board*, 1921, pp. 10-17; *Proceedings, U. S. P. A.*, December, 1920, pp. 42-44.

"Unfortunately, or perhaps intentionally," Mr. Wells said later, "the letter did not state that the executive board would not assume the responsibility for making any change." [39] But when the labor committee met with the executive board at Atlantic City on June sixth, it quickly learned that such was the position of the board.

The manufacturers protested vigorously against this practical refusal to consider their request for an immediate wage reduction and against the postponement of consideration of their proposals for "good workmanship" rules. Yet the decision of the board was undoubtedly a wise one in the circumstances. The board could not have assumed the authority to give the manufacturers any substantial concessions in its own right.[40] It could, of course, have summoned a conference committee immediately, instead of going into conference with the labor committee itself, and if the convention were six months off, instead of less than two, it might have done so. But it is doubtful if an elected conference committee would have agreed to a reduction large enough to induce the manufacturers to accept it as a satisfaction of their claim. More likely it would have submitted the matter to a referendum. The fact that the convention was so near presented an opportunity to get some action in the convention which would give the conference committee countenance in accepting a reduction without a referendum. Then why did the executive board go to a conference, empty-handed, instead of informing the manufacturers immediately that nothing could be done until after the convention? Principally in order to draw the attention of the members more sharply to the fact that the issue of a reduction would have to be met and to prepare the convention for it.[41]

[39] *Ibid.*, 1921, pp. 21, 24.
[40] See below, pp. 130-131.
[41] Statement of President Menge to the writer.

The labor committee decided not to fight to get immediate action but to await a conference with a regular conference committee on August second.[42] After a long conference, extending through a period of eight days, the union side agreed to a reduction of seventeen per cent. The first ten per cent was to date from August eleventh and the remaining seven per cent—of the wages prior to August eleventh—from November third.[43] At the request of the union the agreement was made for but one year—to September 30, 1922—with a provision for a reopening after sixty days' notice, at any time after January 1, 1922.

This conference and its outcome did much to reassure the manufacturers as to their plan of dealing with the Brotherhood. It had been shown that the union could give on a large scale as well as take. Chairman Wells said during the conference that he had been pessimistic before the conference as to an agreement being reached without a strike. At the end he remarked that this was the most difficult situation with which the joint conference committee had ever had to deal and added " we have dealt with this question in a way that fair men should deal with it." [44] However, the settlement was extremely distasteful to a large number of Brotherhood members,[45] and the next year showed that the accep-

[42] Proceedings, U. S. P. A., 1921, pp. 21-22, 24-32; Report of Executive Board, 1921, pp. 17-27; 1922, pp. 12-23.

[43] These were the direct wage-rate terms; the Brotherhood also agreed to the reaffirmation of rules intended to assure improved workmanship.

[44] The source of information for the conferences, from that of 1921 on, is the verbatim reports of the conferences.

[45] It is significant that " there developed opposition to the reduction on the part of unorganized labor, resulting in some interruptions." Proceedings, U. S. P. A., 1921, p. 22.

tance of such a heavy reduction without " consulting the trade " through a referendum vote had left an aftermath of trouble.

The sixty-day clause was not utilized. But when the union convention met in July it adopted a demand for the restoration of the seventeen per cent, from October 1, 1922. The officers of the Association stated before the conference that no increase in wages would or could be granted.[46] Early in the conference the union side retreated from the demand for the restoration of the peak wages to one for the return of the seven per cent taken off November 3, 1921. This demand was not based on changes in conditions since November but was essentially one for a reconsideration of the 1921 decision. Mr. Wells met this issue squarely. The 1921 settlement, he insisted, had been more than fair to the workers under the circumstances. As there had been no change since that time which would warrant an increase, the union demand was one for a repudiation of the 1921 agreement. It would also be a repudiation of the policy accepted by the parties in their dealings for twenty years, that an agreement once made should stand, so far as the general level of wages was concerned, until a radical change in living costs or business conditions occurred.

The conference committee decided to submit the question of making a settlement without the restoration of the seven per cent to a vote of the trade. The manufacturers strongly opposed this course. They urged the union conferees to assume the responsibility for making the settlement there and then and avoid the delay and uncertainty of a referendum as well as the danger of an adverse vote. Some of the members of the executive

[46] *Ibid.*, April, 1923, p. 44; *Report of Executive Board*, 1923, pp. 11-14.

board also urged the conference committee to accept the employers' terms without a referendum.[47] The committee, however, stood by its decision to submit the proposed settlement to referendum. The members denied that they were "afraid to assume responsibility"; they were taking this action because they knew the members at large wanted to vote on whether they should go on working at reduced wages; the conference committee of 1921 had been severely censured because they accepted that reduction without giving the membership a chance to vote on it.

When the question was submitted to the membership in September for a strike vote, the issue was presented as one of accepting the minor concessions offered by the manufacturers or striking for the restoration of the seven per cent in addition. Inasmuch as the conference committee had offered to settle on the seven per cent basis the executive board narrowed the issue to that figure. A statement presented by the manufacturers to the conference committee was sent out to the locals along with the statement of the question to be voted upon. The vote was 1,038 in favor of accepting the employers' terms and 2,731 against, 218 votes above the two-thirds necessary for a strike. Less than sixty per cent of the general ware members had voted. The vote for the strike represented barely forty per cent of the general ware membership. The majority against acceptance in East Liverpool was slightly less than two-thirds. "It was generally believed, and probably true," said the labor committee later, "that the result did not reflect the true sentiment of the trade." The light vote

[47] Statement of Mr. Frank Hutchins to the writer; letter from a member of Local Union No. 4 in *Potters Herald*, February 1, 1923.

and the majority for a strike were ascribed to over-san-
guineness on the part of " the friends of peace." [48]

Doubtless the officers of the Brotherhood would have
much preferred the terms offered by the manufacturers
to a strike. Whatever their opinion might have been as
to the merits of the workers' contention for the seven
per cent and as to what would have been the best policy
for the Brotherhood to follow if the general ware situation had stood alone, there was the complicating fact
that the sanitary division was apparently heading for
a strike. Nevertheless, there the vote was and the board
believed it had no alternative to making it effective.
The strike law did not stipulate that two-thirds of those
eligible to vote must vote in favor of a strike to make
it lawful. It read " a two-thirds vote of the local or
locals affected." [49] The suggestion was made that
because of the small number of those voting the result
should be thrown out by the board and a new vote
taken. This the board would not do on its own initiative. It took the position that it could not disregard the
vote already taken and order a new one on the same
proposal " unless there was an expression of sentiment
on the part of a sufficient number of local unions to
warrant the Executive Board in taking such action." [50]
Such an expression was not forthcoming.

The only hope of averting a strike appeared to lie
in the proffer of new terms by the manufacturers, as in
1917. But this time the hope was vain.[51] Accordingly
the strike order was sent out September twentieth,

[48] *Proceedings, U. S. P. A.,* April, 1923, p. 37; *Report of Executive
Board,* 1923, pp. 15-18.

[49] *Constitution,* 1914, Sec. 86.

[50] *Report of Executive Board,* 1923, p. 19.

[51] *Proceedings, U. S. P. A.,* April, 1923, pp. 37-38; *Report of Executive Board,* 1923, p. 19.

effective September thirtieth. A number of interested persons in East Liverpool attempted in vain to find some basis on which the strike might be avoided. Representatives of the Division of Conciliation of the United States Department of Labor also visited East Liverpool and tendered their good offices but their mediation was also without result; [52] the strike was not due to a misunderstanding or to any lack of conference between the parties.

On September thirtieth the strike began as ordered. It lasted until December sixth. Four firms operating union plants but not members of the United States Potters Asociation had signified their willingness to continue under the 1921-1922 scale plus the 7 per cent and they were allowed to continue under an agreement to observe that scale for one year or until such time as a new agreement should be made by the Brotherhood with the Association.[53] The strike involved all the general ware plants, including china, of the members of the United States Potters Association, except the Onondaga plant in Syracuse, which was not a union plant.

One firm in Trenton with a small china plant, after serving notice upon its employees and giving them a chance to return to their positions, began to operate as an " open shop " in November.[54] With these exceptions none of the general ware members of the Association attempted to operate any of the departments of their factories, whether organized or not, " except for the trifling amount of packing and shipping that were done in some quarters by plant officials." [55] Mr. Wells subsequently testified that " the interruption was remark-

[52] *Potters Herald,* September 28, October 5, 1922.
[53] *Ibid.,* October 5, 1922; *Report of Executive Board,* 1923, p. 19
[54] *Ibid.,* pp. 53-57.
[55] *Proceedings, U. S. P. A.,* April, 1923. p. 38.

ably free from the bitterness and ill-feeling that usually characterize labor troubles. There was no violence or attempted violence reported, presumably because no effort was made to supplant the strikers." [56]

The officers of the two organizations remained on the friendliest terms during the progress of the strike and kept in constant touch with each other to prevent any untoward developments and to examine all possible opportunities for a reconsideration which might lead to a settlement.[57] But the Association officers continued to state that they could make no new offer without a change in conditions and that under no circumstances would they make any concessions while the men were on strike. To do so, they maintained, would be to yield to force and this would make future dealings with the Brotherhood under the conference method impossible. The executive board continued to repeat that it was powerless to order a new vote on the old terms. In fact the board was in a worse position to order a new vote on the old terms after the strike had been initiated than it was before the strike began. It might have decided in September that the vote was inadequate and ordered a new one and then attempted to justify its action on the ground that the law did not cover the case expressly, but to order a new vote on the old terms in October would have been a confession of defeat in the strike.

Several unsuccessful attempts were made by mediators, official and unofficial, to break the impasse.[58] On

[56] *Ibid.*, also *Potters Herald,* September 28, October 19, 26, November 9, 1022.

[57] *Ibid.*, October 5, October 26, 1922; *Proceedings, U. S. P. A.,* April, 1923, p. 38.

[58] *Report of Executive Board,* 1923, pp. 19-21; *Potters Herald,* November 9, 23, 30, 1922.

November tenth, three Commissioners of Conciliation of the United States Department of Labor addressed a letter to President Wood in which they advised the Brotherhood to call off the strike. As the executive board did not see fit to follow this advice the Commissioners departed from the scene.

It was Mr. Wells who made the suggestion that led eventually to the termination of the strike. On December first he suggested that the conference committee be reconvened to give the manufacturers an opportunity to present to that committee the manufacturers' reasons for believing that the conference committee itself should call for a new vote. This was something the executive board could agree to do and it did it immediately. In its call for the meeting of the conference committee, the board plainly showed its preference for a settlement of the strike. It pointed out the seriousness of the situation and its belief that the struggle would be of long duration " unless there is some indication on the part of those engaged at the general ware trade to meet the situation with reason instead of force." [59]

Very early in the conference Mr. Wells went beyond the original suggestion that the conference committee call for another vote, and urged it to renew the agreement then and there. He vigorously attacked the referendum as a method of determining whether the men should return to work. He feared another unrepresentative vote. Moreover, a referendum, even if it brought a settlement, would involve further delay and consequently further wage loss to the operatives. If the vote were unfavorable, as he feared it would be, it was almost certain that the manufacturers would have to attempt to operate " open shops." This question was

[59] *Report of Executive Board,* 1923, pp. 21-22; *Proceedings, U. S. P. A.,* April, 1923, p. 38.

to be discussed at the Association meeting the next day. If the Association decided to make the attempt to operate " open shops " it would mean the end of the system of dealing between the two organizations which had proved so successful up to the present strike. This, he said, was " not a threat " but a " mere statement of the facts in the situation." If the union laws stood in the way of making an immediate settlement the laws were defective and the conference committee members should have the sense and courage to meet the emergency.

At first there seemed little prospect that the union committee would go further than ordering a new vote. Indeed the decision for this course was made by a majority of only one. But Mr. Wells continued to urge the members of the committee not to risk another vote of the trade and in the end the committee voted, 26 to 9, to order the members back to work.[60]

It is fair to assume that the members of the conference committee were influenced somewhat in making their decision by the " open shop " danger confronting the trade. The sanitary manufacturers had already taken that step. The defense fund was being rapidly depleted. On the other hand, there is no doubt that many of them had construed Mr. Wells' remarks in the conference to mean that they would receive an increase in wages if the men were ordered back to work without another referendum. Mr. Wells had not promised an increase but they took such statements as " you will get a better deal if you do than if you do it the other way " (order another vote) and " you will never regret it " and his readiness to meet in conference as soon as the union wished, as meaning that an increase would be given.

[60] *Report of Executive Board*, 1923, p. 23.

The next morning, December sixth, the members were ordered back to work by telegrams sent to all the general ware local unions. They were advised at the same time that a conference would be held at an early date with the manufacturers to make a new agreement. The *Potters Herald* stated that the news "carried with it an electric feeling of joy everywhere." [61] The attitude of Mr. Wells and his associates on the labor committee was characterized by the *Herald* as "magnanimous." There is little doubt that expectation of an increase in wages was widespread among the members. Several of the members of the conference committee told their locals that the manufacturers had given no definite assurance that they would grant an increase, but this did not dull the general expectation.[62]

When the conference convened on December 18, Mr. Wells announced that the manufacturers had decided to grant half the seven per cent. This was given solely because of the misunderstanding that had arisen on the union side as to what was implied at the conference of December fifth. There had been no change in business conditions or living costs since November, or since 1921 for that matter, which would warrant an increase. Nor had he promised at the previous conference, even by implication, that an increase would be given if the men were ordered back to work. However, the manufacturers knew that the members of the conference committee had assumed that there was a promise implied in what he had said at that conference and to avoid even the appearance of disappointing an honest expectation, they had decided to "split the differ-

[61] *Potters Herald,* December 7, 1923.

[62] *Ibid.,* December 14, 1922; *Proceedings, U. S. P. A.,* April, 1923, pp. 38-39.

ence." [63] The kilnmen were to get more—how much more would depend upon the working rules the kilnmen were willing to accept. This offer to the kilnmen had been decided upon before the strike was called off— contingent, of course, upon the termination of the strike by the union—because the manufacturers had come to realize that under the existing rates the kilnmen were compelled to work at too great speed to maintain earnings equal to those received by some of the other branches with which they were fairly comparable.[64]

The union side argued for the full seven per cent. It feared that the members would be greatly disappointed and that the committee would have to "regret" its action in calling off the strike. The discussion was prolonged, each side going over the same ground repeatedly. Finally, Mr. Wells delivered a time ultimatum, something unusual in the conferences. The manufacturers' proposition would stand open until three o'clock that afternoon; if it were not accepted by that time it would be withdrawn. The conference reconvened at 2:30 and President Wood reported that the union accepted the manufacturers' offer.[65] The settlement seems to have been received with satisfaction, all things considered, by the membership.[66]

BIENNIAL RENEWALS THROUGH 1928

With the 1922 settlement the parties went back to the two-year agreement expiring October first as before, but now in the even years. The biennial renewal

---

[63] *Ibid.*, pp. 39-40.

[64] In the 1922 strike vote the East Liverpool kilnmen's local had voted 332 to 21 in favor of a strike.

[65] *Report of Executive Board*, 1923, p. 24; *Proceedings, U. S. P. A.,* April, 1923, p. 40.

[66] *Potters Herald*, December 28, 1922; January 4, January 11, 1923.

has been made in every case with the understanding
that the agreement may be reopened before the expiration of the two years in the event of "pronounced or
radical changes in labor, living or market conditions."
This clause has not been invoked by either party. The
conferences of 1924 and 1926 were uneventful. The
union did not ask for a horizontal increase in either
year, nor did the manufacturers ask for any wage
reduction. In fact, they made no proposals at all.
Their position was in both years that a conference was
really unnecessary, as no proposal from the union side
involving an increase in the cost of production would or
could be granted.[67]

Business continued poor for the next two years. The
employers did not ask for a reopening of the agreement
because with unemployment rife a wage reduction
would but add to the hardship of the workers, and pos-
sibly because the manufacturers anticipated that an
insistence upon a reduction would bring on a struggle
with the Brotherhood which would injure the industry
more than a reduction would help it in meeting the problem of foreign competition.[68] The union was actively
advocating an upward revision of the duties on pottery
and the Brotherhood officers were coöperating with
the officers of the Association in an attempt, which
proved unsuccessful, to secure action by the Tariff
Commission.[69]

[67] Proceedings, U. S. P. A., 1924, p. 32; 1926, pp. 26-27; Report of
Executive Board, 1925, pp. 11-29; 1927, pp. 14-23.

[68] Proceedings, U. S. P. A., 1926, p. 26; 1927, pp. 17, 22-23; Potters
Herald, December 22, 1927; Proceedings, N. B. of O. P., 1928, pp.
11-13.

[69] Ibid., 1927, pp. 7, 9, 17; Potters Herald, July 7, July 14, July 21,
July 28, August 11, September 1, October 13, November 17, December
22, December 29, 1927; January 12, May 3, May 17, 1928; Proceedings,
U. S. P. A., 1927, pp. 15, 19; Report of Executive Board, 1928, pp.
26-28. The Brotherhood officers were also active in a movement

Before the assembling of the 1928 convention the Association sent a letter to the Brotherhood containing several proposals to be considered by the conference.[70] The employers did not propose a general reduction in wages but they did reserve the right, without further notice, to introduce a demand for a general reduction, averaging ten per cent, if their other proposals did not " meet with favorable action by " the union conference committee. The convention spent considerable time on the employers' proposals and finally referred them to the conference committee after putting itself " on record as being opposed to any and all concessions asked for in said letter." [71]

When the conference convened Chairman Wells at once made it clear that his attitude was not what it had been in 1922, 1924, or 1926. Then he had opened with an argument that they should sign the existing agreement for another two years as speedily as possible and go home. Now he proposed at the outset that they agree to give up national collective bargaining and allow the existing agreement to expire peaceably on October first, thus leaving each firm to deal amicably with its own men. The employers, he said, were thoroughly dissatisfied with national collective bargaining. Their dissatisfaction had been greatly intensified by the way in which the agreement had been interpreted by the

inaugurated by a number of national unions affiliated with the American Federation of Labor for an increase in the tariff rates on the products of their respective industries, a movement which resulted in June, 1928, in the formation of a permanent organization, later known as the Wage Earners Protective Conference. *Potters Herald*, May 31, June 21, 1928; *Report of Executive Board*, 1928, p. 29.

[70] *Proceedings, N. B. of O. P.,* 1928, pp. 11-13; *Proceedings, U. S. P. A.,* 1928, pp. 27-29.

[71] *Proceedings,* 1928, pp. 13, 61-62.

Brotherhood, and that interpretation enforced, during the past year—which meant, of course, since the advent of President James Duffy to office.[72] It was not their purpose, Mr. Wells said, to free themselves from the agreement in order to reduce wages. On the contrary, if the restrictions under which they suffered were removed by a cancellation of the agreement, they could get on without a general reduction in the wage level. Undoubtedly there would be some readjustments as between jobs and as between branches, but the general level of wages would not be lowered, and employment would be increased. However, the manufacturers would not insist to the point of a strike on giving up the agreement if the Brotherhood would not give it up peaceably.

It is extremely doubtful that the manufacturers expected the Brotherhood to agree to give up the national system. It is not at all certain that they themselves wished to give it up and face the organized employees individually in local negotiations. Mr. Wells' statement was apparently intended as an extreme form of protest against the administration of the system by President Duffy and as a warning to the Brotherhood conference committee that the manufacturers intended to insist on some relaxation of the existing " restrictions."

President Duffy, of course, argued strongly for the continuance of the national agreement system. He offered to sign for two more years on the existing terms but asked for a better understanding on a few points. The latter were concerned with the recognition of union jurisdiction over some operations and with greater uniformity in decorating prices and some joint

---

[72] *Proceedings, U. S. P. A.,* 1928, pp. 22-23.

machinery for handling decorating disputes. Indeed, a large part of the time of the conference was taken up with the interpretation of the existing agreement. President Duffy's attitude and activities were severely criticized by the manufacturers and defended by him, not without criticism in turn by him of the attitude and actions of a few of the manufacturers or their representatives.

In the end the agreement was renewed with very few changes. The union representatives made some concessions. On the other hand, the union secured an extension of the " unofficial " joint standing committee plan of handling decorating disputes, which, presumably, implies greater recognition of its claim to the right to protect its members in this department from wage reductions.[73] There was undoubtedly relief in both camps that an agreement had been reached and a hope in each that the frank statement of its position on matters that had caused friction as well as on the issues which would have to be faced in the future would make it easier to continue the agreement system.

THE 1930-1931 NEGOTIATIONS AND THE 1931 REDUCTION

The air cleared considerably in the next year.[74] Coöperation of the Brotherhood with the manufacturers' association on the tariff was gratefully acknowledged by the Association.[75] Yet in spite of the increase in the

[73] *Report of Executive Board,* 1929, pp. 15-20; *Proceedings, U. S. P. A.,* 1928, pp. 27-33.

[74] *Ibid.,* 1929, p. 24.

[75] *Report of Executive Board,* 1929, pp. 42-44; *Proceedings, N. B. of O. P.,* 1929, pp. 25-26; *Proceedings U. S. P. A.,* 1929, pp. 17, 24, 54; *Hearings before the Committee on Ways and Means, House of Representatives,* 70th Cong., 2d Sess. (Washington: Government Printing Office, 1929), II, 1302-1306; *Hearings before a Sub-committee of the*

tariff duties the manufacturers were insistent upon the necessity of wage readjustments in the 1930 conference. The union refused the manufacturers' proposals for reductions. The latter declared they would not sign without some decreases. The deadlock was broken by Mr. W. E. Wells, who had retired from the labor committee in 1928, but who now came forward with a suggestion that the agreement be continued until January first in order to await further developments in the condition of the business. This compromise was accepted with the understanding that the conference should be reconvened in December to consider the terms of a new agreement.[76]

After another four-day session early in December the conference committee agreed to continue the existing rates, with slight changes, pending the outcome of the deliberations of a joint committee which was empowered to investigate the manufacturers' complaints of " high spots " in the wage scale and to make such changes as the two sides of the committee should agree upon. The joint committee failed to agree and the manufacturers asked that the conference committee be again reconvened. Finally, on May 23, 1931, the Brotherhood accepted, without a referendum, a general ten per cent reduction from the 1928-1930 scale. The new agreement was signed to hold until October 1, 1932, with the proviso that it may be reopened at the request of either party after sixty days' notice.[77]

Committee on Finance, United States Senate, 71st Cong., 1st Sess., on H. R. 2667, Schedule 2, June 19, 20, 21, 22, 24 and 25, 1929 (Washington: Government Printing Office, 1929), pp. 276-282; *Report of Executive Board,* 1930, pp. 18-26, 53-63; *Proceedings, U. S. P. A.,* 1930, p. 14.

[76] *Potters Herald,* August 14, 21, 28, 1930; *Proceedings, U. S. P. A.,* 1930, pp. 45-46, 51-53.

[77] *Potters Herald,* December 4, 1930; February, 19, 26, April 30, May 21, 1931.

CHAPTER V

THE AGREEMENT-MAKING PROCESS

The " agreement," in the widest sense in which the term is used in the industry, covers everything which is regarded as binding between the parties whether included in the printed " agreement book " or not. In this sense every standing committee settlement, and even every local settlement recorded by the parties with the standing committee, is part of the agreement. Thus the agreement-making process may be said to be almost continuous, in that agreements are being almost constantly entered into which are binding upon both organizations.

In a narrower sense the " agreement " means what is printed in the " agreement book " plus the amendments made by national conferences since the publication of the latest edition of the book and embodied in printed supplements. The " agreement " in this restricted sense cannot be amended by any subordinate committees. Standing committee settlements and local settlements are in the nature of applications of it rather than modifications of it or amendments to it. The agreement itself can be amended or extended only by the two national bodies. This agreement-making function has ordinarily been exercised by the biennial conference. The labor committee of the manufacturers' association and the executive board of the Brotherhood acted for their respective organizations in amending the wage scale between the biennial conferences in the unusual conditions confronting the industry in the period 1916-1920, but the joint conference committee is the normal agreement-making body.

The same biennial conference acts for both china and semi-porcelain.[1] When the Brotherhood submits proposals applying exclusively to china the labor committee allows the china manufacturers on the committee to decide the position which the committee as a whole shall take on them. The china workers have objected to having their wages fixed and their conditions determined by a conference in which they did not have sufficient influence and in which their interests and problems did not, to their way of thinking, receive sufficient consideration, and the Brotherhood has asked that a separate conference be held for china but the china manufacturers are opposed to " dividing china and semi-porcelain."

The printed agreement contains very little about the procedure for the negotiation of the terms of the renewal of the agreement. It provides only that the union shall submit any proposals for change which it wishes to make, " as nearly as may be feasible," sixty days before the conference and that the manufacturers shall submit their proposals, if any, " as nearly as may be possible," thirty days before the conference. This rule was adopted in 1909. As a matter of fact, the conference has in recent years been held much earlier than sixty days after the receipt of the union proposals.

UNION PROCEDURE FOR ADOPTION OF PROPOSITIONS

On the Brotherhood side the first step toward the formulation of the proposals to be presented to the

---

[1] The year 1917 was an exception to this because the china manufacturers and the Brotherhood were working on uniform lists for china.

conference is taken by the local unions. The constitution requires that all resolutions " affecting the wage scale " shall be in the hands of the national secretary not later than sixty days before the date fixed for the convention. This phrase is interpreted to cover all resolutions bearing on the agreement. These must be sent out to the locals thirty days before the convention meets, in order to give an opportunity for discussion in the locals before the delegates leave for the convention.[2] The sixty day rule is seldom waived.

The number of resolutions submitted to the convention is large. In 1921, a year in which the main issue was obviously that of a wage reduction, over one hundred resolutions, many of them calling for wage advances at points along the scale, were sent in by the local unions. In 1922 the number was somewhat smaller but in 1924 it again ran over one hundred. In 1926, another lean year, it was approximately one hundred. And in 1928, with the employers asking for concessions on account of the depressed condition of the industry, it was almost as great. To be sure, some of these resolutions overlap. Frequently two or more resolutions asking for approximately the same thing are sent in by different local unions. But after all such allowances, the number and aggregate content of the resolutions is out of all proportion to what can be obtained and, indeed, to what will be asked.

In a piece-working industry such as this is, the number of proposals for changes in the agreement would naturally be larger than in a time-working industry.[3] But there is no doubt that the union procedure encourages requests from the local unions for changes in the agreement. Presenting a resolution for a change

[2] *Constitution*, Sec. 24.
[3] See below, ch. vi.

is only the first step in the direction of securing it, of
course, and the chance is better than even that it will
go no further, but unless the thing desired is asked of
the convention there is no chance whatever that it will
be obtained. The members believe, too, that the constant repetition of a request will eventually bring about
its adoption by the convention and the conceding of it
by the manufacturers.

When the convention assembles, the resolutions bearing on the agreement are referred to the " committee
on general ware price list." This committee is appointed by the president. In earlier years it showed
a notable predominance of branch local delegates. In
1924 East Liverpool and Trenton furnished 20 of the
26 members and in 1919 all but one came from these
two centers. In 1928, however, the majority was
slight—17 out of 31. The committee has had the same
chairman since 1913—Sixth Vice-President T. M.
Woods, of Sebring.

The task imposed upon the committee is an onerous
one. It is its function to go through all the " demands "
proposed by the locals and decide which shall be recommended to the convention for adoption and submission to the employers.[4] The committee has done its
work well, under the circumstances. The fact that the
majority of the members of the committee are delegates from branch local unions would lead one to expect
that the committee would find it difficult to apply the
knife. At times, too, caucuses of delegates belonging to
particular branches have been held during the convention and agreements reached to " push " certain proposals. Yet in the last five conference years (through

---

[4] A few resolutions bearing on clauses of the agreement are handled
by the committee on law or the committee on health, but the great
bulk of them are referred to the committee on general ware price list.

1928) the price list committee has recommended favorably not more than one-fourth as many resolutions as were offered, on the average. In 1926 the number reported favorably was only 17, but in 1928 it rose to 25, although one of the members of the committee asked to be put " on record as being opposed to adopting any proposition calling for an increase in wages." [5]

The convention follows the recommendation of the committee with few exceptions. It has almost invariably followed it when the recommendation has been favorable to the resolution. Sometimes a resolution opposed by the committee is referred back to it and is subsequently returned by the committee with a favorable recommendation. More rarely resolutions have been adopted in the teeth of an adverse recommendation from the committee. The only two resolutions calling specifically for wage increases which were adopted by the 1926 convention were put through against the advice of the committee.

The net result of the system, in spite of the brake applied by the general ware price list committee, is that the convention adopts too many resolutions, judged by what happens in the subsequent conference. Not only are many included in the list which receive scant consideration in the conference but some are sent to the conference which are shown there to have little or no merit. This is not the verdict of the manufacturers alone. [6]

[5] *Proceedings,* p. 34.

[6] *Proceedings, U. S. P. A.,* 1911, pp. 44-45; *Report of the Executive Board,* 1923, pp. 13-14; 1925, pp. 11-12, 15; 1927, pp. 14-15, 17, 20. In the 1928 conference Chairman Wells characterized the list of union propositions as " the worst jolt we have ever received." The lists of propositions submitted by the Brotherhood have been published in the next subsequent *Proceedings of the United States Potters Association.*

The officers have often urged the conventions not to repeat the mistake of adopting " demands " which are excessive in the aggregate or specific propositions which will be shown later to be indefensible.[7]

THE UNION CONFERENCE COMMITTEE

The convention over, the union officers proceed to the formation of the conference committee. The members of the executive board are members of the conference committee *ex officio;* the other members are elected from their own membership by local unions designated by the executive board; if a mixed local union is designated, the board specifies the branch from which the member is to be chosen. The number of elected members—and the representation to be allowed the several branches as well—varies somewhat with the nature of the proposals to be considered. The majority of elective places on the committee has always gone to branch locals. In 1924, East Liverpool and Trenton furnished 22 of the 26 elected members, in 1926 they had 15 out of 22 and in 1928, 19 out of 28. There have been repeated complaints that this or that branch has not been adequately represented on the committee and attempts have been made to secure mandatory recognition but all such proposals have been defeated or referred to the executive board.[8]

Down to the year 1912 the conference committee was appointed by the president, after consultation with the executive board. In 1912, following the adoption of direct election of the national officers, the convention

[7] *Proceedings,* 1904, p. 9; *Report of President,* 1909, pp. 11-12, 21; 1910, pp. 7-8; 1914, p. 26; 1915, p. 24; 1916, pp. 19-20; *Report of Executive Board,* 1926, p. 21; *Proceedings,* 1928, p. 38.

[8] *Ibid.,* 1917, p. 106; 1919, pp. 62, 81; 1920, p. 54.

extended the election method to the conference committee. The 1913 convention repealed the 1912 legislation
and substituted appointment by the executive board.
Then the 1914 convention established the present
method of choice.[9] The inclusion of the members of
the executive board on all conference committees is
not in the written law; it was added by the board as a
matter of interpretation.

Eligibility for election to the conference committee
is not confined to those who have been delegates to the
preceding convention.[10] In practice the great majority
of the " conferees " have served as members of the
conventions whose demands they have presented to the
manufacturers. In 1928, the number ran as high as 26,
in a total of 28; the same proportion was approached in
1926, with 19 in a total of 22. And close to a majority
of the conference committee members, sometimes a
majority, have been delegates who served on the price
list committee of the preceding convention.

In the matter of continuity of service on the conference committee, the record of the elected members is
not so good. The variation in the number of elected
conferees, the restriction to a specified branch in the
case of a mixed local, and the fact that even a branch
local may be omitted from the designation in some
years,[11] all militate against continuity of tenure. Of
the 28 elected conferees of 1928, but five had served in
1926. Of these five, only two had served in 1924, and
but one of these two in 1922—and he did not serve in

---

[9] *Ibid.*, 1912, p. 30; 1913, pp. 58-59; 1914, pp. 45-46; *Report of
President*, 1913, p. 5; *Constitution*, 1914, Sec. 27; 1925, Sec. 28.

[10] The qualifications for election to the conference committee
are the same as for delegates to the convention. *Constitution*, 1914,
Sec. 27; 1925, Sec. 28.

[11] For example, the dippers' local of East Liverpool in 1926.

1921. Among the members of the executive board the length of service on the conference committee is, of course, far greater. President John T. Wood attended every general ware conference from 1901 through 1926, a record surpassed only by that of Chairman W. E. Wells, who started at the same time but continued through 1928.

One would expect that election of the members of the conference committee by local unions would give less satisfactory results than appointment by the national officers, at least in respect to smoothness in the negotiations with the employers. And it has worked out that way. The elected members are more likely to be influenced by expressions of opinion in the local unions on particular propositions, even if the locals do not attempt to instruct them,[12] and less disposed to be moved by arguments from the other side in the conference. The union officers insist that the elected conferees represent the national organization, not the locals which elect them, and consequently no local has the right to instruct a member of the committee. Nevertheless it is commonly believed that members have at times been practically instructed by their locals and have felt themselves bound by such instructions;[13] there have been cases, too, of elected conferees " pledging " themselves before the conference to stand out to the end for or against particular propositions.[14]

[12] The constitution forbids discussion of any wage proposal in the *Potters Herald,* from the first session of the convention until after the conference is concluded (*Constitution,* 1914, Sec. 137; 1925, Sec. 150), but the returning delegates report the action of the convention to their locals in closed meeting.

[13] For example, *Potters Herald,* December 14, 1922.

[14] It was stated incidentally in the August, 1922, conference, from the union side, that some of the union conferees had come to the 1921 conference " pledged " against accepting a reduction.

The employers did not like the change from appointment to election on the union side. In the 1915 report of the labor committee, Chairmen Wells said: [15]

In former times labor delegates were appointed by officers of the Brotherhood, and, so far as we could judge, men were selected on account of their fitness, their ability, to deal in a fair and judicial way with the questions at issue. The present practice is to select men by vote of locals, and judging by results, the quality that most commends a candidate is immovable obstinacy in contending for his side, right or wrong. There were some notable exceptions at the recent conference, but, as a rule, the delegates conceive their duties to be purely predatory.

In some of the later years, however, Mr. Wells spoke more favorably of the elected conferees. At the close of the 1921 conference he congratulated Mr. Menge on having a " real conference committee " with him. And in 1924, in his report for the labor committee, he said that in that year " the delegates were a well-chosen body, and seemed to be sincere, with very little indication of a radical slant." [16]

The union constitution is silent on the subject of the powers of the conference committee. It is generally understood, however, that it has power to bind the Brotherhood, without the necessity of referring its decisions to a vote of the trade for confirmation. The employers are largely responsible for this development. In the earlier years the employers used to lay it down as a condition of meeting the committee that the latter come with power to make a final settlement and the conventions used to vote such power in order to comply with this requirement. It thus came to be assumed that the conference committee had authority to settle, if the terms were satisfactory to it, even though these fell short of the " demands " voted by the convention.

[15] *Proceedings,* 1915, pp. 49-50.
[16] *Ibid.,* 1924, p. 32.

However, proposals have not been lacking to limit by
law the power of the conference committee to follow
its discretion; the branch spirit had been manifest in
attempts to prevent the committee from jettisoning
particular propositions in conference without previously securing authorization by a majority vote of the
branches concerned.

In 1915 the convention ordered a vote of the trade
on its wage proposals before the conference. The convention had adopted a long list of propositions, of
which twenty-three called for wage increases, directly
or indirectly. Near the close of the convention it was
voted that propositions involving wage increases be
submitted to a vote of the general ware membership
to see if the members were ready to strike for them;
if the vote was not favorable to a strike they were
to be withdrawn. When the ballots were sent out
the members were asked to vote for or against standing out for the twenty-three propositions, *en bloc.*
Only thirty-eight per cent of those eligible to vote
actually voted and fifty-nine per cent of them voted in
favor of the demands. As this fell short of the three-
fourths then required for an affirmative strike vote the
twenty-three propositions were dropped from the list.[17]

Several times in the period from 1916 to 1919 the
executive board acted as an agreement-making body for
the Brotherhood. But the executive board has never
acted as a substitute for the conference committee in
a regular biennial conference. Since the adoption in
1914 of the law providing for the election of the conference committee that would undoubtedly have been
illegal. Except for the agreement of 1917, the only
" agreements " which the board has made have been

---

[17] *Proceedings, N. B. of O. P.,* 1915, p. 62; *Report of President,*
1916, p. 2; *Proceedings, U. S. P. A.,* 1915, p. 40.

"voluntary" agreements increasing the wage rates fixed in a regular agreement, or agreements upon "reopenings" when it was authorized by the convention to act. The board made the regular biennial agreement in 1917 under unusual circumstances. The members had rejected the terms offered by the manufacturers to the conference committee and were on strike in consequence. A second proposal from the manufacturers had just been voted on, and although a majority of the votes cast were against it also, the board decided that it should be accepted. The board now ruled that the conference committee had been discharged by "the trade" in the vote which rejected the terms referred to it by the committee. The manufacturers' subsequent offer was made to the board, not to the original conference committee, and it was the board which submitted that offer to the trade in its own right. The vote which the board construed as an acceptance was also construed by it as a mandate to make an agreement on those terms and it did so immediately without calling the conference committee together again.[18]

THE MANUFACTURERS' LABOR COMMITTEE

On the manufacturers' side the procedure is much simpler. The labor committee performs more functions for the manufacturers than does the conference committee for the union members. It is the labor committee which furnishes the leadership on the manufacturers' side in the formulation of labor policies. It performs for the Association the functions that the executive board, the general ware price list committee and the elected conference committee together perform for the Brotherhood.

[18] Statement of President Menge to the writer; *Report of Executive Board*, 1918, p. 15.

The labor committee was established in its present status as a regular standing committee of the Association in 1906.[19] It then had seven members. It has since been enlarged to eleven. Its personnel is so distributed as to give some representation to East as well as West, to china as well as to semi-porcelain, and to small plants as well as to large. Mr. W. E. Wells was chairman of the labor committee from its establishment until 1929. There has been a large measure of continuity, too, in the personnel of the committee as a whole. It remained unchanged from 1918 to 1921 and from 1922 to 1926. Of the ten members elected to the committee for 1928, at the 1927 (December) meeting of the Association, six had been on the committee since 1915.[20] The Secretary of the Association also sits with the committee.

The labor committee usually consults with the membership of the Association, at a special meeting held for the purpose, before going into a conference with the Brotherhood on proposed changes in the terms of the agreement. Ordinarily this meeting is held after the receipt of the Brotherhood's proposals. If the manufacturers wish to submit proposals to the union officers before the convention a special meeting may be held on these. The meetings are not called for the purpose of giving binding instructions to the labor committee, but rather to allow the committee to ascertain the sentiment of the membership. In practice it serves as an opportunity for the committee to explain in advance to the membership the position which the members of the committee have agreed that it should take. The understanding has always been that when the commit-

---

[19] *Proceedings, U. S. P. A.*, 1905, p. 13; 1906, pp. 5, 17.

[20] *Ibid.*, 1914-1927. It sometimes happens that substitutions are made for the conference in the committee as elected.

tee enters the conference it does so with full power to make a settlement at its own discretion. In fact, in December, 1922, the labor committee decided on its own responsibility, without calling a meeting of the Association, to grant the four and one-fifth per cent advance.[21] Having power to settle, the labor committee also has power, presumably, to stand by its terms to the point of a strike. The question as to whether further concessions should be offered does not become a strike matter unless and until the union membership votes in favor of a strike. In both cases in which this has occurred, the labor committee did, as a matter of fact, report the situation to a meeting of the Association before the date set for the strike. In the first case, that of 1917, the Association decided to offer new terms, which the union subsequently accepted. In September, 1922, however, the Association unanimously endorsed the position taken by the committee in refusing further concessions.[22]

THE CONFERENCE

The convention is over early in July and within a fortnight the Brotherhood sends its list of propositions to the manufacturers' Association. In recent years the conference has been held not later than the middle of August, although the agreement does not expire until October first. The manufacturers prefer an early conference in order to have all uncertainties removed as soon as possible so that they may proceed with their plans for fall production. The conferences are not held in East Liverpool although both national organizations have their headquarters there. The union officers have

[21] *Ibid.*, April, 1923, pp. 39-40.
[22] *Ibid.*, 1917, p. 20; April, 1923, pp. 37-38.

preferred not to have the conference in a pottery center, where their elected conferees would be exposed to discussions with the operatives during the progress of the conference.

There are no rules to govern the procedure of the conference—merely custom. Mr. W. E. Wells always acted as chairman of the conference, at the suggestion of the union side. The proceedings are informal. There is no voting. A proposal advanced by one side is assumed to be adopted when the other side has signified its assent. After agreement is reached on the substance of the matter, the exact wording of the clause is ordinarily left in the hands of the two secretaries, or to these and Chairman Wells and the Brotherhood president, to be attended to after the conference. Beginning with 1921 verbatim stenographic records have been made of the conferences but these reports are not published.

The discussion of proposals is not all argumentative. Much of it is explanatory. It frequently happens that the meaning of a proposition dealing with a " condition " or a rule is not clear to the other side from the wording of it alone. Questions are often asked about the intended scope of such a proposition and what is sought to be attained by it as well as the situation out of which it grew and the number of plants and the number of men which would be affected by it if it were adopted. The explanatory discussion occasionally results in final action on the proposition. If it is one which involves no increase in cost to the employers and appears to have a good reason behind it, it may be adopted at once, with some safeguarding understanding as to its application or actual modification in wording. Or the proposition may be dropped after the explanatory discussion, upon assurance that the situation at which it is aimed will be remedied. Indeed the Brotherhood has at times advanced a proposition more with the purpose of airing a situation and getting an " understanding " on it than of adding a new clause to the agreement.[23] Some of the employers' propositions, too, have been included primarily to get assurances from the union conference committee that the individual employers would be supported in insisting upon their rights under the agreement on these particular points.

After the preliminary, explanatory discussion, and after each group has met separately to talk over the situation in the light of that discussion, the conference settles down to argument on those propositions which have not been accepted but which the proposing side is yet unwilling to withdraw, or to better, as the case may be. The circle of discussion is likely to be drawn more and more closely about a few propositions to which one side or the other returns over and over again. Usually, of course, it is the union side which prolongs the discussion; ordinarily it is the union which is asking for changes. At times the employers express weariness at the tenacity of the union representatives on particular propositions, especially if they have been refused in previous conferences, but they have come to recognize that this is the price of the conference system.

The union caucuses have been an important part of the conference machinery. In 1921, for example, the union side " consumed more time in caucuses than in the conference." [24] In 1922, as a result of conflicting reports on how various members of the committee voted in the caucus which accepted the reduction in 1921, a rule was adopted by the convention that a

[23] For example, *Report of Executive Board,* 1927, p. 22.
[24] Statement of Mr. Frank Hutchins in the August, 1922, conference.

10

"standing vote" should be taken in the caucus whenever one-third of the members of the committee demand it.[25]

Special Committees.—The conference does not employ the device of referring questions on which the two sides are far apart to a joint sub-committee which is to attempt to find a *modus vivendi* and report it back to the full conference. All matters which are acted upon finally by the conference are discussed in full conference and acted upon directly without any intermediary sub-committee discussion or negotiation. But frequently the conference has referred matters to joint special committees to be appointed after the conference adjourns, with full power to bind the parties to any agreement which they may reach. These are matters of a technical nature and, as a rule, involve only one branch. The Brotherhood officers have, on the whole, preferred to have such matters handled through special committees because they can see to it that the branch involved is adequately represented and can select the union representatives for the negotiations. In 1924 the union propositions called for the appointment of special committees on five separate subjects, in 1926 for three, and in 1928 for two.

An agreement in conference to refer a matter to a special committee does not necessarily mean that anything will be accomplished, except, perhaps, to dispose of the question for the time being; unless and until the committee reaches an agreement, things remain as they are. None of the committees authorized by the 1921 conference had accomplished anything by the following June.[26] Of the six committees agreed to in 1922, but one finished the task it was to undertake; another agreed

[25] *Proceedings,* 1922, pp. 43-44; *Constitution,* Sec. 28.
[26] *Report of Executive Board,* 1922, p. 34.

on part of the subject matter referred to it. The one committee agreed to in the 1924 conference brought forth nothing. Of the two appointed in 1926, one reached an agreement.[27] Thus in 1928 several matters referred to special committees by previous conferences were still in abeyance.

The paucity of results from the method of reference to special committees since 1921 can be largely explained by the poor condition of the business during most of this period. In nearly every case it was the union which asked for the committee, and most of them were entrusted with the task of bringing uniformity out of non-uniformity. Undoubtedly the union members, in asking for uniformity, were doing so in the expectation of securing a net gain.[28] If business is poor the manufacturers will not concede much, if anything, and the only uniformity the union can get would involve a reduction for too large a proportion of the members affected to make it acceptable to the union. Consequently, while business conditions are adverse, the union officers are not likely to push for action. If it is generally understood when the committee is appointed that something is to be given, the committee has a better chance of arriving at an agreement.

Each side has complained, especially when it was pushing for conclusive action on a matter in the conference itself, of the barrenness of the special committee method. The union, especially, has objected at times that the reference of its proposals to special committees was merely a method of disposing of the proposals without giving the men anything. In the 1924 conference President Wood specifically complained that the manufacturers had appointed under-executives to special

[27] *Ibid.*, 1927, pp. 25-26; *Proceedings*, 1927, p. 14.
[28] See below, ch. vii.

committees. These men, he said, had pleaded lack of authority to act finally and so had prevented anything being done.

DEADLOCKS AND THE UNION REFERENDUM

In case the two parties cannot agree on terms in conference there is nothing to do but adjourn and await the result of the union referendum. This is in effect a strike vote. To allow the agreement to expire without making an arrangement for its continuance pending the outcome of further negotiations for a new agreement would mean either going back to shop bargaining or going on strike to compel the employers to renew the agreement on better terms than they have so far shown a willingness to concede. In practice it means the latter. The union will not consider the alternative of shop bargaining.

There is no provision of any kind in the agreement for arbitration in case of a deadlock on the terms of renewal. In its earlier years the Brotherhood apparently looked favorably upon arbitration. The 1900 convention instructed its delegate to the American Federation of Labor convention to use his efforts to have the Federation adopt a resolution to petition Congress to enact a compulsory arbitration law on the lines of that then in force in New Zealand.[29] In 1904, Vice-President Hutchins said that the agreement reached in 1903 to submit the unsettled issues to arbitration was one of the two " most noteworthy events " of the year for the Brotherhood.[30] and asserted that it was in line with the principles advocated by all the leading unions of the country.[31] Yet it was the employers who made the

[29] *Proceedings*, 1900, p. 57.

[30] The other was the decision to sign the agreement for two years instead of one.

[31] *Proceedings*, 1904, p. 59.

proposal to arbitrate in 1903, and then only after a strike notice had been served. As late as 1913 the manufacturing potters of East Liverpool entered into an arbitration agreement with the warehousewomen.[32] However, they regarded that experience as an unfortunate one and since then there has been no enthusiasm on the employers' side for arbitration on the terms of an agreement. As time went on both organizations came to favor direct dealing as against arbitration. The officers concluded that if, with all their experience in direct negotiation, they could not agree on terms, it would be a mistake to risk arbitration.[33] Neither in 1917 nor in 1922 was arbitration seriously considered.

The procedure for a strike vote affecting a whole division is not laid down explicitly in the Brotherhood constitution. The laws governing the calling of strikes are still phrased largely in terms of local union action. It is by interpretation of the national officers that they have been applied to the issue of a divisional strike by making the division instead of the local union the unit of decision under the two-thirds rule. Thus in a local union containing both sanitary and general ware members, only those employed in general ware shops vote on whether the general ware division shall strike.[34] This means that there has been divisional autonomy in strike votes, in spite of the fact that a general strike in either division would jeopardize the finances and prestige of the whole organization. The officers have held that those who were to strike, if there was to be a strike,

---

[32] *Proceedings, U. S. P. A.*, 1913, pp. 31-32.

[33] Statements of Chairman Wells and President Menge to the writer.

[34] In 1917, not even the whole general ware division was called upon to vote on the strike issue; the members employed in the china shops did not participate in the vote because in that particular year a separate and later conference had been arranged for china.

should have the full responsibility of deciding the issue. It would be unwise, they believed, to have one division kept from striking by the votes of the other division, when the former was overwhelmingly in favor of striking.

The manufacturers are strongly opposed to the taking of strike votes and have expressed their opposition in vigorous terms, even declaring that the strike vote is an intolerable contradiction of the system of settlement by the conference method.[35] It takes the decision out of the hands of those who have listened to the explanations and arguments and turns it over to persons who have heard nothing of the other side. Many of the members, Mr. Wells has asserted, do not realize fully that they are voting on whether to strike; they think that they are being asked to vote on whether they should have this or that increase. A large proportion of the membership does not vote at all. And the atmosphere in which the voting is done, secret though the ballot is supposed to be, is antagonistic to voting for peace through compromise. In short, argues Mr. Wells, the referendum does not reflect the true decision of the operatives as a whole, much less an intelligent decision on the issues. And whatever the outcome, the referendum involves uncertainty and delay which causes the buyers to hold back orders or place them with importers and thus injures the industry from which both the working people and the employers derive their livelihood.[36]

[35] MS. *Report of Conference*, August, 1922, December 5, 1922.

[36] Mr. Wells' case against the referendum method is summarized in his report for the labor committee to the April, 1923, meeting of the Association. Together with the method of selecting the union conference committee members it constitutes, he held, a menace to the continuance of national collective bargaining. *Proceedings,* April, 1923, pp. 34-35.

CHAPTER VI

THE STRUCTURE OF THE WAGE SCALE

The wages issue in the general ware division of the pottery industry has manifested itself in many forms. Except for the warehousemen and for the mouldmakers on " blocking and casing," all of the branches covered by the national scale are predominantly piece-working. There is a differentiation, too, between semi-porcelain and china. The operations in china are similar to those in semi-porcelain but the " shapes " in china have differed considerably from those in semi-porcelain and the proportion of " small " ware has been larger. More important, from the scale standpoint, has been the assumption that greater care must be exercised by the operatives working with a " china body." [1] In the clay-shop branches, in kilnplacing, and in packing, the rates for china have always been higher than for semi-porcelain.[2] In saggermaking and mouldmaking the base price lists are the same for china and semi-porcelain plants, although in mouldmaking the plussage on the list is higher for china plants.

In several of the branches there has been contention over the " conditions " accompanying the piece rate. These " conditions " questions have to do with the subsidiary operations or supplementary operations to be

[1] Recently the union has been disturbed by the firing of a " semi-porcelain " body in such a way as to get " china " and the refusal of the employer to pay more than semi-porcelain prices for it. *Proceedings,* 1927, p. 15; 1928, p. 40; *Report of Executive Board,* 1928, pp. 23, 26; *Proceedings,* 1930, pp. 45-46.

[2] This does not necessarily mean that the earnings per hour are higher. (See Appendix.)

performed by the journeyman, the facilities to be furnished by the employer, the methods of workmanship upon which the employer may insist, etc. The scale book bears many evidences of attempts to define or delimit the rights of the firm or the men with respect to such matters, in order to put an end to encroachments by some employers, or to reaffirm the rights of the firm, or to universalize a release from some customary obligation which the men had already won in some plants.

There are also alternative time rates in some of the predominantly piece-working branches. For years the employer has had the option of employing the packers at either the piece-price list or an hourly rate fixed in the scale, and in recent years the same option has been recognized in kilnplacing and dipping where "upright" or "periodic" kilns are in use.[3] The relation of these rates to piece-work earnings has at times been an issue; it has an obvious bearing on the choice between the two methods of payment.[4]

---

[3] There is no piece scale for kilnplacing or dipping where tunnel kilns are used; the only rates in the scale for this work are the time rates mentioned above.

[4] For a time the amount of the hourly rate to be paid in the clay-shop branches for work for which no piece rates had yet been set, or when the men were asked to work on a time basis for some other reason, was an issue. Supplementary time rates had been fixed in the scale for these branches but the men complained that they were too far below their normal piece-rate earnings. The question as to the amount of the supplementary time rates in the scale was finally deprived of its significance by the adoption of a rule that the man shall be paid a time rate equal to his average earnings at piece work for the six weeks previous to going on time work. This rule was afterwards extended to hand-saggermaking (there is no piece scale for machine-saggermaking) and even to lining and decalcomania work, for which there is no uniform piece scale.

With a wage-scale structure of this kind the number of particular wage issues to be settled is far greater than it would be if the time system of payment were followed throughout. Nor has the bargaining process on the internal structure of the scale, as distinct from general percentage increases or decreases throughout all branches, been confined to the fixing of the rates in the first instance. Attempts at readjustments within the wage structure have been a continuing feature of the wage bargain and " inconsistencies " in the scale, or in the application of it, have been a fruitful source of local disputes as well.

PIECE WORK

The Price Lists.—The 1900 scale contained descriptive enumerative lists in each of the clay-shop branches and in packing, saggermaking and mouldmaking. The casting list was not made until much later. Changes have been made in these lists from time to time but their general character has remained unchanged.[5]

It has always been understood that the piece prices of the various articles on the list of any branch ought to reflect as nearly as possible the comparative difficulty of making the respective articles. This ideal has not been realized in the waremaking branches.[6] The difficulty of constructing a piece scale which will give wages in exact proportion to the comparative skill and effort expended is in part a technical one and in part due to

[5] The 1900 scale is reprinted in *U. S. Ind. Comm.*, XIV, 613-624, and the scale as it stood in 1925 is reprinted in *Bulletin No. 412 of the U. S. Bureau of Labor Statistics.* There have been no important changes in the piece scale itself since 1924; the change in May, 1031, was a general percentage reduction.

[6] The issue of comparative wages in terms of skill *as between branches* is treated below, in ch. viii.

the inevitable presence of the bargaining approach to the business of rate-making. It is no small task to make a fully comprehensive list, differentiated on the basis of comparative skill and effort required, for a large number of different shapes, of varying sizes, with some variation in the methods of making and in facilities from plant to plant, even if the task were approached entirely objectively, without thought of its bearing on individual wages or labor cost. When the parties who undertake the task cannot be expected to free themselves from at least the subconscious desire to get the best terms possible for their respective sides, the chance that an exact correspondence between rates and comparative skill and effort required will emerge is slight.

How is comparative difficulty in terms of skill and effort to be measured? There is no physical unit of measurement which can be applied as an automatic determinant. The determinant nearest to hand seems to be comparative time required, assuming the same skill and effort on the part of the worker throughout. If one could make that assumption, time studies fairly made would give an approximation accurate enough, perhaps, for practical purposes. But the assumption itself does not hold generally. Few, if any, of the workers in the important clay-shop branches in a large plant are equally adept at all articles on the list; the tendency to specialization, for long periods, at least, has made some of them much more skillful in fashioning a certain limited range of articles. Nor have the rates been based on exact time studies even within the groups of articles made by men of assumed equality of skill in the making of those particular articles. The data ordinarily presented in the discussions are the records of men who have worked on the article or articles for a number of weeks. These records are frequently incomplete in that there is some question as to the exact number of hours worked. The hours of the piece workers are not usually registered [7] and the record of time spent must ordinarily be furnished by the workers concerned. But even on the basis of such data as there are on comparative difficulty, it is evident that there are many departures from the comparative difficulty standard in the lists—many articles which are " underpaid " or " overpaid." That there are such is recognized by both sides, although both would not agree that all the articles alleged to be " underpaid " or " overpaid " belong in those respective categories, or on the degree of deviation.

The wage scale adopted in 1900 was not a structure of rates worked out *de novo* on the basis of comparative difficulty. It was made by assembling the prices in effect in the various plants and striking an average, with departures here and there from the strict average for strategic considerations. Not only were there geographical non-uniformities in the pre-1900 prices, there were also vertical inequalities. Many of these were of long standing and consequently difficult to uproot.[8] Some of them, too, were accounted for by an assumption that the high and the low would offset each other in the run of a man's work; this is a partial explanation of the " lumping " of several different sizes under

[7] *Proceedings, N. B. of O. P.,* 1905, p. 27; *Proceedings, U. S. P. A.,* 1915, p. 49. But in the 1928 conference the Brotherhood agreed that the piece workers should be required to register on a time clock if the firm could arrive at a satisfactory method of controlling it, with a committee of its employees.

[8] The old Trenton list of 1877, a list made by the manufacturers, contained many inconsistencies. Specific instances of prices that were either too high or too low were cited in the report of the labor committee to the manufacturers' association in December, 1878. *Proceedings,* p. 10.

one price, or within a comparatively narrow price range, which is found in many places in the lists.[9] Another cause of inequality was the inability of the manufacturers to pay more for certain articles because of competition from cheaper kinds of earthenware, such as Rockingham; the fact that the prices of these articles had to be left low was used to secure the continuance of some that were admittedly high.

As time went on the inequalities in the original lists were increased. Some new articles were priced on the basis of articles already in the list which are relatively overpaid or underpaid. In some cases, too, inequalities have developed through the acceptance of an assumed degree of difficulty in the making of the new article which was later found to be mistaken. This has not necessarily been due to conscious misrepresentation; new shapes or other departures may involve extra difficulties for the maker because of their very newness, difficulties which are reduced or eliminated in the course of experience. Other inequalities have developed through changes in the methods of making certain classes of articles which have reduced the comparative difficulty without a corresponding reduction, or no reduction at all, in the making price.

A thorough-going revision of the lists has often been suggested, but never achieved. In 1903 a joint committee prepared a revised scale only to have it rejected by the men in a referendum vote. The new lists would have increased some items but they would also, of course, have reduced others and those who feared that the losses would outweigh the gains on their own

[9] Another reason was the desire of the manufacturers to leave themselves a comfortable margin in designing without danger of running into a higher price bracket.

" jobs " were able to muster enough votes to defeat the proposed changes.[10] In 1917 a proposed revision of the list in the jiggering branch was defeated, but not on its own merits. The counter-proposal which the manufacturers made in the September conference that year involved, so far as the jiggermen were concerned, a revised list of prices on the more important items, carrying varying percentage increases, and a uniform percentage increase on all other items. The union conferees were not only willing to accept the revised list but asked that the revision be extended to items not included by the manufacturers. This proposed revision was tied up with other questions on which the parties could not agree and it was rejected as a part of the manufacturers' whole proposal, in the referendum vote.[11]

Something, however, was accomplished in the way of conscious equalization of branch lists when general increases in wages were the order of the day. In the 1919 regular conference, when the employers agreed to grant the dishmakers an increase of ten per cent on base prices, a committee of dishmakers was allowed to apply the increase unevenly to the items on the list for " oval " dishes and bakers. The increase varied from $5\frac{1}{2}$ per cent to 16 per cent on dishes and from $8\frac{1}{3}$ per cent to $12\frac{1}{2}$ per cent on bakers, the larger sizes receiving the greater advances.[12] Moreover, since 1918 a bonus has been paid by the employer to the dishmakers' helper when working on the larger sizes; this is in effect an increase in price on these sizes. The packing list also underwent a considerable measure of revision in the period 1916-1922.

[10] *Circular of* July 7, 1903 (*N. B. of O. P.*).

[11] *Report of Executive Board*, 1918, pp. 7-9, 11, 13-14.

[12] *Ibid.*, 1920, p. 12; MS. *Report of Conference*, 1924.

The opposition of the men making the more highly-paid items has always been an important obstacle to equalization through increases that would be offset by actual reductions in some base prices, as distinct from an approach to equalization through unequal advances. With the increased specialization on certain articles which has developed with the growth of large plants, the better paid items have tended more and more to become the "jobs" of particular men. These men have generally advanced the argument that equalization should take the form of bringing up the more poorly paid articles and leaving the better paid untouched. This argument seems to have been effective within the union.

Nor have the manufacturers pressed the issue of equalization. They have called attention to the better paying "jobs" from time to time and when talking of the necessity of a general wage reduction they have almost invariably expressed the opinion that the decreases should be put on the items which they contend are overpaid. But they have held that real equalization cannot be secured without the coöperation of the union and so long as the union will not face the task they prefer to suffer the lesser evil of inequalities to inviting a strike against a revision.

Another source of difficulty and dissension, especially in the clay-shop branches, is the "size list." Size is an important determinant of wage rates. Not only do articles of the same kind vary in making price according to the respective size groups within which they fall but in some cases size is the essential, and apparently the only visible, basis of demarcation between one class of articles and another class which carries a widely different price. But the limits of the various sizes referred to in the price lists have never been specified, to any considerable extent, in the making-price lists themselves; it has been assumed that these were to be found in a separate "size list." The desirability of making the "size list" both adequate and clear is therefore obvious. Unfortunately, a size list satisfactory to both sides has never been attained. One was adopted for the clay-shop branches, in semi-porcelain, by a joint committee authorized by the 1905 conference. It was not only incomplete but it also gave rise to many disputes in its application. There were constant complaints from the men that articles which were "over-size" were being paid for as of regular size when they should take the rate of a higher class. Joint committees to revise the size list have been agreed to repeatedly, with no result. In china there is no regular size list, although the semi-porcelain size list is not applicable to china; all attempts to draw up a size list have failed.

The "Cubic Measurement" System in Kilnplacing and Dipping.—The unit of payment for kilnplacing, in "bee-hive" or "periodic" kilns, is the "kilnman's day." This is a given number of "cubic feet" of kiln space; each kiln "pays" a given number of kilnman's days, according to the "cubic measurement of the kiln." The "cubic measurement," in this sense is not the total cubic capacity of the kiln. Nor is it the total cubic capacity minus the space in which saggers are not placed. The "measurement" of the kiln is ascertained by a method of reckoning not described in the scale and known in all its details to few outside the circle of those who have to apply it. Once it is determined for a new kiln it remains constant for that kiln unless and until some change is made in the kiln itself.

A kilnman's day in semi-porcelain is now 162 cubic feet in glost kilns and 200 cubic feet in bisque kilns.

In china it is 130 cubic feet in bisque and 112 in glost. As the cubic measurement of the kiln is a constant, and the number of cubic feet in a day also a constant, the number of kilnman's days in a given kiln is a fixed quantity, apart from " extras "—and most of these are also constant for the particular kiln over long periods and are usually expressed as added kilnman's days. Thus a kiln is known as, for example, a " 25-day kiln." Every time it is placed it is paid for as 25 kilnman's days, unless an extra is to be added for some variable which is not ordinarily present. The kilnman's day is no longer an actual day's work for a kilnman, if it ever was. It is common for kilnmen to do more than two " days " in a working day.[13]

Another feature of the system is that the individual kilnman is not paid for an individual output. The men work in crews, usually of from four to six members. Each crew has a " bench boss " or " setter-out," who is in charge of the crew. Each man is paid for the same number of " days," but the firm pays the bench boss $3.78 per " day " for his " days " and the other men $3.17 (in 1928). If a crew of five men makes 75 " days " in a week, each member is paid for 15 " days "; the bench boss receives $56.70 and each other member of the crew $47.55, assuming that all the members of the crew work the same amount of time.

The cubic measurement system was officially adopted by the Brotherhood in 1896, on recommendation of the kilnmen's local of East Liverpool.[14] The custom of paying by the kilnman's day antedated the adoption of the cubic measurement system of determining the number of " days " in the kiln. The earlier practice was to fix

[13] *Bulletin No. 412 of the United States Bureau of Labor Statistics*, pp. 82, 86.
[14] *Proceedings*, 1896; Duffy, p. 24.

the number of " days " in a given kiln in accordance with the number of " bungs "—tiers of saggers—regularly placed in it; under that method non-uniformities had been rife. The cubic measurement was thought to be more " scientific." By 1900 it was general in the West and it was followed in the 1900 scale. However, it was neither common nor well understood in the East and the attempt to impose a new system which would require a recalculation of the " days " to be paid for each kiln was an important factor in the opposition of the Trenton kilnmen to the uniform scale.

Although the cubic measurement system of payment may have been an improvement over the one which preceded it, it has turned out to be far from satisfactory. It has not given wages in proportion to the comparative skill or time required, either as between plants or from time to time in the same plant. The work involved in placing a kiln of given cubic measurement varies with the character of the ware, with the types of saggers used, and with the arrangement of the saggers in the kiln. Even if the number of saggers were the same, the number of pieces to be placed in each sagger is subject to variation with the size and shape of the pieces. Large " hollow ware "—ewers, basins, large jugs, mixing bowls, etc.—gives less pieces per kiln than " small " hollow ware—creams, sugars, cups, etc.—and hollow ware generally gives less pieces than " flat " ware—plates, saucers, oatmeals, fruits, etc. The proportion of flat ware also introduces another complication, in placing glost kilns; ordinarily flat ware is " pinned " and pinning takes additional time.[15] Some types of saggers, too, can take more pieces than others

---

[15] " Pins " are inserted in the sagger to prevent the pieces from coming into contact in such a way as to allow the glaze to run from one piece to another in the firing process.

11

in proportion to the space they occupy in the kiln; and one plan of arrangement of the saggers in the kiln will permit more saggers in a given space than another.

Changes through periods of time in the factors affecting comparative difficulty have raised issues of a more general character than variations between plant and plant at the same time. The kilmen have over and over again put in requests for an increase in the rate of pay on account of changes in one or more of these factors, which, they have contended, have increased the work involved in placing the kiln since the rate was established. Sometimes it has been a demand for an increase in the wage per day or for a reduction in the cubic feet in the day at the same wage per day. At other times it has been a demand for a specific extra for placing an increased proportion of certain kinds of ware, or using a certain new type of sagger, or following a new method of arranging the saggers in the kiln. Demands for specific extras, are essentially requests for internal adjustments in the piece-rate structure. They are independent of general wage considerations, such as cost of living or the condition of the business. If granted, the extra is paid only where and to the extent that the specified condition is present. Inasmuch as the number of cubic feet in a day has been reduced but once since 1900, and then only for bisque kilns, and as the wage per day has been changed only during the period 1917-1922, the demands for extras have had an important place in the attempts to secure readjustment.

In the course of years several departures from " straight cubic measurement " have been recognized in the scale.[16] Most of these have been in the way of

[16] There was only one extra of this sort recognized in the 1900 scale and that applied only to glost kilns.

" extras " for an increased proportion of " flat." Extras
have also been granted for changes in the method of
placing saggers in the kiln. The manufacturers have
been ever on the alert to discover new arrangements
of the saggers which would enable them to utilize kiln
space to better advantage and so permit the placing of
more ware in the kiln. When a new method has been
introduced which accomplishes this purpose, the kilnmen have naturally sought extra payment for using it.

Similar issues have been raised by changes in the
construction of the saggers. An " improvement " in the
pattern of the sagger which permits a better arrangement in the kiln, or more pieces in the sagger, or both,
means " increased work " per kilnman's day to the men.
But in the matter of the type of saggers used, the
employers were for years disposed to fall back on the
argument, in answer to demands for extra, that " give
and take " is implied in the cubic measurement system.
They were willing to grant extras for specific changes
in the kind of ware, when extra work for the kilnmen
was clearly shown, but they contended that in the type
of saggers to be used the cubic measurement system
left them a free hand. They repeatedly called attention to the fact that when changes had been introduced
which made the work easier they had not demanded
reductions from the rate because of them. And they
pointed to the reduction in the time worked per kilnman's day to show that the kilnmen had no cause for
complaint. The latter, on the other hand, have been
prone to compare the time required for the new sagger
with the time required before it was introduced. If it
requires more time to make the same number of days
than it did a month or two before, they believe that they
have a grievance if extra is not paid.

A factor which complicates the situation is that some firms are allowed to use types of saggers without paying extra which other firms may not use without extra payment. This non-uniformity arises from the " established conditions " rule adopted in 1900 which allows a firm to continue any practice without extra which has become an " established condition " in that plant. Naturally it causes irritation among the excluded firms and stiffens their opposition to allowing the extra. The rule also leads to disputes as to whether a sagger which the firm contends it has used before without extra, and is merely reintroducing, falls under the " established condition " exemption. The employers have repeatedly asked that the union admit the right of every firm working under the agreement to introduce any size, shape, or style of sagger or method of placing that may be in use in any other pottery working under the agreement. To this the union will not agree, arguing that some of these practices in particular shops had been established without the knowledge or consent of the national organization and that it would not be fair to universalize every unfavorable condition that any manufacturer has been able to enforce.

By 1921 the employers were willing " in order to prevent the waste of valuable kiln space," to pay the kilnmen something for freedom to introduce " saggers that will more nearly fit the shapes and sizes of articles now being made, or may in future be modeled." [17] Nothing definite was accomplished before the 1922 strike, and in the final 1922 conference the employers brought the matter up again. They now recognized that the pressure the kilnmen were working under to keep up their relative earnings was responsible in some mea-

[17] *Proceedings, U. S. P. A.,* 1921, p. 27.

sure for the kilns not being properly filled and they offered to give a direct increase in wages in return for an agreement to place the kilns to the satisfaction of the employer. They granted the kilnmen twice as great an increase, in percentage, as that granted to the other branches and asked for a joint committee, to which the union agreed, to iron out all unsettled kiln questions.

When the joint committee met, the employers' side proposed rules which would give the employer a free hand in the size of saggers, number of pins, the filling of the saggers, and methods of placing the saggers in the kiln. No change not in conflict with the specifications of the agreement was to be refused by the men because it may be a " change of condition." The men's side was reluctant to agree to such blanket rules; it was afraid that they might operate unfairly under the cubic measurement system of payment. It made the counter suggestion that the day-wage system be adopted. The employers finally agreed to give it a trial in certain plants. Thus the difficulties experienced with the cubic measurement system were recognized as a presumptive reason for going over to time payment.[18]

Except in china, where " day-wage dipping " has long been the rule, the cubic measurement system has ordinarily been followed in dipping wherever it has been used in kilnplacing. Under this system the dipper is paid a given rate per kilnman's day, the days for the dipper or dippers being taken from the count for the glost kilnmen. The dippers get the same number of extra days on the kiln as the glost kilnmen do for pinned ware, but not for such " conditions " as an extra long " carry " of ware to the kiln. The " boss dipper," where there is more than one dipper, usually receives

---

[18] See below, pp. 181-186.

50 cents extra per calendar day for " looking after the shop," but this is not in the scale.

The only differentiation in the dipper's wage per kilnman's day which was recognized in the 1900 scale was one based on the method of dipping. Those base rates have never been changed. Obviously the dippers have been vitally interested in every change in the size or character of the ware, or in the saggers used, or in the method of placing, which has produced an increase in the number of pieces per kilnman's day. Unless and until an addition has been made to the count of kilnman's days because of such a change, the dippers have been as keen as the kilnmen in urging their claims for extra, locally and in conference. And the difficulties and disputes which have developed in the application of the cubic measurement system of payment in dipping have been advanced as an additional reason for substituting day wage for that system in this branch as well as in kilnplacing.[19]

Definition of What is to be Done for the Rate—A full statement of the piece rate in any particular case would include not only the price which the worker is to receive but also specifications as to what he is to do and the facilities which are to be furnished by the employer. When a scale is first adopted not many such specifications are necessary; what the worker is to do and what the employer is to furnish are in most cases so well known to both that it can be assumed as a part of the

---

[19] The male kilndrawers on bee-hive kilns are also paid on the cubic measurement basis in the West. The cubic measurement of the kiln is the same for the kilndrawers as for the kilnmen, but the kilndrawers rate is in terms of 100 cubic feet, as contrasted with the 200 feet unit of the bisque kilnmen and the 162 feet unit of the glost kilnmen. The Brotherhood has not dealt for this branch in recent conferences, but the kilndrawers' rates are still published in the scale book.

scale without the necessity of specific statement. But in the course of time, as the customary practice is departed from here and there, it may be necessary to include specific delimitations in the scale itself. This has been true in the general ware pottery industry. What the employer can exact from the worker without the payment of extra and what the worker can ask from the employer in the way of facilities, if extra is not to be paid, frequently became the subject of local disputes, leading to statements on these points by way of definition or delimitation in the scale. This does not mean that absolute uniformity has ever been attained between plants in what is actually required from the men by the employers or given them by way of facilities. The addition of clauses on such matters has merely defined or reaffirmed the upper limits of what may be exacted or the lower limits of what must be furnished, with respect to certain particulars. The practices on these points are ordinarily called " conditions." [20]

" Conditions " questions have at times been matters of definition and at other times have been analogous to requests for increases in piece rates. A statement in the scale to the effect that the workman shall not be required to do this or that may represent either a protective clause inserted at the request of the union to prevent a change unfavorable to the workman or it may represent the granting of full release from something which the workman was generally held for at the time the scale was adopted. Releases from former customary

[20] Any practice which affects earnings may be called a " condition." For example, the use of a particular type of sagger or the following of a particular method of placing is called a " condition " by the kilnmen. The practices which affect the comparative difficulty of placing kilns have been treated above as factors in the cubic measurement system of payment and they will not be included in this discussion.

obligations will be treated below under the general heading of specific wage changes. The present section is concerned with definitions or delimitations intended to preserve or restore the old practice.[21]

Under the general subject of what the journeyman is to do for the rate comes a considerable body of rules intended to insure good workmanship, added to the scale from time to time at the request of the manufacturers. The piece rate assumes, of course, a quality of product, but this is not narrowly defined. Such expressions as " marketable " and " first class " are used by the manufacturers in the wage discussions to denote the quality of the ware which it is intended shall be turned out by the men for the rate, but these terms have not an unvarying meaning in practice. The quality of the ware accepted and paid for has varied from time to time and plant to plant. As the men put it, the " inspection is closer " in some plants and at some times.[22] This is an element in the rate difficult to standardize by definition. In kilnplacing and dipping, too, it would be difficult, under the cubic measurement system, to handle the problem of deduction for individual pieces even if the quality could be satisfactorily defined in specifications. The employers have attempted to meet the situation in part by insisting on the recognition by the union of their right to require the men to follow certain methods or to spend a specified minimum time on a given output. The latter type of rule will be discussed below in connection with limits of output.

[21] Not all of the conditions which apply in semi-porcelain apply in china. This is at times a source of dispute in china plants as one side or the other denies that a particular condition laid down in the semi-porcelain scale holds for china.

[22] This is another thing which is often included by the men in the general term " conditions."

Requests for the insertion in the scale of rules governing methods of workmanship have come as the result of complaints of the omission by workmen here and there of certain steps, or of the elimination of the use of certain tools, or of the creeping in of the practice of handling a number of pieces at one time—" short cuts " of one kind or another to greater output per hour. Questions of this type are not concerned with auxiliary or supplementary operations, ordinarily, but with things which must be done by the journeyman himself if they are to be done at all.

The year 1905 was the first in which the employers submitted any proposals to the union and these had to do mostly with workmanship.[23] The only rules of importance adopted were those which gave the employer the right to insist on a minimum actual working time for each kilnman's day in kilnplacing and dipping.[24] The employers did not again submit proposals to the Brotherhood until 1913. In that year and in the next two conference years, they again brought in propositions intended to insure more careful workmanship. None of these was adopted. The employers complained that the union conferees " were disposed to treat them (the employers' proposals) lightly as though they did not constitute any real part of the real work of the conference." [25] In 1917 the wage issues overshadowed everything else. In the 1919 conference, although the employers presented no specific proposition on this subject, they complained again of " cutting corners " and urged the necessity of regaining good workmanship, which had been departed from still further in the pressure for speed during the war period.[26]

---

[23] *Proceedings, U. S. P. A.*, 1905, p. 13; 1903, p. 22; 1904, pp. 22-23.
[24] See below, pp. 163-166.
[25] *Proceedings, U. S. P. A.*, 1915, pp. 45-46.
[26] *Ibid.*, January, 1920, p. 32.

With the falling off in the demand for ware in 1921 the manufacturers turned their attention more seriously to insisting on better workmanship. In the spring of 1921 one firm in the East Liverpool district posted a set of rules to be followed by its dippers. This was met by an unauthorized " walkout " of the dippers from that plant and subsequently from several others in which the same rules were posted. The officers of the Brotherhood succeeded in getting the men back to work. The manufacturers' association then drew up a set of proposals embodying rules for dipping, and a number of others of similar purport applying to other branches, and served notice on the Brotherhood that it would insist on the immediate adoption of these rules or rules of similar character, along with a reduction in wages.[27] In the 1921 conference the demand for " good workmanship " rules and that for a wage reduction were closely associated. The employers realized that they were asking that the men be held to doing some things which many of them had not been doing for some time and that the elimination of the " short cuts " which many of the men had been following would mean that they could not reach the same outputs in the old number of working hours; the manufacturers had taken that into consideration in arriving at the percentage reduction which they were asking, putting it at a lower figure than that to which they contended they were entitled on the basis of the reduction in the cost of living.

The union attitude toward rules to insure good workmanship was different from their attitude toward the restoration of conditions covering auxiliary work which had been surrendered by individual employers. The

[27] *Ibid.*, 1921, pp. 20-21, 24-32; *Report of Executive Board*, 1921, pp. 46-50, 17-27.

officers, and the conference committee generally, were willing to agree that the men should be required to follow any established practice necessary to the manufacture of good ware. The discussion on the proposed rules was directed for the most part to whether they were adapted to the end sought—the making of first-class ware and the elimination of losses. Many differences of opinion developed but they were mostly on issues of a technical character, and some of them appeared on the same side of the table. The manufacturers received many suggestions from the men which they recognized as helpful. Indeed, the proposed rules were considerably modified as a result of the discussion. In the end a rather lengthy code was adopted.[28]

On the general subject, of what the employer can exact from the operative for the rate, the employers also moved in the 1921 conference to do away with the "change of conditions" defense of the men once and for all. This is a corollary of the agreement made in 1900 that "established conditions" in each plant should remain as they were until changed by mutual agreement. The manufacturers declared that the term "change of conditions" had "become merely an excuse for failure to comply with ordinary, reasonable and necessary rules of workmanship." They proposed that every employer working under the agreement

shall have the privilege of adopting, introducing and enforcing in his shops any method, or practice, or rule that is being employed, or has been employed, in the shops of any other firm when working under the present, or any previous agreement, between the U. S. P. A. and the Brotherhood, provided only that such practice is not a clear infraction of the letter or spirit of said agreement. . . . .

---

[28] Some of these are included in the china scale—and the china scale has some which are not in the semi-porcelain scale.

The term " Change of Conditions " shall be accepted as a valid excuse for refusal to comply with a request of an employer only when such request involves an innovation that has never been employed in any pottery lawfully working under the agreement.[29]

The union conferees refused to agree to such a sweeping rule.

The packing branch was passed over with the adoption of one rule in 1921. The next year, in the final December conference, the employers asked the packers to agree to a set of rules and expressed a readiness to pay for them. The packers agreed to this in principle and that a joint committee should be empowered to work out the details. A special joint committee was appointed which effected a revision of the price list and also adopted a set of rules intended to secure better packing. In subsequent conferences Mr. Wells testified that much better packing had been secured, with a resulting reduction in breakage, since these rules were adopted although, he added in 1928, it required constant watching to secure observance of the rules.

The rules for good workmanship which did not carry extra compensation were not generally obeyed. The manufacturers have repeatedly complained of this but the union has replied that it had agreed that the men could be held to do these things, that it would support the manufacturer in discharging a man for refusal to do them when ordered to, and it could do no more. The non-observance of the rules, the union contends, was really due to the failure of the manufacturers to insist upon observance. If some manufacturers did not insist upon them it could not be expected that the men could be held to them in the other shops.[30] In the 1926

[29] *Proceedings, U. S. P. A.*, 1921, p. 29.

[30] *Ibid.*, 1925, p. 32. In its 1927 report the labor committee stated that with widespread unemployment and jobs in demand, " workmanship has somewhat improved." *Ibid.*, 1927, p. 17.

conference Mr. Wells admitted that some of the methods which had been reinstated on paper were of doubtful value. He suggested that the rules should be gone over and those which had become dead letters eliminated from the agreement, but there has been no action on the good workmanship rules either by way of revision or strengthening.

As already noted, the manufacturers have at times asked for rules in some branches limiting the output of the workers in a given amount of " actual working time," in the interests of good workmanship. These requests reveal that the enforcement of limits of output by the workers themselves has never been a feature of piece work in the general ware industry.[31] The failure of the men to enforce limits was not due to lack of urging from their officers, at least in the earlier years. President Hughes and President T. J. Duffy repeatedly warned the members that speed had been carried to excess by some of the workers. The evils which they saw flowing from these large outputs were, in addition to the deterioration of workmanship which so disturbed the manufacturers: injury to health, the forcing of men from their trades prematurely, unemployment, and the furnishing of " ammunition to manufacturers who are desirous of reducing wages." [32] The convention did at times adopt limits for some of the branches, but these were not observed in practice.[33] The last of the branches to adopt a limit was the pressers and casters,

[31] See below, ch. xiv, for limits of output enforced by the pressers and casters in the sanitary division.

[32] *Proceedings*, 1895, p. 6; 1898, pp. 9, 10; 1902, pp. 10, 13; 1903, p. 15; 1904, p. 10; *Report of President*, 1906, pp. 5-8; 1908, p. 4; 1911, p. 12.

[33] *Proceedings*, 1894, pp. 15-16; 1905, pp. 34-35; 1906, pp. 19, 49; 1908, pp. 15, 22; *Report of President*, 1905, p. 16; 1907, pp. 10-11; 1911, p. 12.

in 1910.[34] This limit went the way of all the others; a few years later it was recognized as a dead letter.[35]

The movement from the side of the manufacturers [36] for the insertion in the scale of minimum time limits resulted in the adoption by the conference as early as 1905 of such limits for kilnplacing and dipping. The limits were not absolute; the agreement provided only that the employer " may require " that a specified amount of " actual working time " be spent on each kilnman's day.[37] Although these limits were adopted with the hearty concurrence of the union officers there was considerable opposition to the action of the union conference committee from the members, especially from the dippers.[38] Mr. Wells realized that in the face of this opposition, the individual manufacturers might allow the rules to remain inoperative.[39] His fears were well grounded. The employers did not generally insist on the limits and that made it difficult to secure compliance when and where a manufacturer demanded it.[40]

[34] *Proceedings*, 1910, p. 30.

[35] Statement of President Menge to the writer; *Bureau of Foreign and Domestic Commerce, Miscellaneous Series No. 21:* " The Pottery Industry—Report on the Cost of Production in the Earthenware and China Industries of the United States, England, Germany, and Austria " (Washington: Government Printing Office, 1915), p. 317. In the 1927 convention a resolution that " during this depression period casters be limited to $8.00 a day," offered because " so many casters are out of employment," was rejected. *Proceedings*, 1927, p. 12.

[36] See *Proceedings, U. S. P. A.*, 1903, p. 22; 1904, pp. 22-23.

[37] The kilnman's limit was one kilnman's day in five hours. " Whenever kilnmen are unable to place kilns on time by working one and one-half kilnmen days each day, they shall be required to put on additional men." The dippers' limit was one kilnman's day in 84 minutes, and not more than 5¾ kilnman's days in one day.

[38] *Report of President*, 1906, p. 8.

[39] *Proceedings, U. S. P. A.*, 1905, p. 13.

[40] *Proceedings, N. B. of O. P.*, 1907, p. 60.

In the movement for good workmanship rules in 1921 the manufacturers again returned to the idea of scale limits of output, not only in kilnplacing and dipping but in jiggering as well. For the jiggering branch they proposed a schedule of the maximum number of dozens per hour for each of various classes of ware. In the conference they explained that they had attempted to set the limit in each case at the maximum consistent with good workmanship and asked the views of the men on that figure. President Menge said that there was so much difference between men that it might be 25 dozen for one and 35 dozen for another. The jigger-men, although they expressed a desire to reach an agreement with the manufacturers on a limited day's work, preferred not to act on figures until it should be known how much the output per hour would be reduced by the other rules for good workmanship adopted in the conference. It was agreed merely that a joint com-mittee should work out the limits at a later time. Mr. Menge pointed out, however, that the men believed that if business should become brisk again the manu-facturers would ignore the limits and tell the jigger-men "to go to it." As a matter of fact the joint com-mittee was never appointed. In the August, 1922 con-ference Mr. Wells expressed a fear that the "man of extraordinary ability" might be hampered if limits were adopted.

On the proposed limits for dipping [41] President Menge suggested that the other rules adopted on dipping should be sufficient for the purpose, without a limit. One of the dippers on the conference committee opposed

[41] The minimum time proposed for dipping a kilnman's day was 60 minutes, as compared with 84 minutes in the 1905 Agreement; the maximum number of kilnmen's days proposed for one day was 8, as compared with $5\frac{3}{4}$ in the 1905 Agreement.

putting a limit on a man's work; what a man does on any day depends upon how he feels; moreover, if a man is sick it may be necessary to " catch up," in order to keep the kilnmen going. No specific limit was adopted but a clause was added that if a firm could show " proof of injury " as a result of " too much speed in dipping and placing they may insist on more time being taken for the work." The manufacturers also dropped their proposal for a limit on kilnplacing [42] after the inclusion of placing in the above clause. The rapid introduction of day work in kilnplacing and dipping since 1921 has drawn attention away from the question of minimum time limits.

Abnormal Conditions.—Closely allied to questions as to what the employer can demand from the workman for the rate are those concerning the facilities for output to be furnished by the employer. Scale questions of this kind have usually been raised through requests from the men for extra pay for conditions of work which are below a specified standard. This involves, of course, a definition of the minimum conditions to be assumed as covered by the rate. The employers have been reluctant, on the whole, to insert definitions and specific extras of this kind in the scale. If the conditions in a plant are below normal, whether temporarily or because of the construction of the plant or the equipment in use, the Association prefers to have the matter cared for by a " local settlement " between the parties concerned.

A field in which the men have frequently sought delimitation of their obligation, and provision for extra for exceeding it, is that of the carrying of ware. In the

---

[42] The minimum time limit proposed was four hours per kilnman's day, as compared with five hours in the 1905 Agreement.

kiln branch it is still the duty of the men to carry the ware from the green room to the bisque kilns and from the dipping room to the glost kilns. The delimitation of the carry is, with the kilnmen, usually an extra compensation issue inasmuch as the distance which the ware is to be carried can not ordinarily be diminished except by rearrangement of the plant. The principle of extra was recognized in the 1900 scale to the extent that extras were provided for carries of ware over 60 feet, graduated according to the distance, and for half-story and story ascensions. The union has asked for a revision of these scale extras, but without success.

The clay-shop workers still have to carry their finished ware to the green room, so far as the scale is concerned, although this obligation has been greatly reduced in practice through the installation of conveyor belts or similar devices in many plants. The men, having advanced the proposition that they be relieved of what remains of this obligation, but without success, fell back in 1926 upon a proposal that they be paid for carrying out the ware when the green room is located an extra long distance from the worker's bench.[43] They submitted figures showing a variation from 59 feet and 17 steps to 155 feet and 16 steps. They asked that extra be paid beyond a distance of 120 feet, including stairs. The employers replied that the carries had in fact been greatly lessened, in most plants, since the uniform scale was adopted. Some firms had installed automatic carriers, eliminating the carry downstairs entirely and reducing the distance. In some of the newer plants, too, the green room and the jiggering benches had been put on the same floor and not over 60 feet apart. For none of these changes had a reduction been asked.

[43] *Proceedings*, 1926, pp. 20, 22-23, 58-59.

12

Mr. Wells urged the men not to attempt to disturb a situation which had brought benefit to so many of them but to leave the surviving cases of long carries to be corrected by the individual employers as opportunity offered. The union proposal was not adopted.

An issue which has a long history is that of payment for ware which turns out defective before it reaches the green room. The established practice in general ware is to pay for all good ware delivered to the green room. The issue over ware which is not discovered to be defective until after it is fired, which was so troublesome in the sanitary ware division,[44] has therefore not been present in the general ware division. Here the question is confined to ware "lost" before it is brought to the green room, through "cracking" in the moulds or the appearance of some other defect which, the men assert, is caused by poor clay. The waremakers have always contended that they should be paid in full for all ware on which they have exercised proper workmanship, including that which turns out defective through no fault of the worker. The employers concede this in principle. The question is, what caused the defect? It does not assume practical importance unless a man is losing more ware than usual; then he is inclined to find the cause for the abnormal degree of loss in the quality of the clay.

In 1905 it was agreed that

manufacturers shall use due diligence to prevent loss from green ware cracking on moulds and wherever excessive loss occurs and it appears that the manufacturer refuses to make the necessary investigation and take immediate steps to correct such trouble, it shall be a proper matter for adjustment by the standing committee.

What should be considered "excessive loss" was not specified. The jiggermen had asked that the manufac-

[44] See below, ch. xiv.

turer be compelled to stand the loss when it exceeded
five per cent.[45] It was fortunate for the men later that
this figure was not adopted, as firms frequently paid for
losses of smaller percentage.

During the war period there was a large increase in
the number of disputes arising out of charges that the
clay was poor. It was generally known that a number
of firms had " changed the body "—that is, made some
change in clays or in the proportions—and complaints
by the men of the character of the clay multiplied. The
standing committee was then acting on a presumption
that a loss of over two and one-half per cent was
" excessive." In 1922, because of a complaint from the
jiggermen that they could not get settlements from
some firms on this basis, the two and a half per cent
limit was specified in the agreement with the safeguarding clause that the loss should be due to no
fault of the waremaker.

Another question is how long must the men remain
in the plant without pay when conditions are such that
they cannot work? The jiggermen are especially concerned because they employ helpers whom they pay by
the hour. In the 1911 conference the jiggermen succeeded in having a limit of one half-hour set to the
time they can be required to hold their crews in case of
an accident which shuts off the power from the jigger.
In 1919 the kilnmen secured an even more favorable
rule—they are to be paid if required to wait longer
than fifteen minutes for a kiln or material. The packers were granted a similar rule in the same conference.

During the war period some of the clay-shop branches
carried the issue even further by showing a disinclina-

---

[45] *Proceedings, N. B. of O. P.,* 1905, p. 20.

tion to work when their own helpers were absent or when they were unable to secure help. The journeyman obviously cannot earn as much per hour if he has to do for himself work that he ordinarily employs a helper to do at a lower rate of wages, and many of the journeymen preferred to wait until they could get a full quota of helpers, unless, of course, the firm would make up the deficiency in earnings. The position which the employers have usually taken is that the responsibility for securing helpers rests on the journeyman and the firm should not have to suffer curtailment of production or increased labor cost if the journeyman is unable to solve his own labor problems. But when the employers adopted the practice during the war period of paying bonuses to the jiggermen's helpers, in order to keep the journeymen working more steadily,[46] they opened the way to claims from the men for extra compensation if they worked in the absence of their usual helpers.

What the jiggermen asked, in the 1917 conference, was that the firm should make up the difference between the average wages of the jiggerman and his actual earnings when he was required to work without a full crew. The employers would not concede this, but they did agree to pay the jiggerman the *per diem* bonus of 25 cents which would have been paid to the helpers. In 1918 the employers agreed not only to pay the 25 cents *per diem* to the jiggerman for each helper absent but also to give free delivery of clay to the jiggermen working without a full crew.[47] In October, 1920, the

[46] See below, pp. 214-216.

[47] *Report of Executive Board*, 1919, p. 13. In September, 1920, the bonus for working in the absence of a helper was raised to 30 cents. It was reduced to 25 cents in 1921 and brought up to 27 cents in 1922. For the " free delivery of clay " concession, see below, p. 221.

employers also agreed to pay a bonus of ten per cent to the dishmaker when working without a helper on the larger sizes,[48] and in 1922 granted them free delivery of clay.

THE TIME RATE IN THE WAREHOUSEMEN'S BRANCH

The only large branch exclusively on the time-working system is that of the warehousemen.[49] The fixing of a rate for this branch involved the facing of some problems common to the fixing of union rates for time workers in most occupations in which the time system of payment is followed. First, it was made clear that the rate specified was intended to be a minimum; it was not to prevent the payment of a higher rate in particular cases. As a matter of fact men have frequently been paid more than the rate specified in the scale. Second, it was attempted to define those to whom the rate should apply; this was insisted upon by the employers because of the wide variation in the work done by so-called journeymen. Only the " competent journeymen," who not only had served four consecutive years at the trade but also were " competent to properly do all classes of warehouse work " were entitled to the rate. The employer was to be the judge of the competency. Later, further clarification was given the application of the rate. It was to apply only to the men " employed steadily at the more responsible kind of general warehouse work "; it was not to apply to " the man who but occasionally does the more skilled kind of warehouse work,

[48] *Proceedings, U. S. P. A.,* December, 1920, p. 58. The bonus to the helper on those sizes was at that time 19 per cent. The bonus for working alone was not reduced in the general reduction of 1921.

[49] It was not until 1911 that the rate for warehousemen was fixed in the agreement. The branch had not been well organized for any long consecutive period before this.

such as the filling of orders for shipment." Nor was it
to be construed to prevent a journeyman accepting the
less skilled kind of work at less than the scale rate.

The union failed to secure formal apprenticeship
rules in this branch,[50] consequently it was unable to
dispose of the question of competency by that method.
The employers did agree, however, to a scale of wages
graduated according to years of service through four
years, after which "competent journeymen" were to
receive at least the journeyman rate. Then, in the May,
1917, voluntary increase, the employers agreed to pay
the journeyman rate after the third year. A proviso
was added that the "workman must qualify as a warehouseman before he is entitled to draw the wages specified." There are still some men who have served more
than three years to whom the employers will not pay
the minimum journeyman rate, on the ground that they
are not competent warehousemen.

ISSUES AS TO THE SYSTEM OF PAYMENT

The question of whether payment shall be by time
or by piece, which has disturbed the relations of so
many employers and their organized workers, has never
been a matter of serious controversy in the general
ware industry. For most of the history of the agreement the union has been more troubled about systems
under which journeymen employ other journeymen or
helpers than it has about piece work. Generally speaking the national officers and the conventions have favored the substitution of direct employment and payment of all workers by the firm for the employment by
journeymen of either journeymen or helpers. But
internal legislation to this end was largely nullified by

[50] See below, p. 274.

opposition of the members affected. The employers, too, have on the whole been reluctant to decree the abolition of the journeyman-employer, on terms acceptable to the union, and few such changes have been effected by joint agreement.

The Contract System.—Before the days of the national agreement the " contract system " was rather general. The two distinguishing characteristics of the system were that the employees of the employing operatives were themselves journeymen, not apprentices or helpers, and that they were employed at rates lower than those the employing operatives received from the firm. The employed journeymen were ordinarily engaged at day rates which were lower than their outputs would amount to at the piece rates received by the contractor.

Convention resolutions against the contract system were common before the beginning of the agreement system but because of the opposition of members interested in the continuance of it they could not be enforced.[51] In 1902 the convention not only ordered the abolition of the contract system in all branches but the Brotherhood also presented proposals to the employers to make this legislation a part of the agreement. The branches chiefly concerned—the mouldmakers, packers and dippers—refused to obey the law or to support the conference committee in asking the manufacturers to go along with the change.[52] In the face of this oppo-

[51] *Proceedings,* 1894, pp. 16, 17; 1898, pp. 31, 37; 1899, p. 48.

[52] *Ibid.,* 1903, pp. 6-9, 15. The East Liverpool local union of mouldmakers was expelled from the Brotherhood, as was a number of packers who had signed a petition to the manufacturers against the proposed change. The result was that for the next few years the Brotherhood had no organization of any consequence in either branch. *Report of President,* 1908, p. 9; 1909, p. 9.

sition the Brotherhood was unable to secure anything
in the way of an agreement from the employers to do
away with contracting in their plants. The union then
fell back again upon internal pressure and again it was
found that "none of the branches in which this evil
prevails" would take "any steps to eliminate it." [53]
The 1904 convention did force the dippers to give up the
contract system by adopting for that branch a plan
which President Duffy had proposed to the East Liverpool dippers and which their local had refused to accept.
It allowed the head dipper fifty cents more a day than
the others, to be paid by the other dippers, for "running the shop." [54]

In 1909 the Brotherhood again moved against the
contract system in mouldmaking and packing through
the medium of agreement with the employers. President Duffy urged that the Brotherhood "insist upon
this condition being remedied no matter at what cost." [55]
In the mouldmaking branch, in which the blockers and
casers were the contractors, the union proposed that
blocking and casing be put on a day-wage basis and
that all mouldmakers receive the full piece price scale.
The employers agreed to put blocking and casing on
day wage but refused to pay the full list prices for
mouldmaking. In order to get rid of the contract system the union finally agreed to accept a reduction of
ten per cent in the list prices for mouldmaking.[56] In
the packing branch the employers would not accept the
union proposals, although the union "pushed matters
to the verge of a strike." They would go no further

[53] *Proceedings*, 1904, p. 18.
[54] *Ibid.*, pp. 18-19, 105-106, 125; *Rules and Regulations*, 1910, Sec.
215; *Constitution*, 1925, Sec. 270.
[55] *Report of President*, 1909, pp. 8-10.
[56] *Ibid.*, 1910, pp. 4-5. This reduction did not apply to china shops.

than to agree to investigate the system and if any exploitation by the boss packers were found, to remedy the situation.[57] Some employers did this but it was several years before the contract system disappeared from this branch.[58]

The Brotherhood has made no serious demand on the employers for the abolition of the contract system in warehousewomen's work. One of the demands of the warehousewomen in 1913 before they came into the Brotherhood was that the contract system be abolished, but the award of the arbitrators stipulated that " existing contracts may be continued when mutually agreed upon by the employer and a majority of the women in the department concerned." [59] That provision is still in the agreement. The contract system obtains chiefly in the " dressing " of glost ware. The contractor's rates are " arranged between (the) firm and contractor." The piece rates to be paid by the contractor for dressing glost flat ware are not specified in the scale,[60] but the day rate which the girls are to receive for dressing glost hollow ware has, since 1913, been fixed in the agreement. Similarly, if any other part of the work is done under the contract system the contractor must pay the girls the scale rates.

The contract system also prevails in decorating kilnwork in the East Liverpool district. There is no uniform scale for this work. The decorating kiln-fireman—who acts as foreman of the decorating kilns—takes over the placing and firing of the kilns from the

---

[57] *Ibid.*

[58] *Proceedings,* 1911, p. 78; 1912, p. 57. Statements of President Menge and President Wood to the writer.

[59] *Proceedings, U. S. P. A.,* 1913, pp. 31, 35.

[60] The scale provides that this work shall be paid for " at the prevailing piece rate price."

firm at a price per kiln and employs the kiln-placers
and -drawers, usually at piece rates. The union has not
offered vigorous opposition to this system in recent
years. The placers do not object strongly to it; in fact,
in 1919 the kiln firemen employed in the Homer Laughlin China Company's plants " gave in their notices " [61]
in order to force the firm to change from day work to
the contract system. In contrast to the earlier attitude of many of the employers toward the system in
other branches, and of many toward it now in this
branch, Mr. W. E. Wells continued to insist that the
contract system then installed in his company's plants
was unfair. The division of earnings between the fire-
man-contractor and the other members of the crew, a
division worked out by a committee of the local union,
gave the fireman, Mr. Wells maintained, too great a
share in proportion to the work he does.[62]

Payment of Help by the Jiggerman.—The system of
payment in the jiggering branch, whereby the jiggerman employs and pays the finisher, batter-out and
mould-runner has often been the subject of proposals
for change. Some of these have been to substitute direct
employment of the finisher, mould-runner and batter-
out by the firm; these have always come from the union.
Others have gone no further than specifying in the
scale the percentage of the total rate which should be
paid to the jiggerman and to the finisher, batter-out and
mould-runner, respectively, and providing that each
should receive his wages directly from the firm. The
employers have for years been willing to do this but
they have been unwilling to take over the responsibility
for the employment of the helpers or to assume the
" dead work " which would be transferred to them by

[61] See below, pp. 290-292, 359-360.
[62] MS. *Report of Conference,* 1926.

this change. The proposal for a " four-ways " piece scale, which would leave the jiggerman's responsibilities where they are, although agreed to in principle by the employers, has broken down on the inability of the jiggermen to satisfy the employers that they had a division which all three of the helpers' groups would accept.

It is the batters-out and mould-runners who have been both the cause of the proposals for a four-ways piece scale and the problem in working one out. The finishers have since 1903 had a national piece scale, agreed upon between themselves and the jiggermen and ratified by the Brotherhood. Although the relations of the two groups have not always been highly harmonious, and although both have been on record for years as favoring direct employment of the finishers by the firm, the finishers have not been a serious problem to either the jiggermen or the employers.

The jiggermen were especially eager during the war period and the years immediately following to get rid of the responsibility for the batters-out and mould-runners and the " dead work " for which they were in part employed. Even before the war, competition between jiggermen for help had put the time rates above what the jiggermen could afford to pay from their piece rates and above what was paid for other work of similar character in the potteries.[63] The situation became much worse after 1915. Moreover, the turnover was excessive and absenteeism was interfering with production. It was this which made the employers interested in having the batters-out and mould-runners put on a definite piece scale. Eventually the employers themselves offered bonuses to the batters-out

[63] *Proceedings, U. S. P. A.,* 1913, p. 30.

and mould-runners for regular work.[64] However, the direct payment issue has not been pushed in recent years. Since 1924 there has been little talk of the jiggermen bidding up the wages of help.

Piece Work vs. Day Work.—The original constitution of the Brotherhood assumed the prevalence of the piecework system. It also stipulated that all work for which the union had fixed piece prices should be done under that system.[65] This seems to have been due not so much to objection to time work, as such, as to a desire to prevent an employer from having part of the work for which piece prices had been fixed done under the time system and the remainder under the piece system. The union has always opposed this. The men fear that an employer might cull out the " best paying " work in the piece scale and have it done at hourly rates. In 1913 when the employers proposed that " the firm shall have the option of paying day wage or piece price for any part or all of the work done in any department for which a piece work price is provided " the union would not agree to it. The rates proposed by the employers for time work were not acceptable but the union also objected to giving the employer the right to use either system on any part of the work at will.

Nor does the " option of the employer " to use the time system instead of the piece scale, which has been recognized in several branches, allow the employer to give a man part of his work under the piece scale and part at the time rate, even where there is an alternative time rate in the uniform scale. The union is also opposed to allowing the employer to divide work covered by the piece scale between the two systems, within the same branch in the same shop, by employing some

[64] See below, pp. 214-216.
[65] *Constitution,* 1890, Articles IX and XIV.

of the men on one system and some on the other. The
union holds that if the employer wishes to use the time
system for work for which there is a piece scale he
should put all the men in the same branch in the same
shop on the same system. The employers have in practice observed this interpretation, except that glost
kilns may be on the time system and the bisque kilns on
the cubic measurement system.[66]

The employers have twice asked the union to consider the adoption of time work exclusively. In the 1913
conference, when the union refused to agree to the proposal referred to above, the employers asked the men
what rates they would accept for time work throughout.
The wages the union committee proposed were so far
above what the manufacturers were willing to pay that
they dropped the whole matter. In 1917 the manufacturers submitted a proposal for a straight day-wage
system in all branches, to which the individual manufacturer should have the option of adding a bonus system, but this proposal was not pushed in the conference.
Since that time the employers' interest in changing to
the day basis seems to have become restricted almost
entirely to the kiln and dipping branches. In fact, in
1919 and again in 1921, when the union wished to abolish piece work in the packing branch in favor of day
work, the employers refused to agree. Apart from these
three branches there has been no movement from either
side in recent years for the displacement of piece work.

The attitude which each side has taken toward the
substitution of day work for time work in any branch
has been largely influenced by the rates proposed
for the time work. The employers believe that they get
better workmanship under the time system. They also
expect to get lower outputs. Employers have repeatedly

[66] MS. *Report of Conference*, 1924, 1926.

stated in the conference that workers will generally turn out only about two-thirds as much per hour when employed regularly under the time system as under piece work. They have therefore been unwilling to agree to change to time work as a regular method of payment at rates per hour even approximating the average earnings under piece work, except where the necessity of getting better workmanship has become paramount. The men, for their part, although quite willing—and in some branches eager—to escape from the pressure for speed involved in the piece system, have been unwilling to accept much of a reduction in daily earnings or much of an increase in their hours per day to get this relief.

The packers' request for the abolition of piece work grew out of circumstances which developed during the war. Since 1905 the employer had had the option of having his packing done under either system,[67] but the piece system had generally been followed. During the war period the packers in some of the larger plants received concessions which the smaller employers were unable to give. Piece work thus became comparatively less attractive in the small plants and the packers in some of these insisted on day work—a demand which a number of employers had to grant in order to hold their men. The experience of the packers with day work was satisfactory and in order to retain it, they proposed, in 1919 and again in 1921, that the employer's right under the agreement to insist upon piece work be abrogated.

The employers were now unwilling to give up piece work. They maintained that in those plants in which

[67] This option had been inserted in the agreement in order to give the employer the opportunity of employing his packers directly at day wage instead of having the packers employed at day wages by a contractor.

the packers had secured day work, the cost of packing was excessive; it ran from thirty-six to forty per cent above what it was under piece work. Moreover, time payment was inconvenient for the employers, as the practice was to charge the buyer for packing in addition to the price of the ware and when the packing was done under piece work they could tell in advance exactly what it would cost. In answer to the packers' argument that the employers would get better packing under the day-work system the employers replied that the piece prices were high enough to entitle them to good workmanship and if the men were not giving it they were cheating. The next year the employers made a more effective answer to this argument by offering a revision of the piece-price list in return for rules to insure better packing. The resultant agreement of January, 1923, " made piece work packing a better job " and gave the employers better packing.[68] The time rate was not increased at that time and when the packers asked in 1924 that the rate be raised to $1.00 an hour on the ground that 76 cents an hour was not fair pay for packing, the employers refused to increase the rate because they wanted to keep the differential against day work great enough to make the packers prefer piece work.

That the system of payment followed in kilnplacing has given rise not only to many local disputes and non-uniformities but also to repeated demands in conference for extras has already been pointed out. Many of these wage troubles are due to the use of the cubic foot system as contrasted with straight piece work. There have been, to be sure, other subjects of controversy— such as long carries and fetching green saggers [69] —which are not properly chargeable to the use of the

[68] MS. *Report of Conference,* 1924.
[69] See below, pp. 223-224.

cubic foot basis; these could have arisen if payment had been by straight piece work, with a separate price for every kind of ware, every kind of sagger, and every method of placing the saggers in the kiln. But it is the cubic measurement system which has caused most of the trouble, from the employers' standpoint, in kiln-placing.

The most unsatisfactory feature of the cubic measurement system is not its failure to provide automatic adjustment of wages to changes from time to time in the proportions of large and small ware and hollow ware and flat, in the types of saggers used, or in methods of placing. These changes might be cared for more or less acceptably by increases in the rate or by specific extras. The heart of the difficulty is that the cubic measurement system keeps the immediate wage interest of the kilnmen in opposition to the interest of the employers as to the amount of ware placed in the kilns. It offers to the men a temptation to keep the number of pieces in the sagger and the number of saggers going into the kiln as low as possible. On the other hand, what the employer wants is to have the sagger space and kiln space utilized as fully as possible. It costs as much to fire the kiln when only eighty per cent full as when filled to capacity, and practically as much for wear and tear on saggers. But more than that, with dipping, drawing, ware brushing, and other similar operations paid for on the cubic measurement or per kiln basis, it costs the employer more per piece for all of these other operations.[70] The effect of the cubic measurement system of payment on the quality of the ware is logically distinct from it relation to the quantitative placement of

[70] Mr. W. E. Wells estimated in 1923 that the labor cost of kiln-placing, kilndrawing, and dipping was eleven per cent of the total cost of production. *Proceedings, U. S. P. A.*, December, 1923, p. 25.

the kilns. Whatever premium it places on speed at the expense of quality [71] would be present also under a straight piece-work system, unless payment were made only for good ware coming from the kilns—a plan which would raise difficulties of its own.

An important element in the situation, as affecting the ability of the employer to get the kilns satisfactorily placed—both as to quantity and quality—is that the setter-out or " bench boss " of the crew, who has the immediate supervision of the filling of the saggers and the placing of the saggers in the kiln, is not the " firm's man " but a member of the crew, sharing in the crew's earnings, and nearly always a member of the union. The employers have complained of this situation from time to time, declaring that the bench boss can not properly " function as a foreman " because he is under the " control of the local union." They proposed unsuccessfully in 1913, and again in 1915, that the immediate control of the kiln crews should be given over to a kiln superintendent who shall not be a member of the Brotherhood.

In 1919 the Brotherhood proposed the time system for kilnmen. The main reason was that the kilnmen had come to fear the pressure for speed in the cubic measurement system. The pace had been greatly increased during the war period and the belief was general among the kilnmen that they were working too hard. The older men, particularly, were afraid that they would be forced out of the trade if the cubic measurement system were not given up; with the men in the crew shar-

---

[71] In the 1926 conference, after experience with time work on glost kilns in one of his own plants, Mr. Wells said that the reduction in losses had not been as great as had been anticipated, indicating that " a good many of the losses . . . . previously blamed on the kilnmen were probably not their fault."

13

ing the wages equally, the crew was reluctant to retain a man who could not keep up the pace. The kilnmen in some of the plants were also influenced by the fact that they were working under poorer conditions than the men in the newer plants, conditions which were not, to their way of thinking, adequately offset by extras. In a few eastern plants, the kilnmen had insisted upon and obtained day work during the war period by threatening to " give in their notices " and they were not willing to go back to the cubic measurement system.

Some of the manufacturers were inclined to consider day work favorably. They saw in it an opportunity to use any type of sagger or method of placing that they chose, without dispute over extras, and to get the kilns properly filled. Those with superior facilities saw also an opportunity to gain an advantage from them. But the majority of the manufacturers feared that they would lose more by a falling-off in output than they would gain in other ways, at the rate proposed by the men. That there would be a considerable reduction in output per hour they took for granted and, they contended, the proposed time rate did not allow sufficient margin for that. The men, for their part, were not willing to accept a time rate that would satisfy the manufacturers and no change was made.

By 1923, when the union members of the joint special committee on kilnwork which had been appointed after the 1922 conference, proposed a change to the time system as a solution of all difficulties,[72] the employers agreed that it should be tried in three specified plants,[73] but the kilnmen in the three chosen plants were unwilling to undertake it under the conditions laid down. In

[72] See above, p. 155.
[73] *Report of Executive Board*, 1923, pp. 28-30; *Proceedings, U. S. P. A.*, December 1923, pp. 24-25.

the 1924 conference the employers were still too much afraid of day work [74] to agree to the union proposal, strongly urged by the kilnmen on the conference committee, that it be adopted exclusively. The manufacturers concerned finally conceded a renewal of the agreement made in 1923 to give time work a trial. What turned out to be of much more importance was the insertion in the scale that the employer had the option of having his kiln work done on time work at the rate of 90 cents an hour.

By the time the 1926 conference convened the swing to day work under the optional clause was well under way. It was welcomed by both Chairman Wells and President Wood. The latter said that for years he had been in favor of day work from the green room on but had been opposed to forcing it. Mr. Wells expressed the hope that day work in kilnplacing and dipping would be extended until it became universal. He was by this time convinced that day work had proved an unqualified success on tunnel kilns in his plants, both from the standpoint of the firm and that of the men. On the upright glost kilns, on which day work had been tried in one of his plants, the cost was not as much greater as he had feared.[75] The drift to the day system has continued. It is the only system used for tunnel kilns and tunnel kilns are rapidly displacing the upright kilns. The change on the old style kilns has been retarded

[74] *Ibid.*, 1924, pp. 33-34.

[75] *Ibid.*, 1926, p. 30. In the 1928 conference Mr. W. E. Wells said that the time taken to place the glost kilns under the hourly rate system in two of his plants was approximately 50 per cent greater than it had been under the cubic measurement system. At ninety cents an hour the men were receiving about three-fourths as much as they had received per hour, on the average, under the cubic measurement system for placing these kilns; the men on time work put in more hours per day.

somewhat by the dissatisfaction of the kilnmen with the amount of the hourly rate,[76] but in spite of that fact the question of cubic measurement *vs.* day work seems to be solving itself by a peaceful change to time work under the continued influence of the introduction of tunnel kilns and the 1924 clause giving the employer the choice of the two methods of payment.

The day-wage plan won a foothold in dipping earlier and with much less opposition than in kilnplacing. In the earlier years of the agreement system, to be sure, the Brotherhood had been opposed to changing to time payment in dipping. In the 1905 conference, when the employers suggested it, as a means of eliminating what both the manufacturers and the Brotherhood officers regarded as excessive speed in dipping, the union conferees were unwilling to accept the manufacturers' proposal, and a minimum time limit for dipping a kilnman's day was adopted instead. However, day-wage dipping was generally adopted in the china plants, by agreement between the firms and their dippers. There was no uniform scale for dipping china on the kilnman's day basis and none has ever been adopted. During and immediately after the War, too, a few semi-porcelain plants took up the day-wage plan, at rates acceptable to their own dippers. So when the manufacturers asked in the 1921 conference that a uniform hourly rate be fixed in the scale for dipping, the union readily agreed that this should be done and that any manufacturer might put his dipping shop on the time basis at this rate. The hourly rate fixed for dipping was the highest fixed for any branch. One of the union

[76] In *Bulletin 412 of the U. S. Bureau of Labor Statistics* (p. 83) the average hourly earnings of kilnplacers (exclusive of bench bosses) on the kiln day basis, in semi-porcelain, are given as $1.063 in bisque and $1.07 in glost. These figures are for 1925.

arguments for the rate was that inasmuch as the dippers made higher earnings per hour than the other branches at "piece work," they would not willingly accept day work unless the hourly rate were higher. There has been very little complaint of the hourly rate from the dippers, as contrasted with the kilnmen. Doubtless the fact that the dippers' rate is ten per cent higher has something to do with this.

Not only was there much less opposition on the part of the men to trying the day-wage plan than there was in kilnplacing, but there was much less uncertainty on the part of the manufacturers who tried it as to its net advantage over the kilnman's day system. In the 1924 conference one manufacturer estimated that the output per hour was but two-thirds, approximately, of what it had been, but he was not complaining of that as the work was properly done and he did not regard the difference in cost as excessive for the results obtained. Mr. Wells gave similar testimony concerning the results of day-work dipping in his newest plant, but he was not sure that the fact that the kilnplacing in the same plant was done on day work did not have something to do with the improvement in quality.

The amount of day-wage dipping was of course automatically increased at a rapid rate with the introduction of tunnel kilns for glost placing and the change to day-rate placing on the upright glost kilns in many plants.[77] Tunnel kilns have been introduced more rapidly for glost than for bisque placing and on the upright kilns the change to day work has also been more pronounced in glost than in bisque. Consequently day work has become even more prevalent in dipping than in kilnplacing.

[77] It was the kilnman's day in *glost* which was the basis of payment for dipping.

CHAPTER VII

UNIFORMITY AND NON-UNIFORMITIES

Long before the Brotherhood came upon the scene there had been a tradition in the industry that working prices should be uniform. It has been noted that the members of the United States Potters Association throughout the country were urged to follow the " revised and equalized list of the working prices " which the Trenton manufacturers had put in force in 1877. But even that list did not give satisfaction,[1] and as the years went on the differences in conditions and methods between plants made for greater and greater non-uniformity in wage rates. Although many of the manufacturers still believed in the desirability of uniform working prices, non-uniform conditions prevented any effective action toward national uniformity in the lists from the manufacturers' side. When, in 1894, the United States Potters Association sponsored a united movement for a reduction in wages it did not attempt to establish a new uniform wage list.[2]

---

[1] See above, p. 17.

[2] Ex-District Master Workman O'Neill, testifying before the United States Industrial Commission in 1901 (Vol. XIV, p. 652), after referring to his own efforts for a uniform list, stated this conclusion as the result of his experience: " It is a Utopian idea, anyhow—this of uniformity of prices; shops (shapes?) and sizes are different in the different factories, and there are different methods of work, different styles of machinery, used, etc."

THE BROTHERHOOD'S FIGHT FOR A NATIONAL SCALE
(1895-1905)

When, after the 1894 strike, the Brotherhood turned its attention to the question of a uniform wage list,[3] it was confronted not only by the gap between eastern and western wage rates, a problem which it could not handle without the coöperation of the eastern operatives, but also by non-uniformities in rates in the West itself. The "1885 list" was generally assumed by the workmen to be the standard,[4] but it seems to have been in practice rather a standard of reference than a binding list. Working at various "discounts" from the list was general.[5] In addition, many new articles had been introduced and for these there was not even a nominal list.[6] After the failure of the negotiations for a national list in 1897, a committee of the Brotherhood and one representing the western manufacturers did attempt to work out a list for the West alone, to be based on an average of the prices paid in all the potteries west of the Allegheny Mountains. But after the work had advanced a considerable distance the committees deadlocked on the prices to be used in making up the list for jiggering.[7] Thus the first real attempt at a uniform list for the West was wrecked on the rock of the difficulty of applying the basis of "average prices."

[3] In 1900 President Hughes said: "We have been attempting to attain a standard working list ever since the formation of our union." *Proceedings,* 1900, p. 9.

[4] *Ibid.,* 1894, pp. 6, 7; 1895, p. 24. The list proposed by the union in the 1900 negotiations, which was the basis of the first uniform scale, was, the union representatives said, as near the 1885 list as it was possible to get. *Proceedings, U. S. P. A.,* January, 1900, p. 35.

[5] Duffy, pp. 12, 13; *Proceedings, N. B. of O. P.,* 1895, p. 21; 1899, pp. 7, 15; *Report of President,* 1906, p. 12.

[6] *Proceedings,* 1894, p. 7.

[7] *Ibid.,* 1898, pp. 5, 9-10.

In 1899, with the eastern workers in the Brotherhood, the convention decided to try again for a national
scale. The fact that the chance of securing a uniform
list rested on the acceptance of the average of the existing prices throughout the country was not ignored. The
convention not only accepted this basis but voted also
to ask the manufacturers to agree in advance to accept
it, regardless of whether this would increase or decrease
the payrolls of their individual firms; in return the
Brotherhood would agree to " see it is enforced and carried out as far as we are concerned whether it will be an
increase or decrease." Nor was this course of action
adopted without warning that it would mean trouble
with the eastern operatives. The jiggermen and dishmaker's local of Trenton had notified the convention
that it had unanimously instructed its delegates to
oppose the uniform list.[8]

It is doubtful, however, that the Brotherhood leaders realized how strong the opposition to a scale based
on " averaging prices " would prove. What made the
opposition difficult to subdue was its concentrated sectional character. There were some complaints in the
West, to be sure, from individuals here and there who
felt that they had been sacrificed, but on the whole the
West gained by the process of national averaging.[9] It
was the East that was called upon for most of the
decreases.

How important the decreases in the East were, as
compared with the gains, it is impossible to state
exactly.[10] In some branches and on some items the new

---

[8] *Ibid.*, 1899, pp. 9, 15, 17, 18, 19, 26, 41-42.

[9] Mr. Wells said in the 1924 conference that the payroll of every
pottery in East Liverpool was increased by the adoption of the
list.

[10] Price lists for the branches affected are not available for comparison with the uniform list of 1900.

list was to the advantage of the workers.[11] Most of the
complaints of reductions came from the jiggermen's
and kilnmen's locals. The prices for jiggering flat ware
in the so-called "1890 list" in Trenton were higher
than those in the "uniform list"; the difference was as
great as fifteen per cent on some items and on all plates
and saucers it averaged nine per cent. It is true that
many jiggermen were not receiving the "1890 list"
but those who had the "good jobs" were far better
off than they would be under the "uniform list." [12]
There was the further difficulty that the conditions and
facilities were, in general, not as good in the East as in
the West. The 1900 agreement provided, to be sure,
that "where unusual conditions or inconveniences exist
beyond the average the jiggerman shall receive a percentage extra," but the jiggermen, led by those who
clearly stood to lose if the uniform list were accepted,
were in no mood to risk the tedious and uncertain process of exacting allowances for inferior conditions or
facilities. The dissatisfaction of the kilnmen was in
large part due to the fact that the uniform list extended
to the East a system of measurement to which the eastern kilnmen were unaccustomed—the cubic foot system. The attempt to apply a strange system of payment
in potteries in which the conditions were inferior to

[11] *Proceedings,* 1900, p. 10; 1903, p. 10; MS. *Report of Trenton
Conference,* October 28, 1904. All of the branches in the East except
the jiggermen and dishmakers were brought to favor the uniform
list before it was extended to the East, and some were clamoring
for it. There had been no important changes in the list meanwhile,
except "free clay" for the clay workers. Yet when the list was put
into effect in Trenton in November, 1904, a number of branches
gained increases in wages by it. *Report of President,* 1905, pp.
21-24, 25-26.

[12] *Proceedings,* 1903, pp. 10, 17; 1907, p. 46; MS. *Report of Trenton
Conference,* October 28, 1904; *Report of President,* 1905, pp. 24-25

those prevailing in the West was bound to create apprehension and antagonism. As a matter of fact when the uniform scale was applied to the Trenton kilns in 1904, there was a slight increase in the number of days paid, on the average, for both bisque and glost kilns, although there was a reduction of two days on five kilns in one plant. The net increase in wages was nearly five per cent.[13] There had been no change in the uniform scale for kilnplacing meanwhile except a minor one which applied only to bisque kilns.

For a time the Brotherhood had to bow to circumstances and abandon the uniform list in the East. But it had not given up the policy of one uniform list. It was committed not only to a uniform list in the East— for prices were far from uniform in the same branches even in Trenton [14]—but to a national uniform list. President Hughes expressly repudiated, in his report to the 1903 convention,[15] the compromise policy suggested by some that there should be two distinct scales [16]—one for the East and one for the West.

We are of the opinion that there should be a price set for doing a certain kind of work according to regular methods and under ordinary conditions. This is to be our price regardless of the section. . . . . if it is clearly shown that the methods employed and the conditions and the facilities prevailing are not up to the ordinary, then there should be extras so as to enable the men to earn equally as good wages as are earned under ordinary conditions.

The convention applied this principle to the case of the Trenton jiggermen in a resolution that they work under their existing prices until they were given the same facilities as prevailed in the West or " just compensation for lack of facilities "; the uniform list was then

---

13 *Ibid.*, p. 21.
14 *Proceedings*, 1903, pp. 8, 10, 17, 18, 112, 122; 1904, pp. 60, 61.
15 *Ibid.*, 1903, p. 10.
16 *Ibid.*, pp. 117-118.

to be enforced in the East. In the end the jiggermen had to take the uniform list without western facilities and leave the question of "just compensation for lack of facilities" for later adjustment.

The determination with which the Brotherhood leaders strove for national uniformity in working prices in these years shows that uniformity was regarded as something closely akin to a principle.[17] It was the elimination of competition among workmen in the matter of wages pushed to its logical conclusion. They advocated uniformity frankly as the best means of protecting the existing wage level and advancing it. But they also undoubtedly believed that uniformity in piece rates for the same work was demanded by justice not only to the workmen but to the employers as well. Repeatedly during the movement prior to 1900 for a uniform scale the point was made that non-uniform prices were unfair to the employers who paid the higher prices, as well as to the workers who received the lower ones.[18] Meanwhile the connection between uniform piece prices and uniform selling prices and the elimination of competition in both had been discussed in 1897, as has been pointed out, and the union had been favorable to such a program, although unwilling to have either the increase in wages or uniformity in working prices made contingent upon the elimination of competition in selling prices. Undoubtedly the union belief that a uniform list would be a good thing for the manufacturers grew out of a belief that it would make it easier for the manufacturers to pay good wages; nevertheless the opera-

---

[17] One of the union officers told the 1899 convention that they could not be real unionists without a uniform list. *Proceedings,* p. 15.

[18] For example, *ibid.,* 1895, pp. 6, 37; 1899, p. 15.

tives seem to have been sincere in their expressions of a desire to treat all manufacturers alike.

From the side of controlling competition between workmen, the more important aspect of the movement for a uniform list in the beginning was the need for a standard list in each pottery to which all members of the respective branch should conform. The elimination of non-uniformity in working prices between men in the same branch in the same shop logically comes before the elimination of competition between men in different shops, yet it was not secured first. Before 1900 competition between men in the same shop was a frequent source of complaint.[19]

As to differences in working prices between plants, these were regarded as not only unfair to the workers receiving the lower prices but also as exerting a pressure toward the reduction of the higher prices. It was assumed that the manufacturer paying the higher prices would be impelled to reduce them in order to put himself on the same level with the competitor paying the lowest prices.[20] The competitive danger came out most clearly in the East vs. West controversy. In the Knights of Labor days the eastern manufacturers had complained of the competition they were suffering from the western manufacturers through the lower wage rates in the West.[21] Again, in 1897 the eastern manufacturers used the contention that western prices were lower as an argument for not restoring the full twelve and a half per cent.[22] Then, after 1900, when the West was working on the uniform list, the western manufacturers complained of the lower prices paid by their

[19] Ibid., 1894, p. 7; 1895, pp. 6, 7-8; 1899, pp. 42-43.
[20] Ibid.; Report of President, 1905, pp. 5-6.
[21] U. S. Ind. Comm., XIV, 654.
[22] Proceedings, 1898, p. 6.

eastern competitors in some branches.[23] President
Duffy, referring in 1905 to the regrettable fact that
some of the Trenton operatives had been forced to
accept reductions in order to establish a national uniform list, argued that even those who had suffered
reductions in the prices they were then receiving would
ultimately benefit. Their higher prices had not been
safe before; " this menacing condition and downward
tendency " had now been removed and a solid foundation substituted on which better things could be built.[24]

ADDITIONS TO THE UNIFORM SCALE (1901-1919)

Not all of the branches were included in the uniform scale of 1900. The Brotherhood was strongly in
favor of making uniform scales for the other branches
as soon as they could be sufficiently organized to induce
the manufacturers to deal with the Brotherhood for
them.[25] Unfortunately for the rapid success of this
program the lack of uniform scales hampered the work
of organization and at times the Brotherhood found
itself in the difficult position of trying to secure a
uniform list for a branch before it was well organized in
order to use the list as an aid to further organization.[26]

In 1901 uniform lists were added for the clay- and
slip-makers, kilndrawers and printers. The first two

[23] *Ibid.*, 1904, p. 9.

[24] *Report of President,* 1905, pp. 5-6. The officers were confirmed
in their belief in the efficacy of uniformity by the experience of other
piece-working unions which had gone from sectional to national
uniform price lists. *Proceedings,* 1900, p. 19.

[25] *Proceedings, N. B. of O. P.,* 1900, pp. 57, 63, 65-66; 1901, p. 9;
1902, pp. 7, 15, 64, 87-89, 93, 100.

[26] For example, *Proceedings,* 1905, p. 19; *Report of President,* 1907,
p. 10; *Proceedings,* 1907, p. 58.

branches have since left the organization in East Liverpool and the Brotherhood has ceased to deal for them; the printing scale became obsolete because of the supplanting of the printing by the decalcomania process in the semi-porcelain shops. All three lists were made on the basis of the " average of wages and conditions then in vogue." [27] In 1908 a brief uniform list was made for casting. The initiative in this was taken by the employers. It will be discussed below in connection with the introduction of the casting process. A uniform scale was added for warehousemen in 1911 and one for warehousewomen in 1913. In neither case does the scale apply to the East, where these workers have never been organized.[28]

As early as 1907 the Brotherhood began a movement for a general uniform list for china.[29] The action proved premature. In 1915 it was again agreed, at the Brotherhood's request, that joint committees attempt to draw up uniform china lists. Little was done jointly before May, 1917. Then the union officers forced action by coming to East Liverpool with a scale which they had drawn up and asking for a conference with the manufacturers. Before the latter would proceed, they asked and got from the union representatives an

[27] Duffy, p. 40.

[28] The warehousewomen's scale does not include dressing flat ware (glost) which is ordinarily done under local piece work prices and under the contract system. The warehousewomen's scale is not now of much practical importance outside East Liverpool. The work is not done according to the same standards of output and the scale is therefore not generally applied. It is not included in the china agreement.

[29] *Proceedings,* 1907, p. 46. The 1900 agreement contained separate lists for the main waremaking operations in china—jiggering, handling, throwing and turning. The rates on other operations, notably kilnwork, were left as they stood in the several potteries.

agreement setting forth the " principles " on which the uniform scale was to be constructed.

The manufacturers by this time had come to fear that requests from the men for the establishment of uniform lists for work not already so covered meant attempts to raise the general average of the prices above those already paid. Although the labor committee did not " suspect that any such intent or desire was in the minds of the Brotherhood's representatives " in this instance, it wanted it clearly understood that the uniform scale was to be " based upon a fair interpretation of the base list prices generally prevailing in the china shops today." As an example of " fair interpretation " it was stated that " in the main where it is found that a large preponderance of a certain item is made at a certain price, that price shall govern even if comparatively unimportant quantities of the same item are made at a higher or lower price." In other words, the simple average of the prices in different shops was not to be taken regardless of the quantities made in the respective shops. With that understood, the manufacturers were ready to " deal in a reasonable and liberal manner with the prices of items that show a large variation in the present scales." The " principles " having been laid down, the actual details of the scale were left to sub-committees of the respective branches to work out.[30]

The task of the committees, as was to be expected, proved difficult and trying. But they did accomplish the establishment of uniform scales for jiggering, dishmaking, pressing, turning, kilnplacing and packing, in 1918, and in June, 1919, in casting.[31] In mouldmaking

[30] *Report of President,* 1917, pp. 25-27.
[31] *Proceedings,* U. S. P. A., 1919, pp. 26, 33-62; January, 1920, pp. 36-40; *Report of Executive Board,* 1918, pp. 31-32.

and in saggermaking the same base price lists are used
as in semi-porcelain. No price per kilnman's day was
fixed for dipping because of the general prevalence of
the day-wage system in china.[32] Some conditions and
prices in other branches, too, were omitted from the
lists "because conditions were so peculiar and so
extraordinarily different from other plants."[33] The
readjustment of prices in the establishment of such
uniformity as was achieved was, on the whole, highly
satisfactory to the union. Increases were obtained for
many of the workers, "ranging from ten to thirty per
cent."[34]

NON-UNIFORMITIES UNDER UNIFORM PRICES

It is clear from what has been said above[35] that the
establishment of geographical standardization of working prices in the several branches has not brought absolute uniformity in wages for service rendered or in the
labor cost of the various operations. The lack of uniformity referred to here is not the continuance of non-
uniform prices for unlisted articles, or settlements that
leave some existing non-uniformities in price untouched
for the sake of peace,[36] but non-uniformity due to differences in facilities or other conditions. To some
extent such differences are offset by " extras " above the
prices listed in the scale, and to that extent earning

[32] When the china agreement was published as a whole for the first
time, the warehousemen's scale which applies to semi-porcelain in the
West, was not included. However, the Brotherhood officers maintain
that the warehousemen's scale is binding in the china plants in the
West, also, and this position was not contested when President Duffy
stated it in the 1928 conference.

[33] MS. *Report of Conference,* 1921.

[34] *Report of Executive Board,* 1918, p. 32; *Proceedings,* 1918, p. 79.

[35] See ch. vi.; see also, below, pp. 220, 224-225.

[36] For example, the settlement in 1926 as to the price of tulip cups.
See below, pp. 341-342.

opportunities are made more nearly uniform, although labor cost is made to vary. There are, however, many differences in facilities between plants in which the prices paid for the work in question are the same with resultant differences in earnings for equal effort and skill expended by the men. And such differences seem to be increasing.

When the original scale was adopted in 1900 it was realized that some differences in conditions would have to be allowed to remain. It would have been impracticable to prescribe uniform conditions as a prerequisite to the establishment of price lists, even if the members of the joint committee had been able to reach agreement on the conditions to be made standard. The list was therefore adopted with the understanding that conditions not specifically covered in the scale were to remain as they were in each plant, unless and until they were changed by agreement. It was stipulated here and there in the scale itself that abnormally difficult conditions for the men were to be compensated for by extras, but room was left for considerable diversity within the conditions to which the list prices applied. The "established conditions" rule then adopted was a recognition of non-uniformity in conditions with uniformity in prices. Other non-uniformities in conditions crept in during the years that followed. Whether by "local settlements" which were not reported to the respective national officers, or tacit acquiescence, new conditions or practices were allowed in some plants without extras which were refused in others.

Another source of non-uniformity is the improvement of physical conditions and facilities in plants.[37]

[37] This was noted by Chairman Wells as early as 1907. *Proceedings, U. S. P. A.,* 1907, p. 30; also, 1909, p. 25.

14

Except for the elimination of an unusually difficult condition for which an extra is required by the scale, the manufacturer with a new or remodelled plant in which things are more conveniently arranged for the men, carries reduced, etc., receives no reduction in the wage rate. Uniformity does not mean that if more favorable conditions are introduced than those in effect when the scale was adopted there shall be a corresponding reduction in the rate; there is no reciprocal of the rule that extra shall be paid if the conditions are made less favorable. And, generally, the employers have not insisted upon this.

The non-uniformities stand out most clearly, of course, in a comparison of the East with the West. The extension of the uniform list to the East in 1904 did not result in the bringing of eastern facilities and other conditions up to those generally prevailing in the West. It was understood in 1904 that some readjustments would have to be made in the eastern potteries or extras added to the scale prices and it was agreed that all such questions that could not be settled in the shops should be referred to the newly established eastern standing committee, an agreement which started this committee in life with many difficult questions to handle. They were disposed of somehow,[38] but the conclusion left many actual differences beyond the boundary of extra compensation. And the gap has been widened rather than narrowed since that time. The East has been behind the West in introducing those improvements in facilities which have increased earning opportunities under stationary base rates. There has been very little building of new plants or remodelling of old ones in the East in the semi-porcelain division. That earnings

[38] *Report of President,* 1905, pp. 20-26.

are lower on the whole in the East in the organized branches is unquestioned.[39] The eastern employers declare that their men do not work as hard as the western operatives. The operatives, on the other hand, ascribe the difference in earnings to poorer facilities and, to some extent, to more careful workmanship.

In the West the employers have been saying for many years that the uniform scale has been a disappointment in that, instead of securing uniformity of earnings between plant and plant, it has compelled the payment of higher wages to men in the better plants for no greater effort on their part and caused " discontent among men who are fairly paid, but hold less favored jobs." [40] The Brotherhood representatives have not denied that there are considerable differences in earnings for equal skill and effort expended as between one pottery and another; on the contrary, the union conferees have frequently made the point in discussing figures for earnings submitted by the manufacturers in the conferences that these are taken from plants with superior facilities. But the union has never been willing to give up uniformity of wage rates. To get uniformity in earnings by reducing the rates paid by the employers with the better facilities would, it contends, make it harder for the other manufacturers to compete and so produce pressure for like wage reductions in the plants of the latter. Mr. Wells complains, however, that the men do not in practice show any consideration for the employers with the inferior facilities.

[39] The tables of average earnings by occupation, sex and geographical group (in 1925) given in *Bulletin No. 412, United States Bureau of Labor Statistics,* pp. 33-41, show lower average earnings per hour in the Trenton semi-porcelain shops than in the West for most of the organized branches.

[40] *Proceedings, U. S. P. A.,* 1915, p. 43; also *Proceedings, U. S. P. A.,* 1911, p. 44; *Report of Executive Board,* 1918, pp. 12-13; 1925, p. 28.

He charges that when business is brisk the men in the plants with the poorer facilities insist on extras, usually against the letter, if not the spirit, of the agreement, without regard to the effect of the extra payment on the competitive position of these employers. He has also expressed impatience with union proposals to compel the other manufacturers to install improved facilities which have already been introduced by some. Thus non-uniformity in earning opportunities remains an outstanding feature of the uniform scale. Indeed, uniformity in piece rates must embody that feature so long as improvements in facilities are introduced—as it seems likely that they will continue to be introduced—unevenly from plant to plant.

FAILURES TO EXTEND UNIFORMITY OF PRICES

The employers have in recent years been cold toward proposals to extend uniformity to branches not now included in the scale. One reason which they give is that the men's notion of establishing a uniform list is that it is a way of increasing the total wages paid for making the ware in question. This attitude, they charge, makes it almost impossible to secure uniformity on a fair basis, even when the question is merely one of bringing into uniformity the prices of unlisted articles in a branch which already has a uniform list. More important, because fundamental, is an assumption on the part of the employers that conditions in the uncovered branches cannot be made uniform and to adopt uniform lists for them would mean merely an extension of the sphere of uniformity in prices for non-uniform performance. Thus the union proposals have been practically barren of results in late years. This applies both to those for extending uniformity to other branches and those for fixing uniform prices for unlisted articles in branches already included in the uniform scale.[41] With the employers constantly harping upon the impracticability of attempting to set uniform prices in the face of diversity in conditions and with the difficulty experienced in securing agreement upon the relative weight to be given the different prices paid in the various shops, there has been no important extension of uniformity, despite the appointment of committee after committee, since the last of the china lists was adopted in June, 1919.

The outstanding sphere of Brotherhood endeavor in this direction in recent years—and of Association reluctance—is lining. Since the organization of the local union of liners in East Liverpool in 1920 no conference year has passed without a uniform list proposal of some kind from the Brotherhood for this branch.

In the 1921 conference the manufacturers agreed that a joint committee should be appointed to try to work out a uniform list for lining in semi-porcelain but frankly expressed the view that nothing would come of it—the conditions and styles of work in the various shops were too diverse to permit the making of a uniform scale that would be fair. It is significant that one of the non-uniform factors emphasized by Chairman Wells as affecting earning opportunities was the size of the orders. His point was that men working on large orders had better earning opportunities than men working on small orders at the same prices. The liners would not agree that the size of the order was a factor that should affect the price; they maintained that every manufacturer should pay the same price for the same work on the article. In this the liners were contending for a rule that had been followed in fixing uniform piece

[41] For example, *ibid.*, 1926, pp. 15-17.

prices in the other branches. If the size of the order was to be recognized now as a " condition " for which a difference in price should be allowed in all branches, uniformity in prices between large and small plants would be greatly restricted in scope. This has not been proposed by the manufacturers for branches already under the uniform scale but it has its influence, no doubt, in the opposition of some of the manufacturers to extending uniformity to decorating prices.

Another barrier to achieving uniformity, even for the West, is the fact that prices are much lower in " outside " towns than in East Liverpool. As the outside manufacturers will not agree to pay East Liverpool prices, any uniform list that the Association could accept for the West as a whole, Mr. Wells declared in the 1924 conference, would reduce the lining prices in every pottery in East Liverpool.

In 1926 when the union proposed that a uniform list be made for the East Liverpool district alone, it found the East Liverpool manufacturers opposed to this also. The publication of the report of the United States Bureau of Labor Statistics on wages in the pottery industry had apparently brought home more strongly to the East Liverpool manufacturers the differences between the hourly earnings of liners in East Liverpool and those in the " outside " towns in the West, as well as the much greater proportion of women employed in the latter.[42] The East Liverpool manufacturers were convinced it would be " inconsistent " to establish an official price list for the district which would bind them to pay higher prices than were paid in the potteries of other members of the Association. Certainly it would be embarrassing to the Association to have such a scale

[42] *Bulletin No. 412*, p. 39.

embodied in the national agreement with the consequent obligation upon the Association to compel an East
Liverpool member to pay it.

One disadvantage arising from the absence of a uniform scale was the lack of an accepted outside standard
for the settlement of price disputes in the individual
shops and the consequent lack of a competent committee to which these could be sent for decision. The
employers recognized the undesirability of this situation [43] and although unwilling to attempt the uniform
scale solution, they now suggested that an " unofficial "
standing committee be set up to handle decorating disputes for the East Liverpool district, the dispute to be
settled by the committee in each case on the basis of
the prices and conditions obtaining in the particular
shop from which the dispute came. This would not give
uniformity in prices, of course, but it would help to take
care of a situation with which the existing machinery
was unable to cope. The employers wanted the committee to be " unofficial " not because its decisions would
not be binding—in any cases referred to it they were to
be as binding as those of the " official " standing committees—but because they were unwilling to have the
two national organizations made parties " officially " to
the fixing of prices for East Liverpool shops which
would be higher than those paid in the outside shops.
Nor were they willing to have the committee settle disputed prices for the outside shops. The East Liverpool
manufacturers would not agree that even an " unofficial " committee should have authority to fix prices on
a lower level for an outside shop than for East
Liverpool.

The union accepted this proposal. Although less than
it wanted, the conference committee considered it a step

[43] *Proceedings, U. S. P. A.,* 1924, pp. 78-79.

in advance. It did not, of course, satisfy the Brotherhood members. The 1928 convention again asked for a uniform scale for lining in the East Liverpool district, and, going beyond the union's 1926 proposal, asked that the rates for decorating in the outside shops be " governed by the prices in the East Liverpool district." In the conference the union representatives seemed more concerned over the recognition of the right of the decorators in the outside shops to the protection of joint procedure in their price disputes than over uniformity in prices. The only outcome was an agreement that an " unofficial " joint committee should be set up for Sebring, similar to that in East Liverpool, with the same understanding that each dispute was to be settled on the basis of the prices and conditions existing in the particular shop.[44] All thought of using this as means of attempting to fix uniform prices was expressly ruled out by the manufacturers and disclaimed by the Brotherhood.

In the 1928 conference the union also asked that committees be appointed to establish a uniform scale for lining in china. It had experienced considerable trouble over china lining prices since the last conference.[45] The union also volunteered to include the prices paid by the non-union shops in Syracuse in the average to be followed in fixing the proposed scale. The officers did not think this would lower the average and they wanted to put an end to the contention that they were compelling the union manufacturers to pay higher rates than their non-union competitors. To the objection that conditions were not uniform between plants, the union side, while agreeing that prices could not be made uni-

[44] This committee was not set up until 1930. *Report of Executive Board,* 1930, p. 88.

[45] *Ibid.,* 1928, pp. 20-21, 23-25, 45-46.

form unless conditions were also, replied that conditions could be brought into uniformity if a determined effort were made to do so. Chairman W. E. Wells' position was that the labor committee could not bind the china manufacturers to a uniform scale proposal without their consent; the Brotherhood would have to take it up with the china manufacturers. The matter was left there, the Brotherhood officers declaring that they would ask the china manufacturers for a conference for this purpose.[46]

No visible progress has been made toward uniformity in prices for decalcomania and similar work, as distinct from lining. It is in Trenton that the lack of a uniform scale for decalcomania work has caused most trouble. The contention of the manufacturers that their western competitors have an advantage over them in prices has to be faced " every time a new pattern is introduced in the decalcomania department," according to Vice-President Cartlidge.[47] The conventions have urged that a special effort be made to organize the decalcomania workers both East and West, that data on prices and conditions be gathered, and that " every possible effort be made to obtain a uniform scale for decalcomania workers for East and West." [48] It is clearly recognized that some better provision must be made for the fixing of prices in this branch if the Brotherhood is to retain even the membership it now has among these workers, but the situation is not at all promising for the establishment of a national scale.

[46] The conference did not result in the adoption of a uniform list. *Report of Executive Board,* 1929, pp. 21-35; *Proceedings, N. B. of O. P.,* 1929, p. 25.

[47] *Report of Executive Board,* 1928, p. 46.

[48] *Proceedings,* 1927, p. 15; 1928, p. 41.

CHAPTER VIII

ISSUES AS TO WAGE CHANGES

BRANCH WAGE ISSUES

The structure of the wage scale, as has been pointed out above, is such that particular wage issues, as distinct from the question of a general increase or decrease throughout all branches, have inevitably played a large part in the wage negotiations between the Brotherhood and the Association. Branch wage issues have taken up far more time in conference than proposals for a horizontal increase or decrease. The question of a general percentage change has not been pushed prior to 1931 except in the period 1916-1922, whereas the union has presented particular proposals for increases in wages, directly or indirectly, in every conference year since 1900 except 1915.[1] Demands for general percentage increases throughout all branches, on the other hand, were made only in the period 1916-1920 and—in an attempt to recover some of the ground lost in 1921—in 1922. Even in those years the demands for general increases were accompanied by demands for particular increases.

In the first few years after the adoption of the uniform scale the Brotherhood followed the policy of concentrating on " the rectification of a number of evils in different branches of the trade " and on " levelling up "

---

[1] The manufacturers have never submitted a formal proposal for a reduction in a specific piece rate and only once prior to 1930 did they ask for a reduction in a time rate—and that was an over-time rate.

instead of trying to secure a general horizontal advance.[2] This policy was adhered to down to 1917 in spite of proposals from local unions that a general advance be insisted upon because of the increasing cost of living. The facts that earnings could be increased materially by particular piece-rate increases, or by concessions in the field of conditions, and that most branches believed themselves suffering under "inequalities" were important factors in the decision. After 1922, when the cost of living argument for a general horizontal increase was no longer effective, the union reverted to the traditional strategy.

The attitude of the employers, too, has encouraged the union in the policy of concentrating in normal times on particular demands. Long before national collective bargaining was established, the general reductions enforced by the employers were unequal in percentage as between the various branches. Even in the period from 1916 to 1920 the manufacturers favored larger percentage increases for some branches than for others; the increases given were in fact far from uniform throughout the branches. In ordinary times the manufacturers showed such strong opposition to a general increase that the union was practically forced back on branch demands which could be advanced on particular grounds. Indeed, the manufacturers took the position that the plan of working under a joint agreement assumed that, apart from "leveling up the low spots" when possible, an agreement once made should be renewed unchanged unless and until there were some pronounced change in market conditions or the cost of living.[3]

[2] *Proceedings*, 1901, p. 8; 1903, pp. 90, 103-104; 110.
[3] MS. *Report of Conference*, August, 1922.

It is not meant to imply, of course, that the arguments on the general wage level and the arguments on particular proposals have always been kept distinct in the conferences. The particular requests have in some conference years amounted, in combination, to a request for a considerable percentage advance in the total payroll and the employers have been inclined to treat them as tantamount to requests for a general, although not a horizontal, increase in wages and argue against them in bulk on such general grounds as the inability of the industry to pay and the relation of the trend of living costs to the movement of earnings, without neglecting, of course, to reply to the particular arguments. Important branch concessions have also been counted by the employers as part of a general upward advance. Nevertheless it will be advantageous to treat the two types of issues—branch issues and general issues—separately and to take up the former first.

Changes in Base Prices.—Requests for increases in base prices in the waremaking lists, apart from general equalization proposals, have played a very large part in the wage negotiations. These requests have by no means been confined to propositions on isolated individual items. Propositions of the latter type have occasionally been made, to be sure, and a few of them have been granted. Requests which have occupied more attention—and have gained much more for the men in several of the branches—are those for increases on particular types of " edges " or on abnormal " weights," running through many classes of articles, and those for increases on groups of staple articles which loom large in the actual production of the branch in question. These propositions have been supported by the argument that the edges or weights or brackets in question were underpaid but they have been usually regarded by the employers as similar in effect to requests for a percentage increase in the whole list of the branch in question. The latter form of wage increase has also been used, but only rarely.

The jiggering branch ranks first in requests for increases in particular items endorsed by the Brotherhood and it has, in fact, secured more increases in base prices than any other branch. The strategic position of the branch—it has long been the most important of the clay-shop branches from a production standpoint—and the difficulties experienced by the journeymen with their help have won for the jiggermen a relatively large measure of consideration from both the conventions and the employers in the way of increases in base prices, as well as other concessions that do not appear in either the base prices or the plussage. If the price list of September, 1920 be compared with that of 1900, the number of items which show an increase will not appear to be large, nevertheless these items play a far more important part in the ordinary day's work of the jiggerman than those which have not been increased. It should be noted, too, that the plussage was calculated on the new base prices. For example, the jiggerman received eighty-six per cent more in 1928 for making ordinary plain saucers than in 1900—twenty-seven and three-tenths per cent more in the base price and forty-six per cent on the new base price.[4]

In the pressing branch the campaign for increases in base prices was openly directed more toward bringing up the level of earnings in the branch than toward

---

[4] The jiggermen's helpers, who are paid by the jiggermen, were also granted an aggregate bonus of 21½ per cent on the output of the jigger at base prices. Thus the total percentage increase granted this branch was over 100 per cent. For the change in net earnings from 1913 to 1925 see Appendix.

correcting specific " inequalities." Earnings in this
branch were admittedly low in comparison with the
other waremaking branches. Many of the better paying articles on the pressing list had already gone over
to the jigger when the uniform list was adopted. And
the pressers were not enabled to increase their earnings
through the introduction of time-saving methods or
improvements in facilities, as the years went on, as
were some of the other branches. The changes which
were made ran more to transferring the articles from
the pressing bench to jiggering, or to casting, than to
improvements in the methods of or facilities for pressing. In spite of repeated requests for advances in the
pressing list, the only increase received by the pressers before the war period was in one item, in 1907.
However, in the plussages given from 1916 to 1920, the
pressers received the highest percentage.[5] In addition
a few base prices were increased. The number of men
now pressing is relatively small.

The dishmakers were given an increase in base
prices in 1919, in order to raise the comparative level
of earnings for the branch as a whole. The increase
was ten per cent, but instead of a uniform advance on
all items, the increase was distributed unevenly, in the
case of oval dishes and bakers, over the various sizes.
The increases in the form of plussages were the same

[5] Their percentage at the peak, September, 1920, stood at 75; after
the 1921-1922 changes it was 51. Requests for increases on items in
the " sticking-up " list were practically merged with those for pressing down through 1920. The same plussages were given for sticking-
up as for pressing. In 1924 the union asked for a 10 per cent increase on the predominant items on the sticking-up list and obtained
it. This is the only request for an increase granted by the employers
since 1922 and it was granted without argument; it had long been
recognized that the work was relatively poorly remunerated, and it
concerned only a very small number of men.

for the dishmakers as for the jiggermen, except on " hotel " weight, which is heavier than ordinary weight; on this the plussage was greater. The base price for hotel weight was also increased on one item. In 1924 the union presented a demand for an increase of twenty per cent in the base prices of all dishes and bakers. This is an example of a very rare form of branch wage request—that for a percentage increase for the branch, as distinct from a drive on particular items. The dishmakers based their request squarely on the contention that their branch was underpaid. They had not enjoyed the improvements in facilities for increasing output that other branches had and they were falling behind in their earnings as compared with other branches. They were in competition with the jiggermen for help and had to pay wages accordingly, but were not receiving as high prices as the jiggermen. Mr. Wells admitted that the dishmakers deserved more consideration than some other branches but the time had passed for wage increases and the dishmakers got nothing.

The other clay-shop branches received relatively little in the way of base price advances in the 1916-1920 period and have received none since, except an increase in the casting price on one size of jugs which was granted in 1922 without argument.[6] The plussage granted the casters, turners, and handlers was also lower than that granted the jiggermen, as the employers have maintained that these branches were relatively better paid than the jiggermen. They have been especially opposed to granting increases in casting. They hold that the casters' prices, especially those fixed in the settlement of 1914,[7] have allowed them to make high

[6] The casters had declared that the price specified in the published list was a " printed mistake." *Proceedings, N. B. of O. P.,* 1922, p. 38.

[7] See below, pp. 257-258.

wages as compared with other branches and that there is no branch which has less of a case for an advancement in the level of earnings.[8]

In the packing list, as pointed out above, there has been a large degree of equalization. In saggermaking the list has undergone no revision except by way of the addition of a few items. The saggermaker's plussage kept pace from August, 1918, with that received by the casters, turners and handlers. In mouldmaking, no changes in items on the list have been made, and down to 1928 none was asked.[9] On the list as a whole, however, the mouldmakers were trying for years to recover a ten per cent reduction conceded in 1909 as a part of the agreement for the abolition of the contract system. The mouldmakers did not recover the " net list " until the voluntary increase of May, 1917. The plussages subsequently obtained were on the net list, consequently the mouldmakers' plussage at the peak was lower than that of any of the other branches—forty-five per cent. The 1921 and 1922 changes left them with a plussage of twenty-five per cent on the net list, a real advance over 1915 prices of thirty-nine per cent.[10] Mr. Wells declared in the 1921 conference that mouldmaking is the best paid branch in the industry on the basis of the comparative skill required.

Bonuses to Helpers.—During the war years the employers instituted the practice of paying bonuses to helpers employed by the jiggermen and the dishmakers. These bonuses have now come to be assumed as a

---

[8] For the relative hourly earnings, see Appendix.

[9] In 1928 the convention adopted a price demand for moulds for jiggered mugs but this was dropped without argument in the conference.

[10] The china plussage on the same list was 35 per cent, as the plussages were given in china on the net list from the beginning.

permanent part of the wage-rate structure. Whether the granting of the bonuses be regarded as increases in the journeymen's rates, in substance, or as merely a substitute for such increases, the practical effect on the earnings of the journeymen and the cost to the employers is the same. Inasmuch as the helpers are paid by the journeymen it might be expected that the manufacturers would refuse to be drawn into the help difficulties of the journeymen. But even before the war period the employers had busied themselves with the jiggermen's relations with their help.[11] With the increased demand for labor in 1916, the situation became much worse. It was the primary reason for the grant of a " voluntary " increase to the jiggermen, alone among the ware-making branches, in July, 1916.

The advance in base prices in July, 1916, and the second increase in November, 1916, in the form of a plussage of ten per cent, were given to the jiggermen without any stipulation as to what part of the increase should be paid to the helpers. In the third voluntary increase, that of May, 1917, the employers raised the jiggermen's plussage from ten per cent to fifteen per cent with the understanding that the additional five per cent in the plussage was to be given by the jiggermen to their mould-runners, batters-out and finishers. It was at this time that the employers introduced the bonus from the firm to the mould-runners and batters-out as an incentive to regular attendance. A bonus of 25 cents a day was offered to each mould-runner or batter-out who worked not less than eleven full days a " pay "—a period of two weeks. In August, 1918, the employers substituted a percentage bonus on output for the *per diem* bonus and increased the amount consider-

---

[11] See above, pp. 177-178.

15

ably thereby. It was agreed that the jiggermen should " continue to pay the batter-out and mould-runner the present wage only " so that the wages paid by the jiggermen from their own rates should be pegged where they then were and the increase in earnings of the help be derived from the bonus paid by the firm.[12] Mr. Wells expressed the opinion in the final 1922 conference that the bonus to the batter-out and mould-runner had come nearer solving " the boy difficulty " in the jiggering branch than anything else ever tried.[13] The bonus plan was extended to the dishmaking branch, to a limited degree, in September, 1918. A bonus of fifteen per cent, calculated on base prices, was given the dishmakers' helper on the larger sizes. The dishmakers had complained that they could not afford to pay enough to secure helpers on the larger sizes because these sizes were relatively underpaid.[14]

Kilnplacing and Dipping.—One of the union demands submitted to arbitration in 1903 was that the kilnman's day in bisque kilns be reduced from 212 cubic feet to 200, for the same wage per " day." This had been advocated in the convention as necessary to equalize matters between the bisque and glost kilns; the bisque day had been put too high, it was contended, in the 1900 agreement.[15] The arbitrators decided the issue in the negative. It was not until August, 1918, that the

---

[12] It was first put at 10 per cent, raised to 12½ per cent by September, 1920, reduced to 10 per cent in 1921 and came to rest at 10¾ per cent in 1922.

[13] See also *Report of Executive Board,* 1927, p. 19.

[14] This bonus reached 19 per cent in September, 1920, returned to 15 per cent in 1921, and has stood at 16 per cent since 1922. It applies only to the " bench." On the dish-jigger the mould-runner and batter-out bonus applies.

[15] *Proceedings,* 1903, p. 126.

day in bisque was reduced to 200 feet, as a part of a general increase in wages.

In the general wage increases from 1916 to 1921 the form of a " plussage " on a base rate was not followed in kilnplacing. The wage per kilnman's day was increased outright. By September, 1920, it had risen from $2.00, where it had stood from 1900 to 1916, to $3.52, an increase of seventy-six per cent—exclusive of the reduction in the cubic feet in the kilnman's day in bisque. The rate for the bench boss rose from $2.50 to $4.20. The 1921 reductions brought the rates down to $2.90 and $3.50 respectively.[16]

In 1922 the Brotherhood asked for an increase in the cubic foot rate. The increase was sought through the familiar medium of increasing both the wage and the cubic feet in order to establish a new " actual " day, but increasing the former in greater percentage than the latter; the figures proposed would have increased wages five per cent on bisque kilns and seven and four-tenths per cent on glost, exclusive of the general percentage advance asked for all branches. It was on the increase for the glost kilnmen that the union concentrated in the conference. Emphasis was put upon the point that the number of cubic feet in glost had remained the same since 1900, despite the practical disappearance of large hollow ware and the great increase in pinned ware, whereas the bisque kilnmen had been granted a reduction in the cubic feet in their day and had been relieved from carrying green saggers to the kilns as well.[17] The employers' reply was along the usual lines. They asked if the union wished to penalize

[16] After the adoption of the uniform scale for kilnplacing in china, in 1918, the rate per kilnman's day was kept the same as in semi-porcelain.

[17] See below, pp. 223-224.

them for their " liberality " to the bisque kilnmen, and Mr. Wells quoted figures to show that the glost kilnmen were making more days in a given number of hours in his plants than formerly.

In the final 1922 conference, as pointed out above, the manufacturers proposed at the outset to give the kiln-men—both bisque and glost—a greater increase than the other branches, on condition that the kilnmen agree to rules for better workmanship. The wages of the kiln-men were restored to a figure ten per cent below the peak of 1920. This brought the wage per day to $3.17— an increase over the 1900 rate of fifty-eight and five-tenths per cent. Since that time the only specific wage increase asked for the kilnmen, apart from " extras," has been in the day-wage rate.

The dippers have received no increase in their base rate. They were interested, of course, in the unsuccess-ful proposals to reduce the cubic feet in the glost kiln-men's day, inasmuch as their rate is in terms of that day. They have also asked for increases in the base rate on their own account, with the same lack of success. Nor did the dippers fare as well as the glost kilnmen in the percentage increases in the 1916-1922 period. The dippers' increases were given in the form of plussages on a stationary base rate and the dippers were kept on the lower level of plussages along with the casters, turners and handlers, and saggermakers—forty-one per cent in 1922. The smaller increase in the dippers' actual rate is undoubtedly due to the increased speed developed since 1900.[18] The dippers emphasize their

[18] It was assumed by both sides in the course of the 1921 and 1922 wage discussions that the output of the dippers had doubled. The fact that the dippers were receiving greatly increased earnings, apart from the plussage, was recognized in 1921 when an alternative hourly rate was reinserted in the scale for dipping; in 1900 the day rate

own exertions in achieving this result. Mr. Wells, on the other hand, has pointed out that the reduction in the sizes of the general run of ware—which the kiln-men contended had worked against them—and the more convenient arrangements in the dipping rooms have made it much easier for the dippers to turn out a kiln-man's day.

Concessions in Conditions.—Most of the requests which have been urged along this line have been for " relief " from obligations which rested on the workers and were assumed in the rates when the uniform scale was drawn up in 1900. The work in the potteries was still so arranged that there were many tasks which the journeymen had to perform, or pay helpers to perform, in addition to the actual running of the jigger, making of the sagger, placing of the kiln, etc. For example, the obligation of fetching one's clay, or saggers, or ware prevailed in some branches, and in a few the ware had to be carried to the drying room. In some of the branches, too, the men still had to pay, in most pot-teries, for having the clay prepared.

In the 1900 negotiations the union fought hard, but in the main unsuccessfully, for the removal of some of these conditions and for uniformity in those to be retained. " There was very little dispute over prices, but there was prolonged wrangling and debate over conditions, etc." [19] The result was that conditions were left about as they were in the various potteries unless and until changed by agreement of the parties. Ever since that time requests for release from this or that obligation in this or that branch, without, of course, a

---

in the scale was fixed at $3.00, and in 1921 it was put at 70 cents an hour, exclusive of the plussage.

[19] Duffy, p. 35.

reduction in the rate, have played an important part in the conferences. Many of the gains which the workers have made, too, lie in this field of conditions; down to 1916 the concessions which the workers won in conditions loomed larger than those in wage rates proper.

Most of the important changes in conditions which have been legislated into the agreement since 1900 have been placed there only after insistence upon them in conference after conference.[20] The resistance of the Association had meantime been weakened, in some instances, by the grant of the concession by a number of manufacturers individually. Sometimes these employers gave the new conditions voluntarily, in order to attract men. But in some cases the concession was secured by threats to hand in notices. In times when the demand for men was brisk, gains of this kind were rapidly extended from plant to plant. It is difficult for a firm at such times to hold or get men if it insists on the continuance of a condition less favorable than that which obtains in a number of other plants. And once the employer had granted a concession, even under pressure of threats to leave, it was difficult to reëstablish the old condition. The Brotherhood took the position that a concession of this sort, when made without a formal protest by the firm, is " a change of condition by agreement of the parties " and that the union cannot be called upon to force the men to relinquish it.

One of the earliest struggles was over the payment for " pugging " clay in the waremaking branches. Before the introduction of " pug-mills " the journeymen had to " wedge " the clay for themselves and when the employers took over the " pugging " they charged

---

[20] For recognition of this by the workers, see *Proceedings*, 1919, p. 89.

the men for performing this operation for them.[21] In the 1900 negotiations the union failed after a long struggle, to secure " free clay." The charge was then ordinarily five per cent. In 1901, however, the union succeeded in eliminating the discount for clay from the clay-shop branches. This was the most important gain made in that conference.[22]

By 1918 " free clay " had come to mean free delivery of clay to the benches. The agreement provides that the firm must deliver the clay on the floor on which the men work. The obligation still rests on the clay-shop workers, however, to carry the clay to their benches from the elevator or other point at which the clay is left. In 1918 the employers granted free delivery of clay to the jiggerman working without a full crew. They refused to make free clay general in 1919, and in 1921 they refused it to the dishmaker when working without a helper, but in the 1922 August conference they granted the dishmakers' request without argument.[23]

In the saggermaking branch the issue as to the preparation of the clay lasted much longer and caused much more trouble than the similar issue in the clay shop. In the West it had been the custom for the saggermakers to pay for the pugging of sagger clay and the 1900 agreement left this obligation with them. In Trenton, on the other hand, the saggermaking prices were on a " free clay " basis. The Trenton saggermakers did not work under the uniform list in 1900, so the ques-

---

[21] In 1894 the jiggermen in Trenton were not only paying for having the clay pugged but were also paying for the use of the " steam jiggers," in the form of a discount from wages. MS. *Minutes, L. A. 3573; Proceedings, D. A. 160*, 1890, p. 46; MS. *Minutes, L. U. No. 4, Potters National Union.*

[22] *Proceedings, N. B. of O. P.*, 1900, p. 9; 1901, p. 8.

[23] *Report of Executive Board*, 1919, p. 13; 1923, pp. 17-18.

tion was postponed. Meanwhile the Brotherhood was unsuccessful, in 1902 and again in 1903, in its attempts to secure free clay for the saggermakers in the shops under the uniform list, and when the uniform list was put in force in Trenton, in 1904, it was without free clay.[24] In 1905 the Trenton saggermakers demanded a return to the system of free clay, complaining that it was impossible for them, under the conditions obtaining in the shops, to prepare their own clay and that the prices charged for it by the employers were uniform only in being " exorbitant." [25] As no satisfactory agreement could be made with the employers the Trenton saggermakers went out on an unauthorized strike, in May, 1906, announcing that they would not return to work unless and until the manufacturers would agree to assume half the cost of preparing the clay. After the national officers had succeeded in getting the saggermakers back to work the manufacturers agreed to relieve the saggermakers of half the cost.[26]

This stimulated the union to demand free clay everywhere, a demand which was repeatedly refused in conference. Finally, in August, 1916, the saggermakers of East Liverpool went out on an outlaw strike, which lasted six weeks, to secure free clay. They were joined in this action by the saggermakers in other plants in the West. The result was a new agreement " for the purpose of making the conditions under which the clay is prepared for the saggermakers more uniform." Then, in the first 1917 conference, the manufacturers agreed to the union proposal for free clay. According to the saggermakers, the manufacturers had promised

[24] *Proceedings*, 1902, pp. 96-97; 1903, pp. 17, 105-107, 131; *Report of President*, 1905, pp. 21-22.

[25] *Proceedings*, 1905, pp. 23-24.

[26] *Report of President*, 1906, pp. 20-21.

when the 1916 agreement was made, that they would grant free clay in 1917.[27]

The carrying of "green" saggers is another issue with a long history. In 1900 it was the general practice for the saggermakers to carry the green saggers to the door of the sagger room and deliver them at that point to the bisque kilnmen, who carried them to their kiln-shed. Both the saggermakers and the kilnmen early attempted to get rid of their respective parts in the transfer of green saggers to the kilns,[28] but the kilnmen have come off much better in this struggle than the saggermakers. Even before the war period some employers, for the most part those who had new plants in which the distance from the sagger room to the bisque kilns was greater than in the older plants, did excuse the kilnmen from carrying green saggers in order to attract or hold kilnmen.

In August, 1916, the kilnmen's local of East Liverpool decided to put an end to the running-out of green saggers on its own authority. It adopted a rule that kilnmen should cease to carry out green saggers in the plants in which they were still doing it and the rule was given practical effect by the refusal of the kilnmen to carry the saggers.[29] The action of the local union was, of course, contrary to the agreement and the manufacturers' association urged the individual employers to insist upon their rights, but the fact that some manufacturers had previously granted this concession made the other manufacturers reluctant to stand out to the point of losing their kilnmen. In the supplementary agree-

---

[27] *Proceedings, U. S. P. A.,* 1916, pp. 24-25, 31; *Proceedings, N. B. of O. P.,* 1917, pp. 42-43; *Report of Executive Board,* 1917, pp. 3-6; 1018, pp. 2, 9, 14.

[28] *Proceedings, N. B. of O. P.,* 1902, pp. 76, 117, 118.

[29] *Proceedings, U. S. P. A.,* 1916, p. 24.

ment of November, 1916, granting a voluntary general increase in wages, the practical elimination of the carrying of green saggers by kilnmen, except for extra compensation, was recognized. In the plants in which it was impossible to arrange to have this work done by common labor, the kilnmen were to continue to carry the saggers, but were to be given extra compensation for it. The difficulty of getting men who would handle the saggers with proper care and who would be available at the time the work had to be done, had been one of the reasons repeatedly advanced by the employers against relieving journymen of the carrying of saggers.

The release of the kilnmen from their part of the carry made the saggermakers still more dissatisfied with their obligation. As a matter of fact the saggermakers did secure release from their part of the carry in a number of plants in the West during the war period, in some cases by threats to hand in their notices. The employers have since refused union proposals that the saggermakers be relieved of this work where it is still required of them. The saggermakers contend that it takes more time to deliver the saggers to the oddmen than to the kilnmen, as the latter were more proficient in handling saggers and were also eager to finish the work as quickly as possible, in contrast to the oddmen who are paid by the day. The employers have countered with a refusal to have these inexperienced oddmen taking the saggers from the flues.

The argument on this question has also taken a course that it has followed on other requests to make a concession general which has already been won in some plants. The saggermakers contend that it is unfair to exact the carry from the saggermakers in the remaining shops when the men in half the shops have been relieved of it or are paid extra for doing it.

The employers reply that in some of these shops the saggermakers had gained the concession by force and in violation of the agreement, hence the removal of the obligation in those shops can hardly be advanced as establishing the inequity of the carry in others. Furthermore, the fact that some manufacturers have relieved the saggermakers of this work voluntarily, or have done away with the necessity of it through improvements in the arrangement of the plants, should be accepted gratefully and not used as an argument for demanding this relief from the manufacturers not so fortunately situated.

Improvements in facilities without reduction in the rates have affected earnings in the same way, if not in the same degree, as releases from obligations. An instance in point is the installation of automatic conveyors for carrying ware to the green room. Sometimes the men have attempted to compel all manufacturers to give them an improvement which some have introduced voluntarily, or pay extra. The Association has been strongly opposed to taking joint action of this sort to force the hand of the manufacturers.[30]

Warehousemen.—The time-working group which has figured most prominently in requests for wage increases is the warehousemen. Their rate was fixed originally, in 1911, at $2.50 a day, which was much less than the earnings of the skilled branches on piece work. By September, 1920, it had been raised to $6.05, an increase of one hundred and forty-two per cent in the journeyman rate; moreover it applied after three years of service instead of the four years specified in 1911. This relatively large advance had been given the warehousemen because it was recognized that the skilled

[30] For example, see *Report of Executive Board*, 1927, pp. 11, 17-19.

men in this branch had been poorly paid. It was also recognized that, because it was a time-working branch, the men could not increase their earnings through improved facilities or other aids to greater speed. President Menge urged in the 1921 conference that the warehousemen be exempted from the seventeen per cent reduction, on the ground that the branch had always been underpaid before the war increases and it should therefore be allowed to retain the ground that had been gained. The employers had finished " levelling up," however, and insisted that the warehousemen keep their new relative position by sharing in the reduction in the same percentage as the other branches. The 1921-1922 changes left the rate at $5.25 —one hundred and ten per cent above the 1915 rate.

In 1924, and again in 1926, the union asked for an increase for the warehousemen, but unsuccessfully.[31] The warehousemen argued that their branch was still relatively underpaid, on the basis of skill. A part of the work, to be sure, is not skilled work but that part is very laborious. Then, passing on from the test of comparative skill and effort required, they remarked pointedly, in 1924, that " it costs the warehousemen as much to live as the other branches." In 1926 President Wood introduced the argument for a family living wage, pointing out that the warehousemen's wages did not equal the figure necessary for the health and decency budget for a family of five, as found by the United States Bureau of Labor Statistics—$2,099.22. Chairman Wells replied that the manufacturers did not and could not attempt to observe any such minimum. He believed that the wages in the pottery industry were on a par with those in the best-paying industries in this

[31] This was the only wage increase asked in 1926 apart from one in the time rate for kilnplacing.

country, yet only a small percentage of the employees in his plants earned that figure. The potteries could not operate if all male employees had to be paid at least $2,000 a year. Nor did he think that many of the employees in the potteries were not living at a " decent standard " on the wages they were then receiving. As for the warehousemen, they were well paid for what they did, compared with what was paid for work of the same type in other industries.

Warehousewomen.—The original wage scale for the classes in this group was the one awarded by the arbitrators in April, 1913, shortly before they came into the Brotherhood. The employers agreed in the 1913 conference to embody the award in the national agreement, although they tried first to have the day rates for bisque ware brushers and dippers' assistants, which had been set at $1.30 and $1.35, respectively, reduced to the $1.25 rate assigned the other classes of day workers.

The warehousewomen shared in the first voluntary increase, that of July, 1916. Theirs was the only branch included with the jiggermen in that increase. The advances through September, 1920, put the day rates approximately one hundred and twenty-eight per cent above the 1913 level; the percentage increase in the per kiln rates for " drawing " was considerably less. In 1921 Mr. Menge tried to save the warehousewomen, as well as the warehousemen, from the full reduction, on the ground that they had always been underpaid. He was unsuccessful in this also. The 1921 and 1922 changes left the day rates at $2.50 and $2.66, and the per kiln rates at $1.85 for glost and $1.90 for bisque, an increase of approximately one hundred per cent over the 1915 day rates and sixty-three per cent over the 1915 kiln rates. Here again we note that the percentage increase for day workers was greater than that in the piece rates.

In 1924 the union asked for a fifteen per cent increase in the day rates for warehousewomen. The per kiln rate for " drawing " was not included in the proposition. The request was based on the needs of the women for higher wages to meet the cost of decent living. They were earning at that time only $12.50 a week, on the average, as they were not fully employed. The employers were unwilling to oppose the argument that $12.50 a week was not a sufficient wage from a living standpoint. They sympathized with that argument. They pointed out, however, that if the women were employed full time they would receive $15.00 a week, at day rates. The employers fell back, also, on the argument that the women were receiving wages which compared favorably with those received by women in other industries who did work requiring as little skill. Most of the warehousewomen were young girls or old women. The latter were the least efficient class of labor in the pottery; the women who enter the pottery industry as a permanent occupation go into the decorating department, in which the earnings are higher.

WAGE LEVELS AS BETWEEN BRANCHES

A survey of the wages argument reveals that both sides give to comparative skill the most prominent position among the factors which should be followed in fixing wage levels as between the various branches. Both concede that, other things being equal, the net earnings—that is, the earnings remaining to the journeyman after he has paid his help—in any branch ought to bear the same relation to those in every other branch as the degree of skill required for the work. Compara-

tive laboriousness or physical strain has also been recognized as a factor which should be taken into account.
Exposure to special hazards to health has been advanced as an argument for higher wages by the dippers, and apparently not without result; this is doubtless one of the reasons that the dippers are the highest-
paid branch in the potteries.[32] Another element which
the employers are constantly emphasizing is the system
of payment; they will not agree to pay rates to time
workers regularly which will give them earnings
equated on the basis of comparative skill to those of
piece workers.

The contention advanced at times by the Brotherhood on behalf of particular branches—that a " living
wage " should be observed as a minimum—has not been
accepted by the employers as an independent principle
in wage determination. Without admitting that the
rates they were paying in these branches would not be
" living " wages for full-time employment, they have
fallen back upon the factors which they have constantly
emphasized in general wage discussions—what the industry can stand in labor cost and what is paid for work
of similar type in other industries. But when they were
prepared to grant general advances, from 1916-1920,
the employers did favor distributing the general increases between the branches so as to give the branches
which receive the lowest wages, absolutely, larger percentage increases than the others. For example, the
employers' proposals of September, 1917, which were
later rejected at referendum, " represented as nearly as
practicable the same increase in dollars and cents per
week to men in all departments." A uniform percent-

[32] Figures for the hourly earnings in the respective branches are
given in Appendix.

age change would be inequitable, they argued, because the man on a lower wage level "feels the pinch of the times more acutely than men employed in favored positions." [33] And in January, 1920, the labor committee declared that inasmuch as the increases were given only because of the increase in the cost of living "it was not fair to base the change entirely upon percentage, as that plan would give the men in some departments a much larger increase in dollars and cents than in others." [34]

In fixing wages as between the more highly paid branches, the standard of comparative skill has not been strictly adhered to in practice, even where there are no important differences in laboriousness or hazards to health, and where the factor of time payment is not present. The clay-shop branches, for example, are almost identical in these other respects, yet the inter-branch differentiation in wages within this group does not conform altogether to comparative skill. The unevenness in the plussages and in what was given in base-price increases from 1916 on represented an attempt to reduce the departures from the standard of comparative skill, but the differentiation was not carried to the point of establishing conformity between wages and skill. Moreover, equalization at a given time would not mean, necessarily, that the correspondence between earnings and skill would continue. Earnings will advance even without changes in rates if improvements in facilities are introduced unequally between branches.

One might assume that wages would have to be fixed in proportion to skill and effort in order to get the

[33] *Report of Executive Board,* 1918, p. 13.
[34] *Proceedings, U. S. P. A.,* January, 1920, p. 32.

proper distribution of men between the branches. But whatever strength such a force might have under other circumstances, it does not operate to compel a levelling up of the wages of a branch which is experiencing a decline in the comparative demand for its work. Pressing is a notable example of this. And when the dishmakers argued that unless the wages in their branch were increased the necessary supply of men could not be kept up, the employers apparently believed that they would be able to get sufficient bench dishmakers for some time to come. On the other hand, the union rules, reinforced by the agreement, prevent a shift to the more highly paid branches.[35]

GENERAL WAGE CHANGES

General Wage Changes Prior to 1900.—Between the formation of the United States Potters Association and the beginning of national collective bargaining there were three general wage reductions. Following the reduction of 1877 there was a further reduction, both East and West, of approximately eight per cent in 1885 and a still further reduction of approximately twelve and a half per cent in 1894.[36] So far as one can judge from the statements made in the reports of the United States Potters Association, the most important factor affecting the movement of the general wage level during

[35] See below, pp. 281-284.

[36] The 1885 reduction was ordinarily referred to as "the eight per cent reduction." *Proceedings, N. B. of O. P.,* 1895, p. 6. In Trenton the reduction was 8 per cent "from the working list of 1877" but there were some specified exceptions to this in the 1885 agreement. The 1894 reduction was usually called a twelve and a half per cent reduction, although President Hughes in 1894 said it was a reduction "in reality running from 11 per cent to 40, and in some instances 50 per cent." *Ibid.,* 1894, p. 6.

16

this period was the necessity of meeting foreign competition. The measure of tariff protection was therefore accepted as the guide which must be followed in fixing the level of wages. The decline in the cost of living was emphasized at times, too, but the dependence of wages upon selling prices and of selling prices upon the tariff was the wages theory most frequently voiced at the manufacturers' meetings.

The reduction of 1877 was defended by the labor committee on the ground that increased foreign competition had made it necessary. " Owing to the fact that gold has fallen to a trifle over par, of course competition has compelled us to sell our goods at prices very slightly remunerative." The committee then laid it down as a guiding principle that wages should be " based on the price of English labor, as nearly as possible, adding the advantages of tariff protection whether high or low." [37] Fortunately for this standard, the committee found in 1879 that it had not run counter to the maintenance of the level of real wages or the desire to pay wages at least equal to those paid in other industries for work requiring equal skill.

We are glad to know that during the last two years at least, our workmen have been largely benefited by the very low cost of provisions, clothing and rent—which three items compose nearly the whole outlay of a family—and moreover we are satisfied that pottery labor is now, and for years has been, better remunerated than that of the average of trades requiring skilled work.[38]

The reports of the meetings of the Association are silent on the reasons for the 1885 reduction. This cut in wages did not follow a reduction in the tariff rates but

[37] This report was ordered published in the newspapers so that the workmen might read it. *Proceedings,* January, 1878, pp. 35, 42, 43.
[38] *Ibid.,* 1879, p. 11.

an increase, by the Act of March 3, 1883.[39] After 1885 the wage question again appears in the reports. The emphasis now is on the necessity of sufficient tariff protection to make the maintenance of existing wages possible. The coöperation of the workers is sought, too, in the battle for protection.[40] Following the second election of Grover Cleveland, the president of the Association declared, in anticipation of a change in the tariff:

I feel perfectly safe in saying that the American pottery manufacturers have not received one cent of the tariff. The operative potter has not been "vainly waiting for his share." He has had it all and he will continue to get it all, let it be more or less. . . . . I am in favor of basing the wages of all our operatives upon the prices paid by our foreign competitors and add to these prices whatever the tariff may be. This can easily be arrived at as our work is by the piece and the tariff is ad valorem.[41]

President Hughes of the Brotherhood refused to accept the view that the wage reduction of 1894 was necessary. Comparing English and American wages in the light of the tariff, he said: " We fail to see where we get anything like the full benefit of the tariff." [42] The 1895 convention also refused to accept the notion that a wage increase was out of the question with the tariff as it stood.[43] Nevertheless,

during the campaign of 1896 the impression prevailed among the potters, that if McKinley was elected and the tariff rates increased,

---

[39] *Department of Commerce, Bureau of Foreign and Domestic Commerce, Miscellaneous Series, No. 21*, pp. 80-82, 89. These rates were continued in the 1890 act.

[40] *Proceedings*, 1886, pp. 13-20; 1888, pp. 6, 19.

[41] *Ibid.*, 1893, p. 8; 1894, pp. 7, 46 *et seq.*

[42] *Proceedings, N. B. of O. P.*, 1894, p. 6; 1895, pp. 4-5.

[43] *Proceedings*, 1895, pp. 24-25. The Tariff Act of 1894 cut the rates from 60 per cent ad valorem on decorated and 55 per cent on non-decorated ware to 35 per cent and 30 per cent respectively. *Department of Commerce, Bureau of Foreign and Domestic Commerce, Miscellaneous Series No. 21*, pp. 81-82, 89-90.

the manufacturers would restore the rate of wages paid previous to
the 12½ per cent reduction in 1894. And for this reason the potters
seemed to pay more attention to politics than their organization.[44]

In January, 1897, the executive board of the Brotherhood sent a committee to Washington to advocate
before the Ways and Means Committee of the House of
Representatives the restoration of the 1890 rates. The
agreement of 1897, calling for the return to rates paid
prior to the 1894 reduction, was the direct outcome of
the restoration of the duties to the level of the 1883
and 1890 Acts.

1900-1916.—The issue of a general percentage change
in wages was not squarely presented from 1897 to
1916. It is true that in some years the union submitted
lists of specific proposals which in the aggregate involved a considerable percentage advance in the wage
level, but these were argued for on their particular
merits rather than on general grounds, although the
increase in the cost of living was used at times as a
supporting argument.[45]

It was the manufacturers' side which put the argument on general grounds in those years. The condition
of the business was their main argument against
increasing payrolls—and the condition of the business
was generally poor, from the standpoint of selling
prices.[46] This argument was supplemented, of course,

[44] Duffy, p. 24.

[45] For example, *Proceedings, N. B. of O. P.*, 1907, p. 43; 1911, pp.
49, 51; *Report of President*, 1908, p. 4.

[46] The tariff rates on china and white earthenware were not changed
from 1897 to 1913. For foreign competition in the pottery industry
in this period, including comparative labor costs, see *Department
of Commerce, Bureau of Foreign and Domestic Commerce, Miscellaneous Series No. 21.* Of domestic competition this report says (p.
26): "The last two decades have been a period of determined and
even reckless competition among American potteries. This is shown

by the assertion that the earnings of the branches asking for increases compared very favorably with those in other industries requiring equal skill. The fact that earnings were increasing from 1900 to 1916, with practically stationary piece rates, partly because of the granting of outright relief from some customary obligations and the recognition of " extras," partly because of improved facilities in plant and equipment without any reductions in the piece rates, and partly because of increased speed not directly attributable to these changes, helped to subordinate the increase in the cost of living to the " condition of the business " factor.[47]

In 1913 tariff reduction was once again a threatening factor for a time. It made itself evident first in the request of the employers that the conference be postponed and the existing agreement extended for another month in order that the new tariff rates might be definitely known when the parties should go into conference. The union agreed to this after a referendum vote. Early in October the manufacturers presented their proposals. One of these was that the men should agree to such a reduction in wages " as may be necessary to enable the manufacturers to successfully meet the conditions arising under the new pottery tariff rates." [48] But when the conference met the manufac-

---

by the fact that, although the price of materials and the cost of labor have greatly increased, the wholesale prices of the staples of the pottery industry have not advanced in proportion to them or to other commodities."

[47] Mr. W. E. Wells stated to the writer that earnings in 1914 were in some branches twice as great as when the 1900 scale was adopted, although not in all. President Menge stated that in many branches earnings had increased at least 60 per cent.

[48] The 1913 Act differentiated between semi-porcelain and china; the rates on the former were put at 35 per cent for non-decorated and 40 per cent for decorated ware, and the rates on china at 55

turers did not press the demand for a reduction; the matter was left with a proviso in the agreement that the question might be reopened in the summer of 1914. The labor committee believed "that it was hardly proper to insist upon a wage reduction based only upon the probability of a selling price reduction, and that the working men were entitled to the benefit of the doubt until such a time as selling prices under the new tariff should be adjusted to something like a permanent basis." [49]

1916-1922.—The increase in the cost of living was, of course, the main argument from the union side from 1916 to 1920. The employers recognized that they had to meet the union on this ground. They insisted, from the first general increase on, that what they were offering would bring earnings abreast of the increase in the cost of living since the 1915 agreement was made. As theirs was a predominantly piece-working industry they naturally talked more of advances in earnings than of general percentage advances in wage rates. They also maintained that they were advancing wages at a rate that was keeping the earnings of their employees in very favorable comparison with what was being paid for equal skill and effort in other industries.

Although it was the cost of living which was "the controlling factor " [50] in the wage increases during this period, the " ability to pay " of the industry was a feature in the situation which must not be ignored. It was the reason advanced by the manufacturers in July,

---

per cent for decorated and 50 per cent for non-decorated ware as contrasted with the previous rates of 60 per cent on decorated china and semi-porcelain and 55 per cent on non-decorated china and semi-porcelain. *Department of Commerce, Bureau of Foreign and Domestic Commerce, Miscellaneous Series No. 21*, pp. 27-28, 84, 91.

[49] *Proceedings, U. S. P. A.*, 1913, p. 33.

[50] *Ibid.*, 1921, p. 24.

1916, for not making the increase general when the first voluntary increase was granted the jiggermen and warehousewomen. The fact that their contracts with large buyers, made at the old prices, had not expired made it impossible for them, they said, to give a general increase at that time.[51] When the general increase was granted in November, the manufacturers were careful to specify that it was given because of " the unusual conditions that have arisen in the business world " and that it was to hold until the expiration of the 1915-1917 agreement " or while present conditions shall continue in the pottery industry. One feature of the present conditions referred to, shall be understood to be a demand equal to or greater than productive capacity." [52]

It was too much to expect that these two measures should be applied without disagreement between the parties. They were never completely in accord on how much the cost of living had risen,[53] nor was the union side easily brought to agree with the manufacturers' judgment as to how much the market would absorb in selling prices. It has been noted that the first time the union was free to disagree in negotiations for a renewal of the agreement—as contrasted with requesting a " voluntary " increase—there was a strike over the amount of the increase.

In the 1919 regular conference the issue was joined on the manufacturers' announced policy of halting wage advances in order to avoid further increases in selling prices.[54] For the first time since 1916, they were strongly opposed to granting any increase whatever—

[51] Report of President, 1917, p. 2.
[52] Supplements No. 5 and No. 6 to the Chalfonte Agreement; Proceedings, U. S. P. A., 1919, p. 27; 1921, p. 24.
[53] MS. Report of Conference, 1921.
[54] Proceedings, U. S. P. A., 1919, p. 27.

and this in the face of a convention demand for a general increase of 25 per cent. They first attempted to show that no increase was due on the familiar cost of living account. They contended that " the wage increases already granted were equal, in almost every department," to the increase in the cost of living. Their trump card, however, was President Wilson's statement of August 25, 1919, to the Railway Employees' Department of the American Federation of Labor requesting those workers not to embarrass the Government in its campaign to bring about a lowering of the cost of living by pushing their demands for increases in wages at that time and urging that " it was much more in their interest " to coöperate in lowering the cost of living " than to insist upon wage increases which will undo everything the Government attempts." [55] It was manifestly the duty of the pottery industry, said the manufacturers, not to do anything that would make for higher prices. In view of the President's program for reducing the cost of living it would be an " unpatriotic act " to grant any increase in wages at this time that would make it necessary to advance the price of ware. Moreover, it was to be expected that " the cost of living would be reduced as a result of the Government's announced policy to wage a relentless war against profiteering." [56] Although the employers finally offered a general advance they did so, they said, not because they believed the increase was deserved, but merely as the " price of peace." One of the considerations which led the union conferees to accept this offer without a

[55] *Official Proceedings, Fifth Biennial Convention, Railway Employees Department, American Federation of Labor,* April 12 to 21 (inclusive), 1920, Kansas City, Missouri, pp. 25-26.

[56] *Report of Executive Board,* 1920, pp. 11-12; *Proceedings, U. S. P. A.,* January, 1920, p. 30.

referendum on it, was the proviso that if the cost of living advanced the union could have the scale reopened in three months. This the Brotherhood did, with the result that wages were again advanced.[57]

In September, 1920, when the union again asked for an increase, the employers again denied that anything was due the men on the cost of living basis. They declared that " whatever increase in the cost of living may have occurred since January " had already been taken care of in advance; the indications were, too, that the cost of living had reached the peak and the tendency would be downward. However, although they continued to insist that no advance was justified, " except to ware-housemen and one or two of the other lower paid branches," they finally offered a general increase, in order to avoid a strike. That the advance offered did not seem to the executive board large enough is shown by the fact that the board would not accept it on its own responsibility but referred it to the membership.[58] It thus appears that in the application of their recognized standards, the manufacturers three times departed from what they thought these standards called for in the existing situation because of the strike danger. In the fall of 1917 they gave something over five per cent more, in September, 1919, a somewhat similar amount, and in September, 1920, approximately six and one-half per cent.

It is impossible to compare the percentage of increase in wages with that of the cost of living because the plussages were far from uniform in the various branches and important increases were given in several of the branches in addition to the plussages. Moreover,

[57] *Report of Executive Board,* 1920, pp. 11-12.
[58] *Proceedings, U. S. P. A.,* December, 1920, pp. 42-44; *Report of Executive Board,* 1921, pp. 13-17.

the employers' standard was in terms of earnings rather than rates. Mr. Wells stated in the 1921 conference that although some of the plussages did not measure up to the percentage increases in the cost of living, taking all departments together—and in the case of nearly every branch—earnings per hour had doubled since 1914. Vice-President Hutchins said that he did not question this.[59]

Shortly after the increase of September, 1920, went into effect the manufacturers began to talk of the necessity of a wage reduction. The last advance had necessitated " an advance in selling prices just at a time when the market was falling in almost all other lines." [60] But the request for a wage reduction did not come for several months. "Through a combination of favorable circumstances " the manufacturers were able to maintain selling prices and still keep their potteries in " fairly steady " operation for some months longer.[61] And when the market for tableware did slump the manufacturers made an initial cut in selling prices without asking for a wage reduction. It was not until it appeared that a further cut in selling prices was necessary to meet the " clamor " of " merchants and

[59] A comparison of earnings in 1913 and 1925, taken from *Bulletin No. 412 of the United States Bureau of Labor Statistics,* is given in the Appendix. It is stated in this Bulletin (p. 23) that "there is a sufficient number of occupations for which exact comparison is possible to show that hourly earnings in the pottery industry have, as a whole, more than doubled in the 12-year interval." Wage rates were 13½ per cent lower in 1925 than at the peak, in nearly all branches; for kilnplacing they were 10 per cent lower.

[60] *Proceedings, U. S. P. A.,* December, 1920, p. 44.

[61] *Ibid.,* 1921, p. 24. This was due to an accumulation of orders and a shortage of stocks in the hands of the retailers. By April, 1921, the supply had caught up and the employers had to cut prices. MS. *Report of Conference,* 1921.

public alike " for lower prices of tableware " to har-
monize with the downward trend of other commodities," and foreign competition was again to be reckoned
with, that the Association asked for a wage reduction,
in May, 1921.[62]

When the conference convened, in August, 1921, the
manufacturers asked for a reduction of nineteen per
cent in the plussages and day rates—ten per cent off
immediately and nine per cent more (of the peak
wages) on January first.[63] On the basis of the reduction
in the cost of living they were entitled, they said, to a
reduction of twenty-six per cent, at least, but they
refrained from asking for as great a reduction as this
because they were also insisting on the adoption of
" good workmanship " rules which would operate to
reduce somewhat the earnings per hour. The union
side attempted of course to enlarge upon the wage
reduction aspect of the proposed rules. They would
involve, the men said, a reduction in earnings per hour
of fully sixteen per cent. This estimate was offered at a
time when the union committee was attempting to hold
the reduction to ten per cent. The union also insisted
that it was the effect of the proposed rules on earnings
per hour which should be considered in measuring their
effects as a wage reduction, as it was earnings per hour
which the manufacturers had used as a guide in the
years immediately preceding, when the issue was the
percentage of increase necessary to meet the increasing
cost of living. However, the fact that neither side knew
just how much the rules would decrease the earnings
per hour prevented the argument on this point having
much definite effect.

[62] *Proceedings, U. S. P. A.,* 1921, p. 24.
[63] All increases in base prices were left untouched.

The union side was obviously unwilling to have the amount of the reduction determined by the application of any measure of the decline in the cost of living. Vice-President Hutchins frankly expressed the opinion that it was useless to attempt to adjust wages on the basis of cost of living at the moment—that the two sides never had agreed on a figure and could not now. He recognized that the union representatives had promised during the period of increasing wages that they would take a reduction when the cost of living should fall again. What made their side reluctant to take the reduction now proposed, he explained, was " the uncertainty of the situation " as to the immediate future of living costs. To this the manufacturers replied that the chances were all in favor of the workers; the cost of living appeared to be falling rather than rising; the probability was that it would be much lower when the second instalment of the reduction should go into effect. There was considerable—and inconclusive—discussion of different sets of figures put forward by the respective sides as to the trend of the cost of living. There was considerable debate, too, over the union contention that wages had not advanced as rapidly as the cost of living on the upward swing.

There was also much discussion of the reductions in other trades or industries. The union advanced instances of reductions of much less than nineteen per cent and the manufacturers countered with figures of greater reductions. Each side argued that the cases quoted by the other were not comparable to the pottery industry. The union even claimed exemption for the pottery operatives from the general movement for wage reduction on the ground that the men had not received as large wage advances during the war period as the workers in many other industries and, being piece workers, they had not reduced their outputs per hour, an argument which they developed more fully in 1922.

But regardless of the percentage reduction in the cost of living or the wage reductions in other industries, wages would have to be reduced approximately nineteen per cent, the manufacturers declared, to permit the reduction in selling prices which was absolutely essential if the potteries were to keep running. The reduction in selling prices which had already occurred— " conservatively " estimated to average fifteen per cent. and equal in dollars and cents to a wage reduction of thirty-seven and one-half per cent [64]—would not be enough. They intended to put the entire wage reduction into another cut in selling prices immediately. They could not hold off part of the reduction in prices until the second instalment of the reduction in wages became effective even if they wished to; if they attempted it, the buyers, knowing that a further cut in selling prices would follow the second wage reduction would hold off their orders until that time. The amount of employment the operatives would get in the coming year would therefore depend upon the amount of the wage reduction they now accepted.

The union questioned whether a further reduction in selling prices was either necessary or justified. Prefacing his statement with " while it is not any of our business how you folks conduct your business," President Menge said his side believed that the manufacturers would not stimulate buying by reducing selling prices at this time " so long as there are 5,000,000 unemployed." Mr. Wells replied that he believed there was " enough buying power left " to keep the potteries

[64] Mr. Wells estimated that the wages of the branches represented by the Brotherhood were 40 per cent of selling prices.

operating, though not fully, if prices could be cut to what the buyers considered a reasonable point. While agreeing with Vice-President Hutchins' statement that it was unfair of the buying public to expect the potters to cut prices in the same percentage as other manufacturers, because the potters had not profiteered as other manufacturers had, they had to face the fact that the buying public would not recognize it. There was more of a " buyer's strike " against china and earthenware than against any other commodity; the decline in sales was much greater. Moreover, there was danger that what buying would be done would be of foreign ware. During the past year foreign competition had reappeared to a disturbing degree and now threatened to become even more severe than before the War.

In the end it was the statements of the manufacturers concerning the condition of the business which decided the issue. The union side was undoubtedly impressed by the argument that the manufacturers would have to get a large wage reduction if they were to sell their goods and keep their plants in operation.[65] No doubt the fear of a break in relations and a long strike of uncertain outcome entered into the decision of the union committee. It is difficult to assess the relative weight of the logical merits of an argument and of the fear of being beaten in a resort to force, in a situation of this kind.

When the Brotherhood finally receded from its stand for a ten per cent reduction and made a counter pro-

[65] This conclusion is drawn from a reading of the report of this conference and of the August, 1922, conference. The resolution adopted by the 1922 convention (*Proceedings, N. B. of O. P.,* pp. 19, 26) asking for a restoration of the reduction recited that the union was compelled to accept the reduction in 1921 because the labor committee informed them that it would be impossible to operate the plants at the wages then being paid.

posal of seventeen per cent, the time factor was reintroduced. The manufacturers' proposal was for ten per cent off immediately and nine per cent off January first. The Brotherhood's counter proposal reduced the cut on January first from nine per cent to seven. The employers replied that they would accept the lower figure if the second reduction were made effective November first. These were the wage terms finally agreed upon—a total reduction of seventeen per cent, with ten per cent off immediately and seven per cent off November first.[66]

In the August, 1922, conference much of the 1921 argument was repeated. The union's case in 1922 rested primairly on the contention that the reduction in 1921 had been too great. The union representatives did for a time attempt to base an argument on figures tending to show that the cost of living was rising. The manufacturers replied that there were some fluctuations in particular prices in any period—some had gone down a few per cent and some might have risen slightly since November, 1921—but they could not adjust wages to the " slightly wavy line " of the cost of living from month to month. Some of the union members then frankly abandoned the cost of living argument in favor of the right of the workers to a rising standard of living. To this the manufacturers replied that they had always attempted to enable the operatives to improve their standards when the condition of business permitted it, but this was not a period of good business.

The effect of the wage reduction on the rate of speed at which the men worked came in for much discussion. In 1921 the men, as well as the manufacturers, had

[66] The reduction was not exactly 17 per cent in all branches but in none did it vary much from this figure.

assumed that the good workmanship rules would decrease earnings, at least earnings per hour. The union
side was now arguing that the reduction in wage rates
had forced an increase in speed and that this undesirable situation should be cured by an increase in wage
rates. The manufacturers agreed that the rules had at
least not decreased speed. This, they said, was because
they were not generally observed. The remedy for too
great speed was not an increase in wage rates, the
manufacturers insisted, but an observance of the rules,
even if the piece workers had to put in a slightly longer
day.

Having vigorously denied that the 1921 reduction
had been too great on a cost of living basis or that the
men had suffered from the rules adopted in 1921, the
manufacturers were equally emphatic that the conditions of the business and the market prospects would
not permit a new upward movement in wages at this
time.[67] The only thing that had kept them as well
employed as they had been since the last conference
was the large reduction in selling prices which had
followed that conference. The manufacturers had had
to bear most of the price reduction, as the wage reduction had amounted to but 6.8 per cent of the selling
price. The men had made up in earnings approximately the seventeen per cent reduction in wage rates,
through steadier employment, and they should let well
enough alone. If wages should be increased now and
selling prices advanced correspondingly the men would
earn less money than they had made in the past year.

[67] This point had been stressed by the manufacturers in a letter
to the Brotherhood on August 5 (before the conference) and was
emphasized again in a letter of August 26, before the referendum
vote was taken. *Proceedings, U. S. P. A.,* April, 1923, p. 44; *Report
of Executive Board,* 1923, pp. 13-14, 15-16.

The union side did not attempt to ignore the condition of the business and the market prospects. President Wood stated that the members of the Brotherhood believed that the manufacturers could afford to pay the seven per cent; otherwise they would not ask for it.[68] The manufacturers had to stand increases in cost for fuel and materials; [69] why could they not take care of an increase in wages when it is necessary? Some of the union conferees also intimated that selling prices had been cut below what was necessary. There were rumors that there had been a price war among the manufacturers; that the large firms had cut prices to a point that threatened to drive the small firms out of business. This Mr. Wells denied. It was foreign competition, not unreasonable competition between the domestic manufacturers, which had to be feared, Mr. Wells went on to explain. Even at the reduced prices for the American ware, home production had fallen to but fifty-five per cent of the ware sold, measured in value. During the war it was seventy-five per cent. And the drift was still away from the home product.[70]

When the conference was reconvened on December 5 there was some discussion of what the possibilities were of a wage increase in the near future if the men returned to work. The manufacturers had made it

[68] There is no indication in the report of any of the conferences for which verbatim reports are available (from 1921 on) of a disposition on the union side to question the right of the manufacturers to a reasonable profit. There is no trace of a challenging of the legitimacy of profits.

[69] Mr. Wells had stated that labor costs were still 65 to 70 per cent above the pre-war level, fuel 225 per cent above, and the cost of materials 80 per cent above.

[70] See also United States Tariff Commission, *Tariff Information Surveys, B-6,* "The Pottery Industry" (Washington: Government Printing Office, 1921).

17

clear at the outset that if the men returned to work, they would consider a wage advance at any time that increased living costs made it necessary or an improved market made it possible. There was no discussion of the possibility that the cost of living and the market for earthenware and china might move in opposite directions. In their statement of November 15, however, the manufacturers had declared that if there were an increase in the cost of living the manufacturers would increase wages even if they had to stand it for a time themselves,[71] and in this conference they indicated that if selling prices could be advanced wages would be increased, without specifying that an advance would be contingent also upon an increase in the cost of living.

The relation of the tariff rates to selling prices and wages again came in for considerable discussion. The new tariff act had been passed since the August conference, and the union side asked if the increased duties would not make possible an increase in selling prices.[72] This idea the manufacturers took pains to combat. The new rates, they said, would no more than enable them to hold what they had. If the old rates had remained in effect they could not have kept on at the existing wage scale. In fact, if the war had not broken out in Europe the industry could not have stood up under the Underwood tariff rates. With the return of peace and the foreign competitors coming back as strongly as

[71] *Potters Herald,* November 23, 1922.

[72] The duties on semi-porcelain were increased from 40 per cent to 50 per cent and from 35 per cent to 45 per cent on decorated and non-decorated ware respectively, and on china from 55 per cent to 70 per cent and from 50 per cent to 60 per cent on decorated and non-decorated ware respectively. *Tariff Act of 1922,* H. Doc. No. 393, 67th Cong., 2nd Sess. (Washington: Government Printing Office, 1922), Schedule 2, paragraphs 211 and 212.

they were in 1922, the American potters would have lost their business in two or three years under the 1913 rates.

The increase given in the final 1922 conference was not given on the basis of living costs or improved market conditions. It was granted solely, the manufacturers said, because of the misunderstanding which had arisen over what the manufacturers had implied that they would do if the strike should be called off. The manufacturers had not changed their view of the merits of an increase from that which they held in August. However, they did say that so far as the cost of living was concerned, they thought it was a trifle lower. If there should be a slight increase, as the union side seemed to think there would be, the four and one-fifth per cent increase in wages would take care of it.

In 1924, 1926 and 1928 the condition of the business was not only the most important but almost the exclusive note in the general wage discussions in the conferences. The cost of living argument did not figure prominently in these last three conferences. In 1928 it did not figure at all in the discussion. In 1924 the union's proposals involved an amount " almost sufficient to bring the aggregate labor cost up to the peak of 1921," according to the labor committee,[73] but these were argued for on particular grounds. In 1926 the union had but two specific wage demands—for a ten per cent increase for warehousemen and an increase in the hourly rate for kilnplacing. In 1928 the union side did not argue for any of the wage increases requested by the convention; because of the situation confronting the industry the committee refrained from " asking for any increase in anything." However, in all three years, the employers dwelt upon the unhealthy financial con-

[73] *Proceedings, U. S. P. A.*, 1924, p. 31.

dition of the industry, not only as precluding any increase whatever in labor costs but also—in 1926 and 1928—as entitling the employers to a general reduction for which they refrained from asking.

In 1924 Mr. Wells attributed the poor market for American ware to general causes—a decline in production and earnings in the country at large and a postponement of buying due to uncertainty over the election—and to increased foreign competition.[74] In August, 1926, with the condition of the industry worse than in 1924, Mr. Wells found the causes in "conditions that have affected our particular business." [75] The first was the fight being made by foreign potters, aided by low wages and "supported by governmental organizations," to capture the American market; the foreigners were marketing as much ware in the United States as was produced by the American potters.[76] The second was a relative decline in American buying of earthenware and china.

Market conditions continued poor in 1927 and 1928. Selling prices in August, 1928, were thirty to forty per cent below the peak of 1920.[77] In the report of the

[74] At the 1924 meeting of the Association the question was raised as to whether kiln capacity had not been expanded too greatly since 1913. It was calculated that there had been an increase in capacity of sixty per cent whereas the demand would have increased but fifty-five per cent if it had kept pace with the increase in the demand for the products of American industry as a whole. *Ibid.*, pp. 65-66.

[75] *Report of Executive Board*, 1927, pp. 15-17.

[76] See also *Summary of Tariff Information, 1929, on Tariff Act of 1922*, Schedule 2—Earths, Earthenware and Glassware, compiled by United States Tariff Commission (Washington: Government Printing Office, 1929); *Supplement to Tariff Information on Items in Tariff Bill of 1930 (H. R. 2667) Subject to Conference*, compiled by the United States Tariff Commission (Washington: Government Printing Office, 1930), pp. 118-135.

[77] MS. *Report of Conference*, 1928; also *Proceedings, U. S. P. A.*, 1927, pp. 18, 32.

labor committee of the Association in December, 1927, Chairman Wells repeated the familiar declaration that the maintenance of the wage level and reasonably steady employment for the workers were dependent upon the measure of tariff protection given the industry. " In future there must be either a substantial increase in the rate of duty or a radical decrease in the rate of wages." [78]

The employers had maintained from 1925 on that the depressed condition of the business warranted their asking for a wage reduction. They refrained from insisting on it, they said, because they feared it would bring no substantial increase in employment.[79] In the 1928 conference there was some talk from the manufacturers' side of the necessity of a reduction, although no formal proposal for a general reduction was made. The manufacturers' policy was to push for a substitution of less skilled labor for the more highly paid men wherever possible, instead of insisting upon a general reduction in the existing rates. The union alternative was " coöperation with the manufacturers " and a concerted effort to secure an increase in the tariff rates.

[78] Chairman Wells also emphasized that the manufacturers were " handicapped by the national laws forbidding cooperation in establishing and maintaining selling prices." " We are permitted and encouraged," he said, " to establish wages upon a uniform basis, the cost of raw materials and of fuel are nearly uniform, being controlled as a rule by outstanding firms or organizations, prices upon competitive goods from abroad are controlled by cooperation between manufacturers in nearly all countries, and such cooperation is encouraged by national governments. . . . . A modification of the trust laws is second in importance to manufacturers and workers alike, only to the perpetuation of our protective tariff policy. The maintenance of wages is directly involved." *Ibid.*, p. 21.

[79] *Ibid.*, 1925, p. 32; 1926, pp. 23, 26; *Proceedings, N. B. of O. P.*, 1928, pp. 11-12.

The union conferees showed fully as much interest as the labor committee in the tariff question.

1930-1931.—The manufacturers' demand for reductions in the 1930 conference, which finally led to a general reduction of ten per cent in May, 1931, was based primarily on the poor condition of the business. The increase in the tariff duties,[80] they held, were insufficient to support the existing wage rates, especially in the face of the general business depression. They also referred to the decline in the cost of living since the existing scale had been established, and the wage reductions which had already taken place in other industries. Yet, it was once more the condition of the business which was the paramount factor. " We must have relief from our present wage rates if we expect to continue to operate our factories and employ union workmen." [81] To this argument the union conferees, in spite of their invocation of the understanding reached at President Hoover's conference of December, 1929, and their insistence that wage reductions in a time of depression were unwise,[82] had in the end to bow.

[80] The substantial change made by the 1930 act was the addition of a specific duty of ten cents per dozen pieces to the *ad valorem* duties of the 1922 Act (forty-five per cent on undecorated semi-porcelain, fifty per cent on decorated semi-porcelain, sixty per cent on undecorated china and seventy per cent on decorated china). The Act was approved June 17, 1930. *Tariff Act of 1930,* H. Doc. No. 476, 71st Cong., 2d Sess. (Washington: Government Printing Office, 1930), Schedule 2, paragraphs 211 and 212.

[81] *Proceedings, U. S. P. A.,* 1930, pp. 46-47, 48.

[82] *Potters Herald,* May 21, 1931.

CHAPTER IX

CHANGES IN METHODS OF PRODUCTION

In the changes in methods which have affected the work of the skilled journeymen in the pottery industry from the inauguration of the agreement system down to 1928, it has not been the introduction of machinery proper which has played the most important part. The only clear case of the introduction of a machine which vitally affected the work hitherto done by the journeyman is that of the saggermaking machine. Other mechanical devices have been installed, to be sure, but these have been concerned chiefly with the auxiliary work of the journeyman or helpers employed by him. Much more important have been the shift to the casting process, in waremaking, and the substitution of tunnel kilns for periodic kilns in firing the ware. Neither of these changes properly belongs under the head of " the introduction of machinery." They have, however, raised somewhat similar questions.

The Brotherhood has never opposed machinery or new processes. Before the Brotherhood was organized the introduction of the jiggering machine had been resisted for a time by the eastern operatives, according to ex-District Master Workman O'Neill, who declared that the men " stood in their own light for a good many years and succeeded in keeping the machine out." [1] The western operatives had never been well

[1] *U. S. Ind. Comm.*, XIV, 654. Some of the spokesmen for the operatives before the Commission testified, however, that the tardiness with which the jigger was introduced in the East was due to the backwardness of the manufacturers. *Ibid.*, pp. 645, 648. See *Proceedings, D. A. 160*, 1890, pp. 7-9.

enough organized to offer much opposition to the jiggering machine even had they wished. By the time the
Brotherhood began its career in the West the machine
was already well established in the industry and the
operators were an important group of the skilled
workers whom the Brotherhood was attempting to
organize. The inroads of the jigger on the work of the
pressers continued during the early years of the life
of the Brotherhood but there seems to have been no
attempt to oppose this transfer of work from one skilled
trade to another within the organization.[2]

A few years before the inauguration of the agreement system a " dish jigger " was introduced which
threatened to take the making of oval dishes and bakers
away from the dishmakers " at the bench." The Brotherhood was still too weak to oppose it successfully, but
there is no indication that it attempted to. It did try,
however, to secure preference on the machine jobs for
the dishmakers displaced from the bench and to fix a
scale of wages for the work. President Hughes stated
his views on what the wage policy should be to the 1899
convention, saying:

It appears to us that it would be wise for the dishmakers to regulate
a price for ware made in this manner. If it is longer neglected, the
result may be disastrous to that branch. In endeavoring to regulate
such matters, we believe it best to first ascertain just what advantages a man operating a machine has over another working
on a whirler. Then regulate the price to allow for the difference.
In this way we do not antagonize improved machinery, but endeavor to derive whatever benefits that may accrue from the
machine, lightening the labor and at the same time regulating your
prices, so as to enable you to earn the same or as good wages as the
man working by hand.[3]

---

[2] *Proceedings, N. B. of O. P.,* 1895, p. 5.

[3] *Proceedings,* 1899, p. 4.

These two policies of attempting to secure regulation of the wages and conditions for new methods and preference on the new jobs for those displaced from the old have been followed by the Brotherhood ever since. The employers have generally acceded to the request that the journeyman should " follow his work " to the new method. They have made an issue at times of wages, conditions and even hours, on the new method as compared with the old, but have in nearly all cases granted " preference " in manning the new method.

CASTING

The casting process was successfully introduced in general ware before it had made any appreciable headway in the sanitary division. The introduction was not accomplished without considerable friction over wages, but by the beginning of the war period casting was well established as a skilled trade with a wage scale which enabled the casters to make larger earnings than were made at pressing, the branch from which most of the ware made by the casters had been transferred. Thus the coming of casting, which was later a large factor in the breakdown of the agreement system in the sanitary ware division,[4] was so handled in the general ware division as to provide for the displaced journeymen a new skilled trade even more remunerative than that from which they had been displaced.

There was a flurry in 1907 over the attempt of a firm in Wheeling, West Virginia, to employ women to cast some lines of ware. The members of the Brotherhood in the plant threatened to quit unless the women were taken off. The situation was finally taken up by a committee representing the Brotherhood and the labor com-

[4] See below, ch. xiv.

mittee of the Association. A uniform scale was agreed upon for a few lines of ware, and casting and pressing were made interchangeable in apprenticeship and journeyman status. No specific rule was laid down against the employment of women in casting but there was no further attempt of a serious nature to deny in practice the union contention that casting is a journeyman job in which preference shall be given to members of the craft from which the work is transferred.

The question of the piece rates to be paid for casting gave much more trouble. It proved too much for a joint committee appointed by the 1902 conference to formulate a uniform list. The pressers who had gone into casting had in some shops succeeded in retaining pressing prices and these men held that the union ought not to concede less than pressing prices for casting.[5] The pressers supported them in that, apparently with the two-fold desire of keeping their jobs at the pressing bench as long as possible and of establishing a good trading position if they had to go into casting. In the list agreed to late in 1907, which covered only a few classes of ware, the Brotherhood conceded prices averaging about ten per cent below pressing prices but the prices of all other articles were to " remain as paid for at present in the various potteries." [6]

The labor committee charged that the men were holding up the proper extension of casting by refusing to accept a reasonable differential for it. It contended that the skill required was much less than in pressing; that the men could make higher earnings at the prices the manufacturers were offering than at pressing; and, finally, that with the cost of the equipment which they had to install for casting they could not afford to pay

[5] *Proceedings,* 1902, p. 96; 1903, pp. 126-127.

[6] *Proceedings, U. S. P. A.,* 1907, p. 32; *Casting Agreement, effective January 1st, 1908.*

pressing prices for casting. The men denied that the first two points were conclusive. Pressing prices were admittedly too low for the skill required in pressing and the higher outputs permitted by the casting process would, at pressing prices, give earnings that were no more than fair for the skill required for casting; if casting were paid for at less than pressing prices the underpayment from which the pressers were suffering would be perpetuated in the newer method. The manufacturers' contention that there would be no profit in casting at pressing prices they met with a denial; it would cost less to make the ware by casting at pressing prices, they asserted, than by pressing.

In the 1913 conference the employers asked that another attempt be made to formulate a price list for casting. The appointment of a joint committee for the purpose only resulted in another deadlock. The manufacturers' side insisted on a discount from pressing prices of sixteen and two-thirds per cent. The union representatives, chosen from the pressers' and casters' branch, stood out for pressing prices, except on the ware for which "ten per cent off" had been conceded in 1907. They were strengthened in their determination by the fact that some manufacturers were paying pressing prices for casting articles not included in the 1908 list. After further controversy in the shops, and before the standing committee, some firms, notably the Homer Laughlin China Company, announced their intention to abandon casting until the men were willing to go back to it at a proper differential below pressing prices. This led the Brotherhood officers to take the matter into their own hands and they finally reached an agreement with the labor committee on a new scale.[7]

[7] *Proceedings, U. S. P. A.,* 1914, pp. 37-38; *Report of President,* 1915, pp. 2-4.

The two committees took account of the fact that pressing was a comparatively poorly paid branch. They agreed that the prices should be fixed at a level which would allow the casters to make higher earnings than pressers and thus afford relief to the pressers through transfer to better jobs.[8] The new list averaged ten per cent below pressing prices—the same basis as that of the 1908 list.[9] There was resistance in East Liverpool for several days to the new agreement but President Menge succeeded in quelling the opposition.[10] A few years later it was generally recognized in union circles that this was one of the best settlements the Brotherhood ever secured. Mr. Wells has repeatedly declared that the manufacturers were beaten in that settlement.

The growth of casting has continued until the casters are the next most numerous group of waremakers after the jiggermen. In some shops nearly half the ware is cast. The development of casting has been mostly at the expense of pressing and the use of the big jigger. The displacement has been gradual and nearly all of the men displaced were taken on as casters or found other waremaking jobs. Casting has not made much headway against jiggering in the making of flat ware or cups, and these are, in some plants, by far the most important items in the output. Casting is also used to some extent in making dishes; it would be used much more, the manufacturers say, if the dishmakers would agree to a reasonable discount for casting.[11]

[8] Statement of Chairman Wells to the writer.

[9] *Proceedings, U. S. P. A.,* 1914, p. 37; *Report of President,* 1915, pp. 2-4.

[10] *Ibid.,* pp. 4-5.

[11] In 1915 the employers agreed that the dishmakers should have preference on all work on the dishmakers' list transferred to casting.

THE SAGGERMAKING MACHINE

In 1917 the saggermakers' local union of East Liverpool was disturbed over the introduction of a few saggermaking machines in East Liverpool potteries.[12] These machines were operated by odd men. On the initiative of the local the Brotherhood asked that preference be given to saggermakers in manning the machine. The manufacturers agreed, in the first 1917 conference, that " a competent journeyman saggermaker shall be given the preference to operate such machine." There were usually three men on the machine and this meant that but one of them—the man in charge—was to be chosen from the saggermakers; the other two were to be helpers and in choosing them the firm was to have a free hand.[13] The manufacturers' position at the time was that it was not necessary to have a saggermaker skilled in the hand method in charge of the machine but the saggermaker could have that job if he wished it; he was not, however, to expect saggermakers' earnings.[14]

A journeyman and two helpers, the usual machine crew, can turn out at least as many saggers as three journeymen working by hand, yet the machine sagger did not displace the hand saggermakers from the industry to any appreciable extent. For one thing, the machine was introduced at a time when there was a scarcity of saggermakers. Moreover, the hand method is still preferred for many types of saggers. The hand saggermakers are still much more numerous than machine saggermakers.

Not long after the 1917 agreement was made the saggermakers raised the issue of the wages to be paid the

[12] *Proceedings*, 1917, p. 42. Apparently an attempt had been made in 1905 to introduce a saggermaking machine which did not prove successful. *Ibid.*, 1905, p. 38.

[13] *Report of Executive Board*, 1918, p. 6.

[14] MS. *Report of Conference*, 1924.

saggermaker on the machine. There were wide discrepancies between the rates paid in the several shops
in which the machines had been installed and the saggermakers were attempting to secure the same rate in
all. The rate they were trying to establish was 62½
cents an hour. This was less than the hand saggermakers were earning but it was more than was then
paid on the machine in any shop. The issue was finally
taken up by the executive board and the labor committee and an agreement made, which gave the man in
charge of the machine the 62½ cents rate and defined
his duties.[15] The general wage changes ending in 1922
left the machine saggermaker's rate at 76 cents an
hour. In 1924 the men asked that the rate be increased
to $1.00, to bring it into conformity with the earnings
of the hand saggermakers, who were on piece work.
They based their claim primarily on the improvement
in the machine product, which was due, they said, to
the care and skill exercised by the saggermaker in
charge; the work of the saggermaker on the machine
was now more skilled than it was when the rate was
originally fixed. The manufacturers refused to increase
the rate. The work had been done in the beginning by
inexperienced men for much less than the rate they
later gave the saggermakers and, they maintained, they
could again get men to do the work satisfactorily for
less than that rate. Moreover, the machine saggermakers must remember that this was an hourly rate;
their earnings were less than those of the bench men,
to be sure, but the latter were on piece work; the cost
to the manufacturers was greater at the hourly rate
even though the earnings of the men were less.

[15] *Report of Executive Board,* 1918, pp. 34-35; *Proceedings, U. S.
P. A.,* 1919, p. 63.

TUNNEL KILNS

When tunnel kilns were introduced, at the end of the war period, it seems to have been taken for granted that the work would be done by journeymen kilnmen. The ware had still to be carried to the kilnmen's benches and placed in the saggers by hand; the chief difference was that the filled saggers were no longer carried into the kiln and placed in tiers, as in the older upright kilns, but were placed on trucks at the entrance of the kiln. The employment of journeymen kilnmen meant, of course, the payment of journeymen wages. As the existing cubic measurement system of payment could not be applied to the tunnel kilns, the kilnmen went to work on them at temporary hourly rates, based on their previous earnings on the upright kilns, in accordance with the " average earnings " clause of the agreement for work in " the experimental stage." [16] Under the circumstances the kilnmen, so far from opposing the tunnel kilns, welcomed them; there was no threat of displacement, the work was less laborious, and the wages were as good as they had been making on the upright kilns.

It was the manufacturers who made the first move toward fixing a separate wage scale for tunnel kilns. The Association voted, in 1919, that the wages and conditions granted on tunnel kilns were " not to be considered as a precedent in establishing a final settlement "; the matter of making a " final settlement " was to be taken up by the labor committee with the executive board of the Brotherhood.[17] Before the committees were brought together a more or less continuous dispute

[16] Report of Executive Board, 1921, pp. 28, 31-32.
[17] Proceedings, U. S. P. A., January, 1919, p. 75; Report of Executive Board, 1921, p. 28.

began in the plant at Mt. Clemens, Michigan, over the wages to be paid, and, later, the system of payment to be followed, on the newly installed tunnel kilns.[18] A joint committee of manufacturers and union officers, which went to Mt. Clemens to attempt to bring about a settlement, reached agreement on piece rates for this plant. If the rates proved unsatisfactory the question could be reopened in sixty days; the intention of the joint committee was to fix rates which would give the men as good earnings as they had made on the upright kilns.[19] The firm accepted the terms, but, to the great disappointment of the Brotherhood officers, the kilnmen refused them. The Brotherhood thus lost an opportunity to secure a settlement for piece work on tunnel kilns based on the average earnings on the upright kilns, with the approval of a manufacturer's committee.[20] The national joint committee made no serious effort thereafter to frame a separate scale for tunnel kilns. When, in 1921, an hourly rate for kiln

[18] *Ibid.*, pp. 27-38.

[19] *Ibid.*, p. 40. The men's " previous average earnings " were $1.135 an hour.

[20] The dispute at Mt. Clemens developed into a " lockout " of the kilnmen for refusal to work at the piece rates offered by the firm and a strike of the other union members in support of the kilnmen. The firm resigned from the Association. After a few weeks the kilnmen reached a settlement with the firm. *Report of Executive Board,* 1921, pp. 40-46. The firm, however, was no longer a party to the agreement between the two national bodies and even though it operated during the 1922 strike at the terms for which the Brotherhood was striking in the Association plants, the local union found increasing difficulty in securing compliance with the rules and " customs " of the national agreement and in keeping the plant well organized. In the spring of 1923, after the firm had refused to deal with the officers of the Brotherhood, on the ground that it had no agreement with the Brotherhood since the strike in 1921, the Brotherhood called out its members (*Report of Executive Board,* 1923, pp. 32-50), and the plant has since been non-union.

work was added to the scale, it superseded the temporary hourly rates for tunnel kilns in Association plants. The point has been raised by some of the manufacturers that the hourly rate should be lower for tunnel kilns than for upright kilns but the two have not been differentiated in the rate.

Tunnel kilns are rapidly displacing the upright kilns. The advantages are lower fuel cost and a greater percentage of good ware. Most of the employers also report a saving in the labor cost.[21] The men have gained greatly by the change, the manufacturers say, because the work is less laborious and they make as much money, although they put in more hours. Mr. W. E. Wells has repeatedly stated that the introduction of tunnel kilns, under the day-wage plan, has made jobs for many of the older men who would have been forced out of the trade if their only alternative had been continuing on the upright kilns under the cubic measurement system of payment.[22]

DECORATING TUNNEL KILNS

Early in 1924 the Homer Laughlin China Company began operating a decorating tunnel kiln in its new " Number 6 " plant at Newell, W. Va. As this kiln was in a new plant it did not displace any decorating kilnmen employed by the company at the old method. When, however, the company started out with a green crew on the new kiln the decorating kilnmen's local came forward with a request that members of their

[21] *Proceedings, U. S. P. A.,* 1925, pp. 60-61; 1927, pp. 34, 43.

[22] The coming of the tunnel kiln has also raised a new issue concerning hours. The tunnel kiln has made the kiln department a " continuous industry," according to the manufacturers, and has required them to change their position on paying higher rates for work at night and on Sundays and holidays. See below, pp. 286-288.

18

union be given preference for this work. The company would not agree. If the company conceded preference it would mean, objected Mr. Wells, that it would have to discharge the men it then had, who were doing the work satisfactorily, whenever any decorating kilnmen then in the union wanted their jobs. But beyond that was the fact that Mr. Wells did not want the new kiln "unionized" at that stage. He wanted freedom to work out the methods and conditions for the new kiln without any restrictions imposed by the local union and to adjust the wages in accordance with what experience should show the work to be worth, instead of having these fixed in advance by a " settlement " in which the local union would have a hand.

Several months later, in the 1924 conference, Mr. Wells agreed that the men employed on the new kiln might join the Brotherhood if they wished. The company had advanced the rates of wages paid the men over what it paid in the beginning—it was now paying the man in charge 75 cents an hour and the other two men 65 cents—and it was willing to embody those rates in a "settlement" with the Brotherhood.[23] The company would not, however, pay what decorating kilnmen were earning under the old method because the work did not require the same skill. If the decorating kilnmen wanted preference in this work in filling future vacancies they might have it at the existing rates. So the matter was eventually left. There has been no serious trouble over union preference on the decorating tunnel kilns since then.[24]

[23] In 1925, according to *Bulletin No. 412, United States Bureau of Labor Statistics* (p. 40) the average hourly earnings of the decorating kiln-placers and -drawers in the 22 plants in the East Liverpool district were 85 cents (in the 11 large plants, 91 cents).

[24] The number of such kilns installed has been increasing rapidly. *Proceedings, U. S. P. A.,* 1927, pp. 41, 43.

A uniform wage scale has not been adopted for the tunnel kilns. (There is no uniform scale for the old style kilns.) The union has asked for a uniform scale for the tunnel kilns, declaring that the rates paid in some shops, particularly shops outside the East Liverpool district, are too low. But the employers are unwilling to fix a uniform scale for a branch in which the foreman has always been a member of the union and in which the men under him would presumably be paid time rates.

AUXILIARY MECHANICAL DEVICES

The introduction of mechanical devices to eliminate or reduce manual work of an auxiliary character included in what the journeyman has to do, or pay a helper to do, obviously raises less vital issues than changes of the kind we have been considering. The former do not infringe upon the characteristic skill of the journeyman or the essentials of the method to which this skill is attached. If they were introduced in a trade in which the time system of payment prevailed and in which the auxiliary tasks affected were customarily performed by the journeymen, the issue of taking away a part of the " journeyman's work " and thereby reducing the amount of employment open to the journeymen, might be raised. But when the workers displaced were helpers paid by the journeyman—and especially at a time when the journeymen were experiencing help difficulties, as was usually the case in the general ware pottery industry—the journeymen were not so much interested in preventing the displacement as in the effect of the change on their own earnings. And where the change was one which reduced their " dead work," without, of course, any reduction in the piece rate, as in the case of belt conveyors and other automatic devices for carrying out green ware, it was cordially welcomed by the journeymen. It then came under the head of " improved facilities."

Auxiliary mechanical devices have been more prominent in the jiggering branch than in any other. They were stimulated largely by the shortage of helpers during the war period.[25] The most important are improved " stove-rooms " or " dryers," intended to enable the jiggerman to get along without a mould-runner. The introduction of the new stove-rooms did not threaten the jiggerman's base rate but it did raise the question whether the jiggerman using one should receive the bonus for working without a mould-runner. The jiggermen contended that where the McMaster stove-room (the slide type) was used and the mould-runner dispensed with, the jiggerman should still receive the bonus for working with but one helper, apart from the finisher, as his earnings at the regular piece rates were less under these conditions than when working with two helpers and the old type stove-room. After a prolonged local dispute on this point, the manufacturers conceded in the supplementary agreement of August, 1918, that the McMaster stove-room should be " classed as an ordinary stove-room " and the usual bonus allowed the jiggerman for working with one helper. At the same time it was agreed that on a conveyor stove-room job " one helper shall be considered a full crew " and no bonus paid for working with one helper.

Somewhat analogous to the improved stove-room, on the mechanical side, is the " mangle," for use in the dipping shop. The introduction of the mangle, however, gave rise to quite the opposite issue, that of extra pay

[25] *Ibid.*, 1916, p. 49; 1917, pp. 41-42; *Proceedings, N. B. of O. P.*, 1917, p. 32.

above the usual rate per kilnman's day. The mangle is a drying machine with a moving shelf, on which the dipper places the ware after dipping it, instead of placing it on boards near the tub as he does under the older method.[26] In Trenton, where the mangle was first used, the dipper demanded an extra and got it, although the firm contended that the dipper could turn the ware out more rapidly with the mangle than without it.[27] When it was later introduced in the West the dippers objected to using the mangle unless they were given extra pay. The employers complained that this was a " hold-up." However, in July, 1922, one firm made a settlement with its dippers for $1.00 per calendar day for the mangle and the terms of this settlement were then generally followed in other plants. The use of the mangle has since spread rapidly.[28] In 1928 the employers submitted a proposal that the piece rate for dipping should be the same with the mangle as without, but this was not discussed in the conference. The spread of day-wage dipping promises to make the issue of extra for the use of the mangle of little general interest.

DILUTION OF LABOR

Proposals by the employers to substitute inexperienced workers on part of the work hitherto recognized as " journeyman's work " raise the same problem for

[26] The chief advantage of the mangle is that " the ware is not touched while the glaze is still wet upon it. In this way the edges are protected, and come from the kiln more perfectly glazed." However, the firm which first introduced a mangle did so " with the double object of economizing on our dipping cost, and improving the quality of our goods." *Proceedings, U. S. P. A.,* 1914, p. 53.

[27] One of the members of the firm stated that the dipper had admitted this. *Ibid.*

[28] *Ibid.,* 1925, p. 38; 1927, p. 28.

the union as attempts to introduce machinery with inexperienced operators in substitution for journeymen—that of possible displacement. Indeed, a change of the former character is more likely to provoke opposition if the volume of displacement to be expected is serious; just because it is not accompanied by a change in technique, the substitution of a cheaper grade of labor for the journeymen stands out in clear relief.

Proposals of this kind have not been an important issue in the general ware industry until very recently. In the earlier years the union was more disturbed by the delegation of work by journeymen to helpers employed by them than by attempts by employers to give " journeyman's work " to a cheaper grade of workers employed by the firm. The tendency on the part of the journeymen to increase their own earnings by employing helpers to do part of their work for them revealed a conflict between the immediate interest of individual journeymen and what the conventions deemed to be the interest of the trade, which, as in the case of the contract system, was not always settled along the lines laid down by the union. By the time the agreement system was established, the employment of helpers by journeymen was a recognized practice in several branches and the Brotherhood had to fall back upon trying to restrict the kinds of work which the journeyman was allowed to pass on to his helper, with the primary purpose of keeping as many journeymen as possible employed.[29] And during the recent depression in the industry there has been a revival of attempted enforcement of the law, especially against offending journeymen handlers.[30]

[29] For example, *Proceedings*, 1902, pp. 13, 81, 127; 1903, p. 9; 1906, p. 18; *Report of President*, 1907, pp. 10-11.

[30] *Potters Herald*, September 2, 1926; *Report of Executive Board*, 1928, pp. 16-17; MS. *Report of Conference*, 1928.

Recently the employers have proposed that the firm be allowed to turn over to helpers employed by it some of the work hitherto recognized as journeyman's work. These proposals have been advanced as an alternative to a wage reduction and also with the prophecy that they would increase the amount of employment open to the journeymen throughout the industry. They have also been supported by declarations that the work in question does not require journeyman skill. In the 1928 conference discussion the manufacturers attacked the necessity imposed by the union of "paying skilled wages for unskilled work" all along the line but the offensive was especially strong in the case of casting. The proposed dilution of labor in this branch was discussed at great length; both sides seemed to regard it as a test case.

The employers had submitted a proposal that the firm be given the right to take the finishing of cast ware from the journeymen and give it to boys or girls employed directly by the firm, the prices paid by the firm to the jouryneymen to be reduced accordingly. This was accompanied by a guarantee that no caster then regularly employed should be thrown out of employment as a result of this measure; it would, however, affect any vacancies arising in the future or "any new work which may be developed." They maintained that the finishing of cast ware could be done as satisfactorily by unskilled labor and at much lower cost. But it was not merely a question of the injustice of requiring the payment of "skilled wages" for unskilled work, they said; it was essential that costs be lowered if the manufacturers were to get business from foreign competitors to keep the potteries running and they preferred this method to a wage reduction. The manufacturers also urged that what had been done in jiggering should be done in casting. The present practice in casting, they said, was analogous to having the jiggerman do his own batting-out, "run" his own moulds and do his own finishing; they were asking merely that the firm be allowed to do in casting what the jiggermen had done for their own advantage. The difference was an important one to the casters; they were not to make the difference in wages themselves, consequently the surrender of "journeyman's work" was the controlling factor with them.

Before the manufacturers' formal proposal on casting was disposed of, some of the manufacturers expressed a desire to use boys or girls on the entire casting of small pieces. The ware they had particularly in mind was small novelties which were not then made in any union pottery in this country, in any considerable quantity. If they were allowed to employ unskilled labor on this new work they could get the business and thus give the other branches more employment; the mouldmakers, saggermakers, kilnmen, dippers, etc., would all benefit by it. The casters would lose nothing, continued the manufacturers, inasmuch as the ware affected would be ware which the casters were not then making and would never be asked to make because the manufacturers could not make it and sell it if they had to pay casters' prices for making it. The union side was much interested in the possibilities of the new small ware which the manufacturers wanted to make. The casters on the committee finally suggested that they would like to have the casters themselves make this new ware, at special prices, lower than the general level of prices for the articles already listed. They recalled that there are some articles on the list which are priced considerably below the general run of list prices and said that they would be willing to price the new articles on the basis of these low-priced articles. They did not want any outsiders brought into casting but they recognized that they were facing a situation which ought to be met and they proposed to meet it in this way. The manufacturers were at first skeptical. They were afraid the casters would not agree to prices low enough to enable them to get the business. They finally accepted the casters' assurances and it was agreed that a joint committee should be appointed to fix casting prices for new articles of this type.[31]

Having done this, the union side maintained that it had conceded enough in casting. It would not agree to surrender jurisdiction over any part of the casting of articles then made to less skilled labor. With employment poor it was no time to give up any work. The manufacturers' argument that the segregation of finishing would cheapen the total casting labor cost and so enable them to sell more cast goods and thus employ as many casters as before, did not convince them. The proposed guarantee that no casters now regularly employed would be discharged because of the change was not enough. There were too many casters then not "regularly employed" who would be left uncovered. The acceptance of low prices for the new ware was different; it would throw no casters out of work and might give some work to casters not then employed.

A much less important issue has been raised in the dipping branch recently, as an incidental result of the movement toward day work. This is a proposal from some of the manufacturers to substitute " odd help " for journeymen in moving the boards of ware from the mangle to the stilliards. It is of no great importance in

[31] Nothing much came of this. *Proceedings, U. S. P. A.*, 1929, p. 21; *Report of Executive Board*, 1929, pp. 35-37.

itself but it is interesting as illustrating the difference which the system of payment makes in the attitude of the journeymen toward the taking over by the firm of auxiliary work performed by them. More than once dippers paid by the kilnmen's day have sought relief from this carry, or extra pay for unusual distances. And following the agreement in 1921 that the firm might require that flat ware be "boarded," instead of carried in bungs, there were disputes over claims for extra under the proviso that where this was a new condition and involved "real hardship," extra should be paid.

After the change to day work, however, the dippers in a plant at Sebring protested against the attempt of the firm to employ odd men to carry the ware. Inasmuch as the agreement fixing the day rate had not specified that the manufacturer should be allowed to take this work from the dippers, he had no right, the dippers contended, to change the established practice. It would reduce the number of dippers employed; moreover, they contended, it rested the dipper to move away from the tub; it was too unhealthful to stand over the tub dipping all the time and under the piece-work system the dippers could rest when they wished. This dispute was finally disposed of as a special case, the dippers conceding that in "an emergency, in order to keep up production, where dippers are employed at the hourly rate, the firm may have the boards moved by odd labor." But in 1928 the employers, as part of their campaign against "skilled wages for unskilled work," submitted a proposal that "on all plants where day wage dippers are employed, the firm shall determine who shall move the boards of dipped ware." This was one of the proposals not specifically discussed by the conference.

CHAPTER X

OTHER ISSUES

APPRENTICESHIP

In the days of the Potters National Union there were many complaints of a surplus of apprentices.[1] The situation was much more unfavorable in this respect in the West than in the East. As early as 1894 the Brotherhood turned its attention to the " apprentice evil " and adopted apprenticeship rules for several branches— long before it was in a position to enforce them.[2] The members were motivated not only by the desire, so prevalent among skilled craftsmen, to regulate the rate of inflow into their trades, but also by a desire to put an end to the practice of employing men at a discount from the price list under the guise of apprenticeship long after any reasonable period of apprenticeship had expired. In 1895 President Hughes stated that there were men who were still rated as apprentices and working at discounts of ten, fifteen or twenty per cent who had been working at their trades " in some cases as high as ten or twelve years." [3]

The 1900 agreement gave the union apprenticeship restrictions in five branches and in 1905 regulations were adopted for four more.[4] All the branches under the uniform scale then had apprenticeship rules in the

---

[1] For example, *Proceedings, D. A. 160,* 1890, pp. 51, 53-54.

[2] *Proceedings,* 1894, pp. 17, 21-23; 1898, pp. 11, 20, 33, 34, 35, 38-39; 1899, pp. 7, 15, 30, 34.

[3] *Ibid.,* 1895, p. 6; 1899, pp. 7, 30, 34; *Report of President,* 1906, pp. 11-12.

[4] *Ibid.,* p. 8.

agreement except the saggermakers. It was not until 1919 that the saggermaker's helper, who is paid by the saggermaker, was formally recognized in the agreement as an apprentice.

There are no formal apprenticeship rules for the warehousemen's branch. The agreement provides that "no journeyman warehouseman shall be laid off to make room for a beginner" and a graduated scale is specified for three years prior to the application of the journeyman rate,[5] but the term "apprentice" is not used in the agreement. Several times the union has asked that a regular apprenticeship be established, including a ratio of apprentices to journeymen. The union concern in recent years seems to have been primarily to insure that men who wish to learn the warehousemen's trade thoroughly and to qualify for the journeyman rate at the end of three years shall be allowed to do so—and not be kept at common labor for three years and then refused the journeyman scale on the ground that they are not competent warehousemen. The Brotherhood wishes it made clear "when a man is on as an apprentice" and when he is employed merely to do common labor. In the 1926 conference the union was assured by the labor committee that if a young man really entered the warehouse to learn the trade the firm would not refuse to give him a chance. After this clarification of the situation the union dropped its proposal for formal apprenticeship.

The only branch not covered by the uniform wage scale in which the employers have agreed to apprenticeship rules is decorating kiln work. In 1915 the employers acceded to the request from the union that no experienced decorating kilnman should be laid off to

[5] See above, pp. 171-172.

make room for a beginner.[6] In 1921 a union proposal for graduated discounts for apprentices during a two-year term was adopted; no ratio of apprentices to journeymen was established, but the ratios in the other branches had by this time become practically obsolete.

An interesting feature of the apprenticeship system in several of the branches—kilnplacing, dipping, packing, saggermaking, and decorating kiln work—is that the journeymen with whom the apprentices work are credited with their outputs and charged with the apprentice's wages, except where the journeymen themselves are on the time system. In saggermaking the "apprentice" is really the helper of a piece-working journeyman. In kilnplacing and decorating kiln work the apprentice works as a member of a crew which has a collective output. In dipping and packing, the system seems to be a survival from the contract system. In all of these branches, except saggermaking, the rates to be paid the apprentice are fixed in the agreement and are so adjusted that the journeymen have to pay less for the apprentices than their work amounts to at the piece rates, in the later stages of apprenticeship at least. This is because it is assumed that the journeymen give time to the teaching of the apprentice, thus reducing their own outputs.[7]

That the number of apprentices, real and nominal, was regarded as a serious evil in some of the branches before 1900 has already been pointed out. After the

---

[6] This rule was then adopted for the two-year period only, but it has been retained in the agreement without limit of time.

[7] In the case of kilnplacing the agreement states it as follows: "This concession is made to the kiln crew in consideration of the time they give teaching the apprentice, and it is understood that the kilnmen are to be responsible for the workmanship of said apprentice."

initial establishment of joint regulations governing the putting-on of apprentices and the term of apprenticeship and the scale of discounts at which the apprentice should work, the ratio of apprentices to journeymen ceased to be an important issue in most branches. From the beginning, too, the ratios fixed in the agreement had been in several of the branches subject to modifying provisos. One commonly conceded by the employers was that no journeyman should be discharged to make way for an apprentice in order to fill the firm's quota. On the other side, the union conceded in 1900 the proviso that an additional apprentice may be put on " where a scarcity of kilnmen exists." This rule was invoked with great frequency in the earlier years.[8] In 1901 the same concession was made to the manufacturers in return for ratios in pressing and turning. As there was a surplus of pressers, the rule was of little importance in this branch. In turning it was invoked several times in the year following its adoption.[9] The rule in dipping, mouldmaking, and packing was merely that " an apprentice may be put on whenever it is not possible to secure a competent journeyman." [10]

By 1909 the union was asking for a general rule in all branches that an apprentice may not be put on if a journeyman of the craft is available, regardless of the ratio. It was the kilnmen who were most active in demanding such a rule. It was only just, they said, that if the employers were to be allowed to put on apprentices beyond the quota when men were scarce, " thereby flooding the trade with men who must of necessity loaf

[8] For example, *Proceedings, N. B. of O. P.*, 1901, p. 62.

[9] *Ibid.*, 1902, p. 13.

[10] In 1909 a ratio of 1 to 4 was adopted in mouldmaking "for the trade as a whole."

during the dull times," the employers should be estopped from putting on apprentices, even within the quota, " when work is scarce and journeymen kilnmen can be found who are competent to fill vacancies." [11] The employers would not agree to the rule proposed by the union but promised that, " if at any time the adding of new apprentices in any branch of the trade works an apparent hardship, owing to the depressed business conditions, any petition from the N. B. of O. P. to the U. S. P. A. setting forth this situation, will be given proper consideration." In 1913 the promise given in 1909 was reaffirmed and the Brotherhood, on its part, agreed that " if at any time it is found impossible to secure competent journeymen workmen in any branch of the trade, any petition from the U. S. P. A. setting forth such condition, shall be given proper consideration by the N. B. of O. P."

In 1917 the employers asked that for the length of the " labor shortage traceable to the war " the apprentice ratios be suspended in all branches and the manufacturer allowed to put on an apprentice whenever he had a vacancy which the Brotherhood officers could not fill with " a competent, steady journeyman " within ten days. This proposal led to an agreement to set up joint committees which were authorized to allow a manufacturer to start extra apprentices—or women, according to the circumstances. The committee was to assure itself in each case that the manufacturer had first made an honest effort to secure journeymen.[12]

[11] *Proceedings, N. B. of O. P.*, 1909, p. 46.

[12] The East Liverpool " labor shortage committee," which acted for the West, outside of Sebring, was the most active of the committees. As late as the spring of 1924 it was putting on extra apprentices in kiln work.

In 1921, with business poor, the Brotherhood became concerned again about the putting-on of apprentices within the ratio and asked that a rule be adopted specifically prohibiting the starting of an apprentice in any branch when there were journeymen out of employment. The employers agreed to incorporate such a rule if a narrow limit were put on the time within which a journeyman should be supplied, and a twenty-four-hour limit to the period within which the Brotherhood is to furnish the journeyman was set. The employers have not, as a matter of fact, generally insisted on the twenty-four-hour limit in practice.[13] Thus the ratios were expressly made inoperative so long as the Brotherhood can furnish a competent journeyman on short notice—which has been generally the case since 1924. In 1928 the executive board characterized the 1921 rule as the " best law of our entire working agreement." [14]

One effect of the 1921 rule, has been that the employers in the East Liverpool district with the up-to-date plants have not had an opportunity to put on any apprentices in recent years, in most branches. Such apprentices as have been started since 1924 have nearly all gone on in plants outside of East Liverpool. Most journeymen already located in the East Liverpool district prefer to remain there and when a vacancy has occurred in one of the newer plants in the district there has nearly always been a journeyman candidate for it. For example, in the three plants of the Homer Laughlin China Company at Newell, with a capacity of 70 kilns, there were in 1926 only four apprentices and these were in two branches.[15]

[13] *Proceedings, N. B. of O. P.*, 1924, pp. 24, 27, 59; *Potters Herald*, July 10, 1924.

[14] *Report of Executive Board*, 1928, p. 21.

[15] *Proceedings, U. S. P. A.*, 1926, p. 29.

In 1928 Mr. W. E. Wells attacked the 1921 rule because it prevented his company from putting on as an apprentice jiggerman a young man whom it " desired to reward " by this advancement for " five years of good faithful service as a batter-out and mould-runner " and compelled it to fill the vacancy with a journeyman who had never before been in its employ.[16] At first Mr. Wells' complaint was not so much against the rule as against President James Duffy's application of it. The rule was never intended, Mr. Wells maintained, to be applied in this way. But when the national officers insisted on the strict interpretation of the law, the employers proposed to the 1928 conference that it be amended to the effect that if a firm is within the ratio of apprentices prescribed for that branch it " shall have the privilege of filling the vacancy from any of its own employees, provided that they are competent and have been employed by the same firm for a period of at least three years."

The rule, as interpreted by the Brotherhood officers. had been shown to work unfairly, Mr. Wells maintained, both to certain firms and to the young men employed in their plants. The firm was prevented from building up its labor force from within and consequently from encouraging loyal service by holding out the hope of eventual promotion to journeyman status. To this the union side replied that the rule had been adopted to prevent the putting-on of apprentices while journeymen were unemployed; that situation still obtained. Men who are already journeymen are entitled to whatever jobs there are and, declared President Duffy, men who are already members of the Brotherhood are entitled to preference over those who are not

[16] Report of Executive Board, 1928, pp. 21-22; MS. Report of Conference, 1928.

members and not working under the agreement—referring to the helpers; nor would it aid these young men,
in the long run, to be put on as apprentices and swell
the ranks of the unemployed journeymen. The Brotherhood side stood firmly on the rule and refused to make
any concession from it. In this it was undoubtedly following the sentiment of the convention.[17] It was a difficult time for any union committee to agree to give up
any preference for unemployed journeymen.

The term of apprenticeship, like the ratio, has at
times been modified in practice. In some of the
branches the union's insistence upon having a specified
term of apprenticeship fixed in the agreement proceeded in large part from a desire to put a limit to the
time that a man might be employed by the firm at a
discount from the journeyman list.[18] Once that was
accomplished the Brotherhood's position on the length
of the term was determined by the usual considerations—its relation to the proper training of the apprentice and its effect, together with that of the ratio, on the
rate of inflow into the trade.

Even before the adoption of the 1900 agreement the
Brotherhood suspended its own rule requiring a three-
year term for apprentice kiln work and allowed apprentices to be advanced to the status and pay of journeymen at the end of the second year. This action was
taken by the 1899 convention to meet a shortage of
kilnmen and was to hold for a period of one year.
Nearly all of the "two-year apprentices" in the East

[17] *Proceedings,* 1928, pp. 40-41, 59-62.

[18] See testimony of Mr. William Burgess, representing the manufacturers, before the Ways and Means Committee, November 23,
1908. *Tariff Hearings before the Committee on Ways and Means of
the House of Representatives,* 60th Cong., 1908-1909 (Washington:
Government Printing Office, 1909), I, 872.

Liverpool district were thus advanced. The period of
the dispensation was several times extended by union
action, but by the end of 1903 the shortage was over
and the advancing of two-year apprentices to full journeyman status was brought to an end.[19] Then, during
the war period, it was agreed that after the end of the
second year the "apprentice" should receive journeyman wages, although not advanced to full journeyman
status.

For years the manufacturers have believed that the
prescribed term is in most branches longer than is
required by an ordinary young man to learn the trade
but they have not been disposed to make much of an
issue of this since it has been understood that additional
apprentices may be put on when there is a shortage
of journeymen. Moreover, there are now so few apprentices that the question of the length of the term
receives little attention.

CRAFT DEMARCATION IN THE CLAY SHOP

"Industrial unionism" in the general ware pottery
industry has not meant the elimination of questions of
craft demarcation. It is only within the clay-shop
department that the separate crafts are enough alike to
make the question of demarcation a practical one, but
most of the branches in this department have clung
tenaciously to craft preference in filling vacancies and
to the perpetuation of distinct craft lines through separate apprenticeship. The employers, while favoring the
utmost freedom for the firm in filling vacancies, have
generally avoided a frontal attack on craft "rights"
and they have been especially wary of being drawn

[19] *Proceedings,* 1898, p. 30; 1899, pp. 6, 27, 38; 1900, p. 7; 1901,
pp. 7, 62, 63; 1902, pp. 9, 71, 91-92, 120-121; 1903, p. 14.

into the enforcement of the " rights " given a craft by
union law against the members of another craft.

The chief recognition of craft rights in the agreement is in the rule that an apprentice may not be put
on if the Brotherhood can furnish a competent journeyman of that craft. The union recognizes the right of
the employer to put on a journeyman of another branch
instead of an apprentice, if he wishes, when there is no
journeyman candidate from the branch in which the
vacancy occurs.[20] But even in this case the transferring journeyman does not acquire the right to take
another job in that branch until after has has served in
the first job at least a year. This period of protection
against the competition of recent immigrants from
other branches for subsequent vacancies was adopted
in 1921 on the initiative of the turners and handlers of
East Liverpool, who found that some of the immigrants
had been " taking unfair advantage " of the permission given them.[21]

The most serious attempt to break down craft lines
in the clay shop was made in 1909. It was initiated by
the pressers, who were especially eager for the removal

[20] In 1905, when the apprenticeship rules for jiggering were adopted,
no provision for additional apprentices was included in the rules
for this branch; instead it was provided that the employers might
draw men from other clay-shop branches.

[21] *Proceedings*, 1921, p. 17; *Constitution*, Sec. 264. The sanitary
pressers had also obtained union legislation to stop the general ware
pressers from transferring to sanitary ware pressing, except under
restrictive conditions. No general ware presser was allowed to start
at sanitary pressing so long as the union could furnish a sanitary
presser, and then he must remain in the employ of the firm with
which he started for a period of one year in order to be recognized
as a sanitary presser. *Report of President*, 1906, p. 28; *Proceedings*,
1906, pp. 38, 45, 46. The application of this rule made a good deal
of trouble within the organization. *Report of President*, 1908, pp.
12-13, 18-21; 1909, pp. 17-18.

of branch barriers because many classes of ware formerly made by the pressing process were now being fashioned in other ways. The pressers had in fact been given preference, by union rule, in filling jobs at " sticking-up and finishing after the big jigger " and in order to give them a clear field no special apprenticeship had been established for this work.[22] But the pressers were still chafing against union rules which kept them out of vacancies in other crafts, so long as there was a member of the craft in question out of employment. In 1908 the pressers' local union of East Liverpool presented a proposal to the convention that " a legitimate journeyman clay worker shall be permitted to accept a position in any department of the clay shops, without restriction, so long as he receives journeyman pay and is competent to fill the position." The convention would go no further than adopting the rule which allows a transfer in case of a vacancy for which " it is impossible to secure a competent journeyman of the particular branch." [23]

In 1909, when the Brotherhood asked to have the latter rule incorporated in the agreement the manufacturers refused. They did not object to giving a journeyman a position in a waremaking branch other than that in which he had served his apprenticeship, provided he was competent to do the work, but they did object to putting the proposed clause into the agreement. There would be trouble, they declared, " in almost every case " in which it was attempted to apply the rule. They made a counter proposition that all craft distinctions in the clay shop be done away with and the clay shop " made one trade " with a common apprenticeship. This, it will be noted, is practically

[22] *Proceedings*, 1902, p. 76.
[23] *Ibid.*, 1908, p. 56.

what the pressers had been seeking. The conference committee, while not opposed to the proposal, decided that it should not be adopted without giving the members of the clay-shop branches a chance to pass on it, and it was submitted to a referendum vote of those members. In spite of the fact that President Duffy strongly favored it the proposal was defeated by a large majority.

President Duffy's statement of the case for the proposal and his explanation of its defeat are interesting:

If this plan had been put into practice years ago, and all the men now working in the various branches of the clay shop had served their apprenticeship under a system that would have equipped them to do competent work in any department of the clay shop, it would have . . . . precluded such deplorable spectacles as two men, members of the same organization, fighting for a job which either one could competently fill, yet one contests the other's right to it because one is a presser, the other a dishmaker, or one is a sticker-up, the other a handler, etc. It would also . . . . have given the members of each branch six or seven opportunities where they now have one. In isolated potteries it would have enabled our members to help one another in certain cases in which they are now forbidden to do (it). . . . . Many of the journeymen in the various branches are able to do only work in their particular branch; . . . . by opening their branch to others, they felt that they would be lessening their opportunities in their own branch without being able to take advantage of the opportunities that would be opened to them in the other branches. This argument seemed to predominate and was responsible for the rejection of the proposition.[24]

HOURS

The number of hours that shall constitute the normal working day or working week has never been an outstanding issue. This is easily understood when it is remembered that until recently the piece-work system was almost universally followed in the organized

[24] *Report of President*, 1910, pp. 5-7.

branches, except in warehouse work. The piece workers fixed their own hours, so far as the employers were concerned. The Brotherhood has attempted, by internal legislation, to hold the individual piece workers to a maximum day, to be worked within specified starting and stopping times, but the union " hours rule " has not been well observed by the piece workers.[25] In this, as in some other matters in which the Brotherhood has attempted to control its members by union rule alone without a satisfactory degree of success, it has at times sought the coöperation of the employers. And here, too, the manufacturers have been wary of assuming any share of responsibility for coercing the recalcitrant workers in a matter of no great importance to the employers.

The normal day for time workers was fixed in the agreement in 1903 at nine hours. With the spread of the eight-hour day in other industries the members of the Brotherhood came to believe that they ought to establish the eight-hour limit for their industry as a matter of principle and to keep in step with other unions.[26] The employers refused the request for the eight-hour day for time workers. It would mean, they said, the same pay for an hour less a day not only for the warehousemen and for those warehousewomen employed at day wages, but also for all the day workers in the unorganized occupations; they could not give it to the warehousemen and warehousewomen and refuse it to the other operatives. The nine-hour day still stands for warehousemen [27] and, so far as the

[25] *Proceedings, N. B. of O. P.,* 1913, pp. 38-41; 1919, p. 22.

[26] *Ibid.,* 1921, p. 69.

[27] The union submitted a proposal in 1928 for an eight-hour day for warehousemen, for the existing daily wage, with payment at time and one half for overtime, but it was withdrawn without discussion in the conference.

agreement is concerned, for day workers in every other branch except dipping. In that branch the eight-hour day was practically recognized by the employers in the 1905 agreement—in the specification of the maximum output per day. When the day-wage system was introduced in dipping, after the war, the employers made no attempt to hold the dippers to a nine-hour day.[28]

There is no provision in the agreement for more than the usual rate of pay for working outside the normal working times except one for double pay on holidays.[29] However, it has been customary to pay higher rates for overtime.[30] For work on Sundays the more common practice was to pay "time and a half," but "double time" was not unknown. The Brotherhood asked for a general rule for double time in 1917 but the employers insisted that the rate be left to the individual firms and their men.

The advent of tunnel kilns has made the issue of overtime rates much more important. The manufacturers are now taking the position that rules made or customs established when the plants were on a periodic kiln basis should not be applied to continuous kiln plants; Sundays and nights—and holidays, as well—

[28] It is the employers who are contending that the agreement implies that the normal day in day-wage dipping should be eight hours. The dippers insist that it is seven and one-half hours— that is, eight hours minus the half-hour lunch period in the forenoon, which has been an established custom in the dipping trade (and among the kilnmen as well) for many years.

[29] In 1909 "time and a half" was granted the kilndrawers for Sunday work, and in the agreement made with the kilndrawers in 1918, time and a half was granted for the third kiln drawn in one day. The kilndrawers' scale is still printed in the national scale but the Brotherhood has not dealt with the manufacturers for the kilndrawers for many years.

[30] For example, *Report of Executive Board*, 1927, pp. 28-30.

should be recognized as normal working times and subject to the regular rates of pay. The men are benefiting by the tunnel kilns through easier work, the employers argue, and should make some concession in return; moreover, it would help the manufacturers to keep going, by lowering costs, and so work to the advantage of the other operatives.

In 1928 the employers proposed that the double time rule for holidays should not apply to the " kilnplacers, kilndrawers, dippers and their helpers, ware brushers and stampers whose work is necessary for the continuous and steady operation of tunnel kilns." They offered time and a half, although they contended that it should be "straight time." The union would not accept time and a half.[31] In the course of this discussion, however, the employers raised a more important question, one on which they had submitted no proposal. This concerned the payment of overtime rates for Sunday work. It was unfair, they protested, that they should have to pay " penalty " rates for Sunday work in the continuous departments when Sunday work is unavoidable. To be sure, the agreement did not specify that overtime rates should be paid, but the fact was that the men would not work unless they got them. They urged that the union agree to straight time for Sunday work in these departments when it was necessary; if the men would agree to that, the manufacturers would throw every safeguard around it to prevent its abuse. The union side consented to consider a proposal on the matter and when, later in the conference, the manufacturers sub-

[31] It did concede that, for the future, time and a half should be paid, instead of double time, for working on Monday, July 5, or Monday, December 26, when Independence Day or Christmas falls on Sunday and the holiday is celebrated on Monday.

mitted their proposal, the union accepted it. It provides that

when due to conditions over which the N. B. of O. P. and the U. S. P. A. have no control, it is necessary on tunnel kiln plants to work on Sunday in the kiln, dipping and bisque warehouse departments, the work shall be done on the regular scale rate and no extra time shall be allowed.

RIGHT TO DISCHARGE

Nothing was put in the agreement specifically limiting the employers' right to discharge until 1913. Then the limitation was imposed only upon discharge without two weeks' notice. It is only in case of immediate discharge that the cause of the discharge comes explicitly within the purview of the agreement. As a matter of practice, however, the Brotherhood has always taken the position that it will support members against discharge, with or without notice, for union activity or insisting on their rights under the agreement. Even after the no-strike rule of the agreement had been well established, the union constitution made special exception of local strikes against "discrimination" discharges.[32] More than once, too, before 1913, the union went to the length of threatening to close the plant to secure the reinstatement of a man or men whom the officers deemed to have been unjustly discharged.[33]

[32] *Proceedings*, 1904, pp. 112-113; *Rules and Regulations*, 1904, Article VIII, Secs. 4 and 5; *Proceedings*, 1907, p. 58; *Rules and Regulations*, 1910, Sec. 56; *Constitution*, 1925, Sec. 95. Sometimes the union gave the victimized member strike benefits until he secured another position, rather than call a strike in the shop if the former course seemed more prudent. See *Proceedings*, 1904, p. 17. This course had been followed by the Trenton jiggermen's local assembly of the Knights of Labor. MS. *Minutes, L. A. 3573*.

[33] *Proceedings*, 1904, p. 17; *Report of President*, 1905, p. 10; 1907, pp. 5-6; 1911, pp. 10-11.

The silence of the discharge agreement on the point of the reason for discharge after notice does not mean that the Brotherhood accepted the view that the employer has a right to discharge for any reason whatever, so long as he gives two weeks' notice. The employer's original proposals in 1913 read that a workman might resign his position on two weeks' notice or an employer discharge on two weeks' notice " without assigning a reason." The clause just quoted was not included in the agreement. The union view is that arbitrary discharge is precluded by another clause which was included—that " the provisions of this agreement shall be liberally and fairly interpreted in such a manner as not to work an undue hardship upon any of the parties thereto." And in its 1914 report the labor committee "ventured" to suggest " a liberal interpretation of the agreement, and to caution against the possible abuse of the discharge privilege to satisfy personal grievance." [34] The employers have on the whole acted in this spirit. The existence of a permanent joint discharge committee, too, affords an opportunity for investigation and adjustment in any case in which injustice is charged.[35]

In 1922 the union sought to have its position that a man should not be discharged without good reason recognized as a rule of the agreement. The proposal was that " no employee shall be discharged for other than

[34] *Proceedings, U. S. P. A.*, 1914, p. 38.

[35] In the August, 1922, conference when it came to light that a man had been discriminated against for something he had said in a previous conference, Chairman Wells expressed regret that the incident had occurred and also that the man had not brought his case to the discharge committee or to the labor committee. " Had we known it," he added, "you would have been taken care of as no man ever was."

poor workmanship, unless the firm can give sufficient reason to the local union under whose jurisdiction the discharged employee is working." Asking that the employer satisfy the local union as to the sufficiency of his reason did not help the proposal with the employers.[36] Apart from this, however, the employers rejected the proposal as too one-sided. The workman has the right to leave without giving a reason, they said, and frequently workmen have left, just when they were most needed, simply because they were tired of their jobs. Unless that could be stopped the manufacturers would not bind themselves not to discharge without giving a reason. Chairman Wells said he personally thought that a man discharged should be told the reason and another member of the labor committee added that he was perfectly willing to tell the man, or anyone else, why he was discharged, but they would not agree to make it a compulsory rule.[37]

NOTICE OF DISCHARGE OR RESIGNATION

The proposal that " the custom of giving and taking two weeks' notice be made a part of the agreement and that such notice be given in writing " was first made by the Brotherhood, in 1911. In the 1913 conference the employers came in with an elaborate plan covering notice of discharge and resignation and after two days of discussion the essential features of this plan were adopted.[38] It provides that, except in special cases enumerated in the agreement, the employer may not discharge a workman without notice nor may a workman leave without notice. In both cases the notice period is

[36] See below, pp. 315-316.

[37] See *Report of Executive Board*, 1928, pp. 25-30, for a complaint of unfair discharges.

[38] *Report of President*, 1914, p. 11.

two weeks and in both the notice must be in writing on
prescribed forms. After the notice is served the workman " must actually work for said two weeks, and not
loaf without reasonable excuse, unless otherwise mutually satisfactory to both workman and employer."
At the end of the two weeks, if the man has properly
worked out his notice period, he is entitled to a " discharge " paper. The importance of the discharge paper,
as intended by the agreement, is that the employee may
not " legally " obtain another situation without one.

If the employer discharges without notice he must
give the man an " immediate discharge " paper, on
which the reason for the discharge is stated. The discharged employee may take an appeal to the joint discharge committee on the reason assigned and if he is
sustained he is to be reinstated and reimbursed for the
time he has lost, in excess of three days. It was expected when the agreement was adopted that a man
given an immediate discharge would have difficulty in
securing employment. The employers' original proposal was that he could not be employed until after two
weeks. This was not included in the agreement. The
discharge committee later decided that after a man so
discharged had been unemployed—that is, not employed
by a member of the Association—for two weeks he
could secure a " clean " discharge from the secretary
of the Association. Conversely, the workman was given
the right to quit without notice, and to receive a
" clean " discharge paper, " in case he has been sub-
jected to unfair or abusive treatment by his employer,
or in case his employer has violated any provision of
the wage agreement *in dealing with that particular
workman*." [39] If the employer refuses to give him a

[39] Italics are the writer's. See below, pp. 348, 353.

proper discharge paper the man may appeal to the discharge committee. If he is not sustained he must return and work out his notice, or go unemployed for two weeks, before he can secure a discharge paper. The same is true of a man who is adjudged not to have worked out his two weeks' notice properly.

The agreement of 1913 called for the establishment of two joint discharge committees, one for the West and one for the East, " to aid in the operation and correct interpretation of this agreement." Each committee was to have two members from each side. It was specified that the secretary of the Association and the secretary of the Brotherhood should be members of the western committee and that the secretary of the Trenton Potters Association and the first vice-president of the Brotherhood should be members of the eastern committee. The eastern committee never met. To all practical intents and purposes there is no eastern discharge committee nor have the provisions of the agreement covering discharge papers, etc., been followed in the East.

It will be seen that the degree of protection which the discharge agreement actually gives the manufacturers against quitting without serving out the two weeks' notice depends upon the degree to which the manufacturers make it impossible for the workman to get a job without a discharge paper. The protection offered the workman by the agreement can be secured by appealing to the discharge committee; that which it was intended to give the manufacturers can only be secured through the other manufacturers. If a workman who leaves without a discharge paper knows he will be taken on at another plant immediately, there is no penalty. To be sure, he has no redress against discharge without notice if he has not deposited a discharge paper with his employer, but this danger did not prove much of a deterrent when men were in demand. The enforcement of the two weeks' notice requirement upon the men thus depends in practice upon whether the manufacturers as a whole insist upon the deposit of a discharge paper as a condition of employment.

It is at this point that the working of the discharge agreement showed the greatest weakness. Some employers failed to observe the rule that a man should not be taken on without a discharge paper. It was a type of non-observance which tended to provoke others to non-observance. For an employer who had been scrupulously insisting on the presentation of a discharge paper to discover that a man who had left a job in his plant without notice had been immediately engaged at another plant was an experience that did not encourage him to observe the agreement in filling the vacancy.[40] In the shortage of men which began in 1916 the rules were often successfully ignored. The situation became so bad that the Association, in its December, 1920, meeting, adopted a rule that any firm hiring a member of the Brotherhood without a discharge paper should be fined $100.00 [41] With the recession of the demand for men in recent years, the rules have been better observed, but they are not fully observed even now.[42]

DISTRIBUTION OF WORK

What is to be done when the firm has not enough work for all of its regular employees? Is there to be

[40] *Proceedings, U. S. P. A.,* December, 1923, p. 67.

[41] *Ibid.,* January, 1920, p. 71; December, 1920, pp. 79-80. This did not apply to the hiring of men who are brought in to help out temporarily and not taken on as regular employees.

[42] *Ibid.,* 1927, p. 64.

an order of preference, based on seniority or some other factor, within which men are to be fully employed and beyond which they are to be laid off entirely? Or is the work to be divided evenly among the men in the same trade in the same plant? The members of the Brotherhood have from the beginning favored the latter rule. As piece workers, employed at rates which presumably gave wages in correspondence with the amount and kind of work performed, they seem to have assumed that equal opportunity to share in the work to be done was the only fair course. And the employers have agreed to this, generally, in practice. As the employees were, until recently, overwhelmingly on a piece-work basis, the question of the employers' freedom to dispense with the least efficient workers first, which has been an important point in trades working under a union minimum time rate, was not of great moment.

The practice of equal distribution of work in dull times is sanctioned by the agreement as a " request "; it is not a general compulsory rule. " Manufacturers are requested when work is short to instruct foremen to divide work as equally as possible, and not to prefer some men over others in the distribution." This was inserted in 1911 on the initiative of the Brotherhood. In 1926 the union asked that it be made a compulsory rule. In some instances, the union side said, the spirit of the recommendation had not been followed. The manufacturers were unwilling to make the change. They feared that some men might demand a share of work of a kind they were unable to do efficiently. They feared also that it might interfere with the cutting down of the force when one kind of work was permanently reduced in favor of something else. The union conferees disclaimed any intention of insisting upon such interpretations. Nevertheless the manufacturers maintained that a compulsory rule would lead to disputes. So long as the recommendation was meeting with " a good response " they were opposed to substituting a coercive rule which might bring trouble.

THE " CLOSED SHOP "

There has never been any rule in the agreement to the effect that only members of the Brotherhood shall be employed in those branches covered by the scale. That such a rule has not been adopted is not due to failure on the part of the Brotherhood to ask for it. Several times the union has requested the employers to give it this aid in keeping fully organized the branches for which it deals. As the " no-strike " feature of the agreement system has estopped the union from forcing the individual employer by a strike threat to require union membership as a condition of employment, the Brotherhood has sought to meet the situation by securing a statement in the agreement that all operatives in the branches covered by the wage agreement shall be members of the Brotherhood in good standing. The union has urged that the inclusion of a statement to this effect in the agreement would be of itself sufficient for its purpose, without the necessity of coercion by the employer of individual employees to join or remain in the Brotherhood. But the employers have steadily refused to subscribe to any kind of a " closed shop " rule in the agreement.

Before the days of the agreement there was a strong sentiment in the union in favor of insisting on the " card shop "—that is, requiring every operative to have a paid-up union card in order to work in an organized branch in the shop—wherever it was possible to do

20

so.[43] However, this was never carried to the point of making refusal to work with non-members a general rule of the organization.[44] After 1905 the problem was not so much to get the operatives to join the union as " how to keep the members in line permanently." [45] President Duffy believed that persuasion, rather than force, was the proper policy and this was one of his reasons for favoring shop locals as against branch locals, a remedy which the convention would not adopt. Disappointed in this, President Duffy continued to urge that the members could meet the problem, without " interfering with the smooth running of the shop," if they would make a sustained effort.[46]

The 1907 convention was not satisfied with the results of the policy of persuasion. After wrestling with the familiar proposal that members refuse to work with delinquents it handed the problem over to the conference committee with instructions to use its best efforts " to get the ' closed shop.' " [47] The union side accordingly submitted a proposition in that year " that all workmen whose wages and conditions are regulated by agreement between the United States Potters Association and the National Brotherhood of Operative Potters must be members of the National Brotherhood of Operative Potters." As anticipated by the officers, the employers refused to agree to this. When the union repeated the proposal in 1911 the employers again

[43] In the years when the Knights of Labor organization was strong in Trenton the policy of the " card shop " was enforced, in a number of plants, at least. *Official Souvenir*, 1893; *Proceedings, D. A. 160*, 1890, pp. 9-10, 53; MS. *Minutes, L. A. No. 3573*.

[44] *Proceedings*, 1898, pp. 32-33; 1900, p. 52; 1902, p. 6; 1903, pp. 111-112; 1904, pp. 13-14.

[45] *Report of President*, 1906, p. 22.

[46] *Ibid.*, 1907, p. 9.

[47] *Proceedings*, 1907, p. 50.

rejected it.[48] Not only did the employers refuse to become a party to a " closed shop " rule; they refused in the next conference to concede to the men the right, within the agreement, to attempt to enforce union membership by refusal to work with non-members. In the next subsequent conference, that of 1915, they also declined to make it a rule of the agreement that preference be given to union members in filling vacancies in the branches covered by the uniform wage scale.

From 1915 to 1926 the union attempted to meet the problem of maintaining complete organization through its own efforts. However, the policy of handling the problem outside the agreement was not accepted by the 1917 convention until after a long fight for a more aggressive one. The convention declared that the Brotherhood " reserves the right to refuse to allow its members to work with non-union workers " but it was left to the executive board to decide what measures should be taken in each individual case. If as the result of any action decided upon by the board, any members were forced to cease work they were to receive strike benefits for the time lost.[49] This disposition of the question kept the matter ouside the agreement, where the employers had insisted that it remain, and left the executive board free to deal with local sore spots in such a way as to avoid a violation of the no-strike rule of the agreement.

The refusal of members to work with " scabs " stood on a different footing from refusal to work with ordinary non-members, in the eyes of the union, although the agreement gave no more express sanction in the

---

[48] *Proceedings, U. S. P. A.,* 1911, p. 43.

[49] *Proceedings,* 1917, pp. 43, 44, 81, 92-93; *Constitution,* 1920, Sec. 79; 1925, Sec. 80.

one case than in the other. President Duffy had sharply differentiated between the two in 1907. He said:

While we have never objected to working with non-members as long as we were sure they were getting the scale price, I feel that we have a right to refuse to work with out and out scabs, and our members should refuse to work with them. Even though our agreements do not compel the employers to hire none but union men, the employer cannot reasonably ask or expect our members to work with scabs.[50]

This did not mean that the members were to take the matter into their own hands and go on strike, but that they were to leave the case to the national officers to handle. As a matter of fact, it did not become a practical issue in the general ware division. For many years there was only one non-union pottery and for several years more only two, and the manufacturers working under the agreement did not attempt to employ men who had incurred the hostility of the union members by working in one of these plants.

In the matter of withdrawals from membership because of dissatisfaction with the terms accepted or settlements made by the Brotherhood, the employers did agree, in 1905, to insert a clause in the agreement nominally giving the Brotherhood protection against them. The labor committee declared, too, that it stood ready, when appealed to by the Brotherhood officers, to enforce this clause by insisting that the offending persons " pay up " or take notices of discharge. Referring to the withdrawal of some members of the Brotherhood in protest against the casting agreement of 1914 the labor committee said: " If we are to hope for just settle-

[50] *Report of President*, 1907, p. 10; 1911, p. 7. In 1910 the convention declared that members should not work with anyone who had "learned his trade" in the Onondaga Pottery, which had always been non-union. *Proceedings*, 1910, p. 26.

ments in future we must use all our influence and power to see that individuals do not repudiate the work of Brotherhood committees in dealing with us. It is especially recommended that employers go as far the law allows in this respect." [51]

If the exclusion from employment of all who left the union because of dissatisfaction with settlements agreed to by a Brotherhood committee had been rigorously enforced, there would have been little that a closed shop rule could have added to the percentage of organization, down to 1923. There were very few men in the union shops in the branches covered by the agreement who had not been members of the Brotherhood at some time or other. The great majority of the workers in the branches covered by the agreement, it is assumed, believed in the superiority of the method of collective bargaining for the determination of the general terms of employment and willingly supported the organization which made this possible, as they do still. But this is not all. There are other considerations of a more individual character which tell in favor of union membership with some who otherwise might be inclined to leave to their fellow workers the task of maintaining the organization that carries on the negotiation of terms of employment—which apply to all the workers, members and non-members alike.

The fact that so many of the branches in the general ware pottery industry are on piece work has undoubtedly been an important influence in inducing individuals to join the union. The piece worker has many individual concerns—the pricing of a new or changed article, a claim for extra for a changed condition, " excessive loss," etc.—which call for the necessity of particu-

[51] *Proceedings, U. S. P. A.,* 1914, p. 38.

lar settlements. Union membership means the advantage of union support for these individual interests. This factor is not as influential in general ware as it was in sanitary pressing,[52] but it is not unimportant. To be sure, the disappointment of some of its members with the results of the handling of cases of this kind through the joint machinery has itself been a cause of dissatisfaction with the union at times and of some refusals to pay any longer to an organization which "can do nothing" for them. However, there were not enough individual withdrawals for this reason in the years of prosperity to make them a disturbing factor.

There is also an individual advantage in union membership in the matter of securing a job and in the protection afforded against immediate discharge. Although there is no express rule of preference to union members in filling vacancies, it has long been a common practice for employers to apply to the Brotherhood when they need men. The fact that the employer is required to give the Brotherhood a chance to furnish a journeyman before putting on someone not a journeyman in the particular craft has also helped in this. Of course, the employer is free to put on a non-union journeyman of that craft if he can find one but it is simpler to apply to the Brotherhood in the beginning. Thus the union member ordinarily has a better chance of finding a place with the assistance of the Brotherhood than the non-union member has of finding one for himself. In the matter of discharge, although the employers maintain that the non-member has the same rights as a union member and may appeal to the discharge committee to secure protection of them, the union would not take up the case of a non-member with the employer or bring it to the discharge committee.

[52] See below, ch. xiv.

It is those operatives who will not join *willingly* or—of greater importance in the matter of numbers—will not willingly remain in, who furnish the problem for the union in its attempt to maintain a satisfactory percentage of organization without a closed shop rule. In some branches it is of course less difficult for the union members to keep the shop one-hundred per cent organized by quiet pressure than in others. The kilnmen are especially favorably situated in this respect. The system of working in crews, under a bench boss who is himself a member of the crew and of the union, makes it difficult for an individual member of the crew to refuse to keep in good standing. In those branches in which each operative does his work separately, a recalcitrant can go his own way unless the other workers resort to the pressure of the threat to give in their notices.

In many cases the Brotherhood officers have received the coöperation of individual employers in dealing with those who refused to join or keep up their payments. The fact that the Association will not agree to a closed shop rule or even a rule of preference to union members in the agreement itself, does not necessarily mean that individual employers will not indicate their preference, when appealed to by the national officers, that their employees should belong to the Brotherhood; still less does it mean that the employers in general give preference to non-unionists. Most of the manufacturers seem to assume that it is proper that workers whose wages and other conditions of employment are regulated by an agreement between the Brotherhood and the Association should belong to the Brotherhood and pay for its support. Mr. Wells, although emphatic in his opposition to a closed shop rule, and to the giving in of notices by the workers as a means of pressure,[53] often used his influence with workers to get them to join or rejoin the Brotherhood.[54] Other manufacturers have been similarly helpful to the union officers in like cases.

The net result of all these forces tending to bring the operatives in and keep them in was that, down to 1923, the Brotherhood normally had nearly as many members as it would have had under a closed shop rule. The percentage of non-members in the branches for which the Brotherhood had asked the closed shop by agreement was usually very small—barring, of course, the periods in which one branch or another was temporarily disaffected.

After 1922 the situation became decidedly unsatisfactory to the officers. There were many withdrawals in the face of the assessment levied because of the continuance of the sanitary ware strike. The depressed condition of the industry after the middle of 1924 also increased the difficulty of holding the operatives to their dues and assessments. Not only was it harder for the men to find the money but there was much dissatisfaction with the meagre conference results and price settlements on new articles. Men were leaving the union on this account and spreading disaffection by complaining that the Brotherhood was powerless to get anything for them.[55]

In the face of these circumstances the union in 1926 again submitted the proposition " that all workmen, whose wages and conditions are regulated by agree-

[53] *Proceedings, U. S. P. A.,* December, 1920, p. 45.

[54] Statements of President Menge and President Wood to the writer; MS. *Report of Conference,* 1928.

[55] Statement of President Wood to the writer; also *Report of Executive Board,* 1925, pp. 32-33.

ment between the United States Potters Association
and the National Brotherhood of Operative Potters,
must be members of the National Brotherhood of Operative Potters." The union officers did not mean that
the manufacturers should pledge themselves to see to
it that their employees keep in good standing in the
union, but they did want it understood that the manufacturers would not hire anyone who was not a member.
They believed that putting the pressure at the hiring
stage would be sufficient; few men would remain outside if they knew that they could not get other jobs in
case they lost those they had.[56] The union was also
desirous of securing more effective enforcement of the
rule against men dropping out because of dissatisfaction with joint settlements.

In the conference the union emphasis was put on the
latter point. The manufacturers replied that they
would see to it that any man who quit paying because
of dissatisfaction with any agreement or settlement
would " be properly attended to " if the union would
bring the case to their attention; if the individual
manufacturer would not act promptly, the labor committee would. They again refused to go farther than
this. Chairman Wells stated that although the manufacturers preferred their employees to be members of
the Brotherhood, they would not agree to force anyone
to join; such coercion would be foreign to the spirit of
their dealings with the Brotherhood and they would
oppose it to the end. " The one thing that has kept our
faith in your organization more than anything else,"
he said, " is that we are not compelled to do the things
proposed by paragraph twenty-two.[57] You have got

[56] Statement of President Wood to the writer.
[57] The union proposition was numbered 22.

your coöperation a whole lot better by leaving it as it stands today." The union side was accordingly obliged to leave the matter there, although the situation is far from satisfactory to the Brotherhood officers.

HEALTH AND COMFORT OF EMPLOYEES

Proposals from the union for the inclusion in the agreement of measures for the protection of the health and comfort of the employees have figured in a number of the conferences. These have covered such matters as heating, lighting, sweeping of the shops, protection from dust, protection against lead poisoning, and toilet facilities. A few of these have been adopted as compulsory rules and others have been adopted as recommendations. In addition, from 1913 to 1924, the two organizations jointly maintained a system of health inspection for the shops.

The joint provision for health inspection grew out of a proposal for coöperation between the manufacturers and the workers in the care of tubercular operatives. Both the leading figures in this movement— Mr. John A. Campbell, on the side of the employers, and Mr. William Mushet, on the side of the operatives— were in the sanitary division, but their plan was to include both divisions of the industry.[58] The Brotherhood and the United States Potters Association each appropriated $5,000 for this purpose. It was found, however, that the cost would be too great and an alternative plan of inspection of the plants was proposed from the manufacturers' side and finally accepted.[59]

[58] *Report of President*, 1911, p. 14; *Proceedings, N. B. of O. P.*, 1911, p. 59; *Proceedings, U. S. P. A.*, 1911, pp. 38-40.

[59] *Ibid.*, 1912, p. 44; *Report of President*, 1912, pp. 10-12; *Proceedings, N. B. of O. P.*, 1912, pp. 19, 39-40.

Two joint health committees were appointed, one for the East and one for the West. The United States Potters Association acted for the manufacturers, both general ware and sanitary, the Sanitary Potters Association paying the former Association its share of the expense.[60] The operatives also had a health committee of their own in each pottery. It was the duty of that committee to acquaint itself with any condition in the shop which affected the health of the operatives adversely and to report it to an inspector appointed by the joint health committee. " The inspector then makes an investigation of the condition complained of, and if, in his opinion, the complaint is a just one he will report the matter to the firm in writing and suggest the proper remedy to relieve the condition." [61] The inspector was to visit each pottery regularly and make regular reports of his activities to the respective sectional joint health committee.

The workings of the health inspector plan in the West fell far short of giving satisfaction to the union members in the first two years.[62] In the East, however, it worked much more satisfactorily. One important reason was that the chairman of the eastern committee, Mr. John A. Campbell, was the sponsor of the movement on the manufacturers' side, and was determined that it should be a success. The eastern committee did not hesitate to bring pressure upon any manufacturer who appeared unwilling to carry out the inspector's recommendations. The success in the East saved the plan and it was revived in the West with the eastern

[60] The Trenton Potters Association acted for all of the Trenton manufacturers for a time but the United States Potters Association later took over this function.

[61] *Report of President*, 1913, p. 4.

[62] *Ibid.;* 1914, p. 18.

inspector, Mr. William Mushet, acting for the West as well.[63] Complaints continued from western members that they were not receiving benefits from the system equal to its cost—some wanted to abolish it and others wanted to put the inspector under the control of the union exclusively—but the officers and the conventions continued to support the inspector and the system.[64]

The joint health inspection plan proved an interesting and valuable example of the extension of national joint action to the sphere of the health and comfort of the employees. Many improvements were made in the conditions in the potteries as a result of the activity of the inspector and—especially in the East—of the joint committees. The operatives themselves, too, were brought to a much higher level of carefulness and observance of sanitary precautions through the work of the inspector and the shop health committees which coöperated with him.[65] In New Jersey the eastern joint health committee collaborated with the state authorities for the purpose of making the application of the health laws of that state to the pottery industry practicable,[66] and the western joint committee adopted a set of health rules to govern the industry which were approved " with some minor modifications " by the Industrial Commission of Ohio.[67]

It was the collapse of the agreement system in the sanitary division which led, indirectly, to the with-

[63] *Proceedings, N. B. of O. P.*, 1915, pp. 82-83; *Proceedings, U. S. P. A.*, 1915, p. 82.

[64] *Proceedings, N. B. of O. P.*, 1915, pp. 82-84; 1916, pp. 42, 53-54; 1917, pp. 106-107; 1918, p. 91.

[65] *Ibid.*, 1915-1918; *Report of Executive Board*, 1919-1924; *Proceedings, U. S. P. A.*, 1914-1923.

[66] *Ibid.*, 1914, p. 56; *Comm. on Ind. Rels.*, III, 3,000-3,001.

[67] *Proceedings, N. B. of O. P.*, 1916, p. 54; 1917, p. 31.

drawal of the United States Potters Association from the joint inspection system. Seventy per cent of the employers' half of the expenses of the system had been paid to the Association by the Sanitary Potters Association. As a matter of fact, most of the work of the inspector had been done in the East. Moreover, "it was brought out in the discussion" (in the December, 1923, meeting of the United States Potters Association), " that during the ten years in which the inspector has been employed the various State governments had so advanced their health departments in looking after the factory conditions that it was felt it was no longer necessary for us to participate in the employment of an Inspector." [68]

PROPOSED JOINT BENEFIT AND PENSION SYSTEM

In 1920 the union proposed to the employers the establishment of a joint fund for sick and disability benefits and old age pensions.[69] The members of the United States Potters Association seemed favorably disposed and a committee was appointed to work out a plan jointly with the Sanitary Potters Association and

[68] *Proceedings, U. S. P. A.,* December, 1923, pp. 82-83.

[69] Meanwhile the Trenton manufacturers and their operatives had established, in 1916, a joint fund for the provision of hospital treatment for employees, in addition to the sanitarium treatment provided by the Brotherhood for members suffering from tuberculosis or asthma. The fund was inaugurated and administered by the eastern joint health committee, but it had no other relation to either the general ware or sanitary ware agreement. It was open to all employees, whether members of the Brotherhood or not. The employees' contributions were deducted from their wages and were matched by the employers. In the calendar year 1921, the last normal year of the hospital fund experience, the expenditures were $11,178.77. The 1922 strike in the sanitary division ultimately killed this project also.

the Brotherhood.[70] But when a plan drawn up by the
representatives of the latter two was submitted to the
general ware manufacturers in November, Mr. Wells
objected to it. He now advocated that each plant conduct the plan for itself and that the firm pay the whole
expense of it. The Brotherhood could then add to the
manufacturers' payments if it chose.[71] Mr. Wells presented this alternative project to the Association and,
at its December meeting, the Association decided that
the manufacturers " should adopt some plan to take
care of sickness, but pass the insurance feature for the
present." The Association then adopted a " proposed
plan for sick benefits," which had no connection with
the joint agreement. No firm was obliged to accept it
and any firm which did was to operate it independently
and make all the payments itself. There was to be no
contribution from the operatives.[72] Some firms adopted
the plan, with some modifications, but others preferred
to go in for group insurance for their employees.

[70] *Proceedings, U. S. P. A.,* January, 1920, pp. 75-77, 78; *Report of
Executive Board,* 1920, p. 6.

[71] *Ibid.,* 1921, pp. 6-7.

[72] *Proceedings, U. S. P. A.,* December, 1920, p. 77; 1921, pp. 125,
128-130.

CHAPTER XI

THE ADJUSTMENT OF LOCAL DISPUTES

THE CAUSES OF LOCAL DISPUTES

The character of the national agreement makes it inevitable that question should arise in the individual shops, in the period between the biennial conferences, regarding the application of the wage scale. In nearly every branch the introduction of a new shape, method, or condition, or what is alleged by the men to be a "new condition," necessarily raises the question of the price to be paid for it. Several of the clauses of the agreement, too, are of such a nature that it is only to be expected that the necessity of applying them to situations arising from time to time, in one plant or another of the many covered by the agreement, should produce some differences of opinion. But in addition to the grist of questions that may be regarded as inevitable many others have in fact been raised by firms or employees which might have been obviated had the parties possessed both a full knowledge of the terms of the agreement and a willingness to conform to them.

A question is not necessarily a "dispute." It does not arrive at that stage unless or until the local parties confess their inability to settle it themselves. In nearly all cases of local disagreement it is the operative side which makes the matter a "dispute." This is but natural, inasmuch as in most matters which give rise to disagreement it is the employer who has the first move. If, for example, the employer offers a certain price for a new article, or introduces a change in methods, or discharges a man, or puts on an apprentice, the men are in the position of having either to accept or appeal.

The great majority of the disputes which are passed along by the local parties are concerned with the question of price. Most of these relate to the price to be paid for new articles—" new " at least to the shop in which the dispute arises. Sometimes it turns out that a price has already been established for the " new " article in another shop, in which case the question is settled by application of the rule that once a price is properly established in any shop for a particular article it holds for all shops under the agreement. If, however, the article has not previously been so priced, the firm and the men in the shop in which it is first introduced have the authority to fix a price for it and the duty to make a serious effort to do so.

The first guide in pricing new articles, according to the custom of the industry, is what is paid for " similar " articles. But this frequently fails to give an answer acceptable to both sides. Owing to the fact that there are important discrepancies in earning possibilities in existing prices, one side may submit as a " similar article " one which is similar physically to the article in question but which carries a price much higher or lower than another offered by the other side which is equally " similar." [1] Repeatedly one side or the other has refused to accept as a basis for pricing, an article quoted by the other side, on the ground that it is " overpaid " or " underpaid."

---

[1] For example, in a dispute before the western general ware standing committee, in 1925, over the price to be paid for jiggering and finishing an olive dish, four " similar " articles were offered in evidence of which two had been priced at seven cents, one at eight cents and one at eleven cents.

The agreement provides that the price of a similar article shall not be followed if this would give a price manifestly unfair on the " average earnings " basis. In such cases the price of the new article is to be " decided upon merit." This was laid down in 1905, in a clause which is known as the " square deal " clause. Obviously the square deal clause does not preclude disputes. Each side is loath to admit that the articles which it offers as a basis are " out of line." The men naturally try to have new prices set on the basis of the better-paid articles, while the employer is inclined to take the opposite view, especially if the new article is intended to replace or compete with the article which he offers as the basis of pricing.

Pricing upon merit involves another factor on which there is often disagreement between the parties, namely, the quantity of the new article that the man should turn out in a given working time. The practical test which is intended to be applied is how many has the man made in a given time, assuming that he was doing his best? It must be recognized that even without a conscious or subconscious retardation of speed because of the bargaining elements involved, the fact that an article is new may make it more difficult at first. Another fact that has added an element of uncertainty has been the lack of an official record of the number of hours spent on a particular job. Yet there is no doubt that parties have at times tried to overreach in making contentions as to output. In 1906 President T. J. Duffy excoriated those union members who had attempted to increase their earnings by this method.[2] The employers contend that this did not put an end to the practice. The men on their side allege that out-

[2] *Report of President,* 1906, pp. 6-7.

21

puts and earnings cited by individual employers are
exaggerated or that the time taken is understated.

The men complain that it is more difficult to secure
reasonable treatment from the firms in pricing new
articles, and on claims for extra pay for extra work
generally, in dull times than in prosperous periods.
When the market is brisk many manufacturers are willing to make what the men regard as "good settlements." In such times the level of earnings has undoubtedly been raised in the setting of new prices. On
the other hand, when the manufacturers are finding it
difficult to market their goods they are inclined to hold
the prices on new work down as low as possible.[3] Thus
the clause calling for pricing upon merit cannot be
expected to prevent disputes, nor has it done so.

In addition to the disputes arising out of the failure
to reach agreement on the prices of really new articles
there have been many wage disputes which would have
been avoided if the rule for the recording of local price
settlements had been properly observed by the parties.
The rule is that when a firm and its employees agree
upon a price for a new article or a new method or a
new condition, that settlement is to be recorded with
the joint standing committee.[4] It was intended to give
practical application to the understanding that the local
parties who first meet a new price question shall settle
it not only for themselves but for all shops under the
agreement.[5] Once the settlement is recorded with the
standing committee the price becomes the "estab-

[3] For example, *Proceedings, U. S. P. A.,* 1925, pp. 31-32; 1926,
p. 30.

[4] In practice, the recording of prices is important only with the
western general ware standing committee.

[5] This was the union rule from the beginning. *Constitution,* 1890,
Article IX, Sec. 2.

lished " price for that article or method; recorded settlements have, in fact, the same binding effect as settlements made directly by the standing committee.[6]

Failures to record local settlements left the way open to so many disputes on the same questions that the manufacturers' side of the western standing committee proposed, in 1921, that a deadline date be recognized for past settlements—unrecorded settlements made before that date to be regarded as binding and not subject to reopening but none made after that date to be regarded as binding unless recorded. The Association favored January 1, 1920, as the deadline date.[7] Although the union side of the western standing committee did not formally accept this date, the committee gradually came to the practice of refusing to reopen unrecorded settlements which had been in effect for some time.[8]

[6] The manufacturers will not admit that a recorded settlement which gives the men more than the scale calls for is binding on other shops. For example, the manufacturers' side of the western general ware committee refused a few years ago to accept as a binding precedent a recorded settlement fixing $7\frac{1}{2}$ hours as a day's work in day-wage dipping. See above, ch. x. The agreement also explicitly provides that " no price or condition shall be considered settled by reason of the fact that it has been agreed upon by a firm not a member of the United States Potters Association or by a workman not a member of the National Brotherhood of Operative Potters."

[7] *Proceedings, U. S. P. A.*, 1921, pp. 123-124.

[8] In the 1925 convention of the Brotherhood, a rule was adopted that if a shop committee fails to have a settlement recorded within thirty days the local shall be fined $25.00 for the first offense and $50.00 for the second offense. It was recited that " our members have been neglectful in having shop settlements recorded before the standing committee " and " we have lost several good settlements due to carelessness on the part of our members." *Proceedings*, 1925, p. 17; *Constitution*, Sec. 216.

Another source of local disputes has been lack of full familiarity with the terms of the published agreement and the binding settlements or rulings made in accordance with it. Both the operatives and the firm, or its representative who dealt with the men, have frequently been found delinquent in this respect. It must be said, however, that keeping one's self familiar with all that has been agreed to or " established " has been no easy task. The scale book has never covered all the articles for which prices had been established. It is not to be expected that it should; the inclusion of every article on which a price has been established would make the scale book very unwieldy. Many of these articles are produced in but one or two shops, and are well known only to those who are concerned with them. It has been necessary, therefore, to keep in touch with standing committee settlements and recorded settlements in order to be up to date. Failure to recognize an article " new " to the shop as one belonging to a category for which a price has already been established, is also understandable. The classification of shapes by name does not always make for easy identification. The same name is not always applied to the same shape in all shops. For years the officers of the Brotherhood have waged a campaign for more adequate descriptions of the articles priced but even in recent years misunderstandings of this kind have occurred.

In addition to all other explanations of the failure of local parties to handle the questions themselves there is the simple one that in many cases they have not made a *bona fide* effort to do so. The men have often sent price questions to the standing committee without a further attempt at settlement when the prices they asked were not immediately granted. Employers, too, have shown a tendency to let the men's demands go to the committee as a matter of course,[9] taking the position that the employers' side of the committee is better able to handle these matters for them than they are themselves.

As regards local disputes as a whole, each side, although recognizing the failure of some of its own constituents at times to follow the spirit and intention of the system, attributes most of the difficulty in arriving at local settlements to the refusal of the local party on the other side to accept a reasonable settlement. For example, Mr. Wells, in commenting on the comparative lack of troublesome disputes in 1927, assumed that with business dull and jobs in demand, " the workers have been less unreasonable in the adjustment of grievances real or imaginary." [10] From the union standpoint this means that the men were less inclined to stand out for reasonable settlements and less inclined to refuse to submit to encroachments on their rights under the agreement, and were given less consideration when they did.[11]

LOCAL UNIONS AND DISPUTES

The employers have repeatedly complained of the part which local unions have assumed in shop negotiations. The Association has never recognized that a local union has any standing in the system of dealing between the two organizations or that the individual employer is under any obligation to treat with a local union or respect its decisions. In 1900, before the rules of procedure had been worked out, the manufacturers refused the request of the Brotherhood that each manu-

[9] *Proceedings, U. S. P. A.,* 1927, p. 65.
[10] *Ibid.,* p. 17.
[11] *Report of Executive Board,* 1928, p. 30.

facturer first take the dispute up with the local union whose members were involved.[12] Since that time the Association has steadily maintained that if a dispute arises in a shop it is between the firm and its men, not between the firm and the local union, and if the firm and the employees directly concerned cannot settle the question it is to be taken up by an officer of the national union or sent to a committee on which the national union, not a local union, is represented.[13]

However much or little the local union is "recognized" in form, it it difficult to keep the local unions from influencing the course of the negotiations. The men will naturally bring disputed points to the local union for enlightenment or aid and comfort. In fact the union constitution has for years required that "when a grievance occurs in a shop the case shall be reported to the local union by the shop committee." This is before it is referred to the standing committee.[14] And in pricing a new article the union rule clearly indicates that the price is not to be made with the firm by the maker alone but by the maker and the shop committee in conjunction, and, further, that the price must have the approval of the local union.[15] This is in direct

[12] *Proceedings*, 1900, p. 9.

[13] *Proceedings, U. S. P. A.*, 1911, p. 41. In the August, 1922, conference Chairman Wells said: "There is one thing that I have tried to impress on the conference for years, and that is that the United States Potters Association does not officially know there is such a thing as a local; that our dealings are with the National Brotherhood of Operative Potters. The local is not recognized in any feature of the agreement and so far as I have anything to say it never will be."

[14] *Rules and Regulations*, 1904, Article VIII, Secs. 1, 2 and 3; *Constitution*, 1925, Sec. 89.

[15] *Rules and Regulations*, 1910, Sec. 157; *Constitution*, 1925, Sec. 215.

conflict with the employers' contention that the local
union has no right to pass a judgment on the price.
It is the part played by the local union in the pricing
process, especially, which is responsible for most of the
local disagreements, according to the manufacturers.

In disputes which involve conflicting interpretations
of the agreement, the intervention of the local union
has been even more strongly attacked by the employers. These disputes are fraught with much more danger to the no-strike agreement than are price disputes.
More is involved in the former than delayed settlements
and cluttering up the docket of the standing committee.
A price dispute can drag along for months, with the
men doing the work under a " protest " price, without
creating much tension, as the final settlement covers all
work done under " protest," but if a local decides that
an employer is violating the agreement there is a strong
temptation to instruct the men not only to refuse to
concede the employer's position but also to refuse to
continue work unless the employer desists from the
course in question.

In 1913 the employers secured recognition in the
agreement of their contention that the local union had
no right to pass a judgment on a question of interpretation which should be regarded by the men as binding
upon them. It was agreed, first of all, that such questions were to be carried to the proper national officer
of the Brotherhood, and not directly to the standing
committee; the case was not to go to the standing committee unless the national officer failed to bring about
an agreement with the firm on the question. But the
real substance of what the employers had been contending for is in the next sentence. " No local shall
assume to settle upon its own authority disputes or
points of disagreement between its members and their

employers." All that is left to the locals is the right to " carry such matters up to their national officers."

This did not dispose of the locals so far as the pricing of new articles is concerned. The employers continued to object that settlements were prevented or delayed by actions taken by the locals. In the 1926 conference when the union side complained that the individual manufacturers were refusing to make fair settlements, the employers complained in turn that the locals prevented the men from making fair settlements, which the men would have been willing to make if the local had not interfered; they were compelled to bring the matter to the local, which, " being an *ex parte* body, fixed a bargaining price which they did not expect to get." Mr. Wells insisted that if the man himself is satisfied with the price which the firm is willing to pay, it should never go to the local union; the practice of taking the price question to the local was a weakness in the system of adjustment which should be eliminated. But in the end he declared that if the Brotherhood would instruct its members to make an honest attempt to adjust prices on new articles or new conditions with the firm and take them to the local only as a last resort, when it was impossible to reach an agreement with the firm, they would find that the manufacturers would not refuse to settle. The matter was left there.

HIGHER ACTION ON LOCAL DISPUTES

After the failure of the local parties to reach an agreement on any question, it is usual for each side to consult its national officers, if it has not already done so,[16] before referring it to the standing committee.

---

[16] In pricing a new article the union law requires that the national office be consulted before the negotiations with the employer for a final price are begun. *Constitution*, Sec. 215.

The national officers of both organizations have encouraged this, as a means of eliminating unnecessary disputes. The agreement, since 1913, has made it mandatory on the union side to refer the dispute to the national office instead of to the standing committee directly, " in any question as to the correct interpretation of any clause, feature or provision of the agreement."

The national officers of the organizations, especially the president and first vice-president of the Brotherhood and Secretary Goodwin of the Association, have played an important part in the settlement of local disputes. Each has often given his members information on the accepted interpretation of the agreement or an established precedent or an established price which has ended the local controversy.[17] The office of the president and the secretary of the Brotherhood and the office of the secretary of the Association are both in East Liverpool, a propinquity which makes for easy consultation and close relationships. In many cases, too, Secretary Goodwin and the Brotherhood president or secretary have visited the plant together and after ascertaining all the facts have guided the parties to an agreement. The Brotherhood president and first vice-president have also brought about many settlements in the East by direct dealings with the firm. In fact, this has in recent years been more common in the East than settlement by the standing committees.

If the national officers are unable to bring about a settlement, the next step in the plan of conciliation, for an ordinary dispute, is submission of the matter to the proper standing committee. Meanwhile neither side may resort to force; the agreement requires that " all

[17] *Proceedings, U. S. P. A.,* 1924, p. 79.

work in dispute shall be continued pending and subject to the decision of the standing committee." [18] A disagreement over a discharge question goes directly to the discharge committee and not to the standing committee, the parties being under the same obligation to keep the peace. This obligation is not stated in the agreement but it is clearly understood. The discharge committee has had very few cases before it in recent years. It has often gone for more than a year without a meeting. The Brotherhood secretary and Secretary Goodwin, who are permanent members of the committee, have been successful in adjusting nearly all of the cases which have been appealed by the local parties.

In addition to these permanent joint committees the executive board of the Brotherhood and the labor committee of the Association have occasionally functioned as a joint committee for the handling of disputes which have been referred to them directly instead of being sent to one of the permanent joint committees. When this course has been followed it has been at the request of the national officers of one organization or the other and nearly always in a dispute of such a nature that it appeared to be beyond the practical competency of a standing committee to handle it. It was recognized in a clause adopted in 1913 that the national officers of the Brotherhood might submit a disputed matter referred to them by a local union " to the standing committee *or to the labor committee* [19] if they otherwise cannot

---

[18] This rule was not printed in the agreement until 1905. It was implied, however, in the agreement made in 1900 to establish a standing committee. (Statement of ex-President T. J. Duffy to the writer.) It was recognized by the Brotherhood in the revision of the union law governing grievances adopted in 1904. *Rules and Regulations,* 1904, Article VIII.

[19] Italics are the writer's.

adjust amicably." From the context it appears that this was intended to apply only to disputed points of interpretation, but it came to be recognized that any important matter in dispute would be taken up directly by the executive board and the labor committee, without prior reference to the standing committee, if the national officers on either side requested it. In a few cases, too, a dispute involving an interpretation of the agreement, or a matter not expressly covered by the agreement, has been referred directly to the conference instead of being handled by the executive board and labor committee, when the time of the conference has been near at hand.

These supplementary developments in the joint machinery have furnished a valuable element of elasticity to the system and have protected the standing committees from some embarrassing questions of interpretation which they would doubtless have found themselves unable to settle satisfactorily. At times, too, direct handling of the dispute by the executive board and labor committee has expedited action and quieted the local parties in a case which threatened to cause trouble. It has always been understood that the obligation to keep the peace holds in cases taken up directly by the labor committee and executive board, or held over for the conference.[20]

The standing committee is an even-numbered body, with the same number of votes on each side and has

[20] There is one group of disputes over which the regular joint machinery of adjustment has not had recognized jurisdiction—that of price disputes from branches not covered by the uniform scale. "Unofficial" decorating standing committees have been set up for East Liverpool and Sebring (see above, ch. vii.) but decorating disputes outside these localities and disputes from other non-scale branches are still without joint committee coverage.

often deadlocked.[21] The agreement provides, in a clause adopted in 1907, that " disputes referred to the standing committee and not settled within ninety days shall be referred back to the parties interested." [22] But it is not the understanding that the original parties are then free to resort to strike, discharge, or lock-out to enforce their respective stands, although there is nothing in the agreement explicitly forbidding it. First of all, the original parties are expected to make another *bona fide* attempt to settle the dispute amicably.[23] Failing in that, it is now understood that they may resubmit it to the standing committee and, as a matter of fact, many disputes referred back to the parties have later been resubmitted to the committee. But if the parties fail to reach agreement themselves, or the dispute is not disposed of by resubmission to the standing com-

[21] The discharge committee is also an even-numbered body but there has been no serious dispute arising out of a deadlock. The discharge agreement contains a clause providing for the calling of a conference " with authority to amend this agreement " if either party is convinced that any unfair advantage is being taken of any provision of it. Presumably a deadlocked case would also be referred to such a conference, or to the labor committee and executive board. These two bodies did take up directly an appeal of the men who were " locked out " at Mt. Clemens in 1921. *Report of Executive Board,* 1921, pp. 40-43.

[22] The procedure outlined in the 1905 agreement made it obligatory upon the standing committees to submit disputes upon which they could not agree to the decision of a " disinterested man " but this clause has remained practically inoperative.

[23] When matters are referred back to the parties by the standing committee the Brotherhood constitution (Sec. 89) brings the local union in again. In 1915 one of the employers' proposals was that when a matter was referred back to the men and the firm only those directly employed on the job in dispute should have any voice or decision in the negotiations and should be free to settle it in any way agreeable to them—that no outside coercion or pressure should be used. This was not accepted.

mittee, it is expected that neither the firm nor the local union will carry matters to the point of a strike or lockout without first consulting its national headquarters.[24]

Consultation with the national officers opens the way to submission of the dispute to the executive board and the labor committee. In fact, such reference has come to be the capstone of the system of conciliation. It is now understood that if a dispute which has been referred back by the standing committee can be disposed of in no other way and threatens to bring on a local strike or lock-out, the matter will be taken up, at the request of either side, by these two national boards, or, if it is more convenient, by the joint conference, in a final attempt to reach a settlement. It is also understood that neither party is free to resort to local hostilities pending the outcome of the efforts of the two national committees to effect a settlement.[25] As a matter of fact, however, very few of the cases returned by the standing committee to the parties have ever reached the executive board and labor committee.

There remains a debated zone of coercion by the men if a case is referred back by the standing committee. The men making the article may give in their notices, if the employer will neither pay a satisfactory price nor withdraw the article. The Brotherhood has never agreed that this is a violation of the agreement, although the employers maintain that it is.[26] The attempt has also been made to revive an old practice of refusing

[24] On the union side it has since 1904 been obligatory under the Brotherhood constitution to refer disputed matters sent back by the standing committee to the national president and allow him to attempt to secure a settlement. *Rules and Regulations*, 1904, Article VIII, Sec. 3; *Constitution*, 1925, Secs. 89, 90.

[25] *Proceedings, U. S. P. A.*, 1910, p. 27.

[26] See below, pp. 359-360.

to work on the particular article in dispute, without
giving up the job.[27] A resolution was offered in the
1923 convention to make this practice mandatory in
cases in which the standing committee had failed to
reach a settlement after ninety days. This was " ruled
out of order as it is already covered by the agreement." [28] The 1928 convention, however, moved undoubtedly by the number of cases referred back by the
western standing committee at a time when the condition of business made it difficult to get a subsequent
settlement from the employer by peaceful means, and
influenced by the fact that a price dispute which had
stirred the turners of East Liverpool for over a year
had been settled only with the waiver of " protest
money," adopted a long resolution [29] which resulted in
a union proposal " that when a dispute has been before
the standing committee and not settled within sixty
days, the party making the said article in dispute shall
discontinue making same." Needless to say, the employers did not agree to this.

PROTEST PRICES

An agreement that the men may not strike to enforce
their position in a dispute but must allow it to run on
through a joint procedure which may put off a decision
for a considerable time, must, if it is to be satisfactory

[27] Refusing to make particular articles in dispute, and preventing
others from taking the places of those on " individual strikes " as a
result of such refusals, was commonly practiced in the potteries by
the Knights of Labor. The members who gave up their jobs in this
cause were paid strike benefits. MS. *Minutes, L. A. No. 3573; Proceedings, D. A. No. 160,* 1890, pp. 44-45; *U. S. Ind. Comm.,* XIV,
647-648.

[28] *Proceedings,* 1923, p. 24.

[29] *Ibid.,* 1928, pp. 25-26.

to the men, be accompanied by some sort of a guarantee that the men's interest shall not suffer by the postponement. This is carefully provided for in discharge cases. In disputes over prices or claims for extra compensation—and these include a very large majority of the disputes coming to the standing committees—the protection is intended to be furnished by an assurance that the price finally decided upon shall be retroactive. Meanwhile the price paid by the employer is received " under protest." The difference, if any, between the " protest price " and the price finally fixed is to be paid for all the work done since the date of protest. This amount is known as the " protest money."

It is the employer who fixes the temporary price which becomes the " protest price." Usually the employer puts this at the figure he is willing to pay permanently. The Brotherhood is opposed to the employer's paying a price while the article is in dispute which is above that which he is willing to give as a final settlement and therefore above the price which may be fixed eventually. The Brotherhood does not want a situation in which protest money is owing to the employer; it is too hard to collect it from the men if the decision goes against them and they have left his employment in the meantime. In April, 1921, the Brotherhood refunded protest money to a firm to the amount of $1,498.80.[30] The Brotherhood has since taken the position that it will not be responsible for the return of " protest

[30] *Financial Reports of the National Officers,* 1921, p. 122. In this case the firm had paid the men the " protest money " for over a year. When the decision finally went against the men, the firm tried to collect the protest money. It amounted to approximately $2,500. After trying for two years the firm collected but $1,000, approximately. The Brotherhood paid the balance. (Statement of Secretary Goodwin to the writer.)

money." The Association, also, advises its members to retain the amount in dispute until the case is settled.

The protest price rule does not protect the men completely. If the standing committee fails to reach a settlement and the case is referred back to the parties, the employer may withdraw the article with no price fixed for it and leave the men nothing on which to establish a claim for protest money for those already made. In some cases in which the men have made considerable quantities at the protest price they have sent the matter up to the standing committee again with a request to set a price for those already made. If the committee returns it again, as is likely, the men have no further recourse; the case is hardly big enough to be taken to the labor committee and the executive board. The men complain, too, that they have been obliged to waive the protest money at times to get a settlement from the firm in cases returned by the committee.

The protest price method might be eliminated, of course, by paying the men by the hour until such time as a piece price is settled for the new article, but this procedure is not usual. The firm ordinarily puts the article on piece work as soon as possible, even though the price offered is protested by the men. The employers fear that the workers' output will be too low under day wage. There is an unconscious tendency, if not a downright temptation, to the man not to extend himself for output while the piece price is in dispute and the employers believe that this tendency or temptation would be enhanced by keeping the work on an hourly rate. Most of the men, too, prefer piece work.

THE STANDING COMMITTEES

History and Composition.—The agreement of 1900 included an understanding that a permanent joint com-

mittee or "standing committee" was to be appointed
for the settlement of disputes arising out of the agreement. It was also understood that it was to be composed
of three members from each side.[31] The published
agreement, however, was silent on the composition,
authority, and methods of procedure of the standing
committee. Indeed it was several years before the
standing committee system was brought to smooth running order.

There was a hitch at the very outset over the part to
be played by the local unions in the scheme of adjustment. The Brotherhood took the position that before
a case should be referred to the standing committee the
individual employer should first take it up with the local
union. The manufacturers' association refused to agree
to this procedure. The Brotherhood officers conceded
the point, but only to meet with opposition, verging on
defiance, from the "local's rights" party within its
membership. To meet this opposition they proposed
that in each case the branch involved in the dispute
should be represented on the committee. The 1900 convention went further and demanded that two of the
three members of the committee be branch representatives; it also enacted that the two should be elected by
the local union concerned.[32] The manufacturers still
insisted that the Brotherhood give them a permanent
committee representing the trade as a whole with which
to deal, declaring that it would be impossible to get an
impartial decision if the committee were composed of
parties directly interested in the decision.[33] The Brotherhood finally yielded. When the rules for the standing

[31] Statement of ex-President T. J. Duffy to the writer; *Proceedings.*
N. B. of O. P., 1900, p. 9.

[32] *Proceedings,* 1900, pp. 9, 54.

[33] *Proceedings, U. S. P. A.,* 1901, p. 46.

22

committee were adopted in the autumn of 1900, one of them was that it should " be composed of six permanent members," three from each side. That rule has remained unchanged and has been followed in all other regular standing committees subsequently established.[34]

For the first few years the standing committee did not make much headway in disposing of its business. Because the agreement was new and incomplete and many of the men and employers had had little experience in making shop settlements, there were very many questions before the committee, in addition to those specifically bequeathed to it in the uniform scale. In the committee itself, too, the two sides stood far apart, each distrusting the other somewhat and each unwilling to concede. The result was that " the committee for a number of months was meeting on an average of twice a week and was not accomplishing much at that." [35] Then in 1903 it failed to hold any meetings for several months, because the manufacturers were unable to get anyone to act for their side. This seems not to have shaken the faith of the new national president, Mr. T. J. Duffy—who had served for two years on the committee—in the standing committee system, and when the uniform list was extended to the East, in 1904, an eastern general ware committee, modelled on that of the West, was set up at the request of the union.

The china ware standing committees were not established until 1923. Before the adoption of the china uniform lists, china disputes were occasionally sent to the existing standing committees. These disputes were difficult for the committees to settle, as the members

[34] The union side of the East Liverpool " unofficial " decorating standing committee is, of course, made up of members of the local union concerned. *Report of Executive Board*, 1927, p. 26.

[35] *Proceedings, N. B. of O. P.*, 1901, p. 8; 1902, p. 13.

were not familiar with the shapes or conditions in
china and had no uniform list to guide them. Nor was
it altogether certain how many of the general ware
rules applied to china. After the china uniform lists
were adopted it was agreed that a sub-committee of the
larger committee which had made the lists should
decide interpretation questions and settle price disputes. That method of handling disputes also proved
unsatisfactory.[36] The number of unsettled disputes continued to grow, especially in the West, and the union
convention finally decided, in 1921, to ask for a regular
china ware standing committee for the West and, a year
later, for one for the East as well. The manufacturers
did not want " the china business divided " between
two committees. They feared that two committees
would increase non-uniformities between East and
West.[37] They finally agreed to meet two union committees but declared that they would have but one
china ware committee on their side, which would meet
with each of the union committees as the necessity
arose.

The employers' representatives on the standing committees are selected, as are the other committees of the
Association, at the annual meeting of the United States
Potters Association. With the standing committees,
as with the other committees, it has been the policy of
the Association to keep the same men in office as long
as they will serve. The make-up of the western general
ware standing committee has remained the same, on
the employers' side, since 1925. Secretary Goodwin has
served on the committee continuously since 1913. The

[36] *Ibid.,* 1921, p. 51; *Report of Executive Board,* 1922, p. 35.

[37] Vice-President Hutchins also believed that it would be better
to have a single committee, but the members wanted two. MS.
Report of Conference, December 19-20, 1922.

eastern general ware committee had always been separately constituted from the western general ware committee.[38] After the china committees were established, however, the Association decided that its members of the china committees should also act as the employers' side of the eastern general ware committee. The latter committee had by that time become almost inactive and it was concluded that it was no longer necessary to have a separate committee for that purpose. The employers are now represented by the same three men on three of the standing committees—both china committees and the eastern general ware committee. The personnel of this committee has remained unchanged since 1923. Secretary Goodwin, although not a regular member of the committee, sits with it whenever it meets with one of the union committees. Thus Mr. Goodwin's knowledge and experience are available to the employers' side on all four standing committees.

On the Brotherhood side, the original standing committee was made up of national officers. It was not until 1903 that the Brotherhood adopted the policy, followed until 1928, of drawing standing committee members from men holding no other national office.[39] Before 1912 the members of the standing committees were appointed by the president. Beginning with that year, and until 1928, when the convention voted to return to the method of appointment, they were elected by the

[38] In 1905, Mr. W. E. Wells, then President of the Association, advocated the establishment of a permanent labor committee and suggested that it consist of three members from the East and three from the West, who should also act as members of the respective standing committees. This would keep the two standing committees in close coöperation. The recommendation was not adopted. *Proceedings*, 1905, p. 14.

[39] This was given up in the sanitary ware division in 1916. See below, ch. xiv.

members working in the respective divisions and sections. Eligibility for the general ware committees was restricted to members of the East Liverpool and Trenton local unions, respectively. In china any member " actively engaged in the china ware trade " east of the Allegheny Mountains were eligible for the eastern committee, and west of the same for the western committee.[40]

The decision that the union side of the committee should not be made up in any part of revolving members, chosen for each case from the branch involved in the dispute, did not kill the desire to have a member of one's branch on the committee.[41] There were repeated demands on the convention that consideration should be given the branches as such in the make-up of the permanent committee. These were successful to the extent that a rule was adopted in 1911 that no two members of the committee should be chosen from the same branch.[42] In 1914 this was supplemented by a rule that not more than two members should be from the same department, the branches being grouped for this purpose into a " clay department " and a " kiln shed department." [43] In 1921 the rule was further changed, for the western standing committee, to keep pace with the broadening of the organization; the seats were divided equally among three departments—" clay," " kiln-shed," and " shipping." [44]

[40] There is no china ware " center."

[41] In the 1926 conference when the " unofficial decorating standing committee " for East Liverpool was under discussion, President Wood expressed a fear that if a committee were set up for one branch it might stimulate a movement for branch control of adjustment of disputes generally.

[42] *Proceedings*, 1911, pp. 37, 63.

[43] *Ibid.*, 1914, p. 67.

[44] *Ibid.*, 1921, pp. 33-34; *Constitution*, Sec. 38. The western general ware rule that no two should be from the same branch and not

It was the dissatisfaction with the results obtained under the elective plan in the previous two years which caused the union to return to the method of appointment in 1928. As late as 1926 a resolution calling for a return to the appointive method was defeated because the delegates thought the method of appointment " less democratic." [45] In 1928 not only was the proposal to substitute appointment for election adopted but it was decided also to make the national secretary and the first vice-president permanent members of the committees in their respective sections. The convention was now convinced that there was more assurance that qualified members would be secured for the positions through selection by the national president than through nomination and election by the membership at large; most of the members of the union outside of East Liverpool knew little or nothing about the candidates for the western general ware committee. The advantage of having a national officer as a permanent member of each committee had been shown by the efficiency of Mr. Goodwin on the manufacturers' side, and of Vice-President Hutchins on the sanitary standing committee from 1916 to 1921.[46]

The 1905 agreement called for the reference to a seventh " disinterested " man, " for final decision," of " all matters that result in a tie vote in the standing committee," both East and West. This provision was not carried out. The western committee attempted a resort to it shortly after it was adopted, but with no result. A " disinterested " man was found who was acceptable to both sides; he had once worked in the industry as an operative but had left the trade some-

more than one from any of the three departments was applied later to both china standing committees also.

[45] *Proceedings,* 1926, p. 30; *Potters Herald,* July 15, 1926.
[46] *Proceedings,* 1928, pp. 17, 19-20; *Potters Herald,* July 6, 1928.

time before. He sat with the committee through two
night sessions but after considering for some time the
matters referred to him he declared that he was unable
to reach a decision on any of them and withdrew from
the position. In 1915 a seventh-man clause was again
adopted. The operatives were complaining of delays in
the handling of disputes by the standing committees
and had proposed that two committees be set up in the
West, one for the clay department and one for the other
branches. The employers proposed as an alternative
that the seventh-man plan be given another trial. The
conference agreed to this and a new clause was substituted for the much briefer one of 1905. Like the 1905
clause it reads as if it were mandatory. It is still
retained in the published agreement, both for semi-
porcelain and china ware. But it is immediately followed in both by the clause adopted in 1907 requiring
the return to the parties of all disputes not settled by
the committee in ninety days. The 1915 arbitration
provision has never been used in the West and but once
in the East, in 1921.

The Western General Ware Committee.—The workings of the standing committee system are best judged
by the experience of the western general ware committee. It is not only the oldest of the committees but it is
still by far the most important. The number of cases
coming before it each year is many times greater than
the number handled by the other three standing committees combined and the number of firms and workers
upon whom its decisions are binding comprises a large
majority of the firms and workers, respectively, subject to the agreement.

The committee meets in East Liverpool and usually at
night. It holds regularly monthly meetings, except
during July and August, and special meetings when the

volume of business requires. The number and length of
the meetings vary with the number and nature of the
cases to be considered. In each of the two years 1926-
1927 and 1927-1928 the committee held fifteen meetings.[47] Secretary Goodwin, chairman of the manufacturers' side, acts as chairman of the joint committee. The discussion is informal. When decisions are
reached, it is nearly always by unanimous agreement.
The discussion is usually continued until it is apparent
that a particular proposal will be accepted by both sides
or that no agreement can be reached on that case that
night. The practice is not to put a motion to a vote
unless it has been seconded from the other side. Indeed,
a motion is seldom offered until it is apparent from
what has been said that someone on the other side will
second it. Rarely an individual member has asked to be
recorded against a motion made or seconded from his
side and adopted by the committee. In nearly all cases
the action of the committee is an agreement of two
sides, not a majority vote of individuals.

As a rule no attempt is made to reach a settlement on
a dispute in the meeting at which it is " entered." [48]
Usually it is not until the second meeting following the
" entry " that the case is discussed by the members of
the committee. At the regular meeting immediately following the entry the taking of evidence is in order. It
may be that the case will then go over to the next regular meeting but it is much more likely that a special
meeting will be held in the middle of the month to pass

[47] The information on the standing committees was gained from
their minutes and from interviews; comments on the work of the
committees appeared in the *Proceedings of the United States Potters
Association* from time to time, and less frequently in the *Reports
of the Executive Board* of the N. B. of O. P.

[48] For an exception, see *Report of Executive Board*, 1919, pp. 15-16.

on the cases on which evidence has been taken. In recent years so much time has been devoted to the taking of evidence at the regular monthly meetings that the committee has had little opportunity at these meetings to attempt to reach settlements.[49]

The committee has frequently been delayed in its handling of cases by the failure of the local parties to furnish the essential facts when the dispute is submitted.[50] Sometimes the " entering " of a price dispute is delayed for a month or more because no sample of the article is supplied with the original submission. The evidence presented by the parties, too, when they have appeared before the committee, has at times been insufficient to allow the committee to proceed with the case. The committee has occasionally gone so far as to refer the dispute back to the parties, on the ground that it has not been supplied with the information necessary to enable it to make a settlement. Such disputes may be resubmitted later, with more evidence, but the failure of the parties to furnish the necessary facts in the first instance prolongs the life of the dispute and contributes to the impression, rather general among the workers, that the standing committee system involves undue delay.

In some cases the committee has appointed a subcommittee of two—one from each side—to visit the plant and report back the facts. This is particularly helpful, if not indispensable, when the dispute is over what is to be paid for a new method, or a new condition, or an alleged abnormally difficult condition, which no member of the committee has seen. In these cases Sec-

---

[49] For example, *Proceedings, U. S. P. A.*, 1927, p. 65.

[50] *Proceedings, N. B. of O. P.*, 1927, pp. 10-11; *Proceedings, U. S. P. A.*, 1927, pp. 65, 66.

retary Goodwin nearly always acts for the manufacturers' side. The members of the sub-committee have
usually agreed on the facts, however far apart they
may stand on the question of what should be paid under
those circumstances when that question comes before
the full committee.

The rule has always been that a final settlement—
as distinct from a " trial settlement "—made by the
committee will not be reopened unless it is clear that it
was made under a mistaken impression as to the facts
or unless both sides agree to have it reopened. There
have not been many such cases in recent years. If a
price fixed by the committee should turn out to be too
low and the employer is willing to have it raised—
which may be necessary in good times to get anyone to
accept the job—the employer may raise the price
voluntarily.

The original rules of the committee provided that
if it could not reach a settlement within thirty days
after the submission of the dispute, the case should be
referred back to the parties. It was soon realized that
this period was too short and the rule was ignored. In
1907 a limit of ninety days was fixed in the agreement,
at the request of the Brotherhood, but this rule, although never formally repealed, has by no means been
always observed. For most of its history, the committee has been disposed to keep a case which it has not
been able to settle on its docket, regardless of the
ninety-day rule, so long as there was a prospect of
eventual agreement on it. In a number of instances
this extension of the period of consideration has resulted in a settlement. But if the committee has had
to return the case eventually, the prolongation has often
been regarded by the workers concerned as merely
" stalling " on the part of the employers' side of the

committee. The dissatisfaction among the union members with the practice of the committee in retaining cases for long periods led to the presentation of a proposition in the 1928 conference which would have, in effect, taken price disputes out of the hands of the committee and returned them to the men for local coercion, after a period of sixty days. This was rejected by the employers.

It should be clear from what has been said of local disputes that the committee has a large number of questions submitted to it. The number of disputes taken up by the committee in recent years has normally exceeded forty and in some years it has gone over fifty. In many instances several distinct articles, made in the same plant, have been entered as one dispute, so that the number of separate points submitted for decision during the year may run over a hundred.

The committee has not attempted to give a decision in all the cases referred to it. For many years the committee has been wary of disputed interpretations of clauses of the agreement. It has usually referred the case back to the parties, with the recommendation that they take it to the executive board and the labor committee—or to the conference—or has itself referred the case directly to higher joint national authority. This does not mean that the standing committee was not divided in any of these cases on the merits of the question involved, or that one side or the other of the committee did not argue that a particular decision was demanded by the terms of the agreement or at least permitted.

The committee has also referred back a number of cases without attempting to settle them because it believed that the parties had not made a *bona fide* effort to reach a settlement on the issue themselves.[51]   Some of the cases which the committee refuses to consider on this ground, or because of lack of evidence, are eventually referred back to the committee and have to be handled by it, but a few are permanently removed from its docket. Some disputes entered with the committee have been disposed of, too, by agreement between the local parties before the committee has reached the point of attempting a decision. At times the members of the committee, and especially Secretary Goodwin, have given their respective constituents advice, after learning the facts, which has led to settlements of this sort.[52]

The nature of the cases on which the committee has to pass has been discussed above. It is clear that in many of these there is room for honest difference of opinion. There is also the added difficulty that the evidence presented may be conflicting. Yet the committee has reached agreement in an overwhelming majority of the cases presented to it. The members of the committee have undoubtedly attempted to get as favorable settlements as they could for their constituents and they have often allowed disputes to be referred back to the parties rather than surrender their respective contentions, but they have not been mere advocates for the claims of their constituents. If the article is clearly covered by the classification or the size list, or governed by an established price, or the matter is one on which the intent of the agreement is clear or on which there is a recognized precedent, there is little hesitation in the committee. In very many cases in which there is a reasonable doubt, the committee has worked out a com-

[51] *Ibid.*, p. 65.

[52] For example, *ibid.*, 1921, p. 123. During the year 1927-1928 three cases entered with the committee were withdrawn because of local settlements.

promise in order to effect a settlement. Needless to say its task has been a thankless one and its decisions have often been received with disfavor.

When the committee has decided that the making price of an article should be based on merit, or that an extra should be paid for a new condition or a new method, and the men's representatives remain doubtful that the figure offered by the manufacturers' side would enable the operatives to make their average earnings, this figure may be accepted for a temporary or a trial period with the understanding that the question may be reopened at the end of the time specified if the men are not satisfied; otherwise the rate becomes final. The period fixed for the trial has usually been three months, but four months and even six months have been prescribed at times. In very few cases in which a trial price has been fixed have the men asked to have the question reopened.

The proportion of cases referred back has varied from year to year but normally it has not gone above a fourth. Even in 1925 and 1926, when the committee's " work was complicated by an exceptional number of new and unique shapes," the proportion of settlements was kept high.[53] A number of these decisions, however, proved unsatisfactory to the men and in the next two years the proportion of cases returned rose rapidly;[54] the union side was unable to get what it considered satisfactory settlements and refused to accept what the manufacturers' side would give. The addition of Secretary McGillivray to the Brotherhood's side of the committee has greatly increased the proportion of settlements since 1928.[55] As has been already pointed

[53] *Ibid.*, 1925, p. 68; 1926, pp. 30, 63.
[54] *Ibid.*, 1927, p. 64.
[55] *Ibid.*, 1929, pp. 24, 53-54; 1930, p. 47; *Report of Executive Board,* 1929, pp. 40-41; 1930, pp. 91-92.

out, not every case which is returned means that the committee has deadlocked on the issue. However, the great majority of the cases returned have been sent back to the parties because the two sides have stood out for different prices or different rulings on the matter at issue. It is easy to see why in a case involving a ruling, each side may prefer to have it returned to the parties rather than concede the position of the other side. The same is true of some issues over classification or following an established price. Each side may conclude that it is better to leave the particular case to the chance of a local compromise than to agree to a decision which may be invoked against it in later cases. In many disputes in which the question is reduced in the committee to what the man can earn under a proposed price, the employers' side will refer the case back rather than grant more than it believes the evidence warrants, whereas the men's representatives will also prefer to return the case rather than agree to a price which it believes is too low.[56]

Sometimes the union representatives have stood out for a particular price because the men interested have told them that they knew they could get that much from the firm if the case were returned. It must be remembered that the union members of the committee cannot ignore considerations of this kind too far without discrediting the committee with the men in the shops. There have been cases in which the union side of the committee has unwittingly agreed to a price lower than

[56] In the 1928 convention one of the members of the committee complained that the operatives appearing before the committee often failed "to produce the evidence or arguments to back up their requests" and blamed the witnesses "for much of the Brotherhood's failure to get better results than it has" in cases submitted to the committee. *Potters Herald,* July 6, 1928.

that which the men had reason to believe they could get from the firm, and lower than the firm actually did give them subsequently. Of course, the committee should have been informed of the top price the firm was willing to pay to get a settlement.

The majority of the cases referred back disappear from the ken of the committee. In some, the men eventually make a settlement with the firm, with or without the assistance of a national officer. If it is a price dispute the firm may offer more than it did originally, but not as much as the men had asked, and the men may accept the compromise. Or having failed to get anything better by appealing to the standing committee the men may go on working at the employer's terms without a regular settlement. But a considerable number of cases are resubmitted to the committee. In 1927-1928, for example, six cases came back to the committee, one of which was subsequently withdrawn because it was settled locally.

In not a few of the cases which have been resubmitted the committee has been able to reach a decision. New evidence may be presented; a longer experience with the new method or the new article may give a better basis for judgment; or the issue may have been discussed more thoroughly with the national officers on one side or both. Sometimes it is appreciated that it is a case in which some settlement by the committee is highly desirable and both sides may on this account be more disposed to accept a compromise.

An example of a compromise agreement to avoid returning a dispute a second time is furnished by the action of the committee in the "tulip tea" cup case from the Vodrey pottery in 1925. The matter in dispute was whether a proper interpretation of the turning

scale would class this with cups which were priced at
four and one-half cents per dozen or with cups priced
at four cents. The manufacturers' side of the committee supported the firm's contention that four cents
was the correct scale price and produced evidence tending to show that cups of this kind were made many
years before in several plants, including the Vodrey
plant, at four cents. The union side quoted plants in
which the price of four and one-half cents was being
paid for the cups and maintained that this was the price
indicated by the scale. Neither side would give way and
after two sessions had been spent on it, the case was
returned. It was soon after resubmitted. The committee then reached an agreement that " until committees
representing the two national bodies clear up the clause
at the top of page 52 in the scale book, which was
responsible for this entry," those firms paying four
cents should continue to do so and those paying four
and a half cents should likewise continue to pay that
price. The matter was brought to the 1926 conference
through a union request for the four and a half cent
price uniformly. The conference committee finally disposed of it by making the standing committee compromise permanent.

On the other hand, in a large proportion of the cases
resubmitted, the committee has again failed to reach a
settlement. If the evidence is no more enlightening or
if neither side of the committee is willing to recede from
its position sufficiently to meet the other, another deadlock ensues. Of the cases resubmitted in 1927-1928, but
one was settled by the committee. One of the cases,
resubmitted in September, after having been returned
in the previous February, was returned again in January, resubmitted in May and returned for the third

time at the final meeting of the year. The committee may, of course, refer a case which has been resubmitted to it and on which it cannot agree to the labor committee and executive board, or to the conference committee. A few cases have been kept alive by action of this kind, but nearly all of the disputes on which the committee has again deadlocked after resubmission have been simply referred back to the parties.

Most of these cases have caused no subsequent trouble for the two national organizations. A few, however, have had stormy histories. A dispute returned by the committee which caused a considerable stir in the East Liverpool district before it was finally settled by a joint committee was that over the turning price of the " Barbara Jane " cup. The issue was whether this should carry an extra or be done at the scale price. The manufacturers' side would not agree to any advance on the scale price, contending that the men were making good earnings at four cents per dozen, and the case was returned in February, 1927. The local union, after much discussion, decided to refer the question to a committee, which was to take it up with the manufacturers making the cup. However, no settlement had been effected by September and the case was resubmitted to the standing committee. The union side then offered to settle for four and one-half cents but the manufacturers' side still refused to agree to more than four cents. The cup was finally settled in April, by committees representing the turners and the firms making it, at four and one-half cents, with no protest money, but not until after there had been some talk of a " walkout " by the turners to force a settlement.[57]

[57] *Ibid.*, November 24, 1927; April 5, 1928; *Proceedings, N. B. of O. P.*, 1928, p. 11.

23

The Other Standing Committees.—The procedure of the other standing committees follows that of the western general ware committee closely. However, owing to the fact that they meet far less frequently, disputes are often entered, heard and passed on in the same meeting. The eastern general ware committee, which has now but a few plants, all small, under its jurisdiction, held only two meetings in the five years ending in August, 1928. The eastern china committee had held only two meetings down to August, 1928; and had not met since November, 1924. That meeting was taken up largely with a series of disputes over decorating prices at the Scammell China Company's plant. The manufacturers' side of the committee was unwilling to fix higher prices than prevailed in the West and the operatives' side would not agree to compel the workers to accept western prices, with the conditions in this shop. The case was returned to the parties with the understanding that when the firm should give the same conditions that prevailed in the western shops its prices should be readjusted to the western basis.[58] As the manufacturers' side of the committee seemed unwilling to settle decorating price questions definitively and as these are the most troublesome disputes which have occurred in china in Trenton in recent years, the eastern china committee became inactive. Several disputes have been settled by Vice-President Cartlidge with one of the members of the manufacturers' side of the committee who is also connected with the only large plant under the jurisdiction of the committee.[59]

[58] There was a cessation of work over these prices before Vice-President Cartlidge was able to bring about a settlement with the firm. *Report of Executive Board,* 1925, pp. 41-43.

[59] *Proceedings, U. S. P. A.,* 1927, p. 66.

The western china committee held two meetings in each of the years 1924-1925 and 1925-1926 and none in 1926-1927.[60] During 1927-1928 it met twice; once to enter disputes and take evidence on them and again a few weeks later to take action. Of eleven new disputes passed on by the committee at that meeting, eight were waremaking price disputes. In five of the eight the issue turned on size; both the disputes returned to the parties were size disputes. There is no published size list for china.

The committee has been comparatively successful in reaching agreement on the matters referred to it.[61] It has passed no cases on to the labor committee and executive board. At the meeting in January, 1928, eight disputes were settled and but two were referred back to the parties.

Approbation and Complaints.—In the reports of the labor committee, from 1907 on, expressions of congratulation on the existence of such a good system of handling local disagreements as the standing committee method has proved to be and of commendation of the service rendered by the Association's representatives on the committees have appeared almost annually. Frequently, but by no means always, the operative members of the committees have been included in the commendation. In 1915 the change from appointment to election of the union representatives was deplored and it was charged that " it seriously interferes with the efficiency of these tribunals." [62] But in January, 1920,

[60] The committee began business with a long list of disputes inherited from the china special committee. A large proportion of these were eliminated as " dead."

[61] *Proceedings, U. S. P. A.,* 1925, pp. 30, 69; 1926, p. 64.

[62] *Ibid.,* 1915, pp. 49-50. The employers submitted a proposal in 1915 that the union members of the western committee be appointed by

praise of the committees is followed by the statement that " in justice to the Brotherhood members of these committees, they too are entitled to credit for their evident desire to reach just conclusions." [63]

On the Brotherhood side, President T. J. Duffy was a firm believer in the standing committee system from the first. He was strongly supported in this by Vice-President Hutchins. It was not until President Duffy's first report, in 1904, that the system was commended in a presidential report. In the same year Vice-President Hutchins referred to the standing committee system as " a plan which we believe to be the fairest and best plan found in any industry." [64] For several years thereafter these two officers continued to extol the standing committee method of handling disputes which the local parties were unable to settle and to bespeak the gratitude and support of the members for those who served on the committees. In contrast to the attitude of the national officers toward the standing committees and to the union requests for the extension of the system to the china ware division, the record is full of complaints from local unions of delays in the committees and failures to reach settlements, especially in the western general ware committee.[65] On the whole the complaints seem to be more of delays and eventual failure to reach a settlement than of the terms of the settlements which have been made. The most serious weakness of the system, from the standpoint of the men, is that after

---

the national officers. Of course this was not agreed to; it is doubtful if the employers believed that it would be.

[63] *Ibid.,* January 1920, p. 35; 1921, p. 23.

[64] *Proceedings, N. B. of O. P.,* 1904, pp. 18, 60.

[65] For example, in its 1921 report the manufacturers' side of the western committee defended the committee against the charge implied in the nickname " graveyard." *Proceedings,* 1921, p. 123.

making an article for months at a price which they
think is too low, they may find the dispute referred
back without a decision, which leaves them not only
without any protest money for the quantity they have
made but also without any practicable alternative to
going on making the article at an unsatisfactory price.
However, the working of the system, in the West, has
greatly improved, from the standpoint of the Brotherhood, since the addition of Secretary McGillivray to
the western standing committees through the action of
the 1928 convention.[66]

[66] *Report of Executive Board*, 1929, pp. 40-41; 1930, pp. 91-92.

CHAPTER XII

OBSERVANCE OF THE AGREEMENT

It is non-observance of union-employer agreements, rather than observance, which attracts attention. Both national organizations in the pottery industry have very good records in the matter of observance of the agreement and both have, through their national officers, endeavored to secure adherence to the terms of the agreement by their respective individual members. Nevertheless, individuals have at times violated the agreement and it is these violations rather than the usual, matter of fact observance of the terms of the agreement which must be examined.

CESSATIONS OF WORK

The chief form of violation of the agreement on the part of the men is the " outlaw strike." As was explained in the preceding chapter, the " no-strike " feature of the agreement prohibits strikes—in branches covered by the wage scale, at least—over grievances arising during the life of the agreement unless and until the two national bodies have surrendered the matter to those directly involved to fight out for themselves. This the two bodies have never done. All such strikes have therefore been violations of the agreement. The members taking part in a cessation of this kind have frequently contended that their action was provoked by a violation of the agreement by the employer, but even if this were true the cessation was itself a technical violation of the agreement, and of the Brotherhood law as well.

348

The most serious violations of the agreement in the form of strikes have been branch strikes in the trade centers. For the most part they were restricted to the early years of the agreement and to the period from 1916 to 1921. These " outlaw " branch strikes have been not only violations of the agreement but also manifestations of branch insurgency against a national industrial union which attempted to curtail their bargaining and strike autonomy, to what the members of the branch considered to be their disadvantage.

In 1916 there was an outburst of illegal strikes in East Liverpool and Sebring, most of them to secure advances over the agreement terms. There was an abnormal demand for men in the manufacture of munitions and other supplies for the warring nations and stories were current in East Liverpool of the high wages paid to boys and young men without previous experience. The workers in the potteries, both skilled and unskilled, were restless. There were many small strikes of the unorganized workers in the potteries, nearly all successful, in part at least.[1] The first strike approaching branch proportions in the East Liverpool series was launched by the warehousemen. They struck for an increase of fifty cents a day over the rate fixed in the uniform scale. Only a minority of the strikers were members of the Brotherhood; however, the Brotherhood had dealt with the manufacturers for this branch, in 1915. The employers did not grant anything to the strikers while they were out but after they had returned to work, which they did after ten days, the manufacturers gave them an increase of twenty-five cents a day. The practically successful outcome of this strike

[1] There were eight strikes of unorganized pottery workers in Sebring before the first one occurred which was participated in by Brotherhood members. (Statement of President Menge to the writer.)

did much to increase the unrest in the organized branches in East Liverpool.[2]

Three days after the warehousemen returned to work there was a strike of kilndrawers. The East Liverpool kilndrawers had refused to join an outlaw strike started by the kilndrawers of Sebring, which the Brotherhood officers had succeeded in ending after a week,[3] but after a new scale had been adopted for kilndrawing by a special committee authorized by the 1915 conference, they walked out, on May 25, in repudiation of the agreement, in order to compel the manufacturers to give them better terms. The Association refused to deal with the striking kilndrawers and called upon the Brotherhood to compel its members to live up to the agreement.[4] The executive board finally declared that all members who did not return to work by June 12 were to be expelled from the Brotherhood. The strike was broken and all of the plants were in operation on June 12.[5]

The most serious of all the branch strikes was that of the saggermakers.[6] It began on August 15 and lasted until September 28 and involved nearly all of the general ware plants in the West. Mr. Wells estimated the wage loss at half a million dollars.[7] On August 22 the executive board voted to expel all saggermakers who did not return to work by August 28, " or make proper arrangements to do so." Any saggermakers who were

[2] *Potters Herald*, May 18, 25, 1916; *Proceedings, U. S. P. A.*, 1916, p. 23.

[3] *Potters Herald*, May 18, 25, 1916.

[4] Mr. Wells afterwards charged that the kilndrawers were actively supported throughout by the men in charge of Local Number 9— the kilnmen's local. *Proceedings, U. S. P. A.*, 1916, p. 23.

[5] *Report of President*, 1916, pp. 7-14; *Proceedings, U. S. P. A.*, 1916, p. 23.

[6] See above, pp. 222-223.

[7] *Proceedings, U. S. P. A.*, 1916, p. 24.

willing to remain at work, and there were some, were supported in that by the national organization. The employers were allowed to get saggermakers from any source; members of other branches were forbidden to refuse to work with any men who took the places of the striking saggermakers. In the end " an understanding was reached " between the Brotherhood officers and the striking saggermakers that if the saggermakers would agree to return to work the Brotherhood would reinstate them and allow them three months in which to pay their fines, " with the privilege of appeal to a vote of the trade or to the convention " on their fines, and would arrange a conference with the manufacturers within one week after their return to work, to take up their clay grievance. The saggermakers then returned to work, on September 28. A few days later a special committee of the Brotherhood made a new and favorable agreement with the labor committee on the clay question. The saggermakers, in Mr. Wells' words, " had won a partial victory." [8]

After the 1919 agreement the majority of the bisque warehousewomen and dippers' assistants in the East Liverpool district went out on strike on one day's notice because, they declared, they had not been properly treated in the general wage increases. There was something in their contention as " in the hasty conclusion of the agreement these departments had not been fully considered." They were told they would get nothing while on strike. They returned to work " without any promise," whereupon their wages were increased.[9]

Since the war period there have been only two outlaw strikes of branch proportions. In April, 1921, most of

[8] *Report of President*, 1917, pp. 3-6; *Proceedings, U. S. P. A.*, 1916, pp. 24-25.

[9] *Ibid.*, January, 1920, p. 34.

the dippers in East Liverpool were on strike for about ten days against the attempt of the employers to force them to follow a list of "instructions" intended to insure better workmanship, which, the dippers contended, was a violation of the agreement.[10] The executive board finally got the dippers back to work by a threat of expulsion and substitution of other men in their places. In 1923 there was an outlaw strike of kilnmen in the East Liverpool district. The men returned to work in three days, after being threatened with expulsion by the executive board.[11]

By far the larger number of cessations in violation of the agreement have been "walkouts" involving one shop only, and sometimes only one branch in that shop. At times shop walkouts have spread to the men in the same branch in several shops. At other times a cessation by the workers in one branch has been supported by a walkout of the other branches in the same shop. This seems to have happened more often in "outside" potteries than in the trade centers. It is, of course, difficult to ascertain after the event whether the other workers quit to aid the strikers or stopped because the cessation in one branch checked the flow of their work. The cessations have seldom lasted more than a few days, but frequently the intervention of a national officer of the Brotherhood has been necessary to get the men back to work.

The total number of cessations of this type is unknown. Neither national organization has a record of them. The number has varied from period to period and even from year to year. There have been some years practically free of them, at least free of walkouts

[10] See above, p. 160.
[11] *Report of Executive Board*, 1923, pp. 50-53.

that were reported to the national office of either
organization. Generally speaking they were rarer down
to the war period than during the years 1916-1922.[12]
Then, after the 1922 strike things settled down again;
there were no cessations of consequence between 1923
and 1928. The employers attributed this to poor business conditions.[13] Nevertheless, there have been a few
cessations, some even within the past year.[14]

In the majority of cases in which minor cessations
have occurred, the men have quit before the prescribed
procedure of reference to the standing committee had
been complied with. Usually, in such cases, the men
have complained that the employer was violating the
agreement or that they could have secured attention for
their grievance in no other way. In spite of the fact
that straight price disputes have been by far the most
numerous class, they have not been responsible for the
majority of the walkouts. Unless the employer reduces
a price which the men contend has become established
for the shop—because, for example, he has learned that
a lower price is paid elsewhere—the men have been
disposed to let the dispute take its course to the standing committee under the protest price arrangement.
The kilnplacing and dipping branches, on the other
hand, have contributed more than their proportional
share of cessations.[15] This is what might be expected in

[12] *Proceedings, U. S. P. A.,* 1908, p. 41; 1909, p. 25; 1910, p. 27;
1911, p. 40; 1912, pp. 34-35; 1920, p. 32. In 1914 Chairman Wells
stated (to the writer) that cessations had occurred occasionally in
violation of the agreement but they were not important. For cessations in the period 1916-1922, see *ibid.,* 1916, pp. 21-22; 1917, p. 27;
January, 1920, pp. 32-33; December, 1920, p. 53.

[13] *Ibid.,* December, 1923, p. 21; 1924, p. 30; 1925, p. 30; 1926, pp.
25, 30; 1927, p. 17.

[14] *Potters Herald,* April 5, 1928; MS. *Minutes of Western General
Ware Standing Committee; Report of Executive Board,* 1928, p. 24.

[15] *Proceedings, U. S. P. A.,* December, 1923, p. 24.

view of the difficulties in applying the cubic measurement system of payment, with the intensified importance of " conditions " and with the non-uniformities in " rights " as between plants and the uncertainty that prevails over what the men may be compelled to do in a particular plant without extra.

After the war, attempts to take back concessions previously granted resulted in a number of walkouts. President Wood made a vigorous protest in the 1924 conference against this sort of action by the employers. Obviously, it was difficult for the Brotherhood officers to keep the men from striking when the employer withdrew an extra which he had voluntarily granted in good times to get or keep men.

There have been a few cessations after a decision has been made by the standing committee. These are much more serious from the standpoint of violation. In these cases, the men are attempting to force through something that the agreement, through its regular machinery of adjustment, has already denied them. The excuse offered in most of these cases has been that the standing committee did not understand the situation. There have also been some cessations after a case has been returned to the parties by the standing committee. The cessations which have occurred under such circumstances, as has been pointed out, were in violation of the understanding that work is to be continued in such cases, pending appeal to the labor committee and executive board.

NON-OBSERVANCE OF GOOD WORKMANSHIP RULES

Another complaint of the employers, which has loomed large at times, is that the men have refused to perform services or follow methods of production which the agreement gives the employer the right to demand.

The Brotherhood officers have always taken the position that the enforcement of such rules was incumbent upon the individual employers, not upon the Brotherhood. Their position is that when the Brotherhood has admitted the employer's right to exact this or that and has also admitted the employer's right to discharge any man who refuses to conform, it has gone as far as it can; it cannot compel specific performance in the shops. What it agrees to when such a working rule is put in the agreement is that the employer has the right to enforce it, not that the Brotherhood assumes the obligation to see that it is followed by its members.

The Association would not concede in 1906 that this view was correct. In a communication to the Brotherhood, Chairman Wells declared " the manufacturers have a right to assume when they enter into an agreement with the Brotherhood that the conditions thereto will be cheerfully lived up to, and that they shall not be obliged to fight in order to obtain what you have agreed to give them." [16] In 1916, however, he recognized that the manufacturer's right was practically dependent upon his willingness to discharge to secure it, and that in rush times the discharge method was impracticable.[17]

The employer's complaints of non-observance by the men were revived after the reaffirmation of a number of rules for better workmanship in the 1921 agreement. The labor committee realized when these were put in the agreement that the insertion of them would mean nothing unless the manufacturers insisted on compliance with them.[18] President Menge, too, prophesied in the conference that in times of good business the em-

[16] *Proceedings, N. B. of O. P.*, 1907, p. 60.
[17] *Proceedings, U. S. P. A.*, 1916, p. 22.
[18] *Ibid.*, 1921, p. 22.

ployers would encourage the men to disregard the rules in order to get the ware out faster. As a matter of fact, the rules were not observed generally in the busy time following the strike of 1922 and although the labor committee ascribed this to the " spirit of independence which prevails during prosperous times " among the workers,[19] the union officers held that it was primarily due to the failure of individual manufacturers to insist on the methods agreed to.

ACTIONS OF LOCAL UNIONS IN VIOLATION OF THE AGREEMENT

It was pointed out above that the Association has complained at times that local unions have attempted to enforce their own decisions on disputed matters. Local unions have also adopted working rules or rules reducing the hours of time workers. Sometimes the action of the local has resulted in a cessation; at other times it has been carried through to success without an actual cessation, although the threat of one may have been voiced.[20]

The 1916 series of violations included some of this type. In the negotiations resulting in the general " voluntary " increase late in 1916, the employers insisted on adding a stipulation that no workman " governed by action, order or law " of his local union in violation of the agreement was to receive the increase. This was presumably aimed at the kilnmen's local. But in the same conference the employers had condoned the local's worst offense—the enforcement of its rule that no kilnmen should " run out green saggers "—by amending the agreement to bring it into practical conformity with

---

[19] *Ibid.*, December, 1923, p. 21.
[20] For example, *ibid.*, 1911, pp. 41-42.

the local's outlaw rule. Even with this concession the local objected to the clause. It demanded the increase " without any strings whatever " and notified the manufacturers that unless its demands were granted all kilnmen would begin their two weeks' notice. This time the manufacturers accepted the challenge. They threatened that if they suffered any financial loss through any action of the local in violation of the agreement they would institute legal proceedings against the individual property owners for damages. The local then voted 239 to 143 in favor of accepting the agreement.[21]

DEBATED GROUND

It has been noted that there is a difference of opinion between the two national organizations concerning the right of union members to quit in support of other members who are employed in a non-scale branch and who are threatened with a wage reduction or other adverse change by the employer. The problem arises, of course, from the fact that the Association insists that the no-strike feature of the agreement is absolute but will not admit any obligation to extend the protection of the agreement to non-scale branches. The clause in the agreement requiring that " all work in dispute shall be continued pending and subject to the decision of the standing committee " assumes that there is a standing committee which will undertake " to adjust matters that cannot be settled between the firm and the employee." If the standing committee will not take jurisdiction, because the employers' side insists that it is without authority to give a decision binding on the employer, and the Association will not admit that some

[21] *Report of President*, 1917, pp. 6-11; *Proceedings, U. S. P. A.*, 1916, pp. 24-27.

other national joint committee must take up the case, the Brotherhood is free, it holds, to resort to coercion through any or all of its members in that shop to protect those whose existing wages or conditions are threatened. The Association officers hold, on the contrary, that the dispute must be left entirely to the members of the non-scale branch directly involved and the individual employer; any attempt by members of the Brotherhood in scale branches to coerce the employer is a violation of the agreement.[22]

The issue over violations arising out of trouble in a non-scale branch is a development of recent years and it comes from the decorating department. The leading case of a dispute over decorating prices which brought on a strike order for all branches occurred at the Shenango plant, in December, 1927. The company had announced that it would discontinue paying any plussage to its liners from December 21. The liners appealed to President Duffy who advised them not to accept the reduction. As the firm insisted on the reduction, the liners quit. According to the union view, this was a lockout, a violation of the agreement by the employer, inasmuch as the firm refused to employ the operatives longer at rates which could not be changed except by agreement.

The Brotherhood officers did not appeal to the labor committee on behalf of the " locked out " liners because they understood that the officers of the Association had told the firm that " the Brotherhood had nothing to do with decorating affairs so far as our Agreement was concerned." [23] It was the firm which finally appealed to the labor committee, after an ultimatum to the liners

[22] *Ibid.*, 1928, p. 26.
[23] *Report of Executive Board,* 1928, pp. 20-21; Statement of President Duffy to the writer.

that they must return to work by February 14 or their
places would be filled, had been met by a notification
from the local union, with the approval of the executive
board, that unless the dispute with the liners was settled by February 16, all branches would quit work. The
labor committee then asked the executive board to take
up the matter with it. At a conference between these
two bodies a settlement was reached in which the
employer " was conceded the right to discontinue paying his liners the plussage." [24] The labor committee
contended that President Duffy had violated the agreement in ordering the other branches to strike,[25] but
President Duffy would not admit that the Brotherhood
action was forbidden by the agreement in view of the
stand taken against the liners by the Association.

Another matter on which the two organizations differ is the concerted handing in of notices of resignation
because of a dispute over the terms of employment. The
Association holds that it is a violation of the agreement, the union that it is not—that so long as the
employer has the right under the agreement to discharge after notice the men have a right to leave after
notice. Mr. Wells has always contended that quitting
after notice, or even giving in notices as a threat,
because of a dispute over terms of employment, is a
violation of the clause requiring that " all work in dispute shall be continued pending and subject to the
decision of the standing committee " or other joint committee which has jurisdiction. The discharge commit-

[24] *Report of Executive Board,* 1928, p. 21.

[25] Chairman Wells declared: " The Brotherhood administration
. . . . could have been no further off the track if they had called
a strike of jiggermen and dippers at the Shenango because the firm
had a labor dispute with the carpenters and bricklayers constructing
an addition to their plant." *Proceedings, U. S. P. A.,* 1928, p. 26.

24

tee, says Chairman Wells, will not allow an employer to discharge a man because the latter refuses to do something which the agreement does not compel him to do, or to enforce the employer's contention in a dispute not yet passed on by the proper committee—nor would the union men allow anyone to take the place of a man discharged because of a dispute. Consequently no man, or group of men, should be allowed to hand in his or their notices to compel the employer to give something which he cannot be compelled to give through the regular procedure. The fact that the men give notice and leave " individually " does not make it any the less a strike.[26]

In 1917 the employers made a proposal to outlaw the concerted handing in of notices, by three or more men, offering in return to forbid the discharging of three or more men simultaneously even after notice, when done clearly for the purpose of accomplishing some end not specified in the agreement or one that cannot be accomplished legally through the regular channels. The Brotherhood would not agree. It was unwilling to surrender the right of the men to quit in a group on notice so long as the employer retained the right to discharge an individual on notice at any time without giving a reason, and so long as the employers would not agree that only members of the Brotherhood in good standing should be employed.[27]

NATIONAL UNION ACTION ON VIOLATIONS

That the clear violations of the agreement which have occurred on the part of individual union members or local unions have not been encouraged by the na-

26 Statement of Chairman Wells to the writer.
27 Statement of President Menge to the writer.

tional officers, but have on the contrary been discouraged by them has already been emphasized. It has been repeatedly testified to by the officers of the Association, at least down to the autumn of 1927. Even in cases in which the men charged violation of the agreement by the employer, the national officers have urged them to remain at work and allow the national officers to take up the cases, as required both by union law and the agreement.[28] The union officers have also issued general condemnations of their own members who violate the agreement.[29] The convention, too, has several times, through acceptance of the report of the committee on officers' reports, endorsed the statements of the officers in condemnation of those who violate the agreement.[30]

In 1906 the union adopted a rule giving the executive board power " to suspend or expel, without any formality, any local union or member that refuses to observe the provisions of our agreements, or disregards the law governing strikes and grievances, or refuses to obey the instructions of the national officers concerning disputes." [31] Yet prior to 1916, so far as the national president could then recall,[32] no member or local had been suspended under this rule. Members who had gone out in violation of the agreement had always gone

[28] They have, however, warned the manufacturers repeatedly that they could not be held responsible for keeping the men at work if the employer violated the agreement. Statement of President Menge to the writer.

[29] Report of President, 1906, pp. 21, 27; 1907, p. 15; 1908, pp. 6-7; 1911, pp. 9-10, 17-18; 1912, pp. 13-14; 1913, p. 13; 1914, p. 24; 1916, pp. 23-25; Report of Executive Board, 1918, pp. 17-18; Potters Herald, June 11, 1925.

[30] Proceedings, 1906, p. 45; 1908, p. 40; 1911, p. 45; 1917, p. 104; 1918, pp. 78-79.

[31] Ibid., 1906, p. 45; Report of President, 1906, p. 21; Constitution, Sec. 110.

[32] Statement of President Menge to the writer.

back at the bidding of the national officers. Moreover, their employers had wanted them back at work; had they been expelled or suspended and failed to pay their fines and seek reinstatement immediately, the situation would have been awkward for the Brotherhood. The walkouts occurred, as a rule, at a time when the employers were eager to have the men at work; the employers would have been very little pleased at any disciplinary action by the Brotherhood which failed to get the men back to work but, on the contrary, led to a demand from the Brotherhood that they be not allowed to work.

The agreement did not give the union right to order its members to refuse to work with persons expelled from membership and the national officers were never sure that the manufacturer would refuse to employ them if called upon to do so in order to make the Brotherhood's disciplinary action effective. In 1908 President Duffy declared that it was impracticable to enforce the penalty provided in the union laws " without some arrangement with the employers." [33] To be sure, there has been a clause in the agreement since 1905 under the heading of " Penalty for Violation of Agreement" pledging both parties " to discourage any opposition on the part of individuals and to favor in every reasonable way those employers and employees who faithfully and honorably abide by this contract in all its provisions." It seems possible to construe this and similar clauses so as to give the union the right to insist that individuals or members of local unions expelled for ceasing work in violation of the agreement should not be employed in any shop under the agreement unless reinstated by the union. Nevertheless the national officers

[33] *Report of President,* 1908, p. 7.

of the Brotherhood were reluctant to put it to the test so long as the men did not remain defiant.

It was the kilndrawers' strike in East Liverpool in 1916 which called forth the first use of the fine and suspension penalty. The striking members who did not return to work by the date set by the board were expelled from the Brotherhood. About ninety of them failed to pay up and remained expelled. This eventually broke up the local union of kilndrawers in East Liverpool. A few months later the striking saggermakers were fined and then expelled and other men were allowed to take their places, so far as other men could be obtained. The expelled members were later allowed to return to the Brotherhood on payment of the reinstatement fee of $5.00. The 1917 convention sustained the fine and expulsion but allowed those who had become reinstated to retain their insurance status.[34] In 1917 the president, secretary, and treasurer of the insurgent organization which attempted to prevent the workers from returning after the executive board declared the 1917 strike off—and succeeded for several days—were fined $500, $100 and $25, respectively; the president was also expelled from the Brotherhood until he should pay the fine; [35] it was not paid. This action was sustained by the 1918 convention, in a roll call vote, 77 to 19.[36] In punishing these men the Brotherhood was not only punishing a violation of the agreement but an attempt to launch an insurgent organization. Since that time there has been no defying of the board after the members have been ordered to return to work.

[34] *Proceedings*, 1917, pp. 35, 39, 70.

[35] *Report of Executive Board*, 1918, p. 17; *Proceedings, U. S. P. A.,* 1917, p. 21.

[36] *Proceedings, N. B. of O. P.,* 1918, pp. 74, 75, 76, 77.

EMPLOYERS' DEMANDS FOR GUARANTEES

In 1907 the Association made an issue with the national union of violations of the agreement. There had been a number of cessations since the 1905 agreement had been signed. The Association officers were indignant also at the successful opposition of the kilnmen to the time limit for kilnplacing agreed to in 1905. Although the officers did not blame the Brotherhood officers, they did hold that the Brotherhood, because of its inability to secure observance of its agreements by its members, had forfeited its claim to bargain for them.[37] In the 1907 conference the labor committee demanded, before it would consider the union's propositions, that the union put up a money guarantee that its members would not violate the agreement if one were made. The union representatives, in the words of President Duffy:

declined to accede to their demand for a money guarantee and combated their arguments as best we could. We contended that the organization had not encouraged nor sanctioned any violations of the agreement and had always exerted every effort to keep the members at work or have them return to work immediately in cases where they had been so rash as to stop work contrary to the agreement . . . . and that it would not be fair to hold the organization financially responsible for the imperfections of human nature. We offered to cooperate with the employers in fixing a penalty to be imposed upon the individuals who are guilty of such acts. This did not seem to appeal to them and they finally withdrew their request for a guarantee after arguing that point alone all during the first day and part of the second day's sessions.[38]

The cessations diminished in number and importance after 1907 and it was not until 1917 that the labor

[37] *Proceedings, U. S. P. A.*, 1906, p. 14; 1907, pp. 13, 31; *Proceedings, N. B. of O. P.*, 1907, pp. 59-61, 65.

[38] *Report of President*, 1908, p. 4; also, *Proceedings, U. S. P. A.*, 1907, p. 31.

committee again made violations a major issue.[39] In the 1917 conference the manufacturers made two specific proposals. One was that each side should give bonds or post a forfeit of $100,000 to protect the employer from financial loss through violation of the agreement by employees, and vice versa. The second was that the employer might require each employee to enter into an individual contract with him pledging both to a faithful observance of the terms of the agreement. The union refused to agree to either of these.[40] The manufacturers asked again in the 1919 conference, and again unsuccessfully, for guarantees against violations or compensation for loss suffered because of them. " We were . . . . compelled to waive this point," reported the labor committee, " and to depend upon only the good faith and the coöperation of the officers of the Brotherhood, which it is fair to say we have always received in the adjustment of such troubles. Unfortunately, they are as powerless as the manufacturers themselves to control the abuse." [41]

In contrast to the firm tone taken in the official communications addressed by the Association to the Brotherhood and the demands for financial guarantees, it will be noted that the manufacturers have at times given the men concessions after " outlaw " branch strikes which they had refused to give them before. It is also true that individual manufacturers have made settlements after walkouts on terms more favorable to the men than they were willing to give before the violations. These concessions have made the task of the national officers of the Brotherhood much more difficult.

[39] *Ibid.*, 1916, pp. 21-22; 1917, pp. 26-27.
[40] *Report of Executive Board*, 1918, pp. 3-7.
[41] *Proceedings, U. S. P. A.*, January, 1920, pp. 33-34; December, 1920, p. 53; *Report of Executive Board*, 1921, p. 14.

The men have been able to point to concessions obtained by violations of the agreement which the Brotherhood was unable to secure for them by bargaining within the limits of the agreement procedure.

VIOLATIONS BY EMPLOYERS

Down to 1927 there was no complaint from the Brotherhood officers that the Association as such had violated the agreement.[42] There were many charges from members of the Brotherhood, some of which were shown subsequently to be justified, that individual employers insisted upon the acceptance of prices or conditions which they had no right to insist upon under the agreement, or were dilatory in supplying facilities for work or taking measures for the protection of the health of the workers which a competent joint committee had decided they should take, or had disregarded the apprentice rules or some other clause of the agreement, but the Brotherhood officers did not charge that the Association abetted the violator. The Association officers, when appealed to, had coöperated in securing compliance—when they agreed that the employer was wrong. Of course the Brotherhood had to be patient at times with the Association in its attempts to secure specific performance from its members, just as the Association had to recognize the problems of the Brotherhood officers. But in every case in which the union had to declare a strike or recognize a lockout—except in a non-scale branch—the firm had resigned from the Association.[43]

---

[42] President J. M. Duffy holds that the Association officers supported the Shenango Company in reducing the wages of its liners in violation of the agreement in December, 1927. The Association officers deny that this was a violation.

[43] This does not apply to the strike at the Shenango Company's plant which was begun in October, 1928, as a result of an alleged

It must be remembered, however, that the Association cannot compel a member to abide by the agreement if he chooses to resign from the Association and fight it out with the union. It does not pledge itself when it signs the agreement that all firms which are then members will remain in the Association and abide by the terms of the agreement until the date of its expiration. If a member violates the agreement and resigns from the Association the latter is no longer answerable for it. The only redress the Brotherhood has in such a case is to call a strike against the offending firm.

This is what happened in the dispute with the Iroquois Pottery Company, at Syracuse, in 1917. The company had discharged three men without notice. The men charged that they were discriminated against for union activity and the union brought the case to the discharge committee. The firm refused to submit the case to the committee, declaring that the incident was closed. Secretary Goodwin informed the firm that it was bound by the agreement to submit the case or reinstate the men at once and pay them for the time lost. The firm then resigned from the Association and the Brotherhood called its members out on strike.[44]

In recent years there have been charges from the union side of violations by employers in the form of attempted reductions in decorating prices. This, like the charges of violation against union members who quit or threaten to quit in support of members in non-scale branches, is debated territory; the Association does not admit that it is a violation of the agreement. The Shenango case, in December, 1927, has already been noted. Several years before, the Brotherhood sup-

---

violation of the agreement in giving kilnmen's work to a non-kilnman. The Association denied that the kilnmen were entitled to that work under the agreement.

[44] *Report of President,* 1917, pp. 13-14.

ported the decorators against a Trenton china firm [45] which attempted to reduce their wages. The " lockout " of the " decorating shop " lasted for five weeks and the decorators were paid strike benefits for the time they were out. The matter was finally adjusted with the firm by the national officers and the decorators returned at the old wages.[46] Trouble broke out again in the same plant in 1926, and again in 1928, on the same issue. Vice-President Cartiledge held that the firm was violating the agreement by attempting to force what was in effect a wage reduction and the firm charged that the decalcomania girls were in violation of the agreement when they quit work. In 1928 the dispute threatened to involve other branches before it was settled.[47]

[45] The Maddock Pottery Company; this company was soon after succeeded by the Scammell China Company.

[46] *Report of Executive Board*, 1922, pp. 5, 35-36; *Proceedings, N. B. of O. P.*, 1922, p. 70.

[47] *Report of Executive Board*, 1926, pp. 25-26; 1929, pp. 47-50; *Proceedings, N. B. of O. P.*, 1929, p. 26.

CHAPTER XIII

CONCLUSIONS

In trying to account for the rise and continuance of the national agreement system in the general ware division, we shall emphasize factors which have been, if not peculiar to the industry, at least exceptional. The continuance of national collective bargaining through so many years is itself an exceptional experience in American industrial relations and it is only logical to look for unusual conditions, or an unusually favorable combination of conditions, to account for it. In the general ware pottery industry the explanation is apparently to be found in: (1) the importance attributed to the tariff; (2) the localization of the industry largely in a few centers; (3) the system of payment, and the related fact of the tradition that wage rates should be uniform; and (4) the views and attitude toward each other of the men who have been at the helm on the respective sides.

It is significant that the first important movement toward collective bargaining on a national scale grew out of a joining of effort to secure an increase in the tariff, in 1897. Long before this the employers had recognized the desirability of having their employees support them in their tariff requests, but in 1897 the employees had an organization in the West which showed signs of vitality and to which members of Congress might give some attention. The manufacturers were not blind to the strategic importance of having the spokesmen of this organization—which had led such a stubborn fight against the manufacturers in 1894—

now support their claims for increased protection. The willingness of the union to help them cut down the competition of foreign manufacturers enjoying lower wage rates doubtless made the employers more disposed to enter into an agreement with the men's organization to eliminate competition through lower wage rates at home.

The tariff bond has also been important in keeping the manufacturers in the national agreement arrangement when otherwise many of them might have been disposed to force the issue of a wage reduction. Had they fought the union for a decrease in wages in 1913 or 1914, for example, the attitude of the Democratic administration and Congress would likely have been hostile. The industry doubtless escaped more lightly in 1913 because of the support received from the union.[1] In 1922 the situation was different. The union was fighting to recover part of a wage reduction which it had accepted the year before. The employers could argue that there had been no increase in the cost of living nor sufficient improvement in the condition of the industry to warrant a wage increase, and that even the proposed increase in the tariff would no more than enable them to hold their own at the existing wage rates. However, if the employers had turned the wage strike into a fight for the " open shop," as was done in the sanitary division, it might have embarrassed them in their future dealings with the Tariff Commission and Congress. The tariff was perhaps not the most vital factor in the willingness of the manufacturers to resume the agreement system in December, 1922, instead

[1] *Report of President,* 1913, pp. 8-10; *Proceedings, U. S. P. A.,* 1913, p. 25; also F. W. Taussig, " The Tariff Act of 1913," *Quarterly Journal of Economics,* XXVIII, 23-24.

of fighting it out for the " open shop," but it would not be safe to assume that it had no bearing.

In the tense situation in 1928 the tariff factor was undoubtedly an important influence in bringing about a renewal of the agreement for another two years at the old wage terms. One must not take too seriously the labor committee's proposal in the conference that the Brotherhood and the Association part company. Nevertheless, it reflected a far different attitude from that shown in preceding conferences. Moreover, the union did refuse to grant the employers what many of them undoubtedly wanted in the way of substitution of less skilled labor at lower rates for work over which skilled men now have jurisdiction at skilled men's rates. Why then did the employers sign for two more years under the old rates and conditions instead of fighting it out? One may assume that the facts that the tariff rates were still under consideration and that the Brotherhood was working whole-heartedly for an increase in the duties had some influence. The history of peaceful relations between the manufacturers' association and the national union and the energetic support by the union of the employers' claims for more protection was undoubtedly regarded as a valuable asset in dealing with the committees of the House and Senate.

It must be recognized, however, that the tariff bond may not continue strong enough to prevent a fight on the wages issue, or the closely related issue of substitution of cheaper labor. Inasmuch as it is foreign competition which is dwelt on as the reason for the necessity of reducing labor costs, the manufacturers have been stressing the complaint that the union compels them to pay " skilled wages " for much work that can be done by less skilled labor and is so done abroad. They are also complaining that they have not been given the benefit of investments in equipment which have made the work much easier, as in kilnplacing. A few of the manufacturers, too, are now apparently inclined to put their reliance on large scale production of a few lines with the most improved methods, and with wage rates adjusted accordingly, rather than on higher tariff duties. The horizontal reduction of 1931 has not changed the question of comparative wage rates within the scale or the included question of " skilled wages for unskilled work." It has merely lowered the level for all. It is not likely that it has appreciably weakened the employers' dissatisfaction with the internal structure of the scale.

That the industry is so largely located in " pottery towns " in which it is the main, if not the only important, industry, has also been a big factor making for agreement. Employers and men have had a community attitude toward the industry which has bound them together; a break resulting in a strike would mean financial hardship to whole communities. This came out clearly in the 1922 strike and the knowledge that these communities were waiting anxiously for some sort of agreement which would start their industry going again was a consideration with some of the union conferees who voted to send the men back to work.

The fact that the industry was overwhelmingly on a piece-work (including the " kilnman's day ") basis, although it greatly increased the number of wage issues and the number of local disputes, greatly aided the two national organizations to get past the issue of a general percentage increase in wages in the long period from 1905 to 1916. The piece-work system made it possible for the men to increase their earnings in most branches without direct wage increases. " Extras " could be gained, too, through the medium of special joint committees, and even particular rates increased for special reasons by the conference itself, without facing squarely the question of a general advance. Thus the labor committee and the union conferees could " renew the agreement without any substantial change " in almost every conference year through 1915.

The piece-work system also furnished a stimulus to the uniform wage idea. It was assumed that the piece rate was almost an exact, if not an exact, statement of the labor cost of the operation and this led easily to the acceptance of the " principle " that the piece rates should be the same for all employers. The sentiment among the manufacturers in favor of uniformity of selling prices undoubtedly created a receptiveness toward uniformity of wage rates, as a support to uniformity of selling prices, but if the industry had not been on a piece-work basis the realization of a uniform wage scale would have been much more difficult. And the fact that the majority of the employers regarded uniformity in wage rates as a desirable thing for the industry was of great assistance in bringing about national collective bargaining and giving the agreement system valuable momentum in the earlier years.[2]

To be sure, many of the employers have for some time been questioning the advantage of uniform piece rates, as these have functioned in practice. Yet, even though the labor committee did propose in the 1928 conference a return to plant determination of wages, it is doubtful if the employers would wish to see the idea of a uniform wage scale abandoned in favor of making piece rates an

[2] See George E. Barnett, " National and District Systems of Collective Bargaining in the United States," *Quarterly Journal of Economics*, XXVI, 425-443.

added factor in competition between the plants. Although the present scale does not give geographical uniformity of remuneration for skill and effort expended, or uniformity of cost in terms of facilities furnished, it does set a limit of competition in wage rates. The employers with the newer and large plants are apparently not at a disadvantage in competition with the others even though they do not get rebates in wage rates for superior facilities, and the uniform scale does give them assurance against competition based on lower rates at least.

Again it must be recognized that there has been a change. The piece-work system, including the " kilnman's day " basis, is now relatively less important in the industry than it was. The time system is growing rapidly in kiln work and dipping. So far, it has not made much headway in the clay shop. If casting goes over to day work, as has been suggested, and casting becomes the predominant method of waremaking, the piece rates will represent but a small proportion of the labor cost. This might well weaken still further the appeal of a uniform wage scale to the employers.

The mutual confidence and fine personal relations between the officers of the two national organizations, down to 1927 at least, were a great aid in keeping the national agreement going. This is said with full realization that this factor would not have been enough alone. So far as the officers on the two sides were concerned, the same confidence and high personal regard was present in the sanitary division but this could not prevent the breakdown of the agreement. Nevertheless, the attitude of the officers toward each other helped to pull the agreement system in general ware over some rough places. In 1917 and 1922 the fact that the officers wanted to go on dealing with each other led the union officers to seek a way past the adverse vote of the union membership, and the labor committee to coöperate with them. In 1921, too, it was the union officers who convinced the conference committee that Chairman Wells was not "bluffing" and that it should take a reduction which saved the agreement. On the manufacturers' side Chairman Wells more than once persuaded his associates to offer better terms, in order to give the Brotherhood officers something which they could induce their side to accept.

The feeling of confidence entertained by the officers of each side in those of the other, also explains in large measure how so many issues that have greatly disturbed the relations of employers and unions in other trades or industries could be left in an indefinite state without precipitating serious conflict. The handling of the apprentice ratios is a case in point. The elastic rule as to the number of apprentices never could have been adopted if each side had not had confidence that the other would not abuse it. The same is true of the "closed shop" question and the employer's right to discharge after notice. So long as the officers on each side understood the problem of the other with respect to the matter and each could count on the other to smooth things out in practice, it could be assumed that the union would not push matters to a strike to get a closed shop contract or for a clause denying the employers' right to discharge without a reason acceptable to the union.

It might be supposed that one of the greatest advantages to the employers in a national agreement of this kind is the assurance which it offers against strikes over local grievances. It is more than clear, however, that such protection as the agreement gave in practice

25

was at times insufficient. That the occasional breakdown of the agreement at this point did not cause the
employers to abandon the system was largely due to
their knowledge that the union officers were doing their
best to prevent these outbreaks and to get the men back
to work when they occurred. The manufacturers realized that so long as the men were unionized they were
likely to break out, especially in good times, and especially in East Liverpool where they were organized in
branch locals. So long as the men were organized as
they were, a national agreement administered by officers in whom the employers had confidence promised
them a closer approach to freedom from strikes than
they could get otherwise.

The necessity of adjusting local disputes is, under a
no-strike agreement, a necessity of the system rather
than a positive asset in the sense of increasing satisfaction on all sides with the system. To be sure, both
the union officers and the Association officers have, in
pointing with pride to the system of dealing, included
the method of handling local grievances in the reasons
for its success. The joint committee system has undoubtedly worked very well, when one considers that it
depends on agreement and not on arbitration. The elasticity in the machinery of adjustment which allows a
dispute to be carried along subject to some further
joint action, even when the standing committee has
failed to settle it, has been a favorable feature. In
short, the idea that nothing is settled until it is settled
by agreement has been applied with great success,
comparatively. Yet, the necessity of keeping the men at
work through delays and disappointments and the necessity resting on the labor committee and the executive
board of working out some kind of a compromise settlement to avoid a local outbreak has involved a strain.

Here again the personal factor has been important. The officers on both sides have felt confident that when and if the counsel of delay should appear to have been carried to the point where further delay would be dangerous, the leaders of the two organizations would be able, out of their long experience in dealing with each other and their will to agree, to reach some kind of a settlement.

PART III
THE SANITARY AGREEMENT

CHAPTER XIV

THE WORKINGS AND BREAKDOWN OF THE AGREEMENT

THE SANITARY POTTERS ASSOCIATION

The Sanitary Potters Association which entered the inter-association agreement of 1903 for a united front in dealing with threatened strikes,[1] was dissolved on December 31, 1903. One of its chief functions had been the allotment of output among its members and it was feared that a continuance of this activity might bring it foul of the law.[2] For more than two years thereafter the manufacturers had no formal organization for dealing with labor. It was not until May, 1906, that a new association was formally organized, under the old name of the Sanitary Potters Association. The new association was established primarily as an employers' association and especially for collective bargaining. In fact it was the need of more authoritative organization on the manufacturers' side for dealing with the Brotherhood which led to its formation.[3] For many years membership was confined to firms which would abide by the labor agreement. However, in the last few years of its existence the Association opened its doors to some firms which were running non-union shops. This departure seems to have been due to the increasing importance of the trade functions and the growing fear on the part of the union manufacturers of non-union competition.

---

[1] See above, pp. 21-22.

[2] Statement of Secretary J. J. Dale to the writer. There is a brief description of the activities of this Association in the *Eleventh Special Report of the Commissioner of Labor*, pp. 700-701.

[3] Statement of Secretary J. J. Dale to the writer.

At the time of the termination of the national agreement system in the sanitary ware division (October 31, 1922) the Association had 23 members, with 278 kilns. There were then approximately 327 kilns in the industry.[4] The membership of the Association included four non-union plants with thirty-three kilns. Three of these had never been unionized and the fourth had gone non-union a few weeks before. Conversely, there were eight small union plants in the industry which were not included in the membership of the Association, four of which had withdrawn from the Association a short time before, in anticipation of the strike.

The Association had no formal rules of government.[5] Meetings were held only when business required it and meetings on labor matters were not frequent. The president and the secretary were the only officers with important functions. Officers were elected nominally for one year but the formality of reëlection was not always observed. The Association had but two presidents; Mr. John A. Campbell resigned in 1911 and was succeeded in the presidency by Mr. A. M. Maddock. The Association likewise had but two secretaries, Mr. J. J. Dale and Mr. George Dyer; the secretaries were salaried officers. The expenses were met by assessments on the members, levied on the basis of kiln capacity. There was no defense fund. The only defense measure

---

[4] Statement of Secretary Dyer to the writer. This coincides with the statement in the opinion of the court in *U. S. v. Trenton Potteries Company et al* (273 U. S. 394) that these 23 plants produced 82 per cent of the sanitary pottery manufactured in the United States.

[5] The following account is based on interviews with ex-President John A. Campbell, President A. M. Maddock, Secretary J. J. Dale and Secretary George Dyer of the Association. No reports of the meetings were published.

was agreement among the members to lock out all the union members in the sanitary shops in case of a strike against any member who should be sustained by the Association. No such lockout was ever declared.

In August, 1922, the firms constituting the Association and a number of individuals, officers of the several firms, were indicted in the federal district court for the southern district of New York for restraint of trade in sanitary ware. The corporations and individuals were found guilty. They took an appeal. However, the Sanitary Potters Association soon became practically inactive; the labor agreement broke down on October 31, 1922, and the trade activities of the Association had fallen under the ban of the law.[6]

HISTORY OF RELATIONS

The national joint agreement system in the sanitary division had its beginnings in the agreement in 1902 for the pressing branch. Since the organization of the sanitary pressers and some of the other branches within the Knights of Labor, there had been more or less shop bargaining and even negotiations between committees of employers and organized workers.[7] There had been many strikes, too, by the organized workers, chief among which was a strike of pressers in 1891 that lasted five months. The agreement in the pressing branch in 1902 was a long step forward in that it was the first agreement of national scope and was reached without a strike. In August, 1903, the national agreement system was extended to the other

[6] The decision of the District Court was finally upheld by the United States Supreme Court. (*U. S. v. Trenton Potteries Company et al.*, 273 U. S. 392.)

[7] *U. S. Ind. Comm.*, XIV, 625-627.

organized branches and at the same time a regular joint standing committee was established for the sanitary division, after the general ware model.[8]

Like the agreement of 1902, that of 1903 was not signed for a specified period. In 1904 and 1905 some changes in terms were made by the standing committee. In 1906 the Brotherhood submitted a set of sixteen propositions and asked for a conference on them, in the general ware manner. The agreement made in the ensuing conference [9] was allowed by the union to stand for one year only; the same was true of the agreement made in 1907. In 1908 the union conference committee "took it on itself" to make a two-year agreement, as requested by the manufacturers.[10] The two-year period was followed thereafter. From 1908 through 1920 the agreement was renewed biennially without a strike and even without the taking of a strike vote. In 1914 the union conference committee withdrew all of its propositions for increases in wages; these had been adopted by the convention before war had broken out in Europe.[11]

Three times during the life of the agreement which was signed for the two years beginning November 1, 1916, the manufacturers voluntarily increased wages at the request of the union executive board, because of

[8] *Proceedings,* 1904, pp. 11, 60.

[9] *Report of President,* 1907, pp. 3-4, 15-16. The information as to action and arguments in the conferences from 1906 on is taken from the stenographic reports of the conferences, supplemented by interview. References will be given to material bearing on the conferences in the printed reports of the officers.

[10] *Ibid.,* 1908, p. 6, 25-26; 1909, p. 6.

[11] The union officers had Mr. Campbell's statement in the conference printed and sent to the members in the sanitary division. Part of his statement was included in the *Report of the President* for 1915, pp. 12-13.

the increase in the cost of living. The terms of the agreement signed for two years in 1918 were likewise bettered, for the workers, at three different times. One of the advances, given in June, 1919, applied only to the pressers and casters. It was not until January, 1920, that a general advance was given on the 1918 terms. There was such widespread complaint of the " inadequacy " of this increase that the manufacturers a month later conceded another general advance, effective in April. Throughout the period from 1917 to February, 1920, the executive board had been under great pressure from the locals, especially from Local 45, sanitary pressers and casters of Trenton, to demand further increases in wages to meet the mounting cost of living.[12]

It was perhaps unfortunate for the national agreement system that the agreement made in October, 1920, was made for two years. Had it expired in 1921, when the industry was in a depressed condition, the subsequent course of events might have been different. The manufacturers had granted in the agreement which went into effect on November 1, 1920, an increase over the wages fixed in February.[13] Three months later the manufacturers' association asked for a reopening of the wage scale, under the " unforeseen general condition arising in the trade " clause of the agreement, and specifically for a ten per cent reduction. The executive board secured a postponement of a wage conference until after the convention.[14] Immediately following the general ware conference at which the union accepted a seventeen per cent reduction, the sanitary committee

[12] *Ibid.*, 1917, pp. 27-30; *Report of Executive Board*, 1918, pp. 18-26; 1919, pp. 41-43; 1920, pp. 19-32.
[13] *Ibid.*, 1921, pp. 55-59.
[14] *Ibid.*, pp. 66-70.

refused to accept any reduction whatever. Another conference followed, at the request of the manufacturers, with like result. As the time for the 1922 conference approached the manufacturers submitted a wage scale that involved considerable reductions and important changes in the working rules. But the depression of 1921 in the industry had lifted in the meantime and this fact was used by those who had opposed a wage reduction in 1921 as a proof that they had been right and strengthened the determination of the members at large to accept no reduction now. That the conference committee expressed the wishes of the membership when it rejected the manufacturers' proposals, in September, 1922, was evidenced by a "practically unanimous" vote in the ensuing referendum.[15]

The threatened strike was not allowed to materialize without further efforts to avoid it. Many of the union members at first expected that the manufacturers would make another attempt to secure an agreement "because of the fact that all shops were running to capacity and seemed to have plenty of orders." [16] However, when the manufacturers did not ask for another conference "and it was evident," in the words of the executive board, "that they were preparing to take care of their business by the introduction of casting [17] in the event of our leaving the benches," some of the members began to clamor for action by the executive board. The board believed that its hands were tied by the trade vote; it could not ask for another conference without seeming to suggest that concessions would be made by the union. It was ex-Vice-President Hutchins,

[15] *Ibid.*, 1923, p. 81. The vote was 2225 to 9.

[16] *Ibid.*, 1923, pp. 81-82.

[17] For the part played by casting in bringing on the strike and the defeat of the men, see below, pp. 405-412.

now merely an "adviser" to the Brotherhood, and
Mr. John A. Campbell, who had retired from the employers' conference committee, who arranged for a
conference "without prejudice to either side" between
the eastern members of the executive board of the
Brotherhood and the executive committee of the Sanitary Potters Association; it was understood that the two
committees "were not empowered to act officially." [18]

This conference was entirely different in tone and
spirit from the three which preceded it. The union committee was obviously willing to concede as much as it
thought it could persuade the members to give, in order
to save the agreement, and the manufacturers met them
with considerable recessions from their September
ultimatum. The wage terms on which the employers
finally agreed to renew the agreement for one year, and
which the union committee agreed to recommend to the
sanitary membership, were a general reduction of ten
per cent for all branches, except mouldmaking, in which
it was to be five per cent, and casting, in which there was
to be a revision of prices involving a reduction of much
more than ten per cent. The executive board

realizing the determination of the Sanitary Manufacturers to force
a reduction which they claimed was in the interest of the industry
and feeling that a strike at this time would displace for all time
some of those now engaged in the trade and destroy the prestige
of our organization, decided to submit a statement of the conditions of the sanitary trade to be distributed to the members of the
sanitary branch so that they would have a full knowledge of what
confronted them before voting.[19]

In spite of the courageous and trenchant statement of
the board, the sanitary ware membership rejected the

[18] *Report of Executive Board*, 1923, p. 82; *Informal Meeting of
Executive Committees of Sanitary Potters Association and National
Brotherhood of Operative Potters*, October 5 and 6, 1922.
[19] *Report of Executive Board*, 1923, pp. 82-91.

recommendations of its officers—and the manufacturers' terms—by a vote of 2018 to 252.[20] A few small
shops " signed up to continue at the old wage scale "
but all the firms which remained in the Association
refused to give the old terms.

Late in December, after the strike had been going on
for over six weeks, a committee elected by the locals to
act in conjunction with the executive board empowered
the board to settle on the basis of the terms offered by
the manufacturers in the October conference. But it
was then too late to get a settlement on those terms.[21]
In June, 1923, the executive board recognized that the
strike was lost. It ordered the men back to work
" where the firms would consent to take them back as
fast as they could find places for them " but even then
it attempted to lay down terms for other branches than
casting. These were the terms offered by the manufacturers in October. For casting, the members were free
to accept the " wages and conditions prevailing in the
respective shops for casters." A number of firms gave
the members of the board assurances that they would
take back their striking employees on these terms as
rapidly as they could make room for them, but they
refused to make any agreement with the Brotherhood.[22]
As a matter of fact only a small proportion of those
who had gone on strike were taken back.[23] The strike
was continued nominally for another year against the
firms which refused the assurances asked for in June,
1923, but in the summer of 1924 the union members
were allowed to take employment in any sanitary shop

[20] *Ibid.*, pp. 91-92.
[21] *Ibid.*, pp. 93-94.
[22] *Ibid.*, 1924, 33-35; *Proceedings*, 1923, pp. 55-58.
[23] Statement of Vice-President Cartlidge to the writer.

" at the prevailing prices in each shop " and " each shop " was " permitted to make their own settlement " on wage rates.[24] All attempts to reorganize the sanitary industry have failed [25] and in very few shops is the union recognized.

THE AGREEMENT-MAKING PROCESS

The making of the agreement in the sanitary division ran along much the same lines as in general ware. On the union side the same procedure was followed in gathering resolutions from the locals and acting on them in convention and the number and content of the propositions adopted by the convention was all out of proportion to the changes adopted by the conference. The union conference committee, too, was chosen in the same way.[26] As the sanitary pressers greatly overshadowed the other branches in the sanitary ware division, this branch naturally had a controlling voice in the sanitary price list committee of the convention and in the conference committee.

The union conference committee always came with " full power to settle "—and never once did it refer the general terms of the proposed agreement to referendum before settling. In 1920 the convention adopted a resolution to the effect that if the manufacturers did not

[24] *Proceedings,* 1924, pp. 43-44; *Report of Executive Board,* 1925, pp. 45-49.

[25] *Proceedings,* 1925, pp. 10-11; *Report of Executive Board,* 1926, pp. 26-30; 1927, pp. 42-50; 1928, pp. 32-33; *Proceedings,* 1930, pp. 15-17.

[26] In the conferences on general wage advances between the regular biennial conferences, in the period 1916-1920, it was the executive board which represented the union, as in general ware. Some important changes were also made in the agreement by special conferences for particular branches, especially for pressing and casting.

grant in full the demands adopted by the convention, the concessions offered should be submitted to a referendum vote for ratification—" majority vote to decide the issue." The manufacturers refused to go into conference with the union committee unless this resolution were " rescinded or modified so as to give full power of settlement to delegates to the conference, as in all previous meetings." The executive board then submitted the withdrawal of the resolution to a referendum vote and the vote being in favor of withdrawal the resolution was cancelled.[27]

On the employers' side it was the practice to hold one or more meetings to determine their own propositions and to consider those submitted by the union. For years it was usual at these meetings to ask each firm to pledge itself to abide by the action of the employers' conference committee. Of course this committee had full power to settle.[28] The sanitary employers submitted proposals more frequently than the general ware association. Beginning in 1908, the sanitary ware manufacturers submitted propositions to nearly every biennial conference.

The sanitary ware conferences were conducted in much the same way as those in general ware. Mr. John A. Campbell was regularly chosen chairman of the conference, on motion from the union side, down through 1920, and Mr. A. M. Maddock in 1921 and 1922. Prior to the 1921 conferences the tone was nearly always friendly, although the exchange of views and criticisms was frank and the argument frequently prolonged. Mr. Campbell and Mr. Hutchins smoothed out

[27] *Proceedings,* 1920, p. 87; *Report of Executive Board,* 1921, pp. 52-55.

[28] For the situation as it stood in 1914, see *Comm. on Ind. Rels.,* III, 2986-2987.

the rough places, emphasized the common interest of the manufacturers and the men in the welfare of the industry, and proceeded on the assumption that what one side wanted could not be got until the other side was persuaded to give it. The device of reference to a special committee with power to act was used frequently by the sanitary ware conferences, as in general ware. Some important settlements were made in this way. On the other hand, some of the committees failed to reach agreement on the matters referred to them.

THE STRUCTURE OF THE WAGE SCALE

The wage issue in the sanitary ware division, as in general ware, took the form of special branch issues as well as that of the increase or decrease of the level through all branches. Piece work, including the kilnman's day system, was the prevailing system of payment; the mouldmaking branch was the only one on the time basis. There was also a uniform scale in the sanitary ware division.

No more than in general ware was the internal structure of the wage scale accepted as fixed, throughout the years. Demands for increases on the " underpaid " and for reductions on the " overpaid " articles, for extras for work " not properly paid for under the scale," and for changes in " conditions " which involved indirect increases in the rates, characterized the conferences. On the other hand, the story of the branch wage issues in the sanitary division, presents some important differences. The most striking difference on the technical side was the larger size of the articles and the smaller number of staple articles. This not only affected the pricing problem but it also helps to account for the greater importance of the defective ware issue in the

26

clay shop. Another outstanding difference was the fact that the issues particularly affecting one branch, pressing, held the center of the stage most of the time. Indeed, proposals for an increase on lines on which the majority of the pressers were employed were frequently discussed by both sides as if they were proposals for general advances for the industry.

Payment for Defective Ware.—The most troublesome issue concerning " conditions " and the one longest fought over was that of responsibility for defective ware, in pressing and casting. Defective ware had been an issue between the pressers and the employers long before the former came into the Brotherhood.[29] In general, the rule was that the maker should be " charged "— that is, not paid—for any piece of ware which turned out to be defective, if the defect was due to imperfect workmanship on the part of the maker. The inherent difficulty in applying the rule arose from two facts. First, it was impossible to tell whether the piece was properly made until after it had been finished and tested; a piece apparently all right when it left the presser's bench might have a concealed defect. Second, the ware had to pass through several hands and several processes—especially firing—after it left the presser's control. In many cases it was impossible to tell with certainty whether a defect in a finished piece was due to improper workmanship on the part of the presser or to improper handling after it left the presser's control, or to improper firing, or to an improper " mixture " in the clay, or to exposure to unfavorable temperature conditions before firing.

In 1903 the defective ware issue threatened to wreck the national agreement which the pressers and the

[29] MS. *Minutes, Sanitary Pressers National Union.*

employers had made the year before. Several potteries
in Trenton had trouble with ware " dunted " in the clay
state. The manufacturers maintained that the losses
fell within the proper responsibility of the men and
undertook to charge them back. The men held that this
abnormal number of losses was due to inferior clay and
to sudden changes in the temperature of the shops and
green rooms. They refused, under orders from Local
45, to accept responsibility for " dunted " ware except
under protest and elected a committee to present a
demand on the manufacturers that the men be relieved
of responsibility for " dunts." The manufacturers refused to agree to this. While the question of ordering a
strike was pending the executive board secured a temporary settlement of the question. The manufacturers
agreed to keep the temperature in the factories as
nearly even as possible, and not to exceed 75 degrees;
in case the temperature did exceed 75 degrees and dunts
occurred, the firm should bear the loss.[30]

The union continued to try to widen the class of cases
in which the men would not be held responsible. The
employers, however, were very reluctant to give up the
general rule. Their position was, first, that the prices
had been established on the assumption that the presser
should bear these losses. Second—and this was more
important, they said—it would be bad for the industry
to relieve the pressers any further from responsibility.
It was not to save the price of pressing the defective
pieces that they insisted on keeping the rule; it was
to make the pressers more careful and so avoid the
greater loss from the other expenditures on the ware
after it left the presser.[31]

[30] *Proceedings,* 1903, pp. 8, 18-19; 1904, p. 60.
[31] See testimony of Mr. John A. Campbell, *Comm. on Ind. Rels.,*
III, 2987.

The union did secure in practice a considerable reduction in the classes of cases in which the presser was " charged." This was accomplished largely through the decisions of the standing committee. From opposition to letting the presser off in cases in which it could not be shown that something else or somebody else caused the loss, the manufacturers were brought to the position that where there was any doubt the man should have the benefit of it. To quote from the statement of their chairman in the October, 1920, conference, " if we cannot show to fair-minded people that the fault lies with the man in his carelessness in some way or inattention, then I think, as we have said before, it is a matter that the manufacturer will have to assume himself." But in casting, the defective ware rule continued a sore point with the men right down to the collapse of the agreement.[32]

Restrictions on Individual Output.—The limits of output in pressing and casting, although not officially a part of the agreement, were in substance a part of the scale. According to Mr. John A. Campbell they were observed much more strictly than many rules which were published in the agreement. They were taken into account, of course, in fixing piece rates and figured prominently in many of the conferences.

The practice of observing a fixed day's work was an established custom among the pressers " even when there wasn't any union." [33] Before the pressers came into the Brotherhood, the limits were fixed by " common consent of the men in the shops." In the 1904 convention the rules established by Local Union 45 governing

---

[32] See below, p. 410.

[33] *Conference Report,* September, 1922, pp. 74-76; *Eleventh Special Report of Commissioner of Labor,* 1904, p. 703; *Comm. on Ind. Rels.,* III, 2999.

the day's work [34] were accepted by the Brotherhood for the pressers throughout the trade.[35] And when casting was taken up in union shops by ex-pressers the policy of fixing the day's work was extended to casting also. Vice-President Hutchins always maintained that the Brotherhood did not fix the limits; it merely recognized that they were a part of the union rule.

Although the manufacturers' association had no hand in fixing the limits,[36] it recognized the practice. In 1909, in order to secure an agreement that a presser should be allowed to make an extra piece in " overtime "— beyond eight hours—during periods of extraordinary demand, the manufacturers agreed that no presser should make more than the established day's work in eight hours or exceed the limit in normal times. The employers also practically recognized the limits in the October, 1920, conference, by asking for an increase in what they called the " minimum day's work " in certain lines.

The limit was ordinarily a given number of pieces per day. Men were not allowed to add extra pieces in order to make up for pieces " lost " on other days, or for absences. Moreover, the limit was expressed in pieces, not in earnings; it was not a uniform earnings limit applying to all men regardless of the class of ware made. A man working on closets with special features was allowed to make as many pieces in a day as a man making the regular staple line without extra features.[37]

[34] These are reprinted in the *Eleventh Special Report of the Commissioner of Labor*, pp. 706-707.

[35] *Proceedings*, 1904, pp. 116-117.

[36] *Eleventh Special Report of Commissioner of Labor*, pp. 707-708; *Conference Report*, September, 1922, p. 74; *Comm. on Ind. Rels.*, III, 2989.

[37] For ordinary closets, the price of which was $1.84, the limit was 5 pieces; but "where the regular making price of the above

On ware which could not easily be covered in a uniform list of limits, the men were expected to conform as closely as possible to an average money wage per day but as between various classes of ware this ranged from $10.00 a day to $12.00, for pressers.

The policy of the limit was defended by the Brotherhood spokesmen on several grounds. One was that a limit was necessary to insure good workmanship. The officers preached " good workmanship " to their men for years, and good workmanship, the officers always maintained, required, for most men at least, a limited day's work.[38] This is closely connected, of course, with the question of losses. The limited day's work, together with the union rule that a man must spend eight hours on his day's work, was intended to prevent men from hurrying through their work. Another argument was that it makes for more equal division of work between men and throughout the year.[39] The argument that a larger output will result in a reduction in piece rates was not made by the officers in the later years of the agreement system,[40] although they referred at times to the experience of the pressers in the " nineties " as a reason for the opposition of the members to making an extra piece under the 1909 overtime rule, and also pointed out that some of the men have argued that their wages were not increased in this or that case because

closets is increased because of extra thickness, added, or special features, the presser is allowed to earn as near as possible an average net wage of $10.50 a day." *Rules Governing the Day's Work of Clay Workers,* March, 27, 1922.

[38] *Comm. on Ind. Rels.,* III, 2999; *Conference Report,* September, 1922, pp. 75-77.

[39] *Ibid.,* pp. 18, 74.

[40] This was the point " generally and seriously referred to " in 1904. *Eleventh Special Report of the Commissioner of Labor,* pp. 702-703.

they had increased their outputs.[41] The union officers also defended the size of the limits set, except that for casting tanks and washdowns.[42] In 1922 Mr. Hutchins still insisted that the pressing limits were fair, for eight hours work, for the general run of men. He admitted that some pressers could do more but declared that there were some who could not make as many as the allowed number.[43]

The employers repeatedly expressed their opposition to the limits as practiced. Some of them objected to limits " in principle " [44] but the employers' most serious objections were confined to the size of the limits on some particular lines of ware and to the refusal of the men to suspend the limits in " emergencies " when the manufacturers were trying to speed up production.[45] In the last few years of the agreement system they were especially opposed to the limits in casting and these played an important part in the final breakdown of the agreement.

The manufacturers at times tried to get the men to agree to suspend the limits for the duration of an

[41] The fear of reduced wage rates was one of the reasons given by the sanitary price list committee in the 1921 convention for observing the limit. *Proceedings,* pp. 49-50.

[42] *Statement of Facts,* p. 11.

[43] *Conference Report,* September, 1922, p. 76. Some limits were raised after having once been fixed. Before the pressers came into the Brotherhood (in 1899) the limit on ordinary closets had been raised from 4 to 5; it had originally been three. *Eleventh Special Report of the Commissioner of Labor,* pp. 703-704; *Comm. on Ind. Rels.,* III, 2999, 3002; *Conference Report,* September, 1922, p. 76. The pressers' limit on 6-gallon tanks was also increased, from 6 a day to 6 on one day and 7 the next, because of an improvement in the moulds and in the facilities in the shops.

[44] *Eleventh Special Report of the Commissioner of Labor,* pp. 707-708.

[45] *Comm. on Ind. Rels.,* III, 2989.

emergency, but without success. In 1909, however, the union agreed that the presser should be allowed to make one additional piece " in overtime." This concession was made in order to avoid the putting on of a large number of new pressers who would constitute a surplus of labor when the extraordinary demand fell off. It was in return for this permission that the manufacturers practically recognized the union eight-hours rule and the binding force of the limit for eight hours work.[46] Before a man could make an extra piece he must consume the whole eight hours in making the fixed day's work. Moreover, he must employ the same proportional time in making the extra piece. The permission to make an extra piece was also closely safeguarded. The standing committee was to decide when the " conditions of the trade are such as to demand the working of overtime." No presser was to be allowed to exceed the limit unless given permission by the standing committee, and no presser was to be discriminated against for refusing to make an extra piece. The results of the " overtime " agreement were practically negligible; the manufacturers found it impossible to get any considerable number of men to work overtime. In September, 1922, the manufacturers asked that the restrictions surrounding the overtime provision and the corollary forbidding the exceeding of the established day's work in normal times, be abolished. The manufacturers had got nothing from the overtime rule in the way of extra production and they had been embarrassed by the existence of these rules in the proceedings against them under the anti-trust law.[47] No agreement was reached

[46] *Report of President,* 1910, pp. 9-10, 19-20; *Comm. on Ind. Rels.,* III, 2999.

[47] *Conference Report,* pp. 28-29.

on this in September. In the October conference it was agreed to let the question of the working rules go over; [48] the proposed changes in them were not included in the terms submitted to the trade.

Issues as to Systems of Payment.—In spite of the fact that the clay shop was almost entirely on a piece work basis, the men showed a reluctance at times to comply with the manufacturer's requests that a class of work which had been introduced on the hourly basis be transferred to piece work. For example, when the employers asked for a piece-price list for making lavatories, the lavatorymakers were afraid of piece work; they wanted to leave well enough alone. The fear of having ware " charged back " was, of course, a large element in the situation. But so well did the union side of the standing committee, which finally agreed upon a piece-price list with the employers, do its work, that three years later the union had to take a reduction from the list because of the earnings the men were making.[49] The same reluctance to accept piece work was shown by the casters. As late as 1914 the men wanted to go back to day work in casting, " until such time as the process was beyond the experimental stage." [50]

It was in kilnplacing and dipping that the unwillingness of the men to change the system of payment resulted in the most acute issue of this kind. From 1916 on the employers were asking for the substitution of " straight piece work " for the cubic measurement system, but without success, and in 1922 they insisted on it as an absolute condition of a new agreement.

[48] *Informal Meeting,* p. 91.
[49] *Report of President,* 1906, p. 30; 1909, pp. 20-22.
[50] See below, pp. 408-409.

The cubic measurement system of determining the number of kilnman's days to be paid had not been adopted in the sanitary division until 1906.[51] Even then the scale applied only to new or reconstructed kilns; existing prices were not to be disturbed. In 1910 the manufacturers offered, as a counter proposal to a union demand for a ten per cent increase in wages for kilnmen, to give a five per cent increase based on the application of the regular scale to all kilns. The kilnmen accepted this and all kilns were " remeasured." [52] The cubic measurement system produced the same sort of difficulties in sanitary ware as in general ware. Apart from the questions over such " conditions " as fetching and carrying, there were many troublesome issues before the conferences over changes in the character of the ware and in the methods of placing it. There were also many local disputes over extras.[53] The scale obviously failed to give either wages commensurate with time and skill, or uniform cost to the manufacturers. There were charges, too, that the kilns were not properly filled, but this did not play as prominent a part in the discussions as it did in general ware.[54]

[51] *Proceedings,* 1903, pp. 18, 107-108; 1904, pp. 11-12, 60; *Report of President,* 1907, p. 15. The day was then fixed at 236 cubic feet in bisque and 220 in glost, where it remained throughout the history of the agreement. As in general ware, the number of " days " made by the men greatly exceeded the calendar days worked.

[52] Even with the five per cent increase, some kilnmen suffered " severe losses " in their wages by the readjustment, and it was an " open question " whether these were offset by the " decided " gains made by the men working on other kilns. *Report of President,* 1911, p. 22.

[53] In the September, 1922, conference one of the manufacturers stated that in his plant the company had to pay extras on over 50 per cent of the pieces placed. *Report,* p. 84.

[54] Mr. Frank Hutchins declared in the October, 1922, conference that he had long been convinced that the straight piece-work system

There was no uniform scale for dipping, in practice. The scale price applied only to the " standard " size kiln and the regular run of ware. The kilns varied so in size, and there were such variations in the ware, and in conditions, that the firms had frequently to make their own arrangements with the dippers. In many cases the dippers were paid at day rates.

The kilnmen never did work out a straight piece-price list which they were willing to accept. They were also afraid of every specific piece-work proposal made by the manufacturers. They had been afraid of the cubic measurement system when the national officers had urged its introduction and now they were even more afraid of the proposed change from cubic measurement to straight piece work. Vice-President Hutchins labored with them to " interest them in piece work " but without success.[55] In the October, 1922, conference the executive board agreed that a list embodying the ten per cent reduction should be worked out and that the board would see that it was enforced. Under the terms submitted to the trade the reduction was to be effective November first and the new piece-price list was to go into effect not later than January first.[56] The dippers, on the other hand, had not refused to make out a piece-price list; they had simply stood out for the prices they wanted.[57] When, in the October, 1922, conference, Mr. Hutchins proposed that the new list should be based

was the only honest system of payment for kilnplacing. *Informal Meeting*, p. 39.

[55] *Conference Report*, September, 1922, pp. 29-33; 109-112, 115, 116; *Report of Executive Board*, 1922, pp. 57-58.

[56] *Informal Meeting*, pp. 38-39, 56-58, 64-73, 88, 92-93.

[57] *Report of Executive Board*, 1922, pp. 54-57.

on a ten per cent reduction, which was to be effective
November first in any event, the employers agreed that
the making out of the list be again entrusted to a joint
committee, but on the condition that the union executive board be included in the committee.[58]

During this same period the manufacturers were trying to get the men to accept piece work in the only day-
working branch in the sanitary division—mouldmaking—because they were dissatisfied with the outputs
of the men. The mouldmakers maintained that the constantly changing nature of their product, with the large
number of odd pieces and the differences in conditions
between shops, made it impossible to arrive at a fair
uniform piece-price list. These factors, they said, made
the situation very different from what it was in general
ware, where there is a uniform piece-price list for
mouldmaking, apart from blocking and casing. When,
in the regular 1922 conference, the manufacturers concentrated their piece-work proposal for mouldmaking
on washdowns and tanks, the mouldmakers again insisted on the impracticability of piece work, even on
these lines; there was not enough straight work in some
of the shops; the mouldmaker had to run from one job
to another. It might be possible to make piece prices for
straight work in one shop, but it would be impossible
to frame a uniform list for all shops. In the October
conference the manufacturers modified their proposal
to one that in any plant in which the mouldmakers were
willing to work on a piece-price basis, prices should be
established for moulds for casting tanks and washdowns. They did not make the acceptance of piece work
one of the conditions of the proposed agreement.[59]

[58] *Informal Meeting*, October, 1922, pp. 38, 59, 88, 92-93.
[59] *Ibid.*, pp. 13, 58, 88-89.

UNIFORMITY

The tradition of the desirability of uniformity of working prices was as strong in the sanitary division as in general ware. And the belief in uniformity was apparently as strong on both sides just before the break in 1922 as it had ever been. In fact, on the employers' side, one of the reasons for the pressure for the change to straight piece work in kilnplacing and dipping was that this would give real uniformity in prices.

The pressing branch was the group in the industry which had made the most persistent fight for uniformity of prices. After the 1891 "lockout" of sanitary pressers in Trenton, in which the employers succeeded in enforcing a reduction in the list,[60] the sanitary pressers' local assembly of the Knights of Labor had been unable to control prices; competition between men for jobs had brought out about not only greater reductions but great differences in prices. In 1895, the newly organized Sanitary Pressers National Union reduced the price of the ordinary washdown to fifty cents— it had been $1.50 in 1890—in order to get a price low enough to be enforced uniformly in all shops in Trenton, with the hope of raising it once uniformity had been established. A few months after this heroic measure the union was able to raise the price to seventy cents.[61] But it was not until after the sanitary pressers came into the Brotherhood that they were able to secure a national agreement establishing a uniform price list,

[60] *Minutes of Executive Board, D. A. 160,* January 5, 1891; *Proceedings of Convention, D. A. 160,* January 4, 1892; *Report of Executive Board, Knights of Labor, to the Fifteenth Regular Session* (1891), p. 3.

[61] *Proceedings, N. B. of O. P.,* 1895, p. 5; *Eleventh Special Report of the Commissioner of Labor,* p. 704; *Report of President (N. B. of O. P.),* 1906, p. 14.

in 1902. From then on uniformity in clay-shop prices was assumed by both sides to be one of the most desirable features of the agreement.

The devotion on the union side to uniformity in prices did not extend from the national officers to the whole membership. In kilnplacing and dipping, as has been pointed out, the members were not willing to risk much to get real uniformity. The officers favored it, as they did for general ware, primarily because of their belief that it was absolutely essential to the protection of the wage level and the most effective foundation for wage increases. Over and over again they advanced the argument in wage conferences that the employers could afford to give the proposed increase because their costs would be raised uniformly by it and no one would be put at a competitive disadvantage.

The union's failure to make effective this assumed basis of dealing—that all manufacturers would have to pay the same for having the ware made—was an irritating feature of the relations in the last two years of the agreement system. There had been for a long time minor departures from uniformity—due to failure to keep properly informed of standing committee decisions, to concessions obtained here and there in individual shops and the like—but in the important branches of kilnplacing and dipping there was only a pretense of uniformity, as both sides well knew. Uniformity might have been attained if the agreement had continued and if the kilnmen and dippers had gone along with the attempt of the officers to establish practically uniform piece prices in these branches, thus bringing nearer to realization the competitive equality in labor costs which the system of national collective bargaining was intended to secure.

CASTING

It is not too much to say that it was the failure of the union to handle the casting process satisfactorily which was the chief underlying cause of the breakdown of the national agreement. It was competition from non-union plants using this process which was the manufacturers' biggest argument for a wage reduction in 1922, the refusal of which by the union brought the end of the agreement system. The failure of the union on the casting process had two aspects. First, the union failed to organize the shops which started up outside its control and used the casting process as a substitute for pressing. Second, in the face of this non-union competition, the men refused to agree to piece rates for casting which would enable the union manufacturers to meet that competition.

As early as 1910 President T. J. Duffy called attention to the threat involved in the attempts of two non-union shops to make ware with the casting process. The demand for sanitary pressers was at that time very good; the pressers had as yet experienced no injury from the two non-union casting shops. Nevertheless, the president urged that the organization should be forehanded in the matter and attempt to secure the adherence of such of the workmen in these shops as were able to turn out good ware. This would involve recognizing them as " tradesmen," a step not relished by the pressers. However, the convention acceded to President Duffy's request that the executive board be authorized to organize the non-union casters.[62]

The union gesture toward organizing the non-union casters had no tangible results and by 1913 the number of such shops had increased to four.[63] In the spring of

[62] *Report of President*, 1910, pp. 10-11; *Proceedings*, 1910, p. 37.
[63] *Report of President*, 1911, pp. 5-6; 1913, pp. 4-5.

1916, a joint committee, consisting of two vice-presidents of the Brotherhood working in the sanitary ware
division and an appointee of the Sanitary Potters Association, made a tour of the non-union casting shops and
the union shops using the casting process in part, in
order to get an authoritative report on the facts. They
made a common report. It showed 112 casters in 5
non-union plants as against 61 in 6 union shops. One
of the non-union shops was casting a body which was
not semi-porcelain but " vitreous grog." However, it
competed with the cast semi-porcelain product.[64]

The executive board was waiting for an opportune
time to organize the non-union casting shops. It was
opposed to taking the non-union casters in as individuals. To do so would merely leave the non-union
firms free to break in more men to replace those joining
the union and the union would have difficulty in finding
places in union shops for the men admitted.[65] Moreover,
as late as 1918 the board was still hoping that casting
with " unskilled " labor would prove a failure in competition with casters recruited from the union pressers.[66] Only one non-union casting shop was ever
brought into the Brotherhood as a shop—that at New
Castle, which was organized early in 1919.[67]

Meanwhile an agreement had been made in 1912,
on the initiative of the employers, to govern casting in
union shops. It did not work out satisfactorily. The
relation of casting prices to pressing prices, the small
number of pressers going into casting and remaining
in it, the limit on the day's work in casting, and the

[64] Statement of Vice-President Hutchins to the writer.
[65] Statement of Vice-President Hutchins to the writer; also *Report
of Executive Board*, 1922, p. 50.
[66] *Ibid.*, 1918, pp. 26-27.
[67] *Ibid.*, 1919, pp. 38-41; 1920, p. 33.

question of defective ware in casting were brought up
again and again in conferences without reaching conclusions satisfactory to both sides. All of these questions were of course interrelated.

The casting agreement of 1912 recognized the right
of the men already employed at that process in union
shops to continue " at that branch of the trade " at the
prices fixed in the agreement—regardless of their previous experience. However, in the future casters were
to be recruited from the sanitary pressers, if the Brotherhood could furnish the necessary men. If not, journeymen clay-workers from the general ware division or
from the " grogware trade " were to have preference;
if the Brotherhood should be unable to furnish men
from these branches of its organization the manufacturers should have a free choice.

As for the prices set in the 1912 agreement, these
were intended to be high enough to make casting a
" journeyman job." The problem was to put them high
enough to allow a man to make nearly as much as at
ordinary pressing and at the same time low enough to
enable the manufacturers to meet non-union competition in this process. Vice-President Hutchins thought
that both these aims had been attained.[68]

But the sanitary pressers did not offer themselves
for more than a small proportion of the casting jobs.
The manufacturers were " in many cases compelled to
employ labor with no knowledge of the potting industry." [69] In a conference on sanitary casting in January, 1916, the union agreed, as a complement to the
rule giving pressers the first right to casting vacancies, that it was obligatory on the part of the pressers
to do this work when needed and the firm might select

[68] Statement to the writer; also *Report of President*, 1913, p. 15.
[69] *Ibid.*

27

men for casting from among its sanitary pressers. The employers did not in practice insist upon exercising this right of conscription. The union had agreed to it as a means of bringing home to the sanitary pressers the necessity of following their work to the casting bench. But the pressers continued cold to casting. Vice-President Hutchins met their explanation that they could not make good enough wages at casting with the warning that the main question was not whether they could earn as much at casting as at pressing—and that had been proved to be possible and was being done by some—but whether casting was to displace not only the pressing process but the present pressers from the industry. Moreover, the conditions complained of in casting could not be corrected unless the pressers remained at it long enough to acquire the knowledge necessary to sustain their contentions.[70] This warning also went largely unheeded. The pressers never did go into casting in sufficient numbers to satisfy the manufacturers or to man the casting jobs in union shops. At the expiration of the agreement in October, 1922, there were approximately 450 men casting in union shops, of whom two-thirds had not been clay-workers before they took up casting.[71] The pressers would not do casting while they could get pressing jobs—and many who started at it refused to continue in it.

In their desire to make casting more attractive to the pressers, the union officers were constantly contending for a nearer approximation of casting prices to pressing prices, as well as for exemption of the casters from the defective ware rule. As early as 1914 the men asked for an increase in the prices agreed to in 1912. They

[70] *Ibid.*, 1916, p. 21.
[71] *Statement of Facts*, pp. 7, 13.

contended that the methods of casting had been changed after the prices had been set and that the new methods required more time for each piece. Local Union 45 had taken up their complaints and had started a movement in favor of day wage at $4.00 per day " until such time as the process was beyond the experimental stage "; four dollars was then the pressers' day wage on ordinary ware. The manufacturers refused day work at $4.00 and they also refused to increase the piece prices, contending that it had been shown that an inexperienced man could earn as good wages at the union casting prices as the pressers were making. The refusal of the pressers to take up casting and the resultant fact that so many inexperienced men were doing it was undoubtedly a barrier to raising the ratio of casting prices to pressing prices.

Another point of tension between the manufacturers and the men on the casting question was the character of the control exercised over casting in the union shops. Individual manufacturers repeatedly complained that the men, in obedience to orders from the local, hampered the development of the process instead of helping it. These complaints became more bitter after the October, 1921, conference.[72] But their strongest and earliest complaint was against the limit on the day's work. They never conceded that the pressers' practice of working with a limit should have been carried over into casting. And the amount of the limits actually set came in for attack repeatedly. That on tanks was especially low, they insisted, in comparison with what men did in the non-union shops.[73] It was not merely that the limit held

[72] For example, *Conference Report*, September, 1922, pp. 8, 54-57; *Informal Meeting*, October, 1922, p. 43; MS. *Minutes, Standing Committee*.

[73] *Conference Report*, September, 1922, pp. 36, 54-55; *Statement of Facts*, p. 11.

up production from the benches; perhaps more important was the fact that the limit was assumed by the men in comparing the wages at casting with those at pressing.

On the other side, the union contended that the practice of charging for defective ware, as it was actually administered, was even more unfair to the casters than to the pressers because there were more uncertain elements involved. With the refusal of the manufacturers to accept day wage for casting at the price asked by the union, in 1914, the matter of " charging back " defective ware took on renewed importance. Vice-President Hutchins, who was an outspoken critic of the pressers for their refusal to take up casting and of the figure at which some of the limits were maintained in casting, continued to hold throughout that the manufacturers should ease up on the defective ware rule in casting. It was not only unfair to the men, he held, but was unwise from the manufacturers' standpoint because it acted as a discouragement to those men who were willing to give casting a fair trial. As a matter of fact, argued Mr. Hutchins in the October, 1920, conference, the number of cases in which the loss is due to the casters' fault is so insignificant as compared with those in which it is due to causes over which he has no control, that it would be simpler and much wiser to have a rule that no ware " out of the kiln " should be charged to the caster at all. But the manufacturers insisted on applying the same rule to casters as to pressers, and for the same reason. They insisted, too, that they were paying " skilled wages " to casters—and men who received wages that assumed skill should not ask to be relieved of all responsibility.

In the October, 1921, conference the competition from non-union casting plants, which had figured for

years in the manufacturers' argument against wage
increases, was made one of their chief arguments for
a wage reduction. They were increasing the proportion
of casting in their own shops and they declared that
they must be given wage rates on it which would allow
them to use it to meet the non-union competition. After
their failure to secure a wage reduction in 1921 the
manufacturers moved rapidly over to casting. By October, 1922, there were 450 casters in union shops and
nearly all of the union shops were then doing some casting. Of the 32,000 washdowns and tanks produced
weekly in the union shops, 26,000 were cast, as against
6,000 pressed.[74] The manufacturers were not only preparing to meet non-union competition but, if it should
be necessary, to fight a strike with the casting process.
As bearing on the latter possibility, the fact that the
great majority of the men who were doing the casting
were men without previous experience in the industry
was significant.

In the October, 1922, discussion of the terms of the
proposed reduction, it was recognized by both sides that
" the big item . . . . is the casting situation." The deduction from pressing prices and from wages in the
other branches was included to help the manufacturers
" to carry the burden of the competition . . . . on the
staple line of goods " made in non-union shops.[75] The
union representatives conceded, in the proposal to be
submitted to the trade, the manufacturers' years-old
demand for " half pressing prices for casting," which
meant then half of the pressing prices after a ten per
cent reduction in the latter. On some lines, particularly
tanks, this double reduction meant a big total per-

[74] Report of Executive Board, 1919, p. 39; Statement of Facts,
pp. 5-7; also Report of Executive Board, 1922, pp. 49-50.
[75] Informal Meeting, p. 36.

centage reduction from existing prices; it varied from eighteen and one-half per cent on the 8-gallon tank to twenty-seven per cent on the 6-gallon tank, the one by far the most frequently made; the competition from the non-union shops on tanks was keener than on anything else. The officers assumed that the men could escape a large part of this percentage reduction on tanks, by making more pieces in a day.[76] However, the twenty-seven per cent reduction on the 6-gallon tank was a big talking point for those in the union opposed to the reduction and they concentrated on the figure " twenty-seven per cent " with telling effect.

GENERAL WAGE CHANGES

As in the tableware division, branch increases played a very important rôle in raising the general level of wages. Although there was no horizontal advance before the war, there were substantial increases for the great majority of the workers before 1916 [77] and the increases given in the 1916 conference to particular branches or on particular ware involved an increase of twelve and one-half per cent in the payrolls.[78] In the period 1917-1920, too, part of the advance was given in the form of increases in base prices over and above the horizontal percentage increase in all branches; [79] in fact had the manufacturers and the union followed

[76] *Statement of Facts,* p. 11.

[77] There were increases in rates on the great bulk of the pressers' ware, in mouldmaking, and (through an " equalization of prices ") in packing.

[78] The great majority of the pressers, the kilnmen, and the mouldmakers participated in the advances.

[79] The most extreme case occurred in June, 1919, when a special conference to redress " inequalities " in the clay-shop prices resulted in an increase of 15 per cent on most ware and of 12 per cent on the remainder.

the conviction expressed by both, the horizontal method would not have been followed at any time but all increases would have been awarded in discriminating percentages.[80]

The most important factor affecting the general wage level in the sanitary division, taking the twenty years of the national agreement system as a whole, was, as in the tableware division, the condition of the business. It took precedence over the rising cost of living argument down to 1916 and even in 1917 and 1918 it kept the percentage wage-rate advances considerably below the advance in the cost of living. In 1919 and 1920 it was the condition of the business which was the decisive factor in the large increases obtained, especially those secured by the great majority of the pressers.[81]

In sharp contrast to the general ware industry, foreign competition was not an important factor in the sanitary division, during the history of the national agreement at least. The preference for American shapes and construction—again a sharp contrast to the general ware division—had laid that ghost. The competition that the sanitary manufacturers had to look out for (apart from that between themselves) throughout most of the two decades of national agreement, was the competition from cheaper domestic ware, such as enamelled ironware; there was always the danger that a widening of the price difference might turn a considerable volume of orders to the " inferior " ware. In the later years, with the development of the cheaper cast-

[80] The manufacturers were nearly always too busy to work out a detailed revision and adopted the horizontal method to save time.

[81] The price of the ordinary closets, including the " plussage," was advanced from $1.25 to $1.84, in 1919 and 1920, as against an increase from $1.00 to $1.25 between the 1916 conference and 1919.

ing process of making semi-porcelain ware in non-union plants, the latter came to be the most important competitive factor affecting the wage issue.

Comparisons with what men in other industries were receiving were introduced from time to time by the employers as an answer to union requests for increases. But in the later stages of the upswing it was the union which stressed the argument of comparison, especially as applied to percentage increases over the pre-war level, maintaining that they had not received increases equal to those obtained " by many tradesmen who do not possess any more skill." Like the general ware workers they emphasized that, in contrast to many other classes of workers, " because we are piece workers we have to give production for every cent we receive."

What the average increase in wages was in the upward movement which began in the autumn of 1916 and ended in the autumn of 1920, it is impossible to say. The mouldmakers, the only time-working branch, received an increase of one hundred and six per cent. For the piece workers, it is impossible to calculate what the increase was, from the data available. In pressing, the price of the ordinary closets, with seat attachment, was increased ninety-six per cent (including the " plussage ") ; the great majority of the pressers were engaged on this work exclusively. In kilnplacing the rate per kilnman's day was increased sixty-two per cent. The percentage increase for the saggermakers was probably at least that, including two revisions of base prices (in 1917 and 1920). In nearly all the piece-working branches, too, there were changes in prices made by special committees. There were also some changes in conditions which were indirect wage increases. The union estimate of the general percentage increase was

" not over eighty per cent." [82] The manufacturers insisted that the union percentage figures did not take account of incidental increases. Their estimate, based on payroll figures for the same volume of production, was one hundred per cent at least.

The manufacturers' request early in 1921 for a wage reduction was based exclusively on the condition of the business. In the words of the union executive board it proceeded from " an unusual continued state of business depression that caused many of the sanitary potteries to suspend operations completely, together with the constant agitation for lower costs of production as a means of reviving building operations." [83] Throughout the discussions of 1921 and 1922 this factor—the condition of the business—remained the primary, and almost the exclusive argument of the manufacturers for a wage reduction. In the August, 1921, conference the manufacturers did bring in the reduction in the cost of living to supplement their main argument for a reduction but the bearing of the present cost of living on the issue was confused by disagreement as to how much of a reduction had really taken place and by an argument over whether the men had enjoyed the peak wages under declining living costs for as long a period as that in which their increases had lagged behind the rise in living costs. Chairman A. M. Maddock of the manufacturers and Vice-President Hutchins finally agreed that they " would not get anywhere talking about the cost of living." In the October, 1921, conference the manufacturers did not advance the argument

[82] Given by Vice-President Hutchins in the August, 1921, conference.

[83] Report of Executive Board, 1921, pp. 66-67. This is the board's own language.

of reduced living costs at all. Nor did they bring it up
in either of the 1922 conferences.

The refusal of the union conference committee to
grant a reduction in 1921, when the Brotherhood had
accepted a reduction of seventeen per cent in the general ware industry, was supported primarily by the
argument that a reduction in wages would not bring
any more business to the industry. There were other
arguments, such as the lag in wage advances behind
the rise in the cost of living and comparisons with other
trades, but inasmuch as it was admitted that the condition of the business was poor, the union had to meet
the argument that a wage reduction was imperative if
the union plants were to operate. In addition to the
argument that wage reductions were an unwise method
of meeting a general business depression, because they
reduced still further the purchasing power of the
workers and so retarded recovery, the men emphasized
that in their own industry a wage reduction would be
particularly futile because it would not have any appreciable effect on the cost of building and would not
remove the credit influences which were holding back
building; it would be absorbed by the jobbers, who
would insist on reductions in the manufacturers' prices
to the extent of the wage cut and would buy no more
goods than they were then buying unless and until the
other factors affecting building, which were entirely
beyond the control of the sanitary industry, had
changed. As the manufacturers in this industry had
not "profiteered" during the War and as wages had
not been unduly increased or the men's production
lowered, the buyers should be told that there would be
no reduction in wages and no further reduction in
prices.

The manufacturers admitted that they would probably have to give the jobbers the wage cut in reduced selling prices. They also admitted that they could not promise the men more employment if wages were reduced. They could only assure them that unless wages were reduced, employment would fall off still further. But the men were not at all impressed with the proposal that with employment poor and promising to become poorer they should take a reduction as a means of trying to improve the situation, or at least keep it from getting worse. Standing firmly on their thesis that there was no assurance that employment would be bettered by a wage reduction, they declared they would rather face unemployment, or partial employment, at their present wage rates than at lower rates. If employment improved, the holding of their present rates would enable them to recoup their losses to some extent.

Of course, the men had in mind the difficulty of getting the wage rates restored when employment should improve. Nor were they moved by the implied threat that if they did not concede a wage reduction then the employers would not renew the agreement in 1922. The notion had been preached through the trade by men who were not officers of the Brotherhood, and had been accepted by the majority of the union conferees, that whether or not they would get an agreement in 1922, and the terms on which they could get it, would depend on the condition of the business at the time of the 1922 conference, not on what they did in 1921.[84]

In the September, 1922, conference it was the menace of non-union competition which was the outstanding feature of the employers' case for a reduction. Business had been good since the October, 1921, conference,

<hr />

[84] Statement of Vice-President Hutchins to the writer.

and the employers realized that they had to contend
against a belief among the men that the improvement
in business had justified their course in refusing to take
a reduction in 1921. The employers stressed that " all
these manufacturers who do not have an agreement
with you have increased their capacity one hundred per
cent or more " in the past year. The competition of
the non-union manufacturers " for sufficient business
to operate their plants full time " would bring prices
down by the following spring. The union manufacturers would be unable to run their plants in the face
of that competition without a reduction in wages. " We
are not wiped out by some foreign competition that
we can get a tariff to build up to protect us. We are
wiped out by the competition in this country, where no
tariff does us any good." [85] The manufacturers also
stressed the limited day's work of the union men as one
of the things which was standing in their own light; it
was holding them back in competition with the non-
union workmen; if they would make more pieces they
could accept a reduction in rates without reducing their
earnings.

The union conferees would not admit the necessity
of a wage reduction to meet non-union competition.
They urged the superiority of the union-made wares
as an important factor in the competition for business.
They also argued that a reduction in union wages would
not affect the competitive situation because the non-
union manufacturers would enforce the same reduction.
The crux of the matter was that business was apparently good at the time and the men would not accept a
reduction because of a danger which, they insisted, the
manufacturers were exaggerating.

[85] *Conference Report,* September, 1922, pp. 11-12, 28.

The executive board took a different tone a month later when, faced with a strike, it urged the members to accept a wage reduction. In the "Statement of Facts" issued to the members in connection with the referendum on the modified terms offered by the manufacturers in October, it presented figures to show that " the non-union shops have a weekly production equal to one-fifth of the total output of staple sanitary goods that are manufactured in this country." It repeated the manufacturers' statement that the non-union manufacturers, because of their lower costs, could undersell them and still make large profits " when there is an abnormal demand for ware," as well as secure a larger share of the business during periods of depression. The board also adopted the manufacturers' argument that the casters could make up a large part of the rate reduction by making more pieces. In answer to the argument advanced by the union representatives in the earlier conferences that a wage reduction would not check non-union competition because the non-union manufacturers would reduce wages correspondingly, the board said:

But may we not hope that just as soon as the unorganized potter, who up to the present time has been so contented with his condition that he has refused to listen to any appeal to become organized, begins to realize that his welfare is being vitally affected by our action, he will appreciate that there is a very urgent reason why he should join the ranks of organized labor.[86]

It must not be assumed that the board insisted that the manufacturers' arguments were sound. What it was insisting upon was that the manufacturers were really determined to have a wage reduction at this time and that no agreement could be got on better terms

[86] *Statement of Facts*, p. 14.

than those now offered. It believed that an agreement
was worth the reduction "regardless of how we feel
about the merits of a reduction in wages or about the
desirability of adopting such a measure now as compared with some future time." [87]

OTHER ISSUES

There were several other matters covered in the
sanitary agreement or taken up in the conference from
time to time but these had been disposed of to the
apparent satisfaction of both sides or had been carried
along without causing any great tension prior to the
1921 conferences. Most of them were questions which
have also been faced in the tableware division and the
treatment given them was, on the whole, much the
same, allowing for such differences in circumstances
as there were between the two divisions.

The sanitary division, like the general ware, had to
deal with a machine for making saggers, or, more particularly, parts of the sagger. There was some question between the manufacturers and the men whether
the work on the machine used for making the bottoms
of saggers—what the men called the "sagger-helping
machine"—should be thrown open to new men. The
wages to be paid for the various operations were also
still in the stage of local adjustment. The settlement
of these questions on a national basis had been complicated by the fact that the most of regular saggermakers had quit their jobs in November, 1918 (on
another issue—that of carrying green saggers to the
kilns) and machines had been widely introduced during their "lay-off." In the regular 1920 conference both

[87] *Ibid.*, p. 15.

the question of who should make the sagger bottoms and the rates to be paid to the saggermakers and the helpers, were referred to a joint committee. Nothing of importance had been concluded before the issue of a general wage reduction pushed the whole matter into the background.

The tunnel kiln had also made its appearance in the sanitary division before the break but there had been no serious dispute over it. No uniform piece price or day rate was formulated for tunnel kilns. Some settlements for particular plants were made on a piece-work basis. In one case (Kokomo, July, 1919) the standing committee established the piece-work prices; the prices were based on the number of pieces per truck. They were fixed at a figure which, it was expected, would enable the men to make about the same wages as had been averaged on the bee-hive kilns in the same plant for the preceding three months. In the October, 1920 conference the men presented a proposition for the establishment of "what constitutes a day's work in placing sanitary ware in tunnel kilns." But both sides agreed that they did not have sufficient information to do this intelligently. The manufacturers said they were willing to take it up at the proper time—and there it remained.[88]

With respect to apprenticeship, the experience under the sanitary agreement was much like that in general ware. Apprenticeship ratios were emptied of their importance by an agreement that no apprentice should be put on when there was a surplus of journeymen.

[88] One of the companies in Trenton had installed in a new plant, a type of tunnel kiln (for glost ware) in which it was not necessary to put the ware in saggers, consequently there was no need for skilled kilnmen. The union did not oppose the use of unskilled men on this kiln.

The hours issue was unimportant; the only day-work branch was mouldmaking and the employers were trying to get piece work in that. In the clay shop the chief concern of the Brotherhood was the enforcement of the union rule prescribing a minimum day of eight hours for the "day's work." The employers refused for a time to make this rule a part of the agreement, but in 1909 when the union conceded that pressers should be allowed to make an additional piece the employers agreed in effect to make the observance of the eight-hour rule for the ordinary day's work a part of the general agreement. However, the burden of detecting violations of the eight-hour rule remained with the union. As a matter of fact, it was never fully observed.

The right of the employer to discharge a workman was never an issue in the conferences, except in an incidental way, as for example when the rule was adopted in 1912 that no presser shall be discharged in order to make a vacancy for an apprentice. The custom in the trade of two weeks' notice of discharge or of quitting was made a compulsory rule in the 1910 conference. The sanitary division did not, however, adopt anything like the elaborate code or the requirement of the use of printed forms which featured the " discharge agreement " in general ware. The discharge of an individual workman was occasionally, although very rarely, carried as a cause of dispute to the standing committee but all such disputes were adjusted without the necessity of the adoption of formal restrictions on the employer's " freedom to discharge." The men were in fact safe from arbitrary or discriminatory discharge and that satisfied the union. Indeed, Vice-President Hutchins, testifying before the Commission on Industrial Relations, in June, 1914, offered this situation as evidence of the progress which had been made in relations in the industry.[89]

A rule for the equal " division of work " in dull times was adopted in 1912 for the clay shop, the department in which the issue was of most importance. In 1920 the clay-shop men asked that the work be so distributed when there was " short time " that each man be given his share in consecutive full days, as far as the number of moulds available would permit, so that the men should be free to take on something else in the time that they were not employed in the pottery. After some discussion to bring out the modifying " understanding," the employers agreed to this.

The question of the closed union shop was first raised by the Brotherhood in 1906. It was brought up then indirectly, through a union request for a rule that would give it disciplinary authority, under the agreement, over its members. The union was asking not so much for a clause that would force into the union those who had never been in, as for one that would prevent those who were not inclined to obey the rules, or were otherwise dissatisfied, from dropping out. The employers were willing to agree that no one should be allowed to drop out of the union simply because he was dissatisfied with something in the agreement or some decision of the standing committee. This was as far

[89] (Question.) There is little or no such thing, then, in your industry, as what is called industrial unrest? (Vice-President Hutchins): " Well, I won't say that, because there is some; but as to how far they are justified in that, is a question. But this condition don't prevail—there is no man fears losing his job because he is a member of the organization, or because he asserts his rights under the agreement, and there is no more of the condition that prevailed heretofore, that if a foreman came down and discharged you because he wanted to, that you would have to get out and there was no redress." III, 3005.

28

as they would go. In the 1907 conference the union definitely asked " that all workmen whose wages and conditions are regulated by agreement between the Sanitary Potters Association and the National Brotherhood of Operative Potters must be members of the N. B. of O. P." The argument was the same as that advanced for the similar proposition in general ware. Here, too, the union insisted that the manufacturers would not be asked to compel persons to join the Brotherhood. " We feel," said President Duffy, " that the mere mention of that in an agreement would be sufficient without any other force to bring pretty nearly everybody in line and keep them in line." The manufacturers' reply was essentially that they wished to let well enough alone; they saw nothing to be gained for their side by such an agreement. Their chairman added : " We do not see why a mere paper agreement of this kind would add anything to that which is already practically in working operation." The union did not again submit a closed shop proposal in this division.

The Brotherhood did not suffer appreciably because of the lack of a closed shop rule in the agreement, in the sanitary division. The man working in one of the organized branches who refused to join the union was, according to Vice-President Hutchins, non-existent. Occasionally a man fell behind in his dues or assessments, but he was in nearly every case induced to return to good standing.[90] One very important factor in favor of union success in maintaining full organization was the importance to the individual workman in a piece-working trade of the protection of the union in the adjustment of the many issues which concerned him individually. This has been discussed above for the

[90] *Comm. on Ind. Rels.*, III, pp. 2990, 2999, 3000.

general ware division. In the sanitary division it was even more important because of the constant presence of the defective ware issue in the predominant branch. A man who made but five pieces a day wanted all the protection he could get from the union shop committee—and the standing committee—against having any of them charged back. If he did not belong to the union he would not get it. In the next important branch, kilnplacing, the crew system of working kept the possible recalcitrants in line. With these branches safe it was easier to keep the others—even the day-working mouldmakers—in order.

The Brotherhood began as early as 1907 to include in its propositions one or more calling for improvement in the conditions in the shops with respect to ventilation, heating, dust prevention or removal, facilities for washing, etc. Specific health or comfort propositions were, in fact, adopted in several of the conferences. The discussions on proposed measures turned chiefly on what were the most feasible methods of achieving the results desired. Chairman Campbell took a keen interest in health measures and always welcomed suggestions from the union side. The success of the joint health committee system in the East,[91] too, was due chiefly to the coöperation of employers and employees in the sanitary division.[92]

[91] See above, pp. 304-306.

[92] Vice-President Hutchins, in his testimony before the Commission on Industrial Relations, spoke with obvious pride of the work of the joint health committee, and of the fact that the manufacturers and men had secured a provision in the New Jersey law which allowed them "to look after our own industry," so long as they satisfied the Commissioner of Labor that they were doing it adequately. III, 3000.

ADJUSTMENT OF LOCAL DISPUTES

The machinery for the adjustment of local disputes was practically the same in the sanitary ware division as in general ware, up to the point at which the matter was taken over by the standing committee, and the same " no-strike " rule obtained. In the pricing of new ware the procedure on the union side was regulated by the same laws, with the local union retaining the right to pass on every price settlement before it became binding. The standing committee also had the rule that local settlements must be recorded with the committee and that a price so ratified became binding in all shops. The method of working under a protest price was also followed. And, due to ignorance of the provisions of the scale or of binding decisions, or to the unwillingness of shop committees to assume responsibility, or of employers to accept established precedents, the number of disputes sent on by the local parties made the work of the standing committee unnecessarily burdensome.[93]

The Sanitary Standing Committee.—Although the sanitary standing committee was patterned after the general ware committee, the rules of the former differed on two important points. There was no time limit within which the committee had either to reach a decision or refer the dispute back to the parties.[94] Nor was there any rule governing what the committee should do in case of a deadlock or what should be done if the committee referred a dispute back to the parties and

[93] *Report of President,* 1910, pp. 21-22; 1913, p. 15; 1916, p. 23; *Informal Meeting,* October, 1922, pp. 43-44; *Comm. on Ind. Rels.,* III, 2987, 2997-2998.

[94] In 1917 the union convention passed resolutions setting a limit to the time the men should wait before taking further action but nothing came of it. The Brotherhood officers did not push it. *Proceedings,* 1917, pp. 97-99.

they again disagreed. It was thought better to leave these matters to the discretion of the committee, to handle each case as it should arise. It was understood, of course, that a Brotherhood officer could take up an unsettled matter with the firm, but if no adjustment followed, the standing committee would retain jurisdiction. As a matter of fact the "referring back to the parties" feature of the operation of the western general ware committee was not used by the sanitary ware committee except in cases which it regarded as too petty for its consideration or on which it had not been given sufficient information. Nor was it the practice to refer disputes which neither the standing committee nor the parties could settle to the executive board and the labor committee. Indeed, from 1916 on, the eastern members of the executive board were *ex officio* the union members of the standing committee.

The employers' side of the standing committee was nominally elected by the Association, but the practice was to keep the same men on as long as they would serve. From 1903 to 1914 there were only three changes on the employers side.[95] The most important change occurred shortly after that when Mr. Campbell, who had been chairman from the beginning, withdrew.

The union twice changed its method of selecting its representatives. In 1912 it changed from appointment to election, as in general ware. In 1916 it went even further in the other direction, making the eastern members of the executive board the union standing committee *ex officio*.[96] The results under the elective system had not been satisfactory. Some of the elected representatives seemed unwilling to take the responsibility of making settlements; there were instances of

---

[95] *Comm. on Ind. Rels.*, III, 2991.
[96] *Proceedings*, 1916, pp. 86-87.

members of the committee pledging themselves in local
union meetings not to settle except on certain terms;
and there were accusations of " playing politics." The
attitude of one of the union representatives in the meetings of the committee was especially irritating to the
manufacturers. Finally, the manufacturers' side apparently decided to concede nothing to the union committee as then constituted. It was this situation in the
committee, as well as the large number of "petty"
cases, which led Mr. Campbell to withdraw from the
committee. The number of unsettled cases mounted so
high, and there was so much complaint from the men
of the delay, that the union finally put the eastern members of the executive board, headed by Vice-President
Hutchins, on the committee to get action.

The committee had no stated meeting time. It met
whenever the number or character of the disputes pending made a meeting necessary. The number of meetings
was much smaller than in the western general ware
committee. The procedure was equally informal. Discussion was full and free. There was almost no formal
voting. Discussion continued until the assent of both
sides to a particular proposal was indicated or the
question was laid aside to be taken up at a later meeting. Verbatim stenographic minutes were kept of the
meetings, consequently informality did not lead to con-
fusion or misunderstanding as to what had been done.

The committee frequently employed the device of
referring a disputed matter to a special sub-committee
of one or two from each side, appointed for that particular purpose. A matter such as the measurement of
a kiln or a " condition " in saggermaking or kilnplacing, which required a visit to the plant before an
informed decision could be made, was likely to take
that course if the plant was in Trenton or near by.

Finally, in 1919, a permanent sub-committee was set up to handle defective ware disputes, at the request of the union side. The union representatives were the union members of the standing committee; the employers were represented by foremen or superintendents, " practical potters," who were not members of the standing committee. This sub-committee, which came to be known as the " buffer committee," proved to be a great success and was continued until the end of the agreement system. It acted only for the Trenton district, officially, and for defective ware disputes, but it frequently made investigations in price disputes from " outside " shops. In practice it settled defective ware disputes in the Trenton shops on its own responsibility, although its decisions were subject to ratification by the full standing committee. As the defective ware disputes outnumbered those of all other classes combined, it is easily seen how great a relief its work was to the full standing committee. So far as pressing went, the question of responsibility was being handled to the satisfaction of both national organizations at the time the agreement ended. When the strike came the slate was practically clear of defective ware disputes.[97]

As contrasted with the acceptance of the view that in defective ware disputes the committee's function was judicial, in the approach to pricing questions the negotiating spirit seemed to prevail. Yet each side was willing to concede in order to get a settlement, after repeated arguments had made it clear that the other would not accept its original figure. The large proportion of settlements was mainly due to the fact that after 1916 the union vice-president headed the union representation on the committee. His familiarity with the ware, and with the precedents, and the confidence which

[97] Statement of Mr. Frank Hutchins to the writer.

the manufacturers had in him, helped the union side greatly. He was also willing to take the responsibility for accepting a settlement which he believed should be accepted, regardless of what the men concerned in the dispute wished the union side to stand out for.

The sanitary standing committee, as has been made evident, was the most successful of all the standing committees, except for the period 1913-1916, in disposing of the disputes referred to it. It never sent one back to the parties to fight out for themselves. It carried the case along until it could find some answer acceptable to both sides, if the union officers could not reach an adjustment with the firm directly. This laid it open to many complaints from the men—particularly in the West—over the long delays which frequently occurred. But the committee kept the peace, which was its primary function. The spirit shown by both sides in the last meeting of the committee—in June, 1922—was excellent. It was not because of any failure on the part of the standing committee that the sanitary ware agreement system broke down.

OBSERVANCE OF THE AGREEMENT

There was far less complaint of non-observance of the agreement in the sanitary division than in general ware. There were some violations by individual employers, of course, and charges of many more; there were some unlawful walkouts by the men; there were complaints by employers that the men refused to do things at the terms specified in the scale; but down to the period of almost open hostility which followed the second conference of 1921 the record in respect to observance was remarkably good.[98]

[98] Mr. John A. Campbell testified before the United States Commission on Industrial Relations in 1914 that the union kept the

The most spectacular form of violation of the agreement by the men was, of course, the " walkout." There was a number of these in the earlier years of the agreement system and then they became very rare [99] until about 1916 when there was another outbreak. The union officers soon got their men well in hand again and from then on to the end the record was almost clear—in marked contrast with that in general ware· in the same years. The Brotherhood officers were very proud of the way in which their members observed the restraints imposed upon them by the agreement in the years of lagging wages and mounting living costs, with, wages in other trades rising rapidly all around them. In the September, 1922, conference when the manufacturers vigorously, and at times bitterly, complained of the attitude of the union members, and the one-sidedness with which they applied the agreement system, violating the agreement by unauthorized strikes was not one of the things with which they charged the men.

The cessations which occurred were all " shop " strikes. There was no case in the sanitary ware division of a " branch " strike, unless the saggermakers' action in 1918 be counted as such, and the saggermakers had worked out their notices as " individuals." All the shop cessations were ended in a few days; [100] the men never refused to obey the orders of their national officers to return to work.

The causes of the cessations were much the same as in general ware—to put an end to an alleged violation by the employer, to remedy a condition which the em-

---

agreement as well as the manufacturers did. And Vice-President Frank Hutchins stated that neither the Association nor the Brotherhood had ever broken the agreement. III, 2988, 2994, 3004.

[99] *Comm. on Ind. Rels.*, III, 2998.

[100] *Ibid.*, pp. 2988, 2989, 2998.

ployer failed to rectify after repeated protests, to get action without submitting to the " delay " involved in taking the case to the standing committee, and even to force the employer to give something which the men did not think they could get from the standing committee. In some of the cases, too, the men quit with the tacit support, if not at the order of, the local union.

The national officers, of course, vigorously denounced those who quit in violation of the agreement and of union law. But in this division the Brotherhood did not take any drastic punitive measures against men who quit in violation of the agreement. It did not fine or suspend individuals or revoke the charter of any local union. To be sure neither the men nor the local union openly defied the national officers by refusal to return to work except on their own terms. And, as Vice-President Hutchins put it in 1914: " It is hard enough to collect dues without attempting to collect fines." [101]

As in the general ware division, the concerted giving in of notices because of dissatisfaction with the action of the conference committee or the standing committee, or to secure something not yet passed on by either, was regarded by the employers as a violation of the agreement, in spirit at least. The Brotherhood never would concede that this was a violation of the agreement.[102] As a matter of fact, it did not occur frequently. The one outstanding case was that of the saggermakers, in 1918. In that case the Brotherhood conceded that the manufacturers were free to fill the places of the men who had left with whatever men they could get.[103]

[101] *Ibid.*, p. 2998.
[102] See above, pp. 359-360 for the same question in general ware.
[103] *Report of Executive Board*, 1919, pp. 31-34.

The employers complained at times that the men in this or that shop had refused to do things without extra which they were required to do under the agreement and that in order to get the work done employers had been compelled to pay more than the scale terms. In some of these cases, too, the employers alleged, the men were acting under orders from their local unions. It was this type of failure to observe the agreement which the employers stressed in 1922.[104] The men's answer to this charge was that they were but protecting their rights. After the refusal of the union to accept a wage reduction in 1921 some of the manufacturers, according to the men, adopted a hostile attitude, resisting even the legitimate claims of the men, and the men acted in a like spirit. Charges and counter-charges of violating the agreement abounded, especially in connection with casting.

The officers of the Association would not support one of their members in a clear violation of the agreement, any more than the Brotherhood would. If the standing committee decided that an employer's course was in violation of the agreement the Association would ask him to conform or resign from the Association.[105] But if he chose the latter course the Association disappeared from the case and it was left to the union to compel him to conform. This happened in more than one instance. It was undoubtedly a weakness in the system but one which could not easily have been avoided. However, the fact that after the delay involved in going through the standing committee the employer might then resign

[104] *Conference Report,* September, 1922, pp. 44-46, 53-55; *Informal Meeting,* pp. 39-44.

[105] *Comm. on Ind. Rels.,* III, 2989, 3004; *Report of President,* 1906, pp. 15-16.

from the Association and the men have to quit in the end to carry their point made it more difficult for the Brotherhood to keep the men at work under an objectionable condition.

CONCLUSIONS

In the autumn of 1920 the agreement in the sanitary division was apparently on a firm foundation. In the matter of peaceable adjustment the record was much better than in the general ware division. The former division had come through the trying years of wages lagging behind living costs without a strike or even a strike vote and the Brotherhood officers had been able to hold the men to a very good observance of the no-strike rule in spite of "radical" agitation within the ranks for more drastic action. The general wages issue was not threatening. The men had received large increases early in 1920, and although they did not get all they asked in the October, 1920 conference the men seemed pretty well satisfied on the whole with the results of the conference. The war-period wages crisis was apparently safely passed.

The employers, too, were apparently still satisfied with the system of collective bargaining. To be sure they had warned the men that they must coöperate more effectively in the casting process and that there must be real action from the kilnmen and dippers on the introduction of straight piece work. But, assured by the attitude of the union officers on these matters, the manufacturers had followed the usual course of leaving them to be worked out in the months to come and had signed the agreement for two more years with the old-time exchange of friendly sentiments and hopefulness for the future. The atmosphere was friendly, cheerful, and free from tension. The elements which had kept the agreement system going successfully in the industry for nearly two decades were apparently operating as successfully as ever.

Undoubtedly one of the most important of these elements was the belief on both sides—subscribed to by a majority, at least—that it was a great advantage to have wage rates and labor costs set on a uniform basis for the industry and to have them fixed in an agreement for a definite period. A majority on both sides also believed in the superiority of the no-strike rule and the standing committee system of handling local disputes.[106]

There were many evidences of a common interest between the two parties in the welfare of the industry.[107] Although there was not the bond of the protective tariff which united the general ware manufacturers and the Brotherhood, the latter did coöperate with the sanitary manufacturers in dealing with legislative bodies and, for example, with the Fuel Administration in 1918,[108] on matters of concern to the industry. And that the manufacturers, or some of them, at least, were interested in the men beyond the terms of the agreement is evidenced by such activities as the eastern hospital fund.[109]

Too much credit for the success of national collective bargaining in the sanitary industry cannot be given to

[106] Mr. Campbell testified before the Commission on Industrial Relations, in 1914, that the agreement system was preferable to the "old conditions," under which "one man, like a dipper, ... may go out and hold a plant up"; before the days of the agreement the manufacturer had "independence" but paid for it by being "in hot water a good portion of the time." III, 2992.

[107] Mr. Campbell testified before the Commission on Industrial Relations, in 1914, that since the agreement system began the men had shown increased efficiency. III, 2991.

[108] Report of Executive Board, 1918, pp. 21-22; Proceedings, 1918, p. 80.

[109] See above, p. 307 (note).

Mr. Hutchins and to Mr. Campbell. Both believed strongly in the system of dealing which they headed for their respective sides,[110] each had the highest confidence in the other, and each worked hard with his constituents to make the system operate smoothly. It is significant that in October, 1922, with the situation headed obviously for a strike these two men, although each had retired from the headship of the negotiating body on his side, worked together " unofficially " in an attempt to bring about an agreement. It would be a mistake to assume, however, that the breakdown of the agreement system was due to the retirement of Mr. Campbell and later of Mr. Hutchins from the headship of their respective sides. Had Mr. Campbell been chairman in 1921 the tone of the conferences, especially the second one, might have been somewhat different—and the same is true of the September, 1922, conference—but it is very doubtful if the outcome would have been different. The cleavage between the manufacturers and the union conference committee was too sharp and too wide to be closed by even such experienced leaders as Mr. Campbell and Mr. Hutchins.

[110] Mr. Campbell's belief in collective bargaining was expressed in his testimony in 1901 before the Industrial Commission. Asked for his opinion " as an employer " of the system of settling matters by joint conferences, he replied: " I think it is about the best way to handle the subject that I know of. Of course, it depends on whether you get reasonable men on your committees or not. There are hard-headed fellows on both sides, and if they come to the surface, of course, it is a little difficult sometimes to come to a conclusion; but I have served on a great many committees, and my impression is that that is the best way." XIV, 627.

In 1914, he testified concerning the system of dealing in the sanitary ware industry, before the Commission on Industrial Relations:

" The arrangement that we have, I believe, is the best we can get under all the conditions, and the most satisfactory." III, 2994.

The primary cause of the change of attitude on the part of the manufacturers toward the union and the agreement system was the fact that the protection of the uniform scale was not worth as much as it had been. It did not protect them from the rising competition of the non-union shops, which had been a real threat in the depressed year of 1921. Competitive equality among the union manufacturers no longer meant competitive equality throughout the industry. The very prominence of uniform labor costs in the union case for the agreement system and in its wages argument had become a boomerang. The employers insisted that the wage " principle " on which they had proceeded now required a wage reduction to meet non-union competition and the refusal of the union to grant a reduction on this basis was therefore all the more exasperating to the employers.

The policy pursued by the union members with respect to casting was directly related to non-union competition. Their inability to get lower prices in union shops for casting was attributed by the manufacturers to the men's organization; if their casters were unorganized, casting prices would not be artificially inflated by a tie between casting prices and pressing prices, nor by a limited day's work. Inasmuch as the Brotherhood supported the men in these policies, the manufacturers believed it had become a handicap to them in their attempts to compete with the non-union shops in this increasingly important part of the manufacturing process. The employers were irritated, too, by the frustration of their attempts to get the union men to change the system of payment in kilnplacing and dipping, but the casting issue was the one of overwhelming importance.

The employers were also soured by what they considered a changed spirit on the union side—not on the part of the officers, but on the part of the men. The union was now controlled in the sanitary division, they believed, by an element with which they could not deal satisfactorily, an element hostile to the manufacturers rather than coöperative. They attributed the refusal of the union to give them any relief in 1921, when the union had granted a reduction in the general ware division, to the predominance of this element. And some of them, especially Mr. A. M. Maddock, the manufacturers' chairman, found evidence of it in what he considered the hostile attitude of the men in the shops, particularly in relation to the highly charged subject of casting. The attitude of the dippers in the piece-work negotiations was also set down to the same spirit.

On the other side, the refusal of the union to accept concessions in order to ease the situation and preserve the agreement was due to the fact that the members believed that the agreement could be retained without concessions. Naturally they preferred to believe those who told them that is was not necessary to take a wage reduction—that the manufacturers were " bluffing," that non-union competition was unimportant, that casting could not be successfully used to supplant pressing. When it became only too clear that these men were wrong and that Frank Hutchins and the executive board were right it was too late to get an agreement. The majority of the manufacturers were by that time convinced that they were better off without the union and all efforts to restore the agreement were fruitless.

APPENDIX

COMPARISON OF EARNINGS PER HOUR, BY OCCUPATIONS, 1912-1913 AND 1925 (GENERAL WARE)

These figures are taken from Bulletin 412 of the United States Bureau of Labor Statistics: "Wages, Hours and Productivity in the Pottery Industry, 1925," pp. 23-26. The figures for 1925 are for a "representative two-week pay period"; they were furnished by the employees, with the coöperation of the employers. The figures for 1912-1913 are those published in the Report of the Bureau of Foreign and Domestic Commerce, Miscellaneous Series, No. 21. " The occupation terms in that report differ to some extent from those in this study " (Bulletin 412) and " the comparison of the averages for some of the occupations for the two periods cannot, for the reasons stated, be entirely satisfactory."

The order in this table is that followed in the description of occupations in the Introduction.

	Semi-vitreous		Vitreous	
	1925	1912-13	1925	1912-13
Clay- and slip-makers				
Slip makers	74.6	.....	72.7	.....
Laborers, slip house	57.5	.....[1]	50.6	.....[1]
Clay-shop workers				
Jiggermen	90.2	45.66	89.8	44.86
Batters-out	56.5	23.19	41.4	17.25
Cup-ballers	34.0	16.34	....	.....
Mould-runners	47.1	18.74	39.8	14.20
Finishers, female	52.4	25.78	39.5	19.20
Turners	94.2	49.87	85.7	44.35
Spongers, male	35.4	.....	29.2	.....
Spongers, female	31.7	.....	27.3	.....
Handlers	95.5	53.82	92.2	41.67
Handle casters and finishers, male..	52.8	16.64	36.5	15.73
Handle casters and finishers, female.	36.7	.....	39.7	.....
Dishmakers	81.3	44.43	82.1	41.22
Dishmakers' helpers	53.2	.....	....	.....
Pressers	64.9	36.54	88.7	35.87
Stickers-up	59.3	34.16	....	.....
Casters	90.3	38.91	81.5	35.52
Kilnmen				
Kiln placers, bisque	105.2	47.79	100.2	50.48
Bench bosses, bisque	127.3	.....	124.9	.....
Kiln placers, glost	104.2	47.65	96.4	42.03
Bench bosses, glost	124.7	.....	107.8	.....
Kiln firemen	53.1	26.63	62.7	33.16
Kiln drawers, male	71.8	31.87	67.8	23.99
Boss kiln drawers	82.7	.....	81.0	.....

[1] The 1912-13 figures are: " Slip-makers "—semi vitreous 28.64, vitreous 26.30 ; and " clay puggers "—semi vitreous 22.63, vitreous 19.05.

	Semi-vitreous		Vitreous	
	1925	1912-13	1925	1912-13
Warehousewomen				
Ware brushers	32.0	14.61	28.5	.....
Stampers, bisque	33.0	19.63	27.2	.....
Ware wrappers	28.1	13.58 [2]	23.8	12.12 [2]
Ware dressers	34.8	16.29	.... [3]	..... [3]
Ware dressers, forewomen	48.8	.....	....	.....
Drawers (females, in warehouse).....	45.9	19.16	30.0	.....
Dippers' helpers, female	38.4	16.55	33.0	.....
Dippers	123.3	62.34	91.7	53.37
Decorators				
Printers	68.5	42.90	76.6	51.63
Decalcomania cutters	34.8	.....	26.3	.....
Decalcomania and print transferrers..	37.5	20.42	33.2	16.16
Gold stampers	40.2	16.25	23.5	.....
Gilders and liners, male............	75.9	..... [4]	89.3	..... [4]
Gilders and liners, female..........	52.8	..... [4]	63.4	..... [4]
Decorating kiln placers and drawers..	77.2	30.92	61.9	20.43
Decorating kiln firemen............	89.0	48.04	55.3	40.89
Warehousemen	58.5 [5]	29.16	53.1	24.00
Packers	85.1	35.54	65.4	.....
Head packers	96.2	.....	114.4	.....
Saggermakers, hand	96.1	45.28	101.0	58.22
Saggermakers' helpers, hand........	79.3	31.22	68.1	31.56
Saggermakers, machine [6]	62.9	.....	93.5	.....
Mouldmakers	106.4	51.45	101.4	42.20

[2] The 1912-13 figures are for " selectors and wrappers."

[3] The figures in vitreous are: for " dressers, female " 26.3 in 1925 and for " ware dressers, female " 13.25 in 1912-13.

[4] For 1912-13 the figures are: in semi vitreous—gilders, male, 39.80, gilders, female, 27.26, liners, male, 38.03, liners, female, 29.27; in vitreous—liners, male, 55.27, liners, female, 29.22.

[5] The warehousemen's scale, which practically applies only in the West, was then $5.25 for a 9-hour day.

[6] " Includes operators, weighers, and finishers as found in various potteries."

NOTE ON DOCUMENTARY SOURCES

The documentary sources primarily relied on in this study have come from within the industry itself. Some of them were issued by one of the employers' associations or by one of the unions, but some of them—such as wage scales, reports of conferences, minutes of standing committees—are of joint origin. Some are printed and some are in manuscript form. The documents originating within the industry are listed below, grouped according to origin.

I

THE UNITED STATES POTTERS ASSOCIATION

Proceedings of the Annual Conventions of the United States Potters Association, 1875-1930. The title varies; since 1900 it has been " Proceedings of the . . . . Annual Convention."

(MS.) Memorandum of Agreement Between the Western Manufacturing Potters Association, The Trenton Manufacturing Potters Association, and the Sanitary Potters Association, June 11, 1903.

(MS.) Minutes of Special Joint Meeting of Committees from the Western Manufacturing Potters Association, The Trenton Potters Association, and the Sanitary Potters Association, called by the President of the United States Potters Association, held at Philadelphia, September 17, 1903.

II

POTTERS' UNIONS OTHER THAN THE BROTHERHOOD

Proceedings of the Fifth Annual Session of the Operative Potters National Trade, D. A. 160, K. of L., September 1, 2, 3, 4, 5, 1890.

Proceedings of the Executive Board, D. A. No. 160, January 4-6, 1892. (This is really the Proceedings of the " sixth annual convention of the Potters' National Trades District Assembly, 160.")

Proceedings of the Executive Board of the Potters N. T. A. 160, K. of L., December 1, 1890.

Minutes of the Executive Board (D. A. 160), January 5, 1891, January 26, 1891, August 15, 1892.

Constitution and By-Laws of the Operative Potters' National Union and National Trades District Assembly, No. 160, K. of L., Founded July 21, 1886. (Bears imprint of 1887.)

Official Souvenir of the Convention of the Potters National Union of North America, held at Trenton, New Jersey, January 2, 1893.

(MS.) Minutes of Stephens Assembly, No. 3573, K. of L., Feb., 1888–Dec., 1892; and, in same book, of Local Union No. 4 (Potters National Union) June, 1893–March, 1895.

(MS.) Minutes of the Conventions and meetings of the Executive Board of the Sanitary Pressers National Union, Sept., 1895–Dec., 1899.

III

THE NATIONAL BROTHERHOOD OF OPERATIVE POTTERS

Thos. J. Duffy, History of the National Brotherhood of Operative Potters from 1890 to 1901 (Pittsburgh: Commoner and Glass Worker, 1901).

Proceedings of the Annual Conventions of the National Brotherhood of Operative Potters, 1894-1930. (The 1894 convention is called the "fourth annual convention.")

Reports of the President and First Vice-President to the N. B. of O. P. Convention, 1905-1917.

Report of Executive Board to the Annual Convention of the N. B. of O. P., 1918-1930.

Financial Reports of the National Officers to the Annual Convention of the National Brotherhood of Operative Potters, 1905-1930. (The title varies.)

Constitution, adopted 1890.

Rules and Regulations, 1895; 1899; 1902; 1904; 1910.

Constitution, 1914; 1920; 1925.

Unemployment Fund Proposition, Effective April 4th, 1921.

The Potters Herald, April 28, 1904–May 28, 1931. (The numbering of the volumes is irregular.)

Circular issued (by President and Secretary of N. B. of O. P.) July 7, 1903.

Remarks of Mr. John A. Campbell at Opening Session of Sanitary Conference, September 29, 1914.

Statement of the Executive Board Regarding Conditions of the Sanitary Trade, Together with Propositions to be Submitted by a Referendum Vote of the Trade. (1922.)

Uniform Wage Scale for Finishing adopted by the N. B. of O. P., to take effect the first full pay in December, 1903.

Wage Scale for Finishing Jiggered Ware, revised Aug. 10, 1916.

Wage Scale for Finishing Jiggered Ware, revised Aug. 1, 1918.

Rules governing the Day's Work of Clay Workers (Sanitary), March 27, 1922.

IV

GENERAL WARE AGREEMENTS AND WAGE SCALES

(MS.) Basis of Settlement agreed upon between the Committee of the Manufacturing Potters Association and the Executive Committee of the Knights of Labor on behalf of the Operative Potters, to take effect on and after the second day of February, 1885. (Signed by "Thomas Maddock, President of the Trenton Potters Association" and "Frederick Turner, Gen. Sec. Treasurer, K. of L., on behalf of Operative Potters.")

Uniform Wage Scale adopted by the Manufacturing and Operative Potters of the United States of America, to take effect May 1, 1900.

Supplement to the Uniform List, containing Agreement entered into by Western Manufacturing Potters Association and National Brotherhood of Operative Potters on May 1st, 1901.

(MS.) Memorandum of Agreement entered into this first day of October, 1903, by and between the authorized representatives of the Western Manufacturing Potters Association and the authorized representatives of the National Brotherhood of Operative Potters.

Kilndrawing Agreement between the Labor Committee of the United States Potters Association and Kilndrawers Committee, effective on and after Tuesday, August 20, 1918.

The following scales and agreements adopted by, or entered into between, the United States Potters Association and the National Brotherhood of Operative Potters:

Philadelphia Agreement, Sept. 15, 1905.

Wage Scale and Agreements adopted October 1, 1905.

Official Size List applying to all shapes introduced after October 1st, 1905, effective first pay after January 1st, 1907.

New York Agreement, effective first full pay after October first, nineteen hundred and seven.

Casting Agreement, effective January 1st, 1908.

Pittsburgh Agreement, effective first full pay after October 1st, 1909.

Atlantic City Agreement, effective first full pay after October 1, nineteen hundred and eleven.

Wage Scale and Agreements, revised October first, 1911.

Agreement Covering the Preparation of the Saggermakers' Clay (1912).

Agreement Covering Apprentice Kilnmen (1912).

Astor Agreement, effective first full pay after Nov. 1, 1913.

Casting Price List, effective July 20th, 1914.

Chalfonte Agreement, effective first full pay after October 1, 1915.

Supplement to the Chalfonte Agreement—Memorandum of Prices Established for Making Casting Moulds, Jiggering Lemonade or Soda Mugs, Casting Tea Pots and Placing of Bats.

Supplement No. 2 to the Chalfonte Agreement—Uniform Scale for Drawing Glost and Bisque Kilns.

Supplement No. 3 to the Chalfonte Agreement, July 25, 1916.

Supplement No. 4 to the Chalfonte Agreement—Sagger Clay Agreement (effective September 28, 1916).

Supplement No. 5 to the Chalfonte Agreement—General Ware Wage Increase (to apply the first full pay after November 15, 1916).

Supplement No. 6 to the Chalfonte Agreement—China Ware Wage Increase (to take effect the first full pay after November 15, 1916).

Supplement No. 7 to the Chalfonte Agreement—General Ware Wage Increase (to take effect the first full pay after May 8, 1917).

Supplement No. 8 to the Chalfonte Agreement—China Ware Wage Increase (to take effect the first full pay after May 17, 1917).

1917 Agreement.

Corrected Supplement to the 1917 Agreement, effective the first full pay in August, 1918.

Number Two Supplement to the 1917 Agreement, effective the first full pay after September 10, 1918.

Wage Scale for Hotel China—Jiggering and Dish Making, effective first full pay after February 1, 1918.

Wage Scale for Hotel China—Turning and Handling, effective the first full pay in May, 1918.

Wage Scale for Packing Hotel China, effective the first full pay after June 11, 1918.

Wage Scale for Placing Vitreous Hotel China in Glost Kilns, effective the first full pay after June 18, 1918.

Wage Scale for Pressing Vitreous Hotel China, effective the first full pay after July 15, 1918.

Wage Scale for Placing Vitreous Hotel China in Bisque Kilns, effective the first full pay after August 14, 1918.

Wage Scale for Casting Vitreous Hotel China, effective the first full pay after June 2, 1919.

1919 Agreement, effective first full pay after October first, 1919.

Amendments to 1919 Agreement, effective January 22, 1920.

Circular Letter authorized by the New York Conference, January 17, 1920.

Supplement to the 1919 Agreement, effective the first full pay after September 15, 1920.

White Granite and Semi-Porcelain Wage Scale and Size List, by Agreement, Revised September 15, 1920.

Wage Scale for Hotel China, revised September 15, 1920. (Includes price lists for casting, dishmaking, handling, jiggering, kilnwork, mouldmaking, pressing, packing, and turning, but does not include the general rules of the Agreement.)

1921 Agreement, effective on the days of Thursday, August 11, and Thursday, November 3, 1921.

1922 Agreement, effective January 1, 1923.

Packing Agreement, Supplement Number 1 to the 1922 Agreement, effective the first full pay after February 1, 1923.

1924 Agreement, effective October 1, 1924.

White Granite and Semi-Porcelain Wage Scale and Size List by Agreement, revised October 1, 1926.

China Wage Scale and Agreements, revised October 1, 1926.

1928 Agreement, effective October 1, 1928.

V

REPORTS OF JOINT CONFERENCES AND MINUTES OF STANDING COMMITTEES, GENERAL WARE

(All are in manuscript form)

Report of Conference between Committees of the Trenton Potters Association and the National Brotherhood of Operative Potters, at Trenton, N. J., September 22, September 24, and October 28, 1904. (Stenographic report.)

Reports of conferences between the Labor Committee of the United States Potters Association and the Conference Committee of the National Brotherhood of Operative Potters, 1921-1928. (Stenographic reports.)

Minutes of the Western General Ware Standing Committee, February, 1906–June, 1928.

Minutes of the Eastern General Ware Standing Committee, June, 1914–January, 1027.

Minutes of the Western China Standing Committee, May, 1923–January, 1928.

Minutes of the Eastern China Standing Committee, September, 1923–November, 1924.

VI

WAGE SCALES AND AGREEMENTS, SANITARY

Wage Scale adopted by the Sanitary Manufacturing Potters Association and National Brotherhood of Operative Potters, to take effect July 7, 1902.

Supplement to Sanitary Pressers' List; Basis for Placing Sanitary Kilns; Rules Governing Apprentice Sanitary Kilnmen; Price List for Packing Sanitary Ware; Price List for Making Sanitary Saggers, Bisque; Price List for Making Sanitary Saggers, Glost; (all) adopted August 22, 1903. (All are printed on one large sheet.)

Piece Price-List for Lavatories adopted by the Sanitary Manufacturers' Association and National Brotherhood of Operative Potters, to take effect August 7, 1905.

And the following Wage Scales and Agreements adopted by, or entered into between, the Sanitary Potters Association and the National Brotherhood of Operative Potters:

Wage Scale and Agreements, adopted November 1, 1907.

Supplement, Wage Scale and Agreements, adopted October 29, 1908.

Agreements on Underpaid and Overpaid Articles in Sanitary Pressing, to go into effect the first pay in October, 1912.

Sanitary Potters Conference of 1912—Memorandum of Prices, Rules and Recommendations adopted, effective first full pay in November, 1912.

Agreement Governing Casting of Sanitary Ware, effective the first full pay in November, 1912.

Agreement Governing Packing of Sanitary Ware, effective the first pay in June, 1913.

Sanitary Potters Conference of 1914—Memorandum of Prices, Rules and Recommendations adopted, effective the first of November, 1914.

Agreement covering Casting of Sanitary Ware, effective February 1, 1916.

Supplement to Wage Scale and Agreements, effective the first full pay in November, 1916.

Agreement Covering Casting of Sanitary Ware, effective the first full pay in November, 1916.

Size and Making Price of Standard Sanitary Saggers, effective the first full pay after May 14, 1917.

Supplement to Wage Scale and Agreements, effective the first full pay after June 1, 1918.

Supplement to Wage Scale and Agreements, effective the first of November, 1918.

Special Settlement Governing Clay Workers in Sanitary Trade, effective the first full pay in July, 1919.

Wage Scale and Agreements, effective April 15, 1920.

Scale of Base Prices for Making Different Sizes of Saggers, effective first full pay in June, 1920.

Supplement to Wage Scale and Agreements, effective the first pay in November, 1920.

VII

REPORTS OF CONFERENCES AND MEETINGS OF STANDING COMMITTEE, SANITARY

(MS.) Reports of Conference between Committees representing the Sanitary Potters Association and the National Brotherhood of Operative Potters, August 17–August 19, 1903. (Stenographic report.)

(MS.) Reports of Joint Conferences, Sanitary Potters Association and National Brotherhood of Operative Potters, 1906–August, 1921. (Stenographic reports.) These include all the regular conferences from 1906 to 1920, inclusive, as well as "special" conferences and conferences held by joint special committees.

The verbatim reports of the Conferences of October, 1921, September, 1922, and October, 1922, were printed by the Sanitary Potters Association, under the following titles:

Conference Report, Sanitary Potters Association, Atlantic City, N. J., October 25-26, 1921.

Conference Report, Sanitary Potters Association, Atlantic City, N. J., September 12, 13, 14, 1922.

Informal Meeting of Executive Committees of Sanitary Potters Association and National Brotherhood of Operative Potters, Trenton, New Jersey, Thursday and Friday, October 5 and 6, 1922.

(MS.) Reports of Meetings of Sanitary Standing Committee, August, 1903–June, 1922. (Stenographic reports.)